White Water Nepal

A rivers guidebook for Rafting and Kayakir

by Peter Knowles and Da

Good paddling!

Peter Knowles

Rivers Publishing U.K.
Menasha Ridge Press U.S.A.

Front cover photograph: rafting the lower Marsyandi gorge near the confluence with the Trisuli (Himalayan River Exploration).

Back cover photographs: kayaking the upper Marsyandi (Whit Deshner), Bhotia woman porter on the Humla Karnali.

Photographs are by the authors unless individually credited. Drawings and sketches are by courtesy of Jocelyn Wasson, Louise Mathews and Mieke de Moor. Cartoons are by Alan Fox and sketch maps were drawn by Peter Knowles. Cover design by Ivan Cumberpatch.

Disclaimer

The information and advice given in this book were written in good faith as the best available at the time of writing but the reader is warned that nothing in this book should be regarded as 100% accurate: this book was written by humans so there are bound to be errors, rivers and rapids change, and some information is out of date before it is printed. All advice and information should be treated with caution and checked locally. The publishers, authors and contributors can accept no responsibility for any loss, injury, or inconvenience sustained by any person as a result of information or advice contained in this guide.

Published simultaneously by: Rivers Publishing U.K. and Menasha Ridge Press, U.S.A.

Trade enquiries in the U.K. and Europe to Cordee Outdoor Books & Maps, 3a De Montford St, Leicester LE1 7HD; Fax: 0533 471176.

Trade enquiries in the U.S.A. to Menasha Ridge Press, 3169 Cahaba Heights Road, Birmingham, Alabama 35243; Fax: 205 967 0580.

Distributed in India and Nepal by TBI, M-33 Connaught Place, New Delhi 110001; Fax: 11 3325247.

Trade enquiries for other countries to Rivers Publishing U.K. 125 Hook Rise South, Surbiton, Surrey KT6 7NA; Fax: +44 81 391 5114.

Catalogued in the British Library. ISBN: 0-9519413-0-5 Catalogued in the Library of Congress, U.S.A. ISBN: 0-89732-124-3

Printed by Biddles Ltd in England.

The Authors

Dave Allardice's first memories are of being the number three sheep-dog on a small farm in New Zealand – a position he held for five years until the number two dog died. Leaving school without anyone noticing he embarked on a mixed career as a carpenter, sheep shearer and logger before discovering the joys of migratory outdoor recreation.

He has worked worldwide as a rafter since 1984 and now runs 'Ultimate Descents', an international company specialising in river expeditions in Nepal and the Himalaya. In 1989 he was a member of the combined New Zealand and Soviet expedition that made first descents in the Pamirs and Tien Shan Mountains. The following year he was invited to join the International team that ran the unrun Rondu Gorges on the Indus river. This expedition was filmed as an impressive television documentary called 'The Taming the Lion'.

When not rafting and kayaking he is usually off exploring and following his passion for photography in Asia.

Peter Knowles made his first attempts at kayaking in the Scouts but gave it up as a nasty cold wet sport. Ten years later, standing chilled and numb in driving sleet on a rock climb in North Wales he decided that perhaps it was worth trying again. It took him four years to learn to roll (and some epic swims), just in time for a trip down the Grand Canyon in 1973. Pete then fell in love with big-water rivers and hasn't grown up since. In the last twenty years he has run 'quite a lot of rivers' in many different countries and continents, including a few first descents.

Since 1983 he has been exploring and running the rivers of the Himalaya and was recently selected as one of 20 'modern explorers' in an exhibition at Britain's Royal Geographical Society.

He has worked as a raft guide, Outward Bound instructor, throw bag designer, painter, sailing instructor, moonshiner, etc.; but has to admit to spending at least half his life working for famous name companies as a business systems consultant – day-dreaming of course, of that perfect river high in the Himalaya!

Contents

Dedicated to Dr Mike Jones

Mike was one of the world's top expedition kayakers, famous for his 'Canoeing down Everest'. He died trying to rescue a friend on the Braldu River in the Karakorum Mountains in 1978.

Mike's spirit and memory live on. A 'Mike Jones Scholarship' is awarded each year by the Winston Churchill Memorial Fund and over the years this has supported many adventurous kayak expeditions. Entirely separate is the 'Mike Jones Rally' which is run by kayakers and friends of Mike as an annual get-together for recreational white water paddlers: this has become very popular and one of the largest events of it's kind in the world. A brief article about Mike Jones appears on page 174.

Mick Hopkinson and Mike Jones at Everest Base Camp (Eric Jones)

Sun Kosi below 'Rhino Rock'

About this book

Like most ideas, this book started over a beer: we were in 'Rum Doodle's' bar and we got to discussing why more people weren't coming to Nepal to go rafting and kayaking. How about a guide book, we mused – 'It will only take a few months to write'. Over two years later and we're somewhere near finished – but, it has been a fascinating, enjoyable project, and one where we've learnt a lot.

The nicest thing about writing this book has been the support and advice we have had from everyone we approached – we had many contributions – and all freely given because people believed in what we were doing and had themselves had such good experiences in Nepal. So, thank you everyone! We couldn't list all the many people who have helped, but have told some pernicious lies about the main contributors in Appendix E.

We should particularly like to thank Eric Knowles and Michael Manby for correcting the worst of our grammar and spelling, Andy Watt for his outstanding medical contribution and the many paddlers who have put up with us on their trips.

Any mistakes and omissions are our own and we welcome comments and suggestions.

Good paddling! Peter Knowles, Dave Allardice, August 1992.

Why Nepal?

Nepal is a river runner's paradise – no other country has such a choice of multi-day trips, away from roads, in such magnificent mountain surrroundings, with warm rivers, a semi-tropical climate, impressive geography, exotic cultures, wildlife and friendly welcoming people!

But it's not just the rivers – as anyone who has been there will tell you, Nepal is a magnificent holiday in its own right – a fairy tale land of temples, mountains, dramatic festivals, exotic culture, colourful people, medieval villages, superb craft shopping, great food and sights – the bonus is some of the World's best rivers!

Forget the images of hard 'Expedition' boating – yes, there are a few rivers like this – but Nepal is just an outstanding holiday destination for the average recreational boater: most of the rivers in this book are class 1 to 4 – and you don't have to be anyone special to come rafting or kayaking in Nepal. Everyone we know has enjoyed his – or her – holiday here, but the one thing you do need to bring is the right mental attitude: values, especially time values, are different from ours and you do need to be more flexible and tolerant to enjoy your time here and avoid undue stress.

Rafting in Nepal is usually a 'wilderness' experience in that most rivers don't have highways alongside them – but it's a soft, tamed, wilderness with white beaches for camping, clean blue rivers, friendly locals and few 'nasties' – someone described it as 'blissful escapism'!

Incredibly inexpensive, Nepal is a peaceful democratic country where rafters and kayakers get a warm welcome as one of the best forms of ecotourism.

Warm water and great play waves

INTRODUCTION TO NEPAL

The Country

Nepal is a small country, the size of Idaho, or of Austria and Switzerland put together, but a huge country in terms of its diversity: from the highest peaks on earth to steamy jungle. It is inhabited by 20 million people of many different tribes, linked by a rich cultural and religious heritage. Straddling the Himalaya, Nepal forms a boundary and meeting point between the the Indian Sub Continent and the high plateau lands of Asia.

It's a country where, away from the few roads, villages and towns could be straight out of a medieval novel, with a simple life style enriched by deep cultural beliefs and joyful festivals. In modern terms it's a poor, exotic, third world country, with difficult mountain terrain, too many people, little fertile land, and lots of development problems. But it's also a country with a proud history, a sense of unity, fine friendly people, a country with few roads, but wonderful rivers!

Geography

Nepal is long and thin, stretched out along the Himalaya. If we drew a cross section through the country at any point it would look something like this:

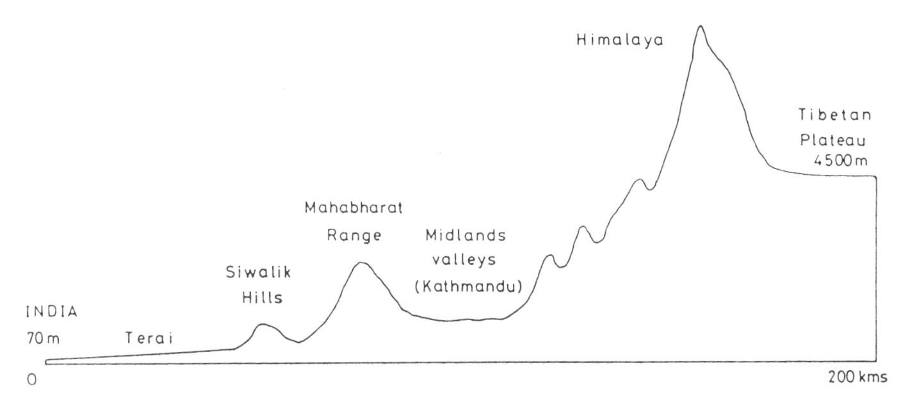

Running parallel to the southern boundary with India is a strip of lowland plain called the Terai. This used to be a mosquito-ridden wilderness and a natural boundary zone, but malaria control programmes since the 1950's have seen massive forest clearance and population settlement in this zone. This is the development zone of Nepal.

Rising from the Terai are the Siwalik (or Chure) Hills and then a higher range called the Mahabharat Hills. The land then drops to the 'Midlands valleys', typified by the Kathmandu Valley at a height of around 1300 metres (4000 ft). These Midland valleys extend across most of Nepal and are followed by lengths of some of the great rivers – the Seti, Karnali, Bheri, Kali Gandaki, Sun Kosi and Tamur. Most of the population used to live in these valleys and historically these were the cultural heartlands of Nepal.

Climbing from the Midland valleys and the surrounding hills are the mighty Himalaya Range, whose highest peaks often demarcate the boundary with Tibet. The Himalaya drop more gently on the northern side to the arid Tibetan plateau.

These different cross section zones also mark the transitional zones for vegetation and wildlife – few areas of the world can show such a marked transition from high arid plateau to lowland jungle. These are differences that you will appreciate on a long river journey.

The Himalaya are being formed by an uplift of the earth's crust as two tectonic plates meet: the Eurasian plate being driven up on top of the Indian one. This means that the Himalaya are young, active, and still growing in height by up to one cm a year. The Himalaya is also an earthquake zone and hot springs may be found on the upper reaches of many rivers where the valley cuts through a fault line. A lot of the geological history of the Himalaya can be read as you raft through the river gorges: rock stata, faults and synclines clearly exposed in the water-carved cliffs.

The Himalaya were pushed up after the river systems had established themselves – this explains the strange way that many of the main rivers have headwaters on the North (wrong) side of the Himalaya. The rivers maintained their courses, established a system of antecedant drainage and eroded deeper and deeper gorges as the mountains kept growing: the upper valleys of the Arun and Kali Gandaki are some of the deepest land gorges on Earth.

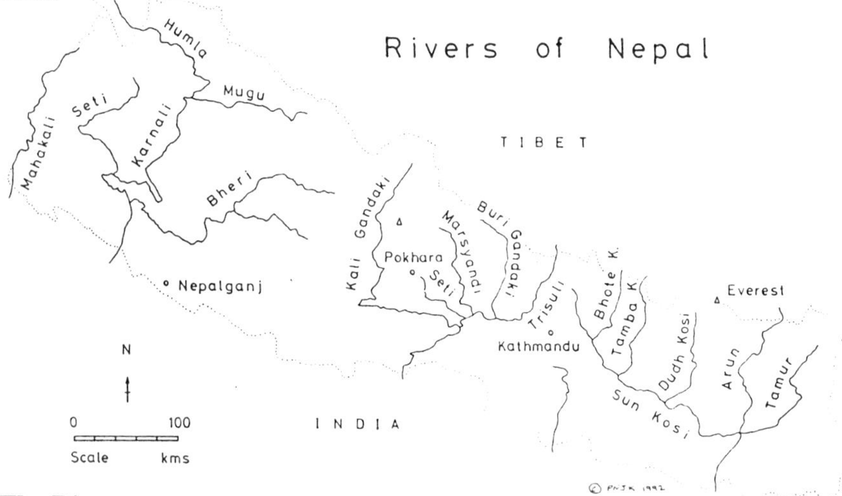

The Rivers

The antecedant system of river drainage partly explains why the rivers of Nepal are so good for rafting and kayaking – they don't just rush straight down to the the plain, but follow convoluted courses traversing the Midland valleys of Nepal and then cutting their way in more mighty gorges through the Mahabharat Range. The profile of the Kali Gandaki (page 109) is typical of many Nepalese rivers in that the gradient eases off at an altitude of around 1000 metres (3500 ft) – this explains why most river running is at relatively low altitude. All Himalayan rivers are actively downcutting and carry a a lot of material as sediment, or as boulders trundling along the bottom – hold a paddle shaft to your ear and you may hear it.

There are tremendous variations in the volume of water in the rivers: typically the mean monthly flow in the monsoon will be over ten times that at low water and the instantaneous highest flow may be 80 times! These are some of the mightiest mountain rivers of the world!

Climate and when to go

Nepal's climate is dictated by the monsoon which arrives in June and usually finishes in late September. The monsoon brings torrential rains that flood the rivers so most people wouldn't want to be kayaking or rafting at this time. Peak season for tourists and for rafting is probably October through November: the monsoon is over, everything is very green, rivers are moderately high but dropping, temperatures are warm and skies are clear with fine mountain views. The only disadvantages with this time of year are that it is the peak season and airline reservations are harder to get; also you cannot be sure when the monsoon will finish: it can be a month late and this can throw your plans into chaos if you are planning on running a river where water levels are critical – as they are on many of Nepal's rivers.

The winter months from late December through to early February are cold, but skies are still clear and river levels will be low. Lots of river running groups come out over Christmas and have a great time, but you certainly should expect cold water and perhaps think in terms of wet suits and dry tops.

From late February through to early April is also a good time for river running – river levels are reliably low, air temperature warm, rivers warm and blue. The disadvantage is that the air is often hazy: you cannot be assured of stunning mountain views and there may be an occasional shower of rain. In the past, many kayakers and rafters have visited Nepal over the Christmas holiday, when the facts seem to suggest that Easter might be a better time.

Pokhara, because of its altitude of 800 metres, probably gives a fair indication of the average temperatures that most river runners may encounter:

Deg. Cent.	Sep	Oct	Nov	Dec	Jan	Feb	Mar	Apr	May	Jun	Jul	Aug
Minimum	19	17	12	7	5	8	11	15	18	20	21	21
Maximum	27	26	23	20	19	21	25	30	30	29	29	29

The People

The physical diversity of this colourful land is mirrored in the numerous different tribes and ethnic groups who make up its population. Each group has its own strong cultural traditions, dress and language. High in the mountains you may meet the Bhotias of Tibetan stock, or the famous Sherpas. These high mountain people were always great traders, supplementing their subsistence farming with trade over the high passes to Tibet. The Thakalis are another tribal group, originally centred on the Kali Gandaki valley, who have become famous as skilful traders and inn-keepers.

On your way down the river you may meet a village populated by Magars, then a few kms later a village of the Rais tribe – your guide may be able to recognise the tribe by its distinctive architecture. You will meet ferrymen whose family have been ferrymen from time immemorial – paddling their dug-out canoes, 'dungas' skilfully against the current.

Most of these people will be Hindus, but usually it is a Hinduism that has strong blends of Buddhism, the older religion. The whole of Nepal seems permeated by its Buddhist past and its philosophy of tolerance and respect for life and people. Despite intense pressures of poverty and limited resources, ethnic or religious strife is almost unknown in Nepal. Most visitors to Nepal are amazed at the tolerance and cheerfulness of the local people and some of your most delightful and vivid memories will be of meetings with local people.

Wildlife

A river journey is one of the best ways of viewing Nepal's abundant wildlife – especially if you float down through the Terai.

You will see a vast number of different birds: from eagles to egrets, vultures to hornbills, over 800 species! Butterflies and moths are usually more visible when you camp, and again there is a huge variety – over 5000 species.

If you are lucky you may sight the rare gharial crocodile (that's the fish eating one with the strange long snout) or the more common mugger crocodile that feeds on anything: fish, small mammals, dead bodies, or other carrion. The occasional rafting group on the Narayani and Karnali rivers have sighted the very rare Gangetic dolphin, one of the few freshwater dolphin species in the world (we suspect that a kayaker stands a better chance of viewing the mammals closely because of the latter's curiosity). If you are a fisherman then you will be interested in the famous Masheer fighting fish – record weight 45 kgs!

There are several species of snakes, but it is extremely rare to see one. River-rafting groups normally see lots of monkeys and deer. If you are lucky and on the right river at the right time you may see tiger, leopard, wild elephant, blackbuck, nilgai, gaur, wild buffalo, rhino, hyenas, wild dogs, civets, wild boars, sloth and black bears. These are of course more likely to be sighted on more remote rivers and those flowing through National Parks.

History

Modern Nepal traces its history as an independent Kingdom back to 1722 when Prithvi Narayan Shah started a war of attrition and expansion. For the next two centuries Nepal grew in power and tested its military strength with wars against Tibet and Great Britain. With the fertile Kathmandu valley as its capital, and wealth from trans-Himalayan trading, the country developed a rich culture. Thoughout these years it remained closed to foreigners and it aquired a reputation as one of the mystery mountain Kingdoms of the East.

From 1846 the country was ruled by a family of dictators, the Ranas, with the King as a puppet figure. The Ranas were overthrown in 1951 and the succession of King Mahendra in 1955 saw Nepal open its doors to the world. Sandwiched between two major countries (China 'liberated' Tibet in 1950), the King did an adroit balancing act to ensure the survival of Nepal. But he ruled as an absolute monarch and the Rana family still retained much power: Nepal in the 1980's was notable for being one of the poorest countries in the world, ruled by wealthy autocrats.

Pressures for democracy came to a head in 1990, with a huge protest by the 'Movement to restore democracy'. After further protests, and a massacre of up to 200 people, this resulted in the King legalising political parties, a new constitution, and parliamentary elections. The elections in 1991 brought the Nepalese Congress Party to power with the King remaining as a constitutional Monarch – one who is apparently still adored by most of his people.

The return to democracy was heartening, but Nepal is still a very poor country (average annual income is quoted as $170 a year) and faces huge economic difficulties. Tourism is one of the biggest sources of revenue so your holiday is a help!

GENERAL ADVICE

Travel to Nepal

Air

From Europe: Royal Nepal Airlines has a direct flight twice a week from London to Kathmandu via Frankfurt – we can recommend this as a convenient and reasonably priced flight. Lufthansa also has a weekly direct flight, but otherwise you will have to change en route, Delhi being the obvious transit point. Delhi now has a nice new International Terminal and the transit is fine, but prices on the Delhi-Kathmandu leg are controlled and so are high ($142 single). You won't save money flying via Delhi but seat availablity is usually better. In 1991 the cheapest tickets from London were with Afghan Air – until they were grounded and their pasengers were left stranded! Aeroflot were next cheapest, followed by Bangladesh Airlines, PIA, Royal Nepal, and then flights via Delhi.

Flying from Asia most pasengers transfer and spend a night in Bangkok, but there are also normally direct flights from Singapore, Hong Kong, Rangoon, Colombo, Karachi and Lhasa.

Try to book early if you plan to travel in the peak season around October. The other thing to mention is that flights sometimes get cancelled in the low season owing to lack of demand. Royal Nepal and Indian Airlines offer a 25% reduction for students or under 30's on some routes. Note that it is possible to fly from other Indian cities to Kathmandu: Calcutta $96, Varanasi $71, Patna $41. A crafty compromise is to take the train from Delhi to Patna and then fly from here to Kathmandu.

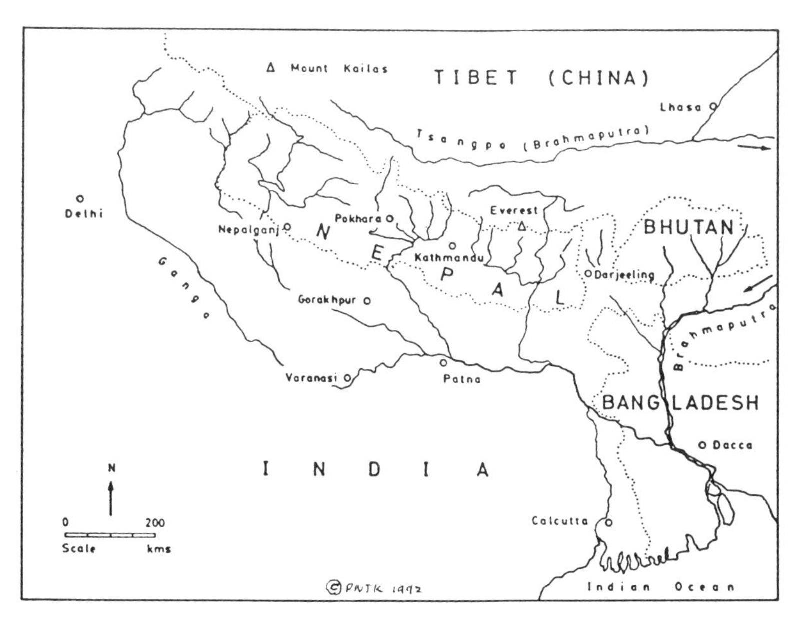

Flying with a kayak

If you're planning to bring a kayak with you, then in our experience you are better travelling with a small friendly airline that has greater scope to be flexible and 'tries harder'. Royal Nepal, Bangladesh and PIA have in the past carried short kayaks on the same basis as surf boards or cycles – no excess baggage charge providing you're within the weight limit (and they are normally nice about this). Thai and Singapore are also pretty helpful. If you are a group, then we suggest you negotiate a deal at the time of booking. If there is just one or two of you then the best thing is just turn up, put all the bulky lighter gear in the kayak, heavy items in your carry-on, and smile sweetly! (Phone them in advance and they have to quote the rule book and start talking about air cargo).

Worst place to fly FROM with a kayak is probably North America, but many airlines will relax the rules if you only have one bag (a long plastic banana-shaped one!) instead of the usual allowance of two.

International airline staff are often not exactly sure what a kayak looks like and get confused between kayaks and canoes; we suggest that it may be helpful to call your boat a 'surf kayak'.

Your Return Flight

It is essential to re-confirm your return flight from Kathmandu, at least 72 hours prior to departure otherwise your seat reservation will be cancelled. Experienced travellers confirm, re-confirm and obtain a computer printout as verification.

Note that there is an airport departure tax to be paid when you fly out. You can change back up to 15% of your Nepalese rupees provided you have the exchange receipts.

Overland

Travelling overland to Nepal saves money but is rarely pleasant or hassle-free: if you are considering it then we recommend that you consult an up-to-date travellers guide book, e.g. Lonely Planet. Reckon on two days for the journey, although with good timing it can be done in less. Second class rail Delhi to Patna (16 hours) will be about $7 and the bus from here to Kathmandu again about $7. Travelling overland makes most sense if you plan to travel in India before or after Nepal. Note that you can save time by finishing a river trip and travelling straight to India rather than returning to Kathmandu. Note also that the new Nepalese highway from East to West (part of the 'Trans-Asia Highway') is now nearly complete and it is smooth and fast where it is finished.

The Indian rail reservation system normally works, but you usually need to book several weeks in advance. We haven't tried carrying a kayak on Indian Trains; we suspect that you might get away with it on local sevices, but not on the express trains. There are a few direct 'tourist buses' that operate between Delhi and Kathmandu. The one we took in 1991 from the Delhi Tourist Camp was a real 'rip off', chock full of Kathmandu 'wide boys' carrying trade goods back to Nepal. Reserved seating was a myth, the seating was 2+3, local regulars took the front seats and left the back seat to the tourists, the journey took 62 hours (only one driver of course!) including a ten hour stop at Nepalese customs (because of all the trade goods). This is only sufferable if you are carrying a kayak or two, but if you are in this position, a better bet might be to look into the possibility of hiring a long distance taxi.

The most spectacular overland route to Nepal is from Lhasa. Tibet is in theory only open to 'organised groups', but we have heard of travellers getting their own group together. Note that Nepal only allows arrival from Tibet via the road through Kodari.

How much will it cost?

Throughout this guide, we have quoted prices in American dollars: this is because although local prices in rupees have risen with the price of inflation, the rupee is regularly devalued in respect to the dollar so that over the last few years prices in dollar terms have stayed the same – indeed, the prices of many things have actually come down.

Probably the most expensive part of your holiday will be staying in Kathmandu – just because there are so many good things there like restaurants to tempt you. Reckon on between $2 and $10 a per person per night for budget hotel or guest house accomodation. Eating well you will spend perhaps $1 on breakfast, $2 on lunch, and $4 for dinner. Add in a few taxi fares and your daily expenses will typically be between $10 and $20 a day.

Most rafting trips cost in the region of $40 to $70 a day all inclusive so if you are coming to Nepal for say a three week holiday, and a ten day Sun Kosi rafting trip then you're probably looking at a total cost in Nepal of around $750.

If you are a kayaker and doing self sufficient trips then your budget will be a lot less: looking back over a few of our trips in 1991, they average out at $5 a day per person, including food and transport. The same is true if you go trekking: in the hills you will find it difficult to spend more than $5 a day.

So if you come to Nepal for a month to go kayaking, do a raft-supported Sun Kosi trip, hire a kayak for another ten days and don't spend too long in the fleshpots of Kathmandu, you would spend about $750. Bring your own boat and go entirely self-contained and it will cost you more like $200 for a month!

Cheap local transport (Foxy)

Money

Nepalese Rupees are not freely convertible and you are not allowed to take them out of the country (not that you would want to). Best way of carrying most of your money is as travellers cheques – easily changed when you get to Nepal. Make sure that you ask for and keep the bank receipt. Currently there is no advantage in converting your money, e.g. sterling, to any other currency like U.S. dollars; you end up paying two lots of bank commission. Credit cards can be used to a very limited extent, but don't rely on them for cash advances. There is a limited black market, but the mark up is only small and for most people this is not worth the risks involved.

Visas

Visas are required for most nationalities; costs vary depending on your nationality, typically around $20 for a 30-day visa. It is straight forward to get this in advance from a Royal Nepalese Embassy and in order to avoid any delays, we recommend that you do this. However, no worries if you don't have time; you can get the same standard 30-day visa on entering Nepal at the airport or border post.

This standard visa can be extended when in Nepal but you will have to produce bank receipts to show that you have exchanged $20 per day (or equivalent) for the additional period. These regulations and amounts can be expected to change but the concept is likely to stay the same; that normal budget travellers staying for a reasonable period are very welcome and can expect no hassle, but the longer you stay and the less money you spend, the less you are welcome! This seems pretty reasonable to us – Nepal is one of the poorest nations on Earth and tourists should bring in revenue, not compete with local people for scarce resources.

Insurance

If you are going to Nepal to go rafting or kayaking then you should check with your insurers to ensure that you have appropriate cover. This is because insurance is a 'goodwill' contract whereby you are duty bound to inform the Insurers of any known facts that could influence the policy. Some insurance companies in the past have perceived river running as especially hazardous (mainly we suspect owing to T.V. documentaries) and applied a 25% loading. More enlightened companies have noted the actual accident statistics and taken the sanguine view that people are more likely to have an accident on the way to the river! If you are going somewhere remote, then we suggest that you also check what the position is if you need to hire a helicopter rescue ambulance.

If you are already in Nepal and thinking about a taking a river trip as part of a longer vacation, then our friends in the insurance business say that there should be no problems if you already have a standard travel policy – unless this specifically excludes rafting or kayaking.

General information

You will find that **English** is spoken by most people you come across in shops and hotels. Engish is taught in all schools and so even in a remote village you are almost bound to find a student who will be delighted to practise his English and translate for you. Note that although Nepalese is the national language, most of the population outside of Kathmandu speak their own local language.

There are many religious **festivals** and public holidays and it is worth checking the dates of these when applying for your visa. 'Dasain' is one of the greatest of these and takes place for ten days in October. The government offices that issue trekking and rafting permits are closed for several days and especially busy before and after the holiday. Like our Christmas festival, it's a time of family gathering so roads, planes and buses are all crowded at this time.

Business hours for government offices and banks are normally 10.00 a.m. to 4.0 or 5.0 p.m. Friday is a half day and Saturday is the day of rest. Tourist shops are open 14 hours a day, 7 days a week.

The **phone system** in Kathmandu is now good and steadily improving to other parts of the country. There are no problems about making or receiving direct dial international phone calls or faxes at reasonable prices. The postal service is less reliable – we suggest that if you are going to have letters forwarded to you, that you have them sent direct to your guest house, hotel or rafting company rather than Poste Restante.

Electricity is 220 volts/50 cycles. Voltage reductions are fairly common and blackouts happen now and again (Always carry a flashlight after dark). Sockets take the one plug that isn't on your 'universal' adapter (better to buy a plug locally?)

Nepal is 5 hours 45 minutes ahead of GMT. If it's noon in London it's 5.45 p.m. in Kathmandu and 7.00 a.m. in New York.

Accommodation

In the main tourist centres like Kathmandu and Pokhara there is a vast choice of all types of accomodation, from five star hotels to a lowly guest houses where the charge may be less than a dollar for a double room. Most river runners stay in guest houses or cheap hotels These are all clean and friendly. The cheapest are obviously a bit basic – but all offer incredible value. A clean room, bed with sheets, hot water, and flush toilets, will cost you between $2 and $8. There is plenty of competition and so a good choice. Most have gardens, or roof terrace, restaurant, room service, phone, and laundry service.

Outside of the main tourist areas then accomodation becomes more basic. On trekking routes you get trekking lodges that offer budget accomodation tailored to westerners. In remote villages you may be offered a sleeping mat on the floor of someone's home.

Note that when away from tourist routes, you will come across few toilets because Nepalese normally use local fields to reconfirm their oneness with nature's life cycle. A favourite, and obvious spot is the local river bank: near large villages and towns these are often fairly unpleasant.

Food

Kathmandu and Pokhara are great places for eating out. There is a wide choice of all kinds of restaurants offering many different cuisines – Indian, Nepalese, Tibetan, Italian, Japanese, Thai, Korean, Mexican, etc. Last time we were there we had a beautiful Japanese meal, served in elegant surroundings; crisp white table cloth, and sparkling glasses: in London this would have cost us over $40 a head, in Kathmandu it cost just $4!

There is a wide choice for vegetarians, and besides the many restaurants, there are bakers and pie shops, fruit stalls, delicatessens, and supermarkets. Obviously there isn't the range of goods that you can buy in western countries, but you can eat very well in Kathmandu and Pokhara – the problem usually is that you can be tempted to eat too well! Yes, it's great to try lots of different restaurants, but it's noticeable that Kathmandu veterans tend to be selective in the number of restaurants they patronise, trying to limit the chances of picking up a bug. If you're not sure about a restaurant, try to have a poke around the back of the kitchen – you might wish you hadn't!

Away from the main tourist centres, food becomes more limited and in the more remote areas it's probably worth avoiding meat. Staple diet of most Nepalese is Daal Bhat, twice a day and every day – rice and a thin lentil soup, perhaps with a spoon of vegetables and chutney. You either love this or hate it. But, there are other local specialities like Indian Samosas and Tibetan Momos – too many to write of here, we're supposed to be a rivers guide book! Note that snacks from local roadside stalls are often delicious and usually quite safe provided they are freshly cooked.

Tea is the reviving national drink of Nepal, but soft drinks and bottled water are widely available. Beer is relatively expensive – $2 a large bottle, but good. Local spirits aren't quite what you're used to at home and it's well worth bringing a bottle of your favourite duty free. (On return, try taking home a bottle of 'Gorkha Wine' for your local wine tasting circle!) The exception is 'Khukuri' rum, that makes a great rafting cocktail when mixed with coke.

We should mention some home produced beverages that you may be offered in riverside villages: 'Chang' is local beer, quite palatable after the first two litres. 'Rakshi' is distilled chang produced in crude home-made stills often set up at the riverside; this is guaranteed to get any beach party going and five free hangovers come with every bottle. The most pleasant and mellow local drink is Tungba, which is made by the sherpas who pour hot water over fermented millet in a big wooden tankard.

On Arrival

Nepalese Customs are unlikely to give you any problems unless you are carrying any expensive gear like a video camera. They might want to enter this in the back of your passport to ensure that you take it back out of the country.

Unless you are being met, you should change some money at the bank in the airport terminal, then wander outside to pick up a taxi to town. Kathmandu airport is only 5 kms from the centre of town so a taxi will only cost you about $2 (bargain and agree the fare before you start). Accomodation is never a problem, there is always a wide choice of rooms available at many different prices. Most people stay in the tourist hub of Kathmandu, an area called Thamel. There are so many excellent guest houses and hotels that it would be unfair and pointless to try and list them all. If you are by yourself and need somewhere to start then we suggest you take your taxi to the Kathmandu Guest House or the cheaper Yeti Cottage a few doors along (both popular with river runners). If these are full then ask them to mind your bags whilst you have a wander around and find alternative accomodation.

Kathmandu is a fascinating, exotic, city and you need a specialist guide book to make the most of it. If you haven't already bought one then we suggest that you walk down the road and buy a half-price guide book at one of the many second-hand book shops. Next, find one of the excellent restaurants and relax with a beer!

Don't forget to confirm and reconfirm your return flight, keep those bank receipts, and take care over what you eat and drink.

Guru on the Marsyandi (Arlene Burns)

Interaction with the Nepalese

Nepal has a fascinating culture built upon a deep, centuries' old foundation of human traditions. We materialistic westerners usually don't appreciate just how important these traditions are to the local people and we can easily offend. This is particularly true of river runners who are coming into contact with remote villagers who rarely see a westerner. If you do offend, the locals are unlikely to say anything – the Nepalese are much too nice to do this – but of course it will affect the way they treat you and the way they view other westerners – family, friends and neighbours will ask 'What kind of people are these foreigners?'

For the westerner, the adjustment to Nepal can be quite a culture shock. We suggest that you build in time to wind down and to adjust to a way of life where human relationships and traditional values are more important than whether a bus leaves on time. Respect and patience are everything; Nepalese do not understand anger or sarcasm – if they have a problem they try to bypass it or laugh and make a joke about it.

'Namaste'

Communication

A smile and cheerful greeting of 'Nameste' will open doors, but add a few words of Nepalese and you will be laughing and communicating across the cultural divide (we suggest that you buy a small phrase book in Kathmandu). Just a few words will go a long way because Nepal has many different languages and people are used to communicating across a language barrier. The questions are often obvious: 'Where have you come from from?' 'How old are you?' 'Father?' etc. If you have a visitor to your campsite, it's always a nice gesture to offer them a cup of tea (chai), the golden nectar of Asia.

If you are seeking information, be aware that out of politeness, people will sometimes tell you what they THINK you would like to hear, so double check and triple check important information. Rarely is information 100% correct; you need to give each statement a credibility rating and then assemble this with information from other sources to fill in a picture – a fascinating detective game! Avoid the leading question: 'Is there a bus in the morning?' will invariably get an answer 'Yes'.

Bargaining

Many things have fixed prices – most bus fares, tea, food, for example; but for many things the accepted norm is to bargain – a means of social intercourse that should give pleasure to both parties – well, that's the idea, but when you're dog tired at the end of a long river trip and bargaining for a taxi back to your hotel, it doesn't seem quite like that! Try to pay the going local rate but give a generous tip for good service. Always agree the rate beforehand. Try to keep a sense of proportion and avoid getting into squalid haggles about a few rupees; bargain hard and carefully agree the details of the really big purchases. Pay too much and the local will try to get even more off the next westerner: renegade on your deal and you will be leaving a trail of turds to be stepped in by every westerner following you.

Begging

We strongly recommend that you never give anything to children begging – this demeans local people and breaks up the fabric of local society. Ask yourself how you would feel if strangers started giving sweets/candy, or money to your children. You will probably encounter adult people begging, some obviously in dire distress, and it is difficult to offer simple advice – except to say that when in doubt you might watch what local people do and respond likewise.

Dress Code

Clothing, or the lack of it, is where many river runners often cause offence. Nepalese are very modest people with a strong sense of decency and are easily offended by skimpily clad foreigners. Stephen Bezrucha asks 'How would you feel if a Papua New Guinea Highlander male wearing only a penis shield came walking down your garden path?' This is the equivalent of a westerner only wearing shorts walking into a Nepalese village. All of us, Nepalese or Westerner are inherently conservative and we judge people by their appearance. Dress discreetly in line with local custom and you will be more readily respected and accepted by local people.

On the river and in the relative privacy of your camp, shorts and bare chests are O.K. for men, but if you are anywhere more public, men should always wear a shirt, e.g. walking up to the road, or to a village, or on top of a bus. If, for example, someone pays a visit to your camp, then the respectful thing to do is to put your shirt on, a gesture that will of course be appreciated. Nepalese men do wear shorts, but only low caste men, so if you are trying to create a half-reasonable impression anywhere, then it's well worth putting on long trousers. Note that there are shorts and shorts – we suggest you try to avoid the tighter or more skimpy style of shorts that can give clues to the wearer's religion.

Avoid nudity and be discreet when going to the toilet or getting changed. Children are often around when you are getting changed and the thoughtful thing to do is to explain beforehand, so that the older girls can retire whilst you change behind a towel.

Women, like men, need to dress modestly. Women should wear a blouse and a long skirt or long trousers when in public (shorts and top are OK. when on the river). A long skirt, with an elasticated top is useful whilst getting changed.

Cultural hints

As in most of Asia, the right hand is used for eating, giving or accepting things; the left hand is considered unclean because it is used with water instead of toilet paper. Yes, it's all right to handle food with your left hand, but you should always use the right hand when offering food, or a cup of tea to someone.

The hearth and cooking area of a house is considered sacred, so don't burn anything on it or walk across it. Feet and especially shoes are considered unclean (they often are) so you should avoid stepping over people and pointing your feet at people or the hearth. It is common practice to take shoes off before entering homes and temples. Peoples' heads are considered sacred so it's not a good idea to go around patting children's heads.

Conservation

Every year the annual monsoon brings a huge deluge that sweeps down the river and scours it clean – this means that camping on riverside beaches in Nepal has a different environmental impact from camping by rivers in North America. We suggest the following guidelines as good practice:

- Try to limit the size of your group. An excessively large group will geometrically compound your impact on the riverside environment.
- Common courtesy dictates that you should leave your camping beach scrupulously cleaner than when you arrived; leaving only footprints behind.
- Paper and cardboard waste should be burnt. We suggest that you keep your own small plastic bag for burnable waste, film cartons, old bandaids, tissues, cigarette butts, and other nas ties. Burn the contents on the fire when directed by your Guide; note that cooking fires are considered holy, so always ask before burning anything.
- All non-biological items, like tins and bottles, should be washed and carried out, off the river (unless local people request these as useful containers). It is environmentally unac ceptable to bury these as the next monsoon will sweep them down the river and expose them on another beach for people to cut their feet on.
- Vegetable waste, such as onion skins and potato peelings should be buried well away from the campsite but below monsoon high water level.
- Food scraps, washing up water, etc. should be disposed of in the main current of the river (not an eddy). Greasy washing up water should first be filtered through kitchen paper and the paper burnt later.
- Toilet pits should be dug well away from camp and below the monsoon high water level. Carry a lighter or matches and burn your toilet paper.

These basic guidelines have the backing of all reputable rafting companies. Don't hesitate to encourage your team if they neglect something. Only if we all show positive concern will we protect this beautiful river environment.

We ask that you please report any flagrant breaches of these guidelines to the Nepal Association of Rafting Agents. Please make the time to do this as Nepal cannot afford river rangers – if you don't bother to write and report matters then no one else will. (The address of NARA is in Appendix H).

Fires

One of the major ecological problems in Nepal is deforestation. The Himalayan Tourist Code says that you should make no open fires, a general rule, that we would whole heartedly agree with when away from the river.

On the large rivers of the Himalaya the monsoon sweeps down huge quantities of drift wood that get deposited on the beaches and in well-populated areas the villagers will gather this for firewood. But on more inaccessible beaches the wood will remain there until the next monsoon washes it further downstream, and we think that it is environmentally acceptable to use this for camp fires and particularly for burning garbage.

It is pleasant to cook on a wood fire, but we don't think that rafting trips should rely on wood fires for cooking (except perhaps on very remote rivers like the Karnali). The normal good rule is that cooking should be done on stoves, with fires only used occasionally. It is unacceptable for any rafting trip either to buy firewood, or to use driftwood that would otherwise be used by local villagers. It is nice to sit around a campfire, but you don't need to do this every night, and there is certainly no place for a roaring great bonfire.

Build any fire below the high water level. Do not build a 'fire ring' (the sign of an urban ignoramus) but rather try to avoid blackening any rocks. Dispose of any ashes or charcoal in the main current (not an eddy) rather than burying them for some one else to find.

Enjoy your campfires – they are a pleasant part of a rafting trip – but treat them as a bit of a luxury and be aware that your fire might be depriving someone downstream of firewood.

The Himalayan Tourist Code . . . *by Tourism Concern*

By following these simple guidelines, you can help preserve the unique environment and ancient cultures of the Himalaya.

Protect the natural environment:

- Limit deforestation – make no open fires and discourage others from doing so on your behalf. Where water is heated by scarce firewood, use as little as possible. When possible choose accomodation that uses kerosene or fuel efficient wood stoves.
- Remove litter, burn or bury paper and carry out all non-degradable litter. Graffiti are permanent examples of environ mental pollution.
- Keep local water clean and avoid using pollutants such as detergents in streams or springs. If no toilet facilities are available, make sure that you are at least 30 metres away from water sources, and bury or cover wastes.
- Plants should be left to flourish in their natural environment – taking cuttings, seeds and roots is illegal in many parts of the Himalaya.
- Help your guides and porters to follow conservation measures.

The Himalaya may change you – please do not change them.

As a guest, respect local traditions, protect local cultures, maintain local pride:

- When taking photographs, respect privacy – ask permission and use restraint
- Respect Holy places – preserve what you have come to see, never touch or remove religious objects. Shoes should be removed when visiting temples.
- Giving to children encourages begging. A donation to a project, health centre or school is a more constructive way to help.
- You will be accepted and welcomed if you follow local customs. Use only your right hand for eating and greeting. Do not share cutlery or cups, etc. It is polite to use both hands when giving or receiving gifts.
- Respect for local etiquette earns you respect – loose, light-weight clothes are preferable to revealing shorts, skimpy tops and tight fitting 'action wear'. Hand holding or kissing in public are disliked by local people.
- Observe standard food and bed charges but do not condone overcharging. Remember when you're shopping that the bargains you buy may only be possible because of low income to others.
- Visitors who value local traditions encourage local pride and maintain local cultures: please help local people gain a realistic view of life in Western countries.

Be patient, friendly and sensitive. Remember – you are a guest.

(The Himalayan Tourist Code was drawn up in close consultation with local people by the organisation Tourism Concern, was launched by Chris Bonnington in 1991 and has had wide support.)

Security

Nepal is one of the safest and most honest countries in the world, but that doesn't mean that there is no crime or that things never get stolen. It means that you don't need to be overtly concerned about security: you can assume that local people are honest, friendly and trustworthy (much more so than their western counterparts!), but at the same time you shouldn't be careless or present honest people with irresistible temptations. Local people are naturally curious, kids doubly so; by all means let them examine a few items under careful supervision, try a helmet on, etc. but keep the rest of your gear in a central spot and make it clear that you do value it all, down to the last grubby pair of socks! We make it a group rule that nothing (even an empty plastic bag) is given to locals until we are packed up and ready to leave camp: this eliminates many misunderstandings.

Be discreet and don't flaunt valuables and money. A useful tip for all travellers is to keep your large denomination money separate in a well hidden wallet or security pocket, and your day to day money in a more handy pocket. Like any country, there are more dishonest people in cities and places like bus stations so take sensible precautions when travelling. If you need to leave your gear anywhere, ask the owner of your tea shop or a local householder to look after it – they will be flattered by your trust.

Our **women** friends tell us that Nepal is a pleasant, friendly country to travel in, and they say there is almost no sexual harassment.

Photography

Nepal is a photographer's dream. Crystal rivers tumble down green valleys with snow-clad Himalayan peaks suspended behind. There are lots of interesting villages and people so that whatever you do, you will need lots of film. This is best bought from home; slide and print film is readily available in Kathmandu, but you may not be able to buy the type you prefer and you cannot be as sure about its quality.

Print developing is good in Kathmandu and quite cheap, a lot of places having computerised colour printing facilities. Slide processing is more variable and probably best left until your return home. Black and white processing is really cheap and good quality. Never send film through the international post for developing – you risk it being lost or opened. Always keep both unprocessed and processed film in your hand luggage and if possible have them hand searched rather than X-rayed. Be wary of buying professional film that is less tolerant of temperature changes and storage conditions.

If you are thinking of buying a camera for your trip then we suggest that you consider one that is high quality, water-resistant, fully automatic and 35mm (not a diving camera, which is heavy and cumbersome). You will get excellent results with one of these. Because these are water-resistant and sturdy, you can carry it on you whilst on the water and get many dramatic action shots that you would otherwise miss if you had a camera that has to be kept in a waterproof container. Most paddlers fasten the camera strap to the shoulder of their life jacket and then tuck the camera down the front of the life jacket ready for quick action. The thing to look out for when using a waterproof camera is water droplets on the lens. Most people we know who have bought cheaper waterpoof cameras have been disappointed with the results.

The general advice for all holiday photos – to concentrate on people, action and close-ups – is just as true for river trips. Your photographs of local people will be the ones that stand out when you get home. Photographing people is normally no problem, but always ask them first – this is normal courtesy. If they are shy and you have an automatic camera then a nice idea is to get one of them to take a group shot of you with them – the whole thing then becomes a game and a lot of fun. Never pay or give rewards for taking someone's photo – this turns an honour into an insult. Automatic cameras are excellent for close-ups of people in that they need no set up – you can get in really close for a full frame, no problems focussing, and the fill-in flash gets rid of contrast problems.

If you are serious about your photography then you will have an SLR camera, associated lenses and need no tips from us! Your camera can be kept safe and dry in a waterproof container. Widely available are 'ammo cans' – often supplied by rafting companies on request.

Better, in our opinion are the American plastic Pelican cases that are available from specialist shops in your home country. A standard roll top waterproof bag is adequate if suitably padded (a towel perhaps). The best waterproof camera container that we have come across is a waist bag made of thick neoprene and sealed by a dry suit zip (made by Brooks Wet Suits in Vancouver).

Photographing white water can be difficult owing to the extremes of light involved. Best times are morning and evening – try to avoid the harsh light at midday. If you have a good shot, then consider bracketing it with slightly different exposures. Most experts recommend that you use a U.V. and/or a polarising filter. Water and sand is the bane of cameras so you need to take extreme care when changing film and a blower brush and lens tissue is invaluable.

Nepal is not a good place to try and get your camera repaired and it is well worth thinking about bringing a second one as a reserve. If you are on a long trip, then a good dodge is to run a print film through your camera in Kathmandu to make sure that everything is working O.K.

A final tip: most cameras and lenses are easily mislaid when put down on rocks, etc. so consider marking them with a couple of strips of dayglow orange tape.

Books

Nepal is such an interesting, exciting and picturesque country that there are many books about it. We will try to recommend a few that we hope will inspire you, and through their bibliographies open doors to further reading.

There are many good guide books, but we suggest as a start that you beg, borrow or buy the 'Insight' guide by APA Publications – this has magnificent colour photographs and illustrations and you will be wanting to rush down to a travel agent to buy an airline ticket! This isn't so good on boring details like where to stay and eat – the Lonely Planet guidebook is very competent on this. Our favourite and recommended best buy is the 'Rough Guide, Nepal' by David Reed (in the USA this is called 'The Real Guide, Nepal'), very readable and well written by someone who has enjoyed exploring the whole country including a lot of out-of-the way places of interest to river runners.

If you are planning a self-sufficient trip, then you should consider buying a trekking guidebook. Hugh Swift's is our favorite; 'Trekking in Nepal, West Tibet and Bhutan' – very readable and inspiring. Stephen Bezruchka's 'A guide to Trekking in Nepal' is also excellent and has more detail on the individual routes. These guidebooks have good chapters on the natural history and the people of Nepal.

There are a few specialised books of interest to the river runner. 'Canoeing down Everest' by Mike Jones tells the tale of the 1976 British Kayak Expedition down the Dudh Kosi. 'Marsyandi, The illusive river of Annapurna' by Alan Barber gives an account of the 1980 kayak expedition. 'River Systems of Nepal' by Chandra K.Sharma is an academic treatise available in Kathmandu bookshops for 150 rupees.

For those who are new to river-running and looking for a book on the subject, then we suggest 'The white-water river book' by Ron Waters, published by Pacific Search Press, Seattle.

Kathmandu has excellent bookshops and also many second hand bookshops where you can buy guides, maps, and other books at roughly half price.

Films and video

Himalayan rivers are highly photogenic and natural subjects for 'expedition films'. Below are listed the films that we know of, that have English commentary. We know that there are several films available in German and believe that French and Italian expeditions have also made their own films. All of these films are about kayaking expeditions; at the time of writing there doesn't appear to be available any video that publicises or promotes rafting in Nepal (There's scope here for someone).

The most famous Himalayan river film is probably 'Dudh Kosi: Relentless river of Everest' which describes the 1976 kayaking expedition led by Mike Jones and filmed by Leo Dickinson. It has won many awards worldwide and is available from Gravity Sports in the U.S.A. or Chrisfilm in Britain.

Ten years later, a follow up film and expedition was made down the Dudh Kosi using microlite aircraft for scouting. This is titled 'Thin air, white water' and again has some excellent sequences of white water kayaking. In Britain this is available from 'Kites and Kayaks'. In the States this is marketed as 'Himalayan river run' and available as a National Geographic Video.

In 1979 the ABC 'Sportsman' programme filmed a kayak descent of the Arun, but we don't know that this is commercially available on video.

'Raging river of Annapurna' documents a descent of the Marsyandi river by kayak in 1980 but also includes some rafting sequences on the lower river. Available from Chrisfilm in the U.K.

'Sun Kosi – River of Gold' describes the 1981 Australian Himalayan Kayaking Expedition down the Sun Kosi. Available from Chrisfilm in the U.K.

Maps

We're dubious about the point in writing this section as most of the paddlers we know can't read maps – one of the reasons they took up going down rivers instead of getting lost on mountains! If you really do want a map (and why not? – they are excellent for impressing people – much better pose value than coffee table books) then it's probably worth waiting until you arrive in Kathmandu where they are cheap and readily available. Available, yes – accurate no; certainly not by Western standards: the Himalaya are a young and active mountain chain; roads, trails, bridges and even villages get washed away. Villages have several different names and sometimes the same name for a village on top of the ridge as the village down by the river. Nothing is 100% certain and the maps reflect this – but it does add interest, and once you accept this fact of life you will probably be pleasantly surprised at the range of maps that are now available.

For a good general map of Nepal, we recommend the one published by Mandala maps at a scale of 1:800,000. This shows the rivers, topographic details, towns, roads, etc. clearly in five colours and is widely available in Kathmandu for about $2 – good value.

Many older guide books recommend the 1:250,000 U502 series of topographical maps produced by the U.S. Army Map Service. These have a 500 ft contour interval so the topographic detail is reasonable, but as they were based on surveys done in the 1930's they aren't that accurate, are expensive (around $8) and the portrayal of roads, trails and villages is often misleading. We think that better maps at the same scale are the **'Main Trail Maps'** produced by His Majesty's Government of Nepal, Ministry of Works and Transport, Department of Roads, Suspension Bridge Division. These were produced in 1989 and 1990 with Swiss help. They are printed in three colours and show rivers, trails and villages in reasonable detail, but relief is only indicated by spot heights. These have a pink cover, six sheets cover the whole of Nepal, and at a price of about $1.50 for each map, these undoubtedly represent a **'Best Buy' for river runners**.

More detailed still, at a scale of 1:125,000 are the 'Central Service Maps' for each District, produced by the same Government Department. These have a blue cover, 73 sheets cover the whole country, and they again cost about $1.50. If you're really keen on the topographic detail, then there is a matching series of maps for each District at the same scale, showing contours at 250 metre intervals. These are such great value at about 30 cents each that there has to be a snag – the names on these topo. maps are all in Nepali script (Tip: hide the map until you're on the river, then watch the reaction as you casually lend it to someone!)

At the time of writing, these H.M.G. maps were only available from the official distributors: 'Maps of Nepal', S.M.Trading Centre, New Baneshwar, P.O.Box 4782. (out on the trolley bus route just before the Everest Hotel). By the way, these maps are printed on environmentaly friendly paper that will disentegrate and recycle itself at the first opportunity – just great for evening papier mache craft sessions.

Various trekking maps are widely available in tourist bookshops, but, compared to the above, most of them are of doubtful accuracy and value to the river runner. However, a few of the rivers in this book are covered on the 'Schneider' topographical maps published in Austria. These are at a scale of 1:50,000 or 1:100,000 and are handsome maps, but quality has a price – in this case about $10.

All the above H.M.G. maps are based on a survey done in the 1960's as a joint exercise by the Royal Nepal, Indian, and British Ordnance Survey; a complete series of maps was produced at a scale of 1:63,360 but these were given a 'restricted' security rating so access is only available to Government Ministries.

The history of river running in Nepal . . . *by Nima Lama*

We Nepalese have always revered and at the same time feared our holy rivers. To ferry across a river in a dugout canoe was a dangerous and fearful experience – no life jackets or floatation and most Nepalese cannot swim. The idea of running rivers, especially white water rivers, for 'fun' seemed quite crazy to us.

The first 'crazy' river runners arrived in Nepal in the late 1960's. Two Frenchman are said to have descended parts of the Sun Kosi in 1968. Kurt Jorguestein from Germany explored the Sun Kosi and Trisuli and two Americans, Teri and Chris Bech, also explored the upper Sun Kosi around the same time. These were exciting times for these early pioneers and all were too busy running the rivers to concern themselves about how you define a 'first descent'. Exploration of the Trisuli continued apace and by late 1976 all of the river and rapids had been run from Trisuli Bazar to TigerTops.

Al Read, a mountaineer, who was at the time with the Ameri can Embassy began exploring local rivers in 1973 as an alternative to climbing and trekking. He began with an inflatable 'duckie', quickly replaced with a folboat and then an Avon raft the following season – Skip Horner of Sobek helped to design an oar frame for this. Al Read realised the commercial potential and started Himalayan River Expeditions in 1976 – this was the first commercial river rafting company in the Himalaya or in Asia. An experienced river guide, Mike Yager was brought in from America to manage the company and to train Nepalese Guides

In 1976 H.R.E. advertised in the 'Rising Nepal' for 'White Water Raft Guide Trainees .' Most of them had no idea what was involved in 'rafting' – but being a Guide sounded a glamorous and well paid job . . . There were over 100 applicants. Mike Yager arranged some capsize drill on the Trisuli and when most of them found out what white water meant, they were horrified and never returned!

Mike finally selected eight men and these started a very thorough training programme that included travel to the U.S.A. for training as Emergency Medical Technicians. In their final exam they scored higher marks than any other group in the whole of the United States.

In the next few years, H.R.E. pioneered commercial rafting in Nepal and explored many of the rivers. Mike Yager was so successful that by 1980 he had worked his way out of a job and one of his original students Lobsang Gyalpo replaced him. The other students formed the nucleus of a strong team of professional guides who then went on to train others and later to split off and form their own companies.

Other rafting companies in these early days were Great Himalayan Rivers, Lama Excursions and Encounter Overland. These imported some of their guides from Europe so there was a fertilisation of international expertise.

At the same time as commercial rafting was developing, 'expeditions' from overseas were arriving:

- In 1975 Major Blashford Snell led an expedition out from Britain to conquer the Trisuli but had the misfortune to break his nose in one of the rapids – now named 'Snell's Nose' in his honour.
- A Czech team of Kayakers attempted parts of the Dudh Kosi in 1973 and in 1976 a British team led by Dr Mike Jones made an award winning film that would put Nepal on the world Kayaking map.
- The Arun river was first explored by Mike Yager and Nepalese Guides in 1976 and an ABC Sportsman program filmed a kayak attempt on the Upper Arun in 1979.
- The Indian Navy descended the Kali Gandaki in the early 80's.
- In 1980 a British Expedition attempted a complete kayak descent of the Marsyandi from its source.
- Bruce Mason led a descent of the Karnali River in 1981.

By the early 1980's Nepalese Rafters were recognised as world class professionals and were invited to lead and support expeditions to other countries in the Indian Sub-Continent:

- The Tista and Rangit rivers in Sikkim in 1980
- Bhutan in 1981
- The Zanskar and Indus rivers in Ladakh in 1981
- The Tuns river in India in 1983.

Nepalese teams were invited to, and attended, International Rafting Rallies: in Switzerland in 1988, in Siberia in 1989, and to the U.S.A. in 1990.

Commercial rafting is now growing fast. It is recognised as an important growing source of tourist revenue by His Majesty's Government and a system of rafting permits was set up in 1985. The principal rafting operators formed a professional body, the Nepal Association of Rafting Agents (NARA) in 1989. Rafting has now become big tourist business – around 5000 client days in 1990 and over 40 rafting companies.

Kayaking has also taken off, with Nepal now seen as a prime destination for the recreational white water kayaker and each year sees more groups coming from more countries.

Mythology of Himalayan rivers . . . *by Mike Yager*

References to the Himalaya and its rivers first appear in the Rig Veda, the world's oldest religious text, written between 1500 and 900 B.C. Throughout its 1028 hymns we find the first myths of creation, of the gods, and of man. The symbolism and metaphors are complex: the activities of heaven are mirrored in the rituals of earth, and the relationship between gods and men is thus revealed, bound inextricably by water.

The Himalaya is the dwelling place of the gods, and its rivers connect heaven and earth. Rivers are the physical representations of the spiritual themes of creation, purity and salvation, and to bathe in a river is to wash away a lifetime of sin. Even today, devout Hindus hold rivers sacred, especially the heaven-sent Ganges, the Mother of rivers.

Until I arrived in Nepal, I had only appreciated the physical reality of rivers. I had thought of them in terms of the factors involved in creating white water: their volume, their flow, their gradient. Certainly river lore exists in the West, but I had never seen rivers so completely entwined in a culture's mythology and daily ritual. The religious reality of rivers was an unexpected fact, something exotic that delighted me.

Wildlife is plentiful

MEDICAL ADVICE

By Dr Andy Watt

Before you go

Everyone thinks of immunisations, but some simpler measures are important too. A physical examination is not necessary, but if you have had the following problems you should discuss them with your doctor before you go.

Jaundice
Peptic Ulcer
Pregnancy
On regular medication
Have any allergies (especially penicillin, sulpha and other drugs)
Diabetes
Asthma
Back Trouble
Previous Shoulder Dislocation
Tenosynovitus
Piles (Injection treatment possible?)
Ear Trouble
Cystitis or Thrush (medicine to take with you?)

Do try and get fit before going – you will enjoy your holiday more, and be less susceptible to minor injuries such as sprains. No special exercises are necessary, much better to do things that you enjoy.

If you are a kayaker, then time playing in a boat is the most important thing. If you are going on a paddle rafting trip then you would be wise to concentrate on exercise for the upper body and arms – ideally canoeing, or swimming (good for the pessimists). Many people practice a daily routine of stretching exercises – these will keep you supple and less prone to strains and have the advantage that they can be done anywhere whilst travelling.

Consider the consequences of a dental problem developing in a wilderness area. We have seen people's holiday ruined by tooth ache. We strongly advise a visit to your **dentist** for a check-up. Do this at least two months before departure in case any work needs to be done.

Immunisations

There are no official vaccinations requirements for entry into Nepal; however it is worth recording your vaccinations on an international vaccination certificate, if for nothing else than to remind you for when you return a couple of years later and start thinking about vaccinations again.

The list below is fairly exhaustive and a bit frightening; however most people will already have had most of these vaccinations and will probably only need jabs for Hepatitis, Typhoid and Meningitis. Start thinking about these about two months before departure. This list can be supplemented by more up to date advice from a specialist source: your family doctor perhaps, a travel medical centre, or a hospital specialising in infectious diseases.

Hepatitis A – Strongly recomended.
Hepatitis A is quite different from the rarer Hepatitis B, see later.

The organism is common in Nepal and is spread by contaminated food and water. It is present in river water – which is why it is of especial interest to rafters and kayakers. The incubation period is commonly 3-4 weeks and common symptoms are an itch, lethargy, fever, diarrhoea, and jaundice. The virus attacks and can damage the liver (N.B. if you enjoy beer and wine!). A bad attack can put you into hospital and leave you very unwell for several months.

The injection of gammaglobulin is not an immunisation in the true sense of the word. It is a collection of antibodies which, after injection, die away with time and therefore the amount of gammaglobulin required varies with the period away from home. A reasonable schedule would be 2ml for the first month and 1ml extra for each additional month up to 5 months. As the protection decreases with time you should have this injection in the week before departure. If you are planning an extended vacation you should consider having the injection renewed in Kathmandu.

Recent research has shown the injection to be effective and very worthwhile. The practical experience of river runners in Nepal confirms this. There is no evidence of AIDs transmission with this injection. A new immunisation for Hepatitis A is expected on the market in 1992 and this will probably make gammaglobulin obsolete.

Typhoid – recommended.
This requires two injections and lasts three years. There is a new oral vaccine which may be more effective, with fewer side effects, and that probably lasts three years. Paratyphoid vaccination is no longer recommended.

Meningitis – Recommended
There was an epidemic of Bacterial Meningitis in the Kathmandu valley in 1983/4 but the incidence of cases has fallen a lot since then. The risk is now low, but this is a serious disease, the vaccination lasts three years, is 90% effective, and is therefore recommended.

Tetanus – Strongly recommended.
You should have current cover for this. If you have not had a booster in the last ten years, then get one now before you stab yourself with a garden fork!

Polio – Recommended.
Again, you should have a booster if you have not had one in the last ten years.

Measles, Mumps, Rubella (German Measles).
Immunization is recommended if you have not been previously infected or vaccinated.

Please Note

The above are the standard immunisations which can be recommended to all travellers in that the advantages of immunisation clearly outweigh any side effects. For the less common, or lower risk diseases below, then it is less easy to make a clear assessment of the risks, which may vary with each individual traveller.

We suggest that the following immunisations are not so necessary for short-term travellers, unless they are particularly concerned. We suggest that they should be considered by long-term travellers, those going to remote regions, and those coming in close contact with local people. When considering these immunisations, we recommend that you get up to date advice from your nearest hospital specialising in infectious diseases. They will have more up to date, and specialised information to complement the advice of your G.P.

Tuberculosis
We recommend that you ask your Doctor for a Mantoux test, then, depending on the result, discuss a BCG vaccination.

Hepatitis B
This is spread by infected person's blood coming in contact with your own through cuts, re-used needles, blood transfusion, swallowing, sex, inhalation, etc. For most travellers this is probably very low risk, but it is a severe and occasionally fatal illness. Immunisation requires three injections and is safe but expensive.

Rabies
If you avoid dogs then the risk of infection is low. If however you do get bitten then very expensive modern treatment with anti Rabies Serum plus immunisation is essential, effective and readily available provided you can return soon to Kathmandu – see Appendix A. If you are planning a remote river trip where you will be away from Kathmandu for an extended period then you may consider that the immunisation is worthwhile. Modern ('Diploid cell') vaccine is safe but expensive: three doses are needed over 6 months and it lasts three years. The expense can be reduced by intradermal injection of one tenth of the dose.

Diptheria
Unless you are working with children, there is little risk of infection. You were probably vaccinated as a child and are still immune. If you are concerned about this disease you should discuss a test or low dose booster with your Doctor.

Cholera
The World Health Organisation no longer recommend Cholera Vaccination for travellers because the vaccine is only partly effective and has significant reactions.

Japanese B Encephalitis
This a mosquito-borne disease so is not found above 1000 metres. Cases have been reported in the Terai, but none affecting tourists. It is, though, a very nasty disease and the vaccine is safe and effective; so if you plan to spend an extended time in the Terai or North India, you should perhaps consider this vaccination.

Malaria Precautions

Malaria is transmitted by mosquitos; these like hot damp conditions, so malaria is fairly prevalent in the Terai (The lowland plain adjoining the Indian Border), especially in the monsoon and post- monsoon period, despite campaigns to control it. Mosquitos are fewer in the dry season and become fewer the higher you go and are not usually found above 1000 metres: so the Kathmandu valley is quite safe. The illness is characterised by fevers and chills which can be easily mis-diagnosed. Modern treatment is normally effective – the disease is only fatal if it is not diagnosed and the parasite invades the brain (cerebal malaria).

Simple preventative measures at evening and night-time to prevent mosquito bites are quite effective – long sleeved clothes, mesh on doors and windows, bed nets impregnated with insect repellent, mosquito coils and insect repellent: only a few mosquitos carry the parasite and these rarely bite in the daytime.

Anti-malaria medicines are not 100% effective but are reasonably safe in long-term use. These need to be some time before arriving in the risk area (normally 2 weeks), taken regularly throughout your stay and for 4-6 weeks after leaving it.

If you are travelling direct to Kathmandu and spending little time in the Terai then the risk is probably minimal and not worth the cost and hassle of a course of fairly nasty-tasting drugs – but do take extra care on the precautions we have mentioned. If you are spending much time in the Terai or in India, then we would definitely advise you to take a course of anti-malaria drugs.

Chloroquine is the most commonly prescribed drug but there are patches of resistance to this; thus European doctors usually prescribe an additional drug, Paludrine to cover these. Mefloquine is the usual drug prescribed by doctors in North America. Doxycycline is occasionally prescribed but should be avoided by river runners because it frequently predisposes to Sun burn.

Staying Healthy

Introduction

Most first-timers to Nepal are concerned about exotic diseases; indeed mention Nepal to most people and the subject of disease is one of the first things that they ask. Happily, the reality is that you are unlikely to experience anything worse than perhaps a mild case of diarrhoea.

A few simple rules are outlined here – follow these and you should be able to avoid common diseases – and perhaps even that one episode of diarrhoea.

More detailed advice on medical problems is given in Appendix A.

Common Diseases

By far the most important group of diseases are the 'faeco-oral' ones that enter your body through your mouth. These are excreted in someone else's stool and by various paths they come to your fingertips – this is the key point where your protection comes in.

The diseases concerned are the diarrhoeas, hepatitis A, Typhoid, Polio and some worms. The reason that these bugs get to within arms reach is that, unlike home, toilet waste is not flushed away or treated, and is in contact with the drinking water supply. Any open water in the third world must be considered as infected. This is of particular relevance to canoeists and rafters as the rivers we use are essentially very, very dilute sewers for the villages we pass, especially in the dry period before the Monsoon. We also camp on beaches that may look clean but which hide disease.

Food is involved because it is usual for local people to defecate in the fields where crops are growing. In addition, most vegetables are washed in open water.

HELP! Does this mean that we dehydrate or starve? – No, a few germs will be dealt with by your bodies' natural defences; it's a lot of germs that can harm you. You can eat well, drink lots and stay healthy if you follow a few simple rules:

Health Guidelines

1. Wash your HANDS before each meal – so simple, so easily forgotten! In the course of the day you will have picked up a few bugs, and hand washing (preferably with soap) will remove these.

2. Consider all water to be infected and not safe for drinking unless you sterilise it or have seen it boiled. Bottled or canned drinks are generally safe as is tea from Chai stalls where both milk and water are boiled. Check the seals on bottled water as some places refill the empty bottle with local water. Ice and ice cream can be made from infected water so are best avoided.

3. Vegetables and fruit should be either cooked or peeled (Hint: carry a small pen knife in your pocket on bus journeys). Salad type vegetables can be washed and soaked in an iodine solution – but avoid green leafy vegetables such as lettuce or spinach that have a large surface area to collect germs and are difficult to wash. It's probably best to think of all green salads and ice cream as dangerous treats – best avoided until you get home.

4. Eat freshly-cooked, hot, simple food – whether cooked in a smart restaurant, on a road side stall, or on your camping stove. Avoid reheated food.

5. Be wary of meat unless fresh and well cooked. Also be wary of dairy products with the exception of plain Yoghurt which is normally safe and good for you. Try to avoid any food with flies on it.

6. Try to eat off clean utensils. On the river trip these can be washed with boiling or sterilised water. On a bus trip, consider carrying a small pack of wipes or tissues for cleaning spoons, cup rims and hands.

   These simple rules should help you avoid most problems; it has been shown however, that even obsessive hygiene cannot prevent the occasional bout of diarrhoea in your group. If you are on a commercial raft trip your guide will be able to advise treatment and medications if needed. If, as is more likely, you have diarrhoea in Kathmandu – from all those lovely cream cakes? – then there is a detailed treatise on the subject in Appendix A.

Three more simple guidelines to keep you healthy:

7. Wear shoes – especially near villages or on popular beaches. Hook worm and scabies are caught by barefoot people.

8. Clean all open cuts, however small, with iodine at the end of each day.

9. Drink plenty so that your urine is always clear or a pale yellow.

Water Sterilisation

Dead easy – two drops of iodine tincture in a litre and wait ten minutes!

This is generally acknowledged by authorities as the best method. Well-proven, convenient, cheap, and almost no side effects. It kills almost all known germs – even Amoeba and Giardia. Iodine is safe for many months – note how many countries routinely add iodine to salt.

Iodine comes in several forms*: the most common is tincture of iodine in alcohol. This is easily purchased in Kathmandu. It is available from your pharmacist back home – but not too readily because it's not in high demand and it is a cheap product with little profit. Your Pharmacist will probably try to sell you some much more expensive sterilisation tablets. Never mind, buy your iodine in Kathmandu and mollify your friendly home pharmacist by buying two plastic dropper bottles off him – he may not have empty ones, but eye or nose drop bottles are normally cheap enough just to empty – these are difficult to get in Kathmandu. (Buy two or three because you're bound either to lose them, or give them to friends). Two drops will sterilise one litre of water in ten minutes, double the dose if the water is cloudy and double the time required if the water is cold. If you don't like the faint taste of iodine then the flavor can be easily disguised with fruit drink powders (Cremola and Tang fans take note) and this is a good idea because it encourages you to drink plenty – important in a hot climate. If the water is very cloudy then it is a good idea to let it stand in a container so that the particles settle out before you transfer to your water bottle for purification. If necessary, cloudy water can be filtered through a clean cloth.

Forget the sales hype for filters and other purifiers – they are expensive, bulky, less effective and more to the point can be dangerous if the filter develops infection or hidden cracks. They may perhaps be useful on large raft trips.

Water can also be sterilised by boiling, but this may be wasteful of precious fuel. It used to be thought that water needed to boil for 10-20 minutes to be safe, but recent research has shown that bringing to the boil, even at moderate altitude, is sufficient.

If you are pregnant, have an over-active thyroid gland, or are allergic to iodine then chlorine based tablets e.g. Puritabs, can be used instead of iodine. These are considerably more expensive and probably do not protect against giardia and amoeba.

Resuscitation

All Raft Guides and kayakers in Nepal will of course have been trained in Cardio/Pulmonary Resuscitation. Yes, its extremely unlikely that someone is going to drown on your trip, but we believe that everyone invoved in water recreation should know the basics of CPR: you may be the only person on the scene at the time to resuscitate your friend. Your local Red Cross Society would be delighted to give practical training on a resuscitation manikin.

We print opposite a basic reminder that you may like to photocopy and waterproof so that you can carry it on you. (This was originally produced by the Mike Jones Rally in Britain as a waterproof self adhesive sticker to go on your kayak, etc. – the idea came from the Alpina Kayak Club in Germany).

**Other forms of iodine are: Lugol's Aqueous Iodine – use 8 drops a litre. Iodine crystals – keep in a small bottle of water and use the saturated solution at 15 mls per litre (careful you don't pour out the crystals). Iodine tablets – expensive and effective, but only have a limited shelf life – use one tablet per litre.*

RESUSCITATION

REMINDER CARD

KEEP CALM

CALL OR SEND FOR HELP

(A) ASSESSMENT

- Is the casualty conscious?
- Is the casualty breathing?

AIRWAY

- Turn onto back
- Check mouth
- Lift chin
- Extend neck

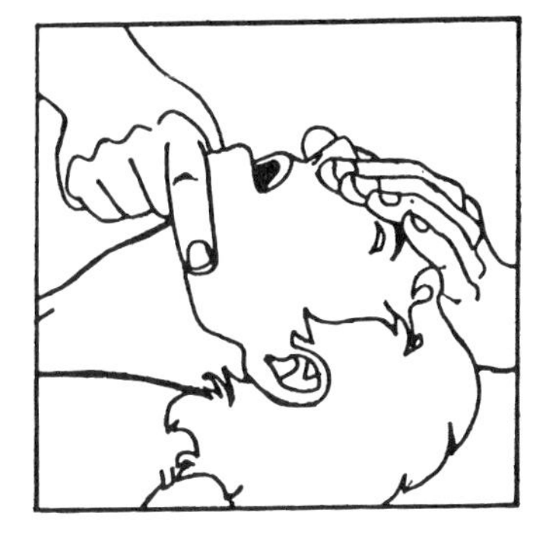

(B) BREATHING

- Pinch nose shut
- Mouth to mouth, 2 inflations
- Check pulse
  ↳ if present ......
- Continue, one inflation every 5 seconds

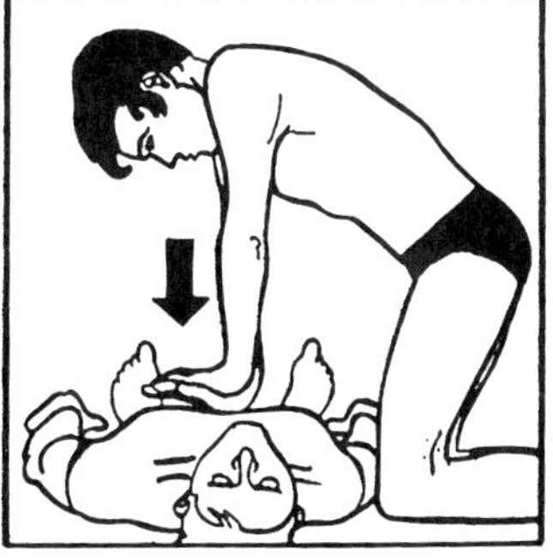

(C) CIRCULATION

IF NO PULSE

- Remove any Buoyancy aid
- Place hands on centre of lower half of breastbone
- Compress 60 – 80 per minute
- Give 2 inflations after every 15 compressions

CHECK PULSE EVERY 3 MINUTES

CALL AGAIN FOR HELP

CONTINUE UNTIL MEDICAL HELP ARRIVES

On recovery, put in recovery position

LEARN ON A COURSE AND REMEMBER!

Produced by the MIKE JONES RALLY, in conjunction with  **RLSS UK**

AIDS

There is little AIDS in Nepal at the moment. You are most at danger from casual sex with fellow travellers. If lust wins over better sense then the male partner should wear a condom.

Oral Contraceptives

If you are are taking 'the Pill' (Combined oral contraceptive pill) then note that there may be problems of reduced absorption if you have to take antibiotics or have a gut infection.

Probably the simplest way to manage is to keep taking the pill, the only proviso being that you miss out the fourth (placebo or sugar pill) week and go on to the next packet directly. In addition, start your alternative method of contraception and continue this for a week after the illness or antibiotic has finished. By then, you will effectively have started a new course of the pill and will be back to the same level of protection.

If vomiting occurs within four hours of taking your pill, then take a second pill. If further vomiting, start using the alternative method of contraception and continue the pill as above. It is a sensible precaution to carry an alternative method and a spare supply of the pill in a different bag.

Dysentery? . . . *by Foxy*

5 a.m. in the morning; the darkness is diffusing into a cold grey. I lie snug in my sleeping bag aware of the river side around me coming to life, but mainly listening to the rumblings of my stomach. I can feel the pressure building up, and, as there's no one around I am confident about breaking wind to relieve the pressure. It's a mistake, I can sense a follow through . . . Panic! Terror! I claw my way desperately out of sleeping bag and bivi bag, buttocks clenched tight, leap ten feet, trousers down and explode.

Dysentery, dysentery, dysentery; the thought ached in my bowels. The stool inspection is not too promising and I'm still two or three days from the next road. I have to resign myself to further trauma. Fortunately my fears are unjustified; by mid-day I'm feeling better and even hungrier so I cook up double rations and put my upset down to twenty hours of travelling, lack of food, and heat. Once again I can relax into the flow of the river.

RAFTING WITH A COMMERCIAL OPERATOR

Introduction to Rafting

Will I enjoy rafting?

If you have taken the trouble to beg, borrow or buy this book; then the answer to this has to be YES! There are many kinds of rafting trips and the important thing is to choose the right trip for you. Of course, there are people who don't enjoy rafting – if you hate water activities and the outdoors, then stop right here!

Why go rafting?

- The rivers of Nepal take you away from the busy trekking routes and penetrate the heart of rural unspoilt Nepal where there are no roads.
- Rafting offers an attractive alternative to trekking, something to note if you don't enjoy walking. It also complements trekking, in that you see the country from a different viewpoint.
- Rafting 'leaves no footprints', has minimal ecological effect, and causes little disruption to the social patterns of local life.
- Rafting gives you the unique and enjoyable experience of river travel and if you chose a white water river, the exhilaration of running rapids.
- There can be few better ways of viewing wildlife, than quietly drifting along in a boat.

White water or flat water?

Rafting has this image of crashing through horrendous rapids and monstrous waves and, yes, there is plenty of this type of rafting in Nepal, but there are also many rivers which we call 'flat water' where you lazily float along admiring the scenery, with only a few very small rapids or riffles, to add minor interest. Rafting in Nepal is a great experience in it's own right; the thrill of running white water rapids is the cream on the cake for those who enjoy it!

Rivers are graded for difficulty on an international scale of 1 to 6 and if you prefer a leisurely flat water trip then you should chose a river that is class 1 or 2 and that we call 'easy' – examples are the Bhote Kosi, and the lower Kali Gandaki. On rivers like these, you'll hardly get your feet wet!

Most people are naturally a little bit apprehensive if they haven't been on white water before, but after the first rapid are 'hooked' – most active people would be happy booking on a river of moderate difficulty, class 3+ or 4−: examples are the Trisuli and upper Kali Gandaki. Remember that we grade a river on the hardest sections – most rivers have days of easier water and long stretches in between the rapids in which to relax. You can usually walk around any rapids that you feel are too big.

More difficult, class 4, white water rivers are really exciting and add a spice of danger. To book a trip on one of these rivers you should be active and comfortable around water – and preferably have some previous rafting experience (Note that it is not necesssary to be able to swim, but swimmers are more able to relax and will be be more comfortable and safer in this alien watery environment).

Time of Year

As we explain elsewhere, the time of year always makes a big difference to the difficulty of water. After the **monsoon** in September and October, **water volumes are huge** and all rivers much more difficult or too dangerous. Later in the year, rivers become much more pool/drop, and there is time to recover and sort yourself out between rapids. You need to think carefully about this; as one raft guide put it 'water levels are critical to people's enjoyment'.

Paddle rafting versus oar powered rafts

Any raft can be paddled, or rigged with an oar frame and rowed. Each method of propulsion has it's advantages and appeals to different people.

With an **oar-powered raft** the Guide sits in the middle and rows it down the river, manoeuvreing in rapids using 'ferry glides'. – this gives him or her time to react. On bigger rapids (class 4) it is possible that the rafters may be asked to act as human ballast by using their weight to balance the raft as it goes through big waves – but mostly it's just a case of holding on tight and enjoying the thrills.

Paddle rafting is all about group participation and teamwork. All (or most) of the rafters have paddles, propel the raft down the river and manoeuvre it through the rapids with the Guide wielding a steering paddle at the back of the raft and 'calling the shots'. Paddling your own raft is a lot of fun, challenging, satisfying, and builds a great team spirit; but it's also hard work at times and there is greater scope for things to go wrong, so it is obviously not everyone's choice.

Many raft guides and companies prefer oar rigs because they feel that they are more in control than if they had to rely on a paddle-wielding crew. They point out that things are less likely to go wrong with an oar rig, and that if a client is injured, or if equipment is damaged or lost, then it is the guide who will get blamed. However, many guides prefer paddle rafting because it is more participatory and challenging – if the rafters have more fun, then so do they!

I asked Cam MacLeay about the differences (Cam is one of the World's top raft guides – and rowed the raft on the 'Taming of the Lion', Indus Gorges Expedition). He opinioned that a good paddle crew can show up any performance by an oar powered rig; the paddle crew has more power and can perform more difficult manoevres – remember the Grand Canyon of the Stikine film? He was also of the opinion that being a good paddle raft guide is more difficult than being an oar guide: because it's more of a team effort the guide has to discuss in greater depth the reasons why a rapid has to be run in a particular way; he has to train the paddle crew in different strokes and manoevres, to weld them into a cohesive team, and on a rapid he has less time to react, so he has to read the water better and plan ahead, then he has to communicate and motivate the crew to do what he wants, and finally, also make corrections for any mistakes they make!

One thing to note is that on both paddle rafts and oar rigs you spend quite a lot of time drifting along quietly, letting the current do the work and enjoying the scenery and wildlife.

'Upset' rapid, Trisuli (Anders Blomquist)

Different Styles of Rafting trip

Like trekking agencies, commercial operators offer many different styles of rafting trip to suit different people's idea of a holiday. We suggest the main choices are between:

- Participatory versus everything done for you.
- Lots of gear and comfort versus light and manoeuvrable.
- Large group versus 'small is beautiful'.

Rafting trips can be quite luxurious with lots of equipment. You can be rowed down the river and a full team of staff do everything for you; your tent is put up, you are served drinks as you sit in a camp chair and eat delicious meals off a white table cloth. Because labour is cheap in Nepal, a 'luxury' safari-style trip like this is not expensive and represents incredible value when compared with other parts of the world.

At the other extreme, you can paddle the raft, load and unload it, put up your own tent, help the Guides cook the meals and wash up, etc. Surprisingly perhaps, there may be little difference in price between these two styles of trip – as we mentioned, labour is cheap in Nepal, a good Nepalese cook will be more economical with food, and participatory trips are more expensive in terms of wear and tear and loss of equipment. Proponents of the participatory style of trip are mainly paddle rafters and they also adopt a lightweight philososphy so that the rafts are lighter and easier to paddle. Outdoor enthusiasts will know that lightweight, hi-tech gear is good but expensive.

There are many variants on these two extremes, and it is a matter of personal philosophies and life styles which you will prefer. The enthusiasm of your guides will obviously affect the style of your trip and you should try to talk to them prior to booking a trip.

Size of group is again a matter of personal philosophy and what you want to get out of a trip. We have been with groups of 35 on a river trip and had some great non-stop partying, but a large group will make it difficult to interact with local people and also have an adverse environmental impact. Most people come away on a river trip partly to enjoy the quiet and beauty of getting away from the noise and tempo of civilisation – to 'listen to the sounds of time and the river flowing'. You need to be in a small group to do this. But on the other hand, a river trip should be an enjoyable social experience and a small group who don't get on with each other can be a pretty boring and even miserable experience.

How Long?

Undoubtedly the best value trips in both terms of the overall experience and value for money are the long multi-day trips such as the Sun Kosi, Tamur or Karnali. Rafting trips like these, where you are away from the highway and 'civilisation' for a week or two are immensely uplifting and memorable holidays – talk to anyone who has been on one and they will enthuse for hours and convince you that if you can possibly afford it, you should try to book on one of these 'World Classics'.

Sad to say, if your time is limited, then you won't get anything like this 'World Class' experience on a 3 or 4 day trip: however, in this length of time you will start to become a proficient rafter and will settle into the pleasant routine of camping on the riverside. You will have time to slow down to the pace of the river and to enjoy the natural surroundings. It will also, importantly, give you time to relax and to get to know your guides and fellow rafters. Most people's vacation time is limited, and these trips do represent a reasonable compromise of time versus holiday experience.

A one or two day trip should be regarded more as a 'taster' where you will only get a partial flavour of the full rafting experience.

Who enjoys Rafting?

Women in particular in our experience – for many different reasons, so don't ask us – ask them!

A rafting trip can be a wonderful holiday and an excellent experience for **older children** – but this obviously depends on your family and how confident they are about water. Most rafting companies suggest that 14 years and older could consider more adventurous rivers such as the Sun Kosi. 7-13 year olds would usually be happier and safer on class 2-3 rivers. Points to note are that camping beaches are relatively clean, safe and friendly places. Kids like to be active and involved so a paddle rafting trip is better for older kids (We suggest a deal: you allow them to go paddle rafting, provided they agree to walk around the more difficult rapids). An oar rig, and a quieter river like the Seti or the lower Trisuli would be better for younger children.

There is no upper age limit for rafting: the nice thing is that it can be as leisurely or as active as you wish. In our experience, **older people** enjoy the river experience, the natural surroundings and the relaxed pace of camp life. (Cam MacLeay tells of two 70-year old widows who booked on a raft trip down the Zambesi Gorges (BIG water class 4+) in the mistaken idea that it was 'a Gin and Tonic sunset cruise' and he says 'they just loved it'!)

If you or friends are **disabled**, then rafting and kayaking offers the freedom of getting out into the real Nepal and we strongly recommend that you discuss the possibilities with one of the more reputable companies. One possible option is to paddle your own kayak or 'duckie'.

Joining a Group

If you have a group of six or more then you should be able to choose your own river and negotiate a deal with a rafting company for a customised trip. Make sure it is clear whether this is a private trip for just your party, or whether the rafting company can sell spare places.

If you are by yourself, or just with a friend or two, then you will be limited to the trips that are being advertised by the companies at the time. Many companies will advertise a trip, but of course will only run it if they can get enough people to make the trip economic. The key question is, 'Have the other would-be rafters paid their deposit?' Now, you yourself don't want to pay your deposit unless the trip looks like it's definitely on, so you can end up in a catch 22 situation where no one wants to pay their deposit because no one else has paid theirs! If you don't trust what the company is telling you, then if possible we suggest you go and talk to the other would-be rafters.

If you are keen to do one particular river, then why not advertise for other people and put your own group together? This way you will get the trip you want, with the Company you want, at the right time for you, and at the best possible price. You should find it surprisingly easy to get people to join you, in that would-be rafters are always delighted to have someone else do all the work of putting a trip together, checking out rafting companies, etc.!

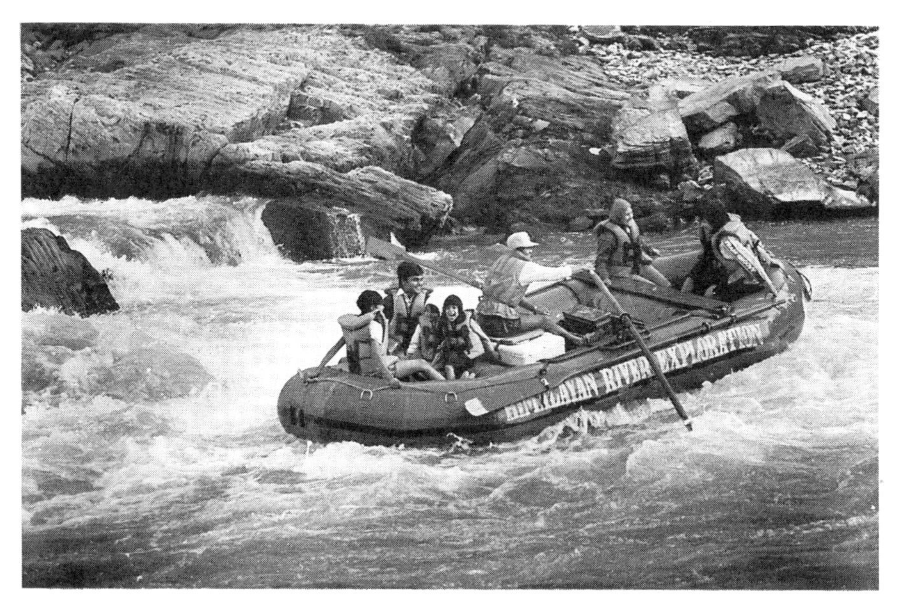

Family group on the Trisuli (H.R.E.)

Safety

Most people's image of white water rafting is one portrayed by films and the media and almost everyone who hasn't done it imagines it as a horrendously dangerous sport. The truth is the reverse: accidents, even minor ones, are rare and rafting has a much safer accident record than say trekking, cycling, skiing, or probably walking around Kathmandu!

This is because when you are on the river you are in a relatively protected vehicle – a nice big bouncy rubber raft directed (we hope) by an experienced professional guide – in effect in a controlled situation. This isn't to say that rafting doesn't have risks; if you run class 4 white water then there is always the possibility of a capsize, moving water isn't a rigidly structured, precise environment, it wouldn't be much fun if it was! However, if the worst does happen, and you do take an accidental swim – then because water is a nice soft landing, it's not likely to be anything worse than an involuntary ducking.

But, having given you this reassurance, we have to stress that white water rafting IS an assumed risk sport; it relies on good practice to keep it relatively safe and you should carefully check the experience of your guides and the quality of the equipment.

At the time of writing there were no minimum safety conditions recommended by any official body in Nepal. We have talked to many international Guides and based on their experience, and regulations in other countries, we suggest the following check list for your guidance.

'They make it look so difficult'

Basic Safety Guidelines

1. Minimum of two rafts per trip.
2. The person in charge of the raft must be a qualified, trained guide with a minimum of 50 days rafting experience.
3. Raft guides should have done at least one previous trip on the river.
4. The Trip Leader should have done a minimum of five previous trips on that river.
5. All Guides should have a current First Aid certificate.

Guideline one is a basic rule everyone agrees is good sense, but many guides still feel that it doesn't apply to them! Some of the worst international rafting accidents have occurred where there has only been one raft. Note that many experts accept that one (or preferably two) safety kayakers could replace the second raft – at times with advantage. In high water conditions, three rafts are safer than two.

Like all guidelines, there are exceptions which need to be made in rare circumstances – but it is important that these are discussed and the implications understood by all concerned – particularly by the customer who is paying for the trip.

Personal Safety Points

Your Guide will give you a safety talk at the start of your trip and give basic guidance. May we suggest the following points:

1. Normally wear your life jacket at all times when on the water – check with the Guide before taking it off, even just to don a sweater. Wear your helmet when directed by the Guide (or more often if you don't trust the way your team mates wield their paddles!). Wear your life jacket and helmet properly with the straps done up comfortably so that they will protect you and not just fall off at the first bump. It is also a good idea to keep your life jacket on if scrambling along the sides of a rapid to scout or take photographs – it's all too easy to slip and fall into the water.
2. Keep your legs and arms inside the raft. If you are going to hit a rock, then let the raft bounce off, don't try and fend off: rafts are tougher than human bones and cost less to repair.
3. If you do take an accidental swim:
   - try not to panic
   - hold onto your paddle (this makes you more visible)
   - swim to the raft if close
   - get into the white water swimming position, on your back with feet downstream (so you can see where you are going and can push off rocks with your feet)
   - relax, practise breath control and enjoy the ride!
4. NEVER, at any time, or in any circumstance, tie or wrap a rope around any part of you – this can hold you underwater and drown you.

Which River?

Your choice of river for a rafting trip will depend on a multitude of factors, many of course personal to you, but here are some ideas to get you started. The introduction to the rivers of each Region in the second half of this book should also prove helpful.

Remember that time of year is critical to your choice; in high water conditions, September and October, some rivers are too dangerous and all others are much more difficult.

Long multi-day trips

If you have seven days or more, are looking for white water and a really exciting and memorable experience then the choice is between the Tamur, the Sun Kosi, and the Karnali – these are all World Classics, with excellent white water, stunning scenery, unspoilt villages away from all roads and beautiful beaches. These surpass all other rafting trips in Nepal!

The **Sun Kosi** is the cheapest of these trips because the start is close to Kathmandu and you can drive to both start and finish points, it's good at any level and has rapids all the way down the river. Often described as one of the 'ten best rafting trips in the World', this is an excellent choice for most people and especially for those doing their first river trip in Nepal.

The **Karnali** is our pick as the best overall trip. The rapids are more challenging than the Sun Kosi, but not too difficult; add to that a fine two-day trek, superb canyons and pristine wilderness; finish with a couple of days at the Royal Bardiya Wildlife Reserve and you have a rafting trip that is probably 'Best of its kind' anywhere in the World.

The **Tamur** could be described as a mini-Karnali, with a spectacular trek in to the start and lots of white water interest – at the right water level probably more challenging than the above rivers.

Another river that should also be considered is the full length of the Kali Gandaki. This offers a good multi-day rafting trip, particularly recommended when combined with a trek in to the Annapurna Sanctuary.

If you are looking for a long multi-day trip, but with easier water, then the best are in the Far West: the Seti/Karnali, the Bheri, and the Mahakali; all remote and beautifully unspoilt.

Medium length trips

If you still want an exciting multi-day white water raft trip, but your time is more limited, then four rivers suggest themselves – the Trisuli, upper Kali Gandaki, Arun, and Dudh Kosi/Sun Kosi.

The cheapest trip is likely to be on the Trisuli but this is spoilt by the main highway that runs alongside most of it. For a little more cost you should be able to get a trip on the **upper Kali Gandaki**, a much finer river in our opinion. The Arun and Dudh Kosi/Sun Kosi are good choices if you would have liked to do a full Sun Kosi trip but cannot afford the time; you have to fly in to the start of these so they will be more expensive.

If you prefer easier water, then two rivers in the Far West, the Babai and lower Bheri (from Surkhet) offer superb wildlife, unspoilt scenery and easy rafting, but at a price. More accessible and cheaper options are the lower Kali Gandaki and the Seti: both offer good scenery, jungle, wildlife and unspoilt beaches.

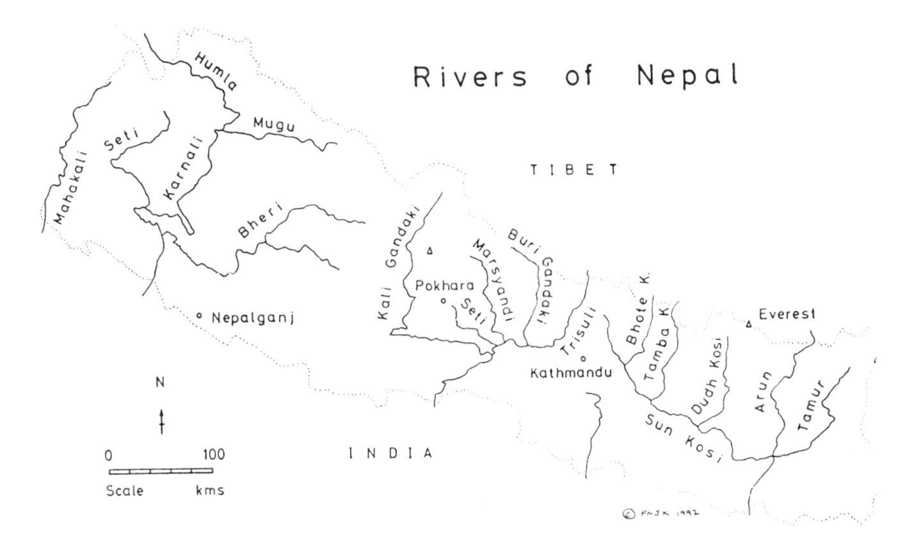

Short Trips

The most exciting two-day white water trip is probably the lower section of the Tamur river – great if you've little time, but plenty of money (for the air flights). The **Trisuli** is an obvious and popular choice if you are looking for a day or two of exhilarating white water and at the cheapest possible price.

If you only have a day and would like to try an easy water rafting trip then we recommend the **Bhote Kosi** (upper Sun Kosi) which is relatively unspoilt and yet close to Kathmandu.

Summary of the 'Bests'

Best **long, white water** trips, 'World clasics' – Karnali, Tamur, and Sun Kosi.

Best rivers for **wildlife and fishing** – Babai, Bheri, Karnali, Mahakali.

Best **3-6 day white water** trips – Arun, Dudh Kosi/Sun Kosi, upper Kali Gandaki, Trisuli.

Best **4-12 day easy water** trips – Bheri, Seti/Karnali, lower Kali Gandaki.

Best **1-3 day white water** trips – Tamur (lower), Trisuli, Marsyandi.

Best **1-3 day easy water** trips – Babai, Seti, Bhote Kosi.

Best combined **treking** and **rafting** trips – Tamur, Kali Gandaki, Karnali.

Best **budget** trips – Sun Kosi, Kali Gandaki, 1-3 day Trisuli white water.

Combining Trips

If you have the time, you will want to do as many rivers as possible, and it is relatively cheap to add a couple of days on the front or back of your trip. Popular choices are a warm-up day on the Trisuli on the way out to the Karnali, or to combine a float down the Babai with a

Karnali trip. A trip down the Sun Kosi finishes at Chatra, only a few hours drive away from the bottom section of the Tamur – a magnificent stretch of white water and a great climax to a rafting holiday. The Marsyandi is another technically difficult river that is popular as an additional trip, especially with paddle rafters.

It's a fine idea to **combine a trek with a raft trip** and this to most people adds to the total experience and the enjoyment. The Tamur is the obvious star here, with a wonderfully scenic three day trek in to the start. The Karnali is special in that the only way in to this remote river is to trek in along a trail that sees few Westerners.

The other option is to trek down from the high Himalaya to the start of your rafting trip. Probably the best river for this is the Kali Gandaki – you can trek in to Annapurna Sanctuary and then raft down the Kali Gandaki all the way to Chitwan National Park – a fine 3 week trip. It would also be possible to combine treks to Everest Base camp with descents of the Dudh Kosi/Sun Kosi or the Arun. People who have done this type of combined trek and rafting trip are very enthusiastic about the experience of travelling from the high Himalaya to the dusty plains as one journey and describe it as 'immensely satisfying'.

Rafting Summary

River	*Class*	*Volume Cumecs*	*Total days*	*River days*	*Scenery/ wildlife*	*Star rating*
TRISULI	2/3+	300	2–8	1–7	**	**
Kali Gandaki upper	4–	120	6	5	**	***
Kali Gandaki lower	2	250	5	4	**	**
Seti	2	40	3	2	**	*
Marsyandi	4	80	3	2	**	**
Buri Gandaki	3	90	5	2	*	*
SUN KOSI	4–	400	10	9	**	***
Bhote Kosi	2	90	1–2	1	*	**
Indrawati	2	40	1–2	1	*	*
Dudh Kosi/Sun Kosi	4–	400	7	6	**	**
Arun	4–	215	4	3	**	**
Tamur	4	150	7–11	6	***	***
KARNALI – lower	4	300	10–11	7	***	***
Mahakali	3	300	9–11	6	***	*
Seti/Karnali	3	130	8–10	7	***	**
Bheri	2	170	6/12	4/10	**	*
Babai Nadi	1	35	4	2	***	**

Notes:
Total days = days to and from Kathmandu or Pokhara.
Star rating is our subjective view of the river as a rafting trip – taking into account logistics and cost.
*** Highly recommended, ** Recommended, * Specialist interest.

Selecting a Rafting Company

(This section is written by Peter Knowles – an impartial river-runner with no commercial involvement with any rafting company or ageny.)

Value for money

In 1991 the typical price for a rafting trip on the Sun Kosi varied between $400 and $800 for a ten day trip. This is excellent value when compared with similar multi-day trips in other countries – for example a trip on the Grand Canyon of the Colorado will typically cost you $1900. Rafting trips in Nepal are such good value that I suggest your priority should be quality of experience before price.

In 1991 there were 45 companies in Kathmandu claiming to be rafting operators: a few of these were well established companies with an excellent reputation, some were agencies sub-contracting to other companies, others were newly formed by ambitious, but inex perienced people keen to get into the 'glamour business' of white water rafting, a few were new, with modern equipment and well trained guides, most were small, competent, but owned only a few rafts and a minimum of equipment.

In a market like this you need to be very careful when selecting a company – especially for a more remote trip or one in high water conditions.

The Quality Trip

The best companies in Nepal have river guides with international training, modern equip ment and standards that excede many overseas operations. These offer a quality trip at a reasonable price. It's very difficult to recommend particular companies, but at the risk of offending others, I feel duty bound to mention some of the longer established companies that appear to have a particularly high reputation. To do this, I asked around some of the acknowledged top guides and rafting operators as to who else they would recommend.

Himalayan River Exploration (H.R.E.) stand out as the foremost rafting company in Nepal. Part of the Tiger Tops and Mountain Travel group, they have historically had an up-market clientele, with an accent on oar rigs and comfort for the client. In recent years they have responded to customer demand and run more participatory style paddle trips.

Himalayan Encounters are the Nepali company closely associated with Encounter Over land. They have an accent on group participation and paddle rafting, reflecting their clientele who are mainly young overland travellers. However their customers seem to have got older and more up-market and I have even heard rumours that they were considering employing cooks – heresy!

Two smaller companies both get high praise from other outfitters and agencies: G.H.R. and White Magic. And then I'm afraid I couldn't get a consistent pattern of recommenda tion: there were several new companies who hadn't had time to establish a reputation, lots of smaller companies who would be highly recommended by 5 people but dammed by others (probably unfairly!) and one or two companies who everyone identified as real cowboys, but who I can't unfortunately name for legal reasons.

Smaller companies in Nepal change rapidly and some of their most senior and experi enced guides break away and form new companies. In a changing market like this, any recommendations are likely to be misleading and out of date; better for you to ask about the experience of the senior guides behind the company – I suggest that this is the key thing.

The budget trip

Many experienced guides claim that some would-be customers have been their own worst enemies by making it sound as if the price of a trip is the only thing they are interested in. A few companies have responded to this market demand and run really cheap 'bargain basement' rafting trips: be warned, from the stories I've heard from customers, many of these trips can be miserable, nasty and dangerous.

I suppose that broadly speaking, like most things in life, we get what we pay for, but why pay good money for a trip if it's of such a low standard that you won't enjoy it – surely, better to not go at all? Pay a little extra though, ask the right questions, select a reasonable company and you can have the trip of a lifetime. The vast majority of rafting companies in Nepal offer a really enjoyable trip of good standard and at a very reasonable price.

There are some real bargains to be had if you have the time to hunt them out: the most typical situation is where a trip has say 10 people and just two spare places – the operator can heavily discount these places. You have to be in Kathmandu at the right time to grab the opportunity. Another possibility is a newly formed company, with good equipment who are prepared to make a loss in their first year just to break into the market and establish a reputation; but make sure you ask the right questions.....

General advice

Jim Traverso, a travel specialist, gives the following advice:

- Even if your trip is being arranged by your travel agent or trekking outfitter, ask to speak with the rafting guides in person. This will give you a chance to form an impression of the people who you'll be spending time with.
- Ask if a group has recently returned, or is due to, from the same river. Make time to speak to these customers about their trip; this will be your best source of information about food, transportation, and the quality of the trip.
- Safety is of paramount importance. Ask about the age of the equipment and about the training and experience of the boatman.

Read our safety guidelines carefully and quiz the company on these. If you are planning a remote and adventurous river like the Sun Kosi, Tamur, or Karnali then double check the experience of the guides and the quality of the equipment; this particularly applies to any trip done in high water conditions in June, September or October.

We've mentioned the different type of trips you can have: talk to the company about the organisation of the trip and try to get a feel for how it runs . . .

How will you get to and from the river?
How long is each day?
How many actual hours paddling or rowing?
How many in the river team and what are their jobs?
Where will you camp each night?
Do the river team prefer to camp near or away from villages?
What happens after you arrive at the campsite?
Do the rafting guests participate in camp chores – how much?
Ask to see the menu.
What do you cook on – fires or stoves?
What happens to garbage?
What do people do in the evenings?

Look through the photo file that most operators have, this can be very helpful and give you an idea about equipment and safety.

How old are the rafts – who actually owns them?

How old are the life jackets – ask to see one?

What spares are carried?

Your Raft Guide

If possible, ask the guides about their experience (many guides keep a log book recording all their trips and training), but also ask them more general things such as why do they like rafting and what kind of a trip do they like to run. Try to decide whether you relate to them or not. Do you have confidence in them? Do they communicate well? Are they fun to be with or are they quiet and competent?

The best Nepali guides have trained and worked overseas, have years of experience of running rivers in their own country, and you will enjoy their local expertise, enthusiasm and sense of humour. A few raft guides come from overseas each season: although their knowledge of Nepal and Nepalese rivers is limited, they do bring in variety, new ideas, and create an international depth of knowledge that is good for the rafting industry in Nepal. More and more, as in skiing, top guides are international – Nepalese guides work in the off season in the Alps, Norway, North America, Ladakh, etc.

N.A.R.A.

Nepal Association of Rafting Agents, was formed as an independant body to represent the rafting companies in discussions with the Government. At the time of writing, membership of NARA does not mean much else: most rafting agencies in Nepal are members including at least one well known 'cowboy' operator! Talking to NARA members, I am led to believe that this may change in the near future, and that there are plans to introduce and enforce standards that will guarantee the quality of rafting trips.

Trisuli

Equipment

Quality equipment obviously makes a huge difference to the safety and comfort of a trip, but good rafting equipment is expensive and difficult to obtain in Nepal . . .

Rafts come in various sizes: the most popular is 16ft (5 metres) long, and this will a take a crew of six plus guide and gear, or up to 9 plus guide without gear. The best example of this size is the famous Avon Professional. Rafts like this are very tough and rugged so it's rare for them to be damaged or punctured. Even if the latter happens, this is usually not serious as they have several compartments to keep them afloat. For really hard rivers, where swamping, or a flip is likely, then a self-draining model with an inflatable floor is recom mended and should be considered obligatory for high water trips.

Smaller rafts are more manoeuvrable but are more likely to be 'flipped' on a wave. Really small one or two person boats, known as 'Duckies' are fairly new to Nepal. You paddle these yourself, and it's up to you how you get down the rapid; potentially more dangerous, but tremendous fun!

Good **life jackets** (Buoyancy Aids or Personal Flotation Devices) are essential. Modern ones are comfortable and well-fitting and have adjustable straps and buckles to ensure a snug and secure fit. They should ideally have a minimum of 9 kgs (20lbs) of buoyancy for a large adult. The important thing to ask is the age of the jacket – the foam in the jackets perishes with time and also absorbs more water so that after 3 to 6 years it may only have half the buoyancy.

Helmets should be considered as obligatory on any white water trip. The main danger on an oar rig is banging your head on the frame or oars if you get thrown across the raft. On a paddle raft, the helmet is more to protect your head from the paddle strokes of your over-enthusiastic team mates! Contrary to popular belief, it's very rare to actually bang your head on rocks when taking an accidental swim. Try to select and adjust your helmet so that it fits well and provides good protection for your forehead.

The **paddle** is to a rafter, like boots are to a trekker. The best modern paddles these days are plastic and alloy – light, strong, and comfortable to use. Nicely crafted wooden ones can be a delight to use, but beware any ones made locally which may be clumsy and heavy.

For white water trips, the raft should be rigged with 'flip lines' so that it can be righted in the event of a capsize. It should carry throw lines or throwbags for rescuing swimmers. Obviously all trips should carry comprehensive first aid and repair kits and spare oars or paddles.

What kind of waterproof containers does the company provide? How old are these? Modern roll top bags are excellent and will keep your gear dry even in a flip. Do they provide 'Ammo cans' or a waterproof barrel for cameras and video gear?

Camping gear varies widely. If you are rafting in the spring, then good rainproof tents or flysheets are essential, but from October to December rain is unlikely and many people like to sleep out under the stars. A tent is nice as a cosy, private and relatively sand-free bedroom – best ones are free standing dome tents with a built in groundsheet. This type of tent is expensive and so most companies provide a more basic model. Riverside beaches are pleasant, friendly environments and you need have little fear of insects, snakes, scorpions, or other nasties.

Personal Equipment

One of the nice things about a river trip is how few things you need, we can remember several instances where guides, in all the hurly-burly of oranising the group gear, have ended up leaving their own personal gear behind – and no problem, all you really need is a pair of shorts and a thermal top!

However, here is the complete list of what to take based on that supplied by H.R.E. (one they have perfected over more than ten years of rafting in Nepal):

For Autumn and Spring trips:

One-day trips:

Shirt (long sleeves and collar if you need sun protection)
Shorts (or loose, light cotton trousers for sun protection)
Sports sandals or old trainers or sneakers
Light Thermal top (in case it gets cold)
Light nylon waterproofjacket (….. and wet/windy)
Swim suit
Sun hat with brim
Sunglasses (plastic lenses are safer) and tie
Suntan cream (high factor)
Personal water bottle
Very small amount of money (for cold drinks on the return)
Towel and a complete change of clothes, including shoes, for the return drive (and camp wear).

In addition, for two days or more:

Sleeping bag
Foam sleeping mattress or thermorest
Washing kit
Light woollen sweater or thermal top for camp wear
Extra pair of shorts
Extra shirt(s)
Small flashlight or headlamp

Optional extras:

Reading and writing materials
Personal medications
Contraceptives
Camera and film
Binoculars
Pocket knife
Walkman and tapes

For a Winter trip (December to February), the following extras:

Extra thermal top
Thermal long trousers
Light nylon waterproof trousers
Wet suit boots or thick woollen socks (all to wear on the raft)
Warm trousers
Warm jacket (pile, pelt or down)

Quote: *'The most important thing to bring is the right mental attitude'* (Cam Macleay).

Hints

Take old comfortable clothes that you don't mind getting lost, damaged, and of course wet!

Cotton clothing is really pleasant for hot sunny days but is cold when wet. Wool stays warm even when wet. Modern **thermal underwear** made by companies like Helly Hansen, Patagonia or Sub Zero is quick drying and ideal wear for cool days on the river, often worn under a pair of shorts.

Ideal **footwear** are modern 'sports sandals' like 'Teva' or 'Alps' (our favourites): these let your feet breathe and dry out, and can be worn with woollen socks on cold days. Any rafting shoes need to be well secured by laces or buckles so that you don't lose them; Flip flops, Thongs, etc. are useless on the raft but O.K. for wear around camp.

A small headlamp is more useful than a flashlight – great for reading in bed. Best is probably the Petzl micro.

Probably the one thing that makes for comfortable camping is a good campbed or mattress. Many companies provide a sleeping pad made of insulating foam but these can be quite hard. If you value your sleeping comfort, we suggest that you consider taking your own **thermorest** or similar modern mattress. On a recent ultra-lightweight trip down the Tamur, some of our team didn't bring spare clothes, others no sleeping bag (not a good idea), but everyone carried a thermorest.

On longer trips it is nice to have a supply of sweets or chocolate as a treat for yourself and others. Most rafters enjoy alcohol around the campfire and local rum makes an excellent punch. Check that you have an adequate supply and likewise if you enjoy a smoke.

Kathmandu and Pokhara have lots of shops that buy, sell and **hire trekking equipment** so don't worry if you have arrived in Nepal without something. It often makes sense to hire: if for example you have an expensive 3-4 season down sleeping bag, it may be better to hire a lightweight two-season hollofill one that you won't have to worry about.

Lunch stop on the Sun Kosi

What happens on a Rafting trip?

Getting Started

After you have paid your deposit, the Company will ask you to complete a booking form and they will apply for the necessary rafting permit. They will usually give you a gear list and arrange a briefing meeting for all participants a day or two before departure.

All companies provide waterproof bags for your gear and your guide will explain how to pack these. Assume that the bag will be dropped, jumped on, etc. so pack accordingly. They may offer to store your extra luggage for you whilst you are on the river, but we suggest that to avoid confusion, you store any extra gear at your hotel. If you want a bag taken down to meet you at the end of the river, the company can normally arrange this, but do make sure it is well labelled.

Most companies will provide a bus, mini bus or taxi to take you to the river and will arrange a convenient meeting point. The first day is always a frantic scene of activity, 101 things that have to be done or haven't been done, so don't get frustrated if there is a fair amount of hanging around; come prepared with a good book. Typically you will arrive at the starting point on the river sometime mid-morning and then the rafts will be blown up and assembled, gear sorted out and loaded. The Trip Leader will give you a briefing; introducing everyone, telling you where you are going, and covering the important safety points. Then after lunch you will set off down the river. In the first km down the river your raft guide will give you a little training course about what to do and when.

When you come to a small rapid the Guide will explain what is happening and why you are running a particular route – if he doesn't, don't be afraid to ask him! You will soon build up confidence and look forward to each rapid. In between rapids, you may just drift along with the current, or the raft may be rowed or paddled a little. Normally the first day will be fairly short and you will make an early camp so that people have plenty of time to sort themselves out.

Camping

The raft will swing into the camping beach, the front people leap out and pull the raft up, and then everyone heads ashore to stretch their legs and survey the campsite for the night. Meanwhile your guide is untying the gear and then the traditional shout of 'Duffle Line!' echoes down the river. Everybody pitches in to pass all the gear up onto the beach. You are now free to pick a pleasant spot for your tent; everyone has their own preferences, but important things to consider are that you don't want to be too close to the kitchen or toilet. The other important factor is the early morning sun: the ideal is to be woken up at just the right time by the sun shining through your tent door! Always camp well above water level in case the river rises.

The usual thing is to stake your spot by dropping your bags there and then go back to sort out your tent and other gear. One of the raft team will give you a hand if you need help to put your tent up. Meanwhile, back at the ranch, the kitchen gear has been unloaded and a kettle has been put on the stove for a reviving cup of tea. If there are reasonable supplies of drift wood then you may have a campfire later: please help gather firewood before you relax for the evening.

Hygiene

Cooking arrangements and dining arrangements will vary depending on the style of trip, but all rafting trips have strict hygiene rules and routines for doing things so as to avoid infection. Before handling food or eating, everyone has to wash their hands, first with soap and water, and then rinse them in a disenfectant solution. Water is normally sterilised with iodine and your team will have a system for marking untreated water, water that has been iodised but needs to stand for a while, and sterilised water that is safe to drink. There will be another system for washing up. It's important to familiarise yourself with these as good hygiene leads to a happy and bug-fee trip!

A minor point is to use untreated water for boiling to make tea or coffee or other cooking. Tea tastes foul when made with iodised water.

Evening Activities

The time before dinner is always one of the most pleasant times of the day: time to relax, perhaps a leisurely wash and change, to sit with a cup of tea and write up your diary? Perhaps a gentle stroll to explore the river bank (do let your Guide know where you are going, just in case). Or, if you are still feeling active, perhaps a game of volleyball, or ask one of your guides to show you Kabatti, the Nepalese version of touch rugby.

Dinner is always the high spot of the day and a social occasion with the rum and cokes flowing as the high lights of the day are relived and laughed over. After dinner, more drinks and stories around the campfire perhaps, but no one will think you strange if you quietly fade into the warm surrounding darkness and sit looking at a black mirror of a river, bright dancing stars above, and fireflies dancing in the bushes. And so to bed and one thing a river trip almost guarantees is the most perfect sleep.

People . . . *by Mark Baker*

It was the people and their living which for me, made everything so different and often special. As we passed down the river, no matter how many days from a road, there were people; fishing, washing, waving, burning their dead, crapping, smoking, or just sitting.

Gathered round the fire at night, whilst relaxing and chatting, a sub-group of locals sometimes formed and would start beating a drum, chanting, dancing and singing, but never in any competitive way, just in a graceful wandering manner for their own and our entertainment. Pleasures are natural, values so different, living rudimentary and conditions harsh; and yet the people appear so happy that by the end of your river trip you question all your western beliefs.

Onward down the river

It's much better to start and finish early on a river trip, so typically the cooks will be up at 6.00 a.m. to serve and wake everyone with a cup of tea or coffee at 6.45 a.m, breakfast will be at 7.30 a.m., and with luck you will be on the water at 9.0 a.m. You can help by having most of your gear packed by breakfast, leaving just the things that need to air, like sleeping bags and towels, for last minute packing.

When you come to big rapids, the guides will often beach the rafts and everyone will walk along the shore to 'scout' the rapid and work out the best routes. The problem with scouting rapids is that the longer you stand and look at them, the more frightening they appear . . . However, if you really don't want to run the rapid there's usually no problem in walking round, and the 'ploy' here is to say that you would like to take photos!

Lunch stop will often be at a nice swimming beach and if you have any kayaks along, this is a good chance to try out this deviant activity. Lunch will be a help-yourself picnic with salads, breads, fruit, etc.

Hints to enjoy your trip

Most people under estimate the strength of the sun and get painfully **sunburnt** on thighs, arms, shoulders and necks. The sun is particularly strong because it is also reflected off the river, but the water makes it feel deceptively cool on the raft. We strongly advise you to cover up well whilst rafting and to get a nice even suntan, if wanted, by sunbathing on the beaches at camp and lunch.

Sunglasses should ideally have plastic lenses and you need to tie these on so that you don't lose them; either with a proprietary device or, at a fraction of the cost, with a thin piece of nylon string tied through two small holes drilled through the tips of the plastic ear pieces. We particularly recommend polaroid sunglasses; as sailors know, these cut through the reflected glare off the surface of the water. Another very useful device is a peak to keep the sun out of your eyes and off your face; either a peaked cap worn under the helmet when necessary, or a peak made out of closed cell foam and stuck on to the helmet.

Learn the correct method of sealing up your dry bag and take care each time to do this up properly; wet sleeping bags are not nice!

Whilst rafting and around camp, be aware of where your gear is and don't leave valuables lying around as unfair temptation for normally honest local people; a watch left clipped to a life jacket may represent a year's wages to a local farmer.

Nepalese rivers are of such large volume, that it is quite O.K. to wash and bathe in them, but do take care for your personal safety, the sandy shore will often collapse under your weight and throw you into the river. It is always safer, and more sociable, to bathe together.

The one snag with camping on beaches is that sand seems to get everywhere! Tread very carefully and slowly around the kitchen so that you don't kick sand into food. It's a good idea to try and keep your sleeping area/tent as a relatively sand free environment and it's useful to keep an old towel or T shirt by the door to wipe your feet on.

If you are paddle rafting, be careful when doing any fancy strokes not to extend your arm up and behind your shoulder – this may lead to a dislocated shoulder. Straight arms are fine when leaning forward to commence a stroke – but at all other times you should keep your arms comfortably bent. Do check your paddle shaft is smooth to grip; any rough bits will soon lead to blisters.

Nepal – first time round . . . *by Tim Raw*

Our first day in Nepal felt slow. We knew very little but then talking around we met a rafter who lent us some boats and gave us some information on the best kayaking rivers. Some of the rivers sounded hard but he left us to decide what we could or couldn't do.

The next day we had two boats packed for our trip. At 5 o'clock in the morning we were on the bus and starting our journey for real. We spent days paddling, pulling up on beaches and cooking on open fires. We stopped at villages and sat in the glorious sunshine with blue skies and breathtaking views of the mountains.

Villagers greeted us most evenings. I have memories of them crowding round us, looking at our equipment and sitting in our boats. My strongest memory is laughing and smiling with them; that's what they did nearly all the time – laugh and smile. We felt on many occasions as though we were the first westerners to visit them. Whole villages would span a bridge and and wave and shout at us as we passed. This friendship, and closeness with Nepal and its people, added a truly unconditional acceptance to our kayaking and our being there.

It wasn't all smooth. One night we slept in a stream – where it came from at 3.00 a.m. I still don't know. On our first night we took over two hours to cook a cup of tea and a bowl of noodles. We sat in the dark giggling as we ate and thought what a fine effort it was for two people who together had spent nearly twenty years working in the outdoors. We had lost our torch in the sand along with countless other items and we laughed at the bloody shambles. If only our friends could see us now – the Himalayan heroes!

It was great kayaking and there was some mighty water. We had a memorable time and I want to tell you to go and do the same – you don't need sponsorship, hordes of porters and a jumbo jet to move all your equipment around. I don't know why there aren't more people coming out here to paddle – there is something here for everyone, and in retrospect my experiences were too powerful to ever contemplate missing.

PLANNING A SELF-SUFFICIENT TRIP

Introduction

Ten years ago, if you said to anyone that you were going paddling in Nepal, most people would think either that you were crazy or that this was some death-defying expedition. But slowly the message has spread around that you don't have to be some hairy, aquatic gorilla to paddle here, rather that Nepal is a paradise for the average white water recreational boater on a budget – as one Kiwi group said: **'Any ordinary dude can do it'.**

Nepal is an exotic friendly country with many easy rivers, as well as more difficult ones, but it can be particularly recommended for it's magnificent multi-day white water trips. Many of the larger rivers can be paddled with a commercial outfitter supplying raft support and this of course has many advantages, particularly if this is your first trip and/or your time is limited. The Sun Kosi is a popular and recommended choice for a raft-supported kayak trip; and many paddlers choose to do this as their first river with raft support and then move on to run other rivers on a self-sufficient basis.

Doing your own thing will save you money, but the prime reason for going self-sufficient must be for the quality of the experience – there are few more satisfying experiences than starting out with all your personal gear for the days ahead packed in your boat – the backdrop of the Himalaya behind you and the promise of a mighty river ahead.

We reckon that for a self-sufficient kayak trip, the ideal size of group is four paddlers; 'less than three there should never be' is a good safety rule; more than six persons gets unwieldy. If you are a lone kayaker it is usually fairly easy to link up with other paddlers if you hang around Kathmandu for a few days. Ask around the rafting companies to see if they know of any kayak groups, put up a few notices and generally keep your eyes and ears open.

Choice of boats

We have written these notes mainly for the white water kayaker, but the advice is usually relevant for any other boats that you may be planning to use.

Modern white water kayaks are ideal craft for river trips in Nepal: they are lots of fun and can cope well with all the different rivers and conditions. They can carry enough gear for trips of several days and can be transported easily on local buses, taxis, etc. Many of the rafting companies have a small fleet of kayaks that are available for rent: a typical charge in 1991 was $15 a day. We reckoned as a rough estimate, that there were over 60 kayaks in Kathmandu at the time of writing, some in private hands, but anyone just turning up on spec. and wanting to hire a couple of kayaks should normally have no problems and a wide choice, if they spend a day or two asking around.

It is very difficult to hire rafts for a 'do it yourself trip'. If you do manage to negotiate a rental, the company will probably demand a deposit of the market value of the raft, which may be twice the western price. It is probably better to think about bringing your own raft with you.

Many of the longer and easier rivers in Nepal would be ideal trips for a traditional open canoe, but we haven't heard of anyone using one, probably because of the costs of transporting one to Nepal. If you look at the list of rivers, you will see that there is considerable scope for folding boats, and these could easily be flown to the more remote rivers.

There are now several small inflatable boats in Nepal, often called 'duckies'; these are a lot of fun for novice paddlers but in expert hands these can also be used on quite difficult rivers. There are also some cat-a-rafts. If you are a Huck Finn type on a shoe string budget and know what you're doing, then it probably isn't too crazy to consider a home made raft out of inner tubes and bamboo for one of the easier river trips.

Choice of Rivers

Important points

The time of year is critical to your choice of river. After the monsoon, in September and early October, water volumes are huge and many rivers are too dangerous. This varies tremendously from year to year depending on whether the monsoon is early or late – as the hydrograph below illustrates. Do seek advice on current river conditions from a reliable expert on arrival in Kathmandu.

Note well that Nepal is an adventurous country where roads are few, rivers BIG and WILD, rescue services are non-existent, and medical facilities are very limited. We advise you to be suitably conservative in your choice of rivers and be particularly cautious in which river you plan to run first. Plan to start on easier and smaller rivers and then build up experience for the harder and more remote trips.

Please start by reading the introduction to each region that outlines the characteristics of the rivers. On their first trip to Nepal, most kayakers run rivers in the Central and Eastern regions that are more easily accessible to Kathmandu. As mentioned earlier, a raft supported trip down the Sun Kosi is a popular first choice and one that we can recommend – many of the suggested itineraries below are built around this. If you are interested in doing other rivers with raft support then please read the 'Choice of rivers' advice in the section on rafting with a commercial operator.

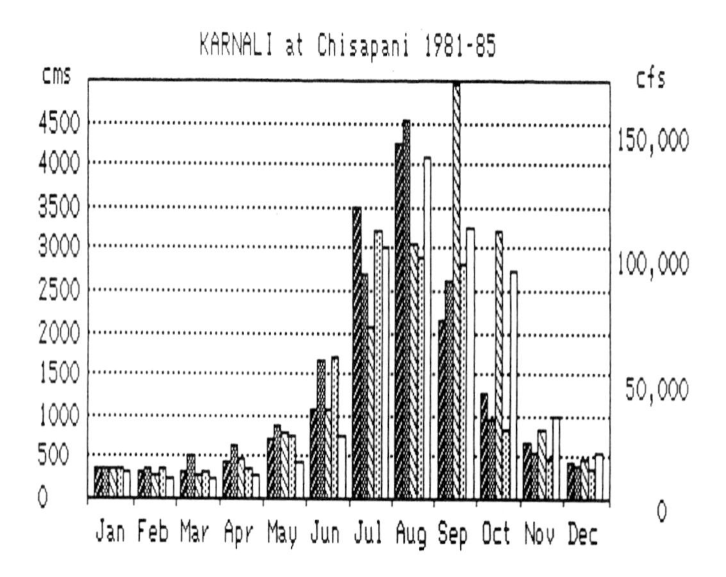

Kayaking Summary

River	*Class*	*Volume Cumecs*	*Total days*	*River days*	*Scenery/ wildlife*	*Star rating*
TRISULI	3+	300	2–6	1–5	**	**
Modi Khola	4	20	5	2	***	***
Kali Gandaki upper	4−	120	5	3	**	***
Kali Gandaki lower	2	250	4	3	**	**
Seti	3	40	3	2	**	**
Marsyandi	4+	80	5	3	***	***
Buri Gandaki	3	90	4	1	*	*
SUN KOSI	4−	400	8	7	**	***
Bhote Kosi	2–6	90	2–5	1–4	**	**
Indrawati	4+	40	1–2	1	*	*
Tamba Kosi	4+	80	3	2	**	**
Dudh Kosi	5	100	13–20	10	**	*
Arun	4−	215	4	3	**	*
Tamur	4	150	81	4	***	***
KARNALI – lower	4	300	9	5	***	***
Humla Karnali	5−	200	20	18	***	***
Mahakali	3	300	8	4	***	*
Seti/Karnali	3	130	7	4	***	**
Bheri	2	170	5/9	3/6	**	*
Babai Nadi	1	35	4	2	***	**

Notes:
Total days = days to and from Kathmandu or Pokhara.
Star rating is our subjective view of the river as a rafting trip – taking into account logistics and cost.
*** Highly recommended, ** Recommended, * Specialist interest.

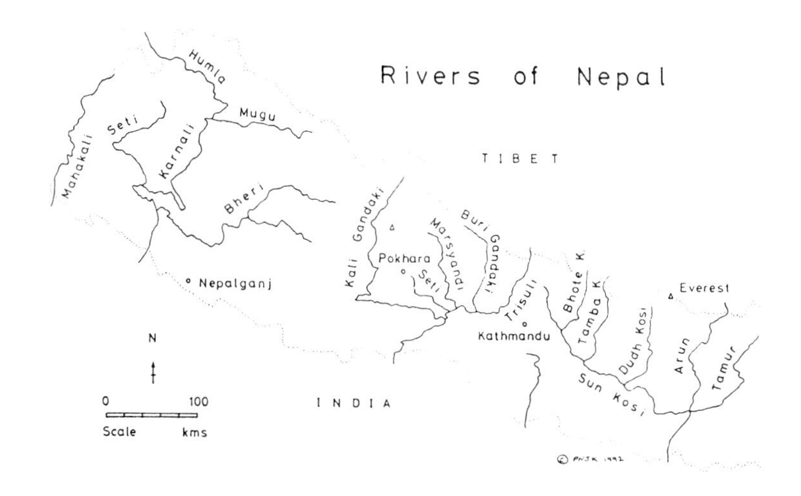

Possible itineraries

Most of the suggested itineraries below are designed to minimise driving and progress in difficulty (the notable exception is the 'asset stripper'). They give you an idea of how rivers can be combined in a reasonable time span, but note that, unless you are hiring your own transport, you should allow at least one reserve day for delays waiting for local buses, etc. You need at least 2 days at the start of your trip either in Kathmandu or Pokhara sorting out permits, and getting ready.

The 'Asset Stripper', for the expert kayaker

General opinion has it that the best kayaking rivers are the Marsyandi, Tamba Kosi, Modi Khola and Tamur; so a four week itinerary that would cream off most of the best paddling might be:

Day 1-2 in Kathmandu sorting out boats, permits, etc.
Day 3, One day warm up on the **Bhote Kosi**.
Day 4-5, 1½ days on the **Tamba Kosi**.
Day 5-12, run the **Sun Kosi** (with raft support).
Day 13, run the bottom (hardest) bit of the **Tamur** river.
Day 14, Chitwan National Park (get scared by the Rhinos).
Day 15, Pokhara, rest, recuperation and resupply.
Day 16-17, Bus and trek into the Modi Khola (towards Annapurna),
Day 18-19, Run the **Modi Khola**
Day 20, Pokhara for some more R,R, and R.
Day 21-22, Bus and trek up the Marsyandi.
Day 23-26, Run the **Marsyandi**.
Day 27, Back in Kathmandu.

Eastern mountains to the plains, for the expert paddler

This is an immensely satisfying 3 week itinerary that gives you plenty of variety, excellent paddling and minimum time in buses.

Day 1-2, in Kathmandu sorting out boats, permits, etc.
Day 3, one day warm up on the **Bhote Kosi**.
Day 4-5, 1½ days on the **Tamba Kosi**.
Day 5-12, run the **Sun Kosi** (raft support?).
Day 13-15, trek into the upper Tamur (incredible scenery).
Day 16-19, run the **Tamur** river.
Day 20, Chitwan National Park (get scared by the Rhinos).
Day 21, back to Kathmandu for R. and R.

Sun Kosi warm up

If you are looking for a warm up and practice for a Sun Kosi trip, especially a self-sufficient one, then a couple of days on the **Trisuli** starting from the Tadi Khola would be a good alternative choice to the Bhote Kosi.

Annapurna to the plains, for the expert paddler

Another itinerary that gets you away from roads and combines some fine white water with one of the world's most famous treks.

Day 1-2, in Kathmandu sorting out boats, permits, etc.
Day 3-5, run the **Trisuli** from Betrawadi down to Mugling.
Day 6-7, R. and R.in Pokhara.
Day 8-16, bus to the Modi Khola and trek up to Annapurna Sanctuary.
Day 17-18, Run the **Modi Khola**.
Day 19-21, run the **upper Kali Gandaki.**
Day 22-23, run the **lower Kali Gandaki**.
Day 24, Chitwan National Park.
Day 25, back to Kathmandu.

Itinerary for aspiring intermediates

Here's a three week itinerary designed to build confidence, 'to do your own thing', and you'll actually paddle on 8 rivers. (If you feel the upper Kali Gandaki is a little too remote, then build in a Trisuli trip instead of this.)

Day 1-2, in Kathmandu sorting out boats, permits, etc.
Day 3-4, practise on the Sun Kosi near Dolalghat & run the **Indrawati**.
Day 5, rest and recuperation in Kathmandu.
Day 6-8, drive to, then run the **Seti** into the Trisuli.
Day 9, rest and recuperation in Pokhara.
Day 10, drive to Modi Khola, put in near Chuwa, run the last few kms.
Day 11-14, run the **upper Kali Gandaki**.
Day 15-16, run the **lower Kali Gandaki** into the Narayani.
Day 17, Chitwan National Park.
Day 18, bus to the Marsyandi.
Day 19-20, run the **Marsyandi** from Besishahar or Bhote Odar.
Day 21, Kathmandu for R. and R.

'Softies special'

Here's a relaxed itinerary for people wanting to tour on easier rivers. This completely disproves all that macho hair-boating nonsense!

Day 1-3, in Kathmandu sorting out boats, permits, etc.
Day 4-6, practise on the Sun Kosi near Dolalghat & run the **Indrawati**.
Day 7-8, rest and recuperation in Kathmandu.
Day 9-10, drive to, then run the **Seti** from Damauli.
Day 11-12, rest and recuperation in Pokhara.
Day 13-15, run the **lower Kali Gandaki**.
Day 16, continue down the Narayani to Chitwan.
Day 17-18, Chitwan National Park.
Day 19, back to Kathmandu.

Safety

This is a 'where to do it book' not one on 'how to do it'. Nepal is a wild and adventurous country and the rivers deserve respect and prudent planning. Before paddling here you should obviously have reasonable experience, commonsense , basic outdoor skills, and a sense of 'awareness'. There are no rescue or paramedic teams to help you if you get into trouble and you may be several days from a hospital or doctor.

Safety Guidelines:

- If you are the kind of person who is a bit accident-prone – things happen to you through no fault of your own – then perhaps you should think about joining a commercial river trip which should give you added protection and back up.
- Be conservative in your choice of rivers – particularly the first one.
- Seek advice from local experts on river levels and difficulty.
- Allow yourself plenty of time to paddle the river so that you are not in a hurry and do not have to paddle when tired.
- Don't paddle what you can't see – never hesitate to scout or portage.
- Most newcomers to Nepal are surprised by the power of Himalayan rapids – build up experience gradually and mentally train yourself to 'go with the flow' so that you do not strain muscles or dislocate a shoulder.
- Consider a higher volume boat than you would normally paddle at home: you will be carrying extra gear, it will be less prone to pins, and the water is probably bigger than you may be used to.
- Carry essential first aid, survival and rescue gear on ALL trips.
- Check end loops are adequate and consider a central deck line; this makes it easier to keep hold of your boat when swimming big rapids, handy for passing boats up and down cliffs and also in the event of rescue.
- Paddle as a team, encourage good safety habits, and foster a stronger group awareness than you are probably used to at home.
- We recommend bright colours for boats, paddles and helmets so that you can more readily see a swimmer. (White helmets are really bad in this respect – almost like camouflage in big white water: consider marking them with orange day glow tape: 3m company make a stick-on film called 'ScotchCal' that is used on the sides of police cars – yes, it can be unstuck and re-used!).

Accidents and rescue

In the event of an accident or emergency, then you are very much on your own, and you will have to rescue the victim, render first aid and evacuate as necessary. It is obviously sensible if your group realise this and are reasonably prepared and trained for accidents. In the sad and unlikely event of a fatality you will have to recover the body and deal with it yourselves and it is helpful if people are at least mentally aware that this is a remote but real possibility.

Evacuation

After a careful evaluation of the patients injury and incapacity you need to consider the options. In Europe or America we are trained to make the patient comfortable and wait for an ambulance. This is not a viable option! If the patient can move with help, even if, as it probably will, this involves pain; then you should consider either continuing down river or walking out; this will depend on many factors, but this may be the fastest, least complicated and most certain way of getting the patient back to expert medical help. In these situations, our perceptions of further injury are usually exagerated – consider climbers with fearsome injuries who have crawled down mountains.

If evacuation is necessary then you can normally hire local porters to carry the patient. In real need it may be possible to hire a helicopter to evacuate a patient, but payment has to be guaranteed by an agent in Kathmandu (this may be several thousand dollars). If you are planning to do a remote river then we suggest that you find out more about this from the Himalayan Rescue Association and set things up in advance with your Embassy or a reliable agent. Bill O'Connor's book 'The Trekking Peaks of Nepal' has some useful advice on emergencies and rescue. Our own experience is that trying to communicate in an emergency by radio messages to Kathmandu is difficult, uncertain and unbelievably frustrating. It may well take two or three days to get your helicopter....

Local porters will not carry a body, neither will government helicopters, so on a remote river you may need to consider local burial or cremation. This should be witnessed by local police and officials, photographs taken (relatives will appreciate these), and a report prepared and signed by all present. The leader should make an inventory of personal items, have this witnesed and then look after them until delivery to embassy officials.

Getting to and from the river

Most of the rivers in this book are surprisingly easy to get to: transport in Nepal is cheap and you don't have to set up expensive shuttles. If you use local buses then your transport costs will be minimal – for example a bus to the Sun Kosi will cost about $1 and the return from the take-out to Kathmandu, about $5.

Whilst the journey to the river may be relatively easy and cheap, it's rarely smooth, comfortable or boring. Talk to people who have paddled in Nepal and some of their most vivid memories are of their travels to and from the river: this is part of the total cultural experience of paddling in a third world country.

Local Buses

There aren't that many roads in Nepal, but it's a well populated country so wherever there is a road, there's usually a frequent and cheap local bus service. These buses are an ethnic experience; they are usually incredibly overloaded, slow and uncomfortable. What can't go inside, people, animals, bales of goods, furniture, crates, boxes, and barrels goes on the roof rack. Kayaks, paddles, rafts etc, are no problem!

Best thing is to pack most things inside the kayaks where they will be protected from damage and loss. Keep ropes and karabiners handy to tie the boats on with. Note that sharp bolts and edges of roof rack can wear a hole in your boat before you even get it to the river – best place for kayaks is tied together as a block on their sides on the very front of the roof rack, or alternatively again on their sides, tied singly outside and along the sides of the roofrack. Expect that, as the bus fills up, crates, people and goats will end up on top of them. It is usual to pay extra for a kayak: we suggest that half the adult fare is reasonable.

Where do you sit? There are two ideas on this: one is the 'sandwich' theory: get yourself a place in the middle of the inside of the bus so that you have lots of human cushioning to protect you if it goes off the road. The alternative theory is the 'Seal launch' – a nice spot on the roof where you can hope to jump clear if anything bad happens. On standard local buses with 2+3 seating, most river runners favour the roof; this is a great place for watching the scenery go by, chatting with the locals, and generally hanging loose. Up here, you can also keep an eye on your gear. It can be cold if the sun goes in, so keep some warm clothes or a sleeping bag handy and something as a cushion to sit on. Look out for low branches, and in towns, especially whilst loading, power lines!!!

More comfortable than the local buses are **'Night buses'** or 'Tourist buses' that operate on the long distance routes. These have, or should have, 2+2 reclining seats and half reasonable leg room. You get a reserved seat when you buy your ticket so if you buy your ticket several days in advance you'll get a seat near the front; buy it at the last minute and you end up on the back seat bouncing a foot in the air on every bump. As the name implies, a lot of these buses travel through the night; a good time to travel in that it is cooler, the roads are less busy and it saves you time. Tip: take a stuff bag of clothing as a pillow.

On some of the more popular routes, like Pokhara to Kathmandu you may be offered seats in a minibus. The ticket agent will tell you that this is faster and more comfortable. Yes, they are fast, but they have a bad accident rate as most of them have young crazy drivers – as the saying goes, you get old drivers, and crazy drivers, but never old crazy drivers!

Taxis and private minibuses

It can save you a lot of time and hassle to hire your own minibus or taxi, particularly for the shorter journeys. Again, costs are very reasonable; e.g. $60 for a 15 seat minibus for the 3 hour ride to the put-in on the Sun Kosi. This saves you lugging your kayaks across to the bus station, transferring, haggling about the amount and then having to hang around for an hour or two before the bus goes. From a safety viewpoint, your own vehicle is money well spent; you can check it out in advance (note the state of the tyres), it won't be grossly overloaded, and you call the shots – don't hesitate to tell the driver to drive slower or more safely.

Almost all minibuses have substantial roofracks. Quite a few taxis also have roofracks – where they don't this is no problem, you can rest two kayaks flat on the roof on a towel or foam pad. Tie one line through the kayak seats and tension up through the open doors. Tie other lines from the end loops down to the bumpers/fenders. If the roof is strong, another kayak can rest flat on top of the bottom two. Kathmandu taxi drivers seem to be getting quite used and happy at the idea of carrying 'dungas' on their roofs – as long as you pay them extra (for a short journey, we suggest 50% extra for one kayak, double rate for a full load). If you need a reliable and helpful 'Mr Fixit' to arrange transport, try Mr Harry of Natraj Travels in the courtyard of the Kathmandu Guest House.

Other vehicles

If it moves, you can probably hire it to carry your gear. One kayak will fit very comfortably on an auto-rickshaw (we did hear of a group of Kiwis who managed to get 3 boats on one!). One kayak can be carried quite easily on a pedal rickshaw or with more difficulty over your shoulder on a mountain bike. At different times we have hitched lifts with kayaks on tractors, lorries, jeeps, handcarts, ponies, yaks, elephants and of course porters. It's a bad day when you have to carry your gear yourself! Note that, like most third world countries, all vehicles come with a driver (they are not going to trust their valuable vehicle to some strange foreigner, not when labour is so cheap) – this is just great for river runners in that you automatically get a shuttle driver: one who will, for a few rupees extra, quite happily sit at the take-out until you appear.

Porters

Where you need to trek in to the start of a river, the usual thing is to hire porters to carry the boats and other gear. If you have a large group then you may want to hire a guide/sirdar from Kathmandu to arrange things for you and do the negotiating, but this is probably not worth while for a short trek. You will normally find that a local lodge keeper will be happy to advise you and help you with the translation. Hiring your own porters can at first appear a bit daunting – but it's really very straight forward and like any negotiation it can be frustrating but enjoyable. Take your time, don't appear in any rush, shrug off the 'wide boys' who are hanging around at the road head, over-keen to help you (and rip you off). Best thing, if you have time, is to book in a lodge overnight and spread the word by the lodge keeper that you are looking for some reliable porters; this gives time for them to come in from their homes, fields or other work.

Look your would-be porters in the eye and trust your instincts when choosing them. Standard porter load is 30 kgs (66 lbs). Daily rate is currently about $2 to $4, but it is better to negotiate a rate based on each stage – see the 'Tamur' write up. Make sure that it is clear whether the porters have to buy their own food (strongly recommended) and whether the negotiated rate includes their return payment (if you pay a daily rate then it is usual to pay for the return journey at half the daily rate). The porters will argue for an increased rate for carrying kayaks because they are an awkward load – they don't seem to mind if the kayak weighs 20kgs or 30kgs.

You will probably find that your porters are a group who are used to working together and who will have their own unofficial leader. Porters are professionals at their work so you should trust their judgement on how to carry the loads, (they will probably use tump lines around their foreheads) where and when to stop, etc. but be firm and fair on what you have agreed. On the trek you are responsible for the health and safety of your porters and a couple of your team should always bring up the rear behind them. Try to establish a social rapport between your porters and the rest of the team; it helps if each kayaker gets to know the individual porter carrying his boat, helps him load it, and assists on any awkward places.

Trekking with porters is usually slow, sometimes frustratingly so, but working directly with local people will give you insights into the rural way of life and the social interface can be a satisfying and memorable experience. Hugh Swift's trekking guide book has some excellent advice on hiring and working with porters.

Air

Royal Nepal Airlines have a well-developed network of services into even the most remote parts of Nepal. Flying to the more remote rivers is usually cost-effective and saves a lot of trekking time.

The most commonly used plane is the Twin Otter, a 19 seater that can operate off short dirt airstrips. This only has small luggage hatches in the nose and the tail, but a single kayak will fit in the main cabin down the gangway. This probably breaks a few international regulations but on local hops in the more remote areas of the country, everything is possible, and RNAC personnel are noted for being really helpful. If there are not many people on the plane then it is possible to get up to eight kayaks in by removing most of the seats – this can be done for a charter flight.

Note that a charter flight can be especially cost-effective for the right size raft group.

Because Nepal is long and narrow, local routes operate out of regional hubs such as Nepalganj or Pokhara. If you are trying to keep your costs down then the thing to do is to travel by bus to the regional hub and then fly into your river from there.

Tourists have to pay more than locals for their tickets and pay in dollars, but this does give them priority on reservations – a pretty good system in most people's view. Fares, routes and timetables change, so up-to-date information should be obtained from an RNAC office.

Charter flight to Simikot

What to bring

Most river trips in Nepal are at a low altitude so that typically you will find the water pleasantly warm and the climate sub-tropical: in truth, this is one of the pleasures of paddling here: much of the time all you need to wear is a pair of shorts and a thermal top. If you are doing a multi-day trip you won't normally need to carry lots of heavy cold weather gear.

Here is a suggested gear list for a self-contained trip down the Kali Gandaki or Sun Kosi in November:

Personal Gear

For paddling: Kayak, spray deck, paddle, life jacket, helmet, paddling jacket, thermal top, shorts, thermal bottoms (for cold days), sports sandals, throw bag, karabiner, water bottle, sponge, flotation bags (or waterproof dry bags).

Carried on the person: whistle, knife, trekking permit and/or photocopy of passport, money, matches and fire starter, wound dressing, iodine dropper bottle, watch.

Camp and travel: waterproof dry bags, sleeping pad, sleeping bag (2 season), small towel, spare lightweight change of clothes: underpants/shorts, trousers/skirt, socks, shirt and warm top; toothbrush, soap, mug, spoon, toilet paper, sun hat, sunblock cream, lip chap, headlamp, batteries, diary, pen, camera, film, book? razor?

Team Gear

Nylon flysheet, cooking pot/s, cooking gear, food, plastic bags, matches, spare paddles, repair kit, nylon string, map, first aid kit, toothpaste, extra rescue gear.

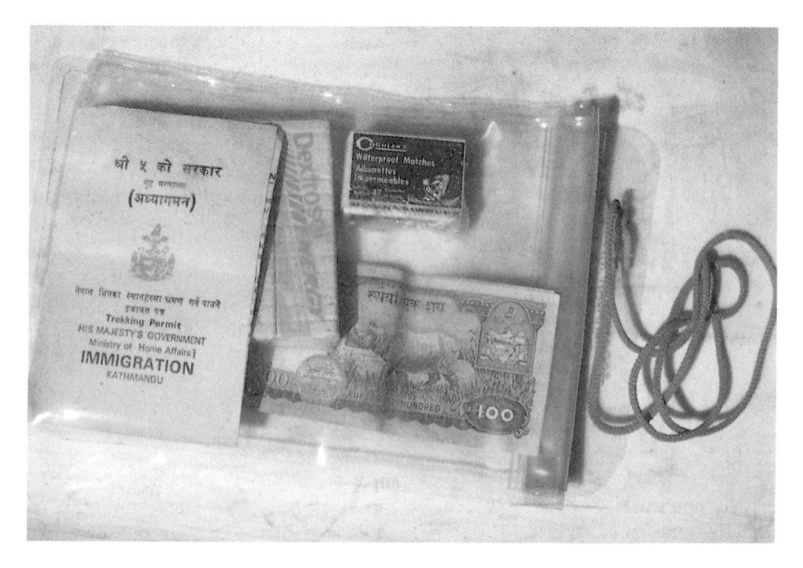

Notes

The gear you should take obviously depends on the time of year, the river, and the altitude of your start point. When we did an expedition down the Humla Karnali, we started at 2000 metres in December and we were grateful for our wetsuits and extra warm clothes. For more difficult rivers like this, there is a strong case for long john wetsuits in that they give you more protection if you do have a bad swim.

Paddling Wear

For white water kayaking, on the top half of your body, you can't go far wrong with a 'dry top' and under that a thermal top – ideally long sleeves and a zip turtle neck so that it gives you sun protection when worn by itself.

The nether regions are a sensitive zone and every one has their own ideas for promoting paddling comfort. If its really hot, then a pair of 'baggy' type swimming shorts are just fine; if it gets a bit colder then a pair of thermal bottoms or tights worn under the shorts works well (the shorts stop the tights ending up around your ankles in the event of a swim). Your Himalayan veteran compromises with 'Green Slime's Nebulous Knickers', thermal shorts cut to be long, baggy and comfortable – these haven't quite made it into Patagonia's latest catalogue! More fashion-conscious deviant kayakers favour figure hugging rubber wet suit shorts. Pile (Helly Hansen) or pelt salopettes are another favourite garment; these are warmer than the items above, and more flexible than wetsuits. Note that full dry suits would only be advantageous for winter trips on really cold rivers (and who wants to go paddling in those conditions?).

The sun is normally intense – please see the rafting section for notes on sun protection.

When selecting equipment and clothes for a multi-day trip, try to select items that are not too specialised, but rather that are practical, durable, lightweight, flexible and have more than one function – remember that besides paddling, you will probably be riding on the tops of buses, trekking and visiting villages. Bring old gear so that you won't get upset when it gets damaged, which it surely will. The other other thing to bear in mind are local weather conditions. Cold winds are unusual and in the main paddling season, late October though December, rain is very rare – days are sunny and nights clear and still.

On the person

Back in 1985 we were kayaking the Doda river up at 3,500 metres in Ladakh. On a cold black day with driving sleet, in an evil little gorge we lost Mike's kayak – never to be seen again (somewhere down the Zanskar or the mighty Indus). Lost was his passport, sleeping bag, clothes, and all the team money. We had a mini-epic but have learnt from our mistake: we always now carry an essential survival kit as itemised above on the person. Things can be sealed in a waterproof bag and either hung around your neck, or kept in a small waist pouch, or probably best of all if you have one, in a well secured life jacket pocket (perhaps tacked shut with big stitches?).

Tents

A tent might be an idea for spring paddling, but for the main paddling season we recommend a lightweight nylon flysheet that can be rigged using paddles and throwbag. A flysheet 3 metres square weighs about 600 gms and will comfortably shelter 4 persons – keeping off the dew (usually heavy) and any rain (unlikely). It also makes a great raft sail!

Footwear

We've probably tried every kind of footwear over the years and have come to the conclusion that for most moderate trips, sports sandals such as 'Tevas' or 'Alps' (our favorites) are best. These let your feet breathe, dry quickly and are comfortable for paddling and trekking. They can be worn with woollen socks (or thin wet suit socks) for cold rivers or evenings. They do not provide as much protection for your feet as trainers or wet suit boots, so these should be used for more difficult rivers or longer treks.

Paddles

Split (break-down) paddles are excellent in that, broken apart and stashed in the kayaks, they don't get damaged on bus journeys, etc., one less item to get lost. They of course, also have the advantage that they can be used with either a right or left control.

Repair kit

Besides the ubiquitous duct/canoe tape you probably should think of: sewing thread and needles, epoxy glue, rubber cement, aquaseal (for wetsuit, drytop, thermorest and drybag repairs), spare kayak nuts and bolts, half a hacksaw blade and a small spanner.

Packing

Good waterproof dry bags are needed for packing your gear and food. Our experience is that you need a couple of long medium-size bags for packing sleeping bag and clothes; being light and bulky these go down the back of the boat with your thermorest. You then need 2 to 4 smaller bags in which to pack food and heavier items so that you can shift these around to balance the boat. Really heavy items like tins are best carried as close as possible to the middle of the boat – perhaps jammed behind the seat? Split paddles often fit snugly tied down at the the side of the seat. In the group we always carry one or two large lightweight nylon kit bags, like sailbags, that we can stuff gear in for bus journeys – the fewer bags you have, the less you have to lose.

Consider the consequences of a swim and tie everything in so it won't come out when the boat is trashed. Our favourite system is to block the opening to the back of the boat with a spider's net of nylon cord, little loops coming out from the sides, laced together by a central tie.

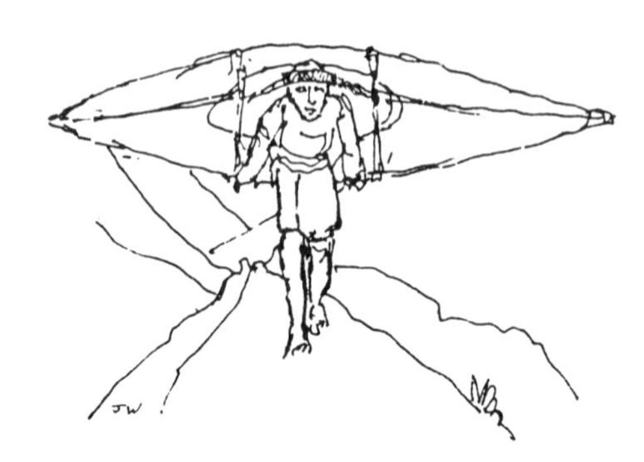

Food and Cooking

Accommodation

Most paddlers in Nepal like to camp on the riverside because the beautiful campsites are one of the pleasures of a river trip. But, like trekking, there is the option on many rivers to stay in local villages; in lodges, tea houses, or people's homes. This is a convenient idea on the way to the river, and it can save carrying cooking gear and food if you eat meals in local tea houses. On the river, this is an inconvenience in that you either have to carry your boats with you or leave your gear in the safekeeping of a reliable householder near the riverside.

Cooking Gear

Cooking on a stove is normally cleaner and easier than a driftwood fire, but of course you will need to carry a stove plus fuel. If you prefer the idea of a fire, on most rivers you will find sufficient driftwood for a small one pot cooking fire. Locals normally build their fire using three stones to support the pot and feeding fuel in the gaps between. This 'star fire' seems pretty well standard all over Asia and is very fuel efficient.

If you plan to cook on a fire then it's probably better to buy your pots from the local bazar rather than ruining a hi-tech stove set; local pots are cheap and their design has evolved over centuries for use on wood fires. Minimum gear is one fair size cooking pot plus lid. For more than one night, we would take a second pot.

Think about some plastic plates (we use frisbees and they also make good fire wafters – see what we mean about more than one function!). A wooden spoon or spatula is a good idea, and also a spare plastic cup that you can use as a scoop/ladle or as a guest cup – these weigh very little. Don't forget a tin opener, cigarette lighter/matches, scourer and a very small amount of biosoap for washing up.

As our second pot we normally take a folding non-stick frying pan – this is our favourite luxury item in the kitchen – it releases us from the constraints of boiled sludgey type dishes into the realms of omelettes, pancakes, bacon and egg, chapatis, fried trout in butter, etc.

Food

You can eat really well on a paddling trip: you're not quite as limited by weight as when trekking, and you are normally in a more relaxed atmosphere, next to a river and with plenty of time. Cooking on a wood fire is more difficult and challenging, but gives you a lot more scope for variety, it's fun and normally there's no shortage of fuel. Your diet is really only limited by your imagination.

Bear in mind that on many rivers it is possible to eat in local tea houses and it is usually possible to buy limited supplies in local villages – rice, dahl, tea, sugar, perhaps vegetables. Fresh vegetables are often best bought en route to the river at the last town on the road.

Shops in Kathmandu have a wide variety of dried foods suitable for trekking and lightweight river trips. Trekking guidebooks and backpacker's cookbooks will give you ideas for menus if you need them. We normally reckon that you can eat well if you carry about one kg of food per person per day. This includes a few tins, but keep tinned food to a minimum – only buying high protein and high calorie items. Go for tinned foods that contain oil and fat as these have the highest calories – so buy tuna in oil or corned beef. Don't buy tuna in brine or meat in gravy, because you're carrying 50% water = 50% waste and 50% extra weight.

Dried fruit and nuts are excellent, peanut butter is of high calorific value, likewise hazelnut spread. Mars bars and chocolate are good for a boost for the last rapid of the day, but generally, sugar is NOT good for you: you need to get your energy for paddling from a high carbohydrate diet, as athletes do. A good and simple diet might be muesli for breakfast; wholewheat bread, cheese, nuts, dried fruit for lunch; soup, tuna pasta, stewed fruit and biscuits for dinner. Keep chocolate as emergency rations, a 'pick me up' or a treat. Build in plenty of hot drinks – these are good for you. Take a few 'magic' ingredients like onions, oxo cubes, stock cubes and tomato puree that give flavour, besides salt, herbs and spices. Try to avoid dried foods like Indian soup powders and quick noodles that contain too much monosodium glutamate – after a while everything seems to taste of this.

Take time to pack food carefully. Transfer all items in glass jars into plastic containers. Seal everything into double plastic bags. For longer trips we normally have a 'brew kit' bag with sugar, tea etc. and a separate 'cook's' bag containing things like spices. Other food is split up and packed in one or two meal quantities, and labelled e.g 'muesli day 1 & 2', 'dinner day 3', etc. Boring sensible people write the contents on tins with a permanent marker before the labels get washed off.

When weight is not too critical it's nice to build more fresh vegetables into the menu. This might for example be on the trek, and also perhaps for the first day on the river.

Quote: 'Don't pack the red peppers in with the toilet paper'! Gerry Moffat.

Food to bring to Nepal

The following food items are not readily available in Nepal, or are expensive, or poor quality; so if you have spare bagage allowance you might like to consider including some of them:

Oatmeal porridge (wheatmeal porridge is available), old fashioned bacon, salami, high quality freeze dried food, american pancake mix (no added ingredients necessary), dried omelette mix, sultanas, trail mix, chocolate, granola, granola bars, stock cubes, quality soup powders.

Marsyandi (Arlene Burns)

Permits

Introduction

Nepal has a system of permits for trekking, rafting, mountaineering and expeditions – at first these seem unnecessary bureacracy but in reality are fairly simple.

Why does the Government have permits?

- It brings in a useful source of revenue.
- Gives a means to help trace missing tourists.
- It helps regulate who goes where (certain areas are restricted because of the undesirable impact that tourists would have on a fragile culture and environment).

Trekking Permits are for individuals trekking anywhere outside the Kathmandu valley (You don't need a permit if you're travelling on the roads between towns). These are the most common form of permit. For the individual the trekking permit does have the advantage that the only identity document that you need to carry is your Permit – you can leave your passport with other valuables in safe keeping in Kathmandu.

Rafting Permits were instigated to regulate commercial rafting but technically cover all boating on all rivers of Nepal.

Expedition Permits are issued under the Mountaineering regulations for groups doing 'expeditions' to remote areas.

You may be asked to show your permit at any Police Check Post that you pass. In practice, this seems to be mainly on, or on the way to, main trekking routes – in one three-month's period of river running I think I was only asked to produce a permit twice. Most check posts are only familiar with Trekking Permits and only on the way to the main rafting rivers – the Trisuli and Sun Kosi – are you likely to be asked for a Rafting permit (or are the officials likely to know what one is).

This system of permits has now become fairly well established and I am told that it is not likely to see much change over the next few years.

How does this affect me?

If you are going with a commercial operator then the company will obtain the necessary rafting permit and you have no worries.

If you are arranging your own raft or kayak trips on one of the approved rafting rivers then we advise you to get a **rafting permit** for your group – cost is minimal and it is fairly straight forward to obtain – see below. The list of approved rivers for rafting is updated regularly, so please enquire locally in Kathmandu: it includes all the popular rivers such as the Trisuli, Sun Kosi, and Kali Gandaki.

If you are planning a major expedition to some remote area of the country – for example the Mugu Karnali, then you should apply for an **Expedition Permit**. This costs a lot more money than other types of permit because you are required amongst other things to take and pay for a Liaison Officer (typically $1500 for a group). The Trekking Agency who are handling your logistics will insist on this permit, and obtain it for you.

The grey area is where you are a kayaker and want to run a river that doesn't fit in these categories – some in this book. Normally these are smaller volume rivers that are fairly accessible from a road, or involve a few day's trek up the valley to then come down it. In the past, most kayakers have obtained a **trekking permit** for their route and shown this if requested.

We haven't heard of any river runners having problems where they have followed the practice above. Most officials in Nepal couldn't be nicer and as long as you have some kind of permit and stay out of restricted areas you are very unlikely to have any kind of problem.

Obtaining a rafting permit

Rafting permits are obtained from the Ministry of Tourism in Kathmandu (near the Football Stadium) or in Pokhara. In 1991 they cost $5 per person for each river trip. You need a list of all your group names, passport numbers, etc. This doesn't have to be obtained in person and we recommend that you pay a local agency to fill out the forms and do the running around for you. Do check though that they have obtained all the necessary government rubber stamps and signatures.

Obtaining a trekking permit

These have to be obtained in person by each individual from the office of the Ministry of Immigration Kathmandu (in Thamel) or in Pokhara. This is the same office that processes visa extensions, but note that these two things are now quite distinct and separate – a trekking permit no longer extends your visa and bank receipts are not required for trekking permits. But, the routine and the regulations change from year to year so the best thing to do is do pop along there the day before, check out the queue (often there is a big line up at opening time, none at closing) and find out the cost (currently about $5), what the rules are, and how the procedures work, from some knowledgaable old-hand trekker.

Remember that this is Nepal: things don't work as they do in the West, if you want everything to be super-efficient you shouldn't be here! If you are not sure about something, talk to other travellers to find out how the system works. At times, we have been appalled at how rude, crass, and ignorant western tourists can be because they expect things to work as they do in their home town. Local officials are really nice guys, at times under a lot of pressure and harrassment to do a routine job – be pleasant with them and make their day with a smile!

Because kayaking on the smaller rivers is a bit of a grey area, it would be foolish and cause a lot of unnecessary problems if you tell officials that besides trekking, you may also be kayaking (or butterfy collecting, kite flying, mountain biking, etc.). Try to give them the information they want and no more, in the format they are used to; keep things simple and routine; avoid complications and discussion. This makes their life a little easier – and yours!

Boating in the Monsoon

. . . by Don Weeden

Most travellers avoid Nepal during the monsoon months, June through September. Torrential rains, leeches, and landslides can turn a normally pleasant trekking route into an epic waiting to happen. What's more, views of the Himalaya are rare in the rainy months. The monsoon is the time when when Nepali rivers go amok, running wild with sometimes 100 times their winter low volumes. For the white water boater this means that runs such as the Marsyandi and the Tamba Kosi – pushy during low water – would be suicide missions at the peak levels. But for the more gradual sections of rivers like the Trisuli, monsoon water levels can provide world-class BIG water kayaking and rafting.

In September one year, after it had been raining for a solid week, I set out with six other kayakers to run the **Sun Kosi**. En route to the put-in by truck we were stopped by a huge mud slide across the road. It looked as if we would be dragging our heavily loaded kayaks the remaining miles until someone noticed that the trickling stream usually paralleling the road had become a raging river . . . Why not? We named this tributary of the Sun Kosi the Coca Khola for its dark brown colour and bubbly character. One two metre waterfall, a tricky portage around an unrunnable rock jumble, ten kilometres of class 3-4 rapids, and four hours later we reached the Sun Kosi. Monsoon kayaking demands that you roll with the punches.

Sun Kosi

Entering the Sun Kosi was like hitting fast forward: this river was in a hurry to reach the Bay of Bengal. By the time we reached the most significant rapids 100 kms downstream its flow was something like 3000 cumecs (100,000 cfs). From the start it was a high speed roller coaster of up to four-metre waves, with the occasional temple-swallowing hole to avoid. Perhaps the biggest hazards were the monstrous wall pillows formed by the 90 degree turns the river occasionally makes. Most of the big rapids, such as Meatgrinder, Hakapur and Big Dipper were definitely NOT washed out. One of the kayakers swam through Meatgrinder and only alerted the others by repeatedly thrusting his paddle up vertically – so big were the waves that the others could not otherwise see him. He wasn't rescued for another two kilometres downstream. Should you swim in a monsoon river, expect it to be a long one!

We ran the 270 kms of the Sun Kosi from Dolaghat to Chatra in four days with six or seven hours of paddling a day. That's fast: in low water this normally takes nine days. Monsoon trips generally take half or less than the usual number of days for a low water descent. The **Trisuli** River from the Tadi Khola to Mugling can be done in an exhilarating day and a half as opposed to the normal four days. Better yet, take an extra day and also paddle the spectacular, but easier Narayani Gorge from Mugling to Narayanghat. Another possible one day monsoon trip would be the Seti river from Damauli.

The rainy season is the time to seek shelter in village huts as opposed to camping, as it can rain hard for hours during the night. A pleasant alternative is the thatched open air huts found in most rice fields alongside the rivers. These structures are built off the ground on stilts and will keep you dry even in the worst downpours. A thermorest pad will make sleeping morc comfortable on the uneven platform. If you are planning to camp out, then bring a sturdy tent rather than a lightweight tarp and a stove is very advisable. Both river and air temperatures will be reasonably warm, despite the intermittant rain. A paddle jacket and light polypros (thermals) and a dry change of clothes will be enough.

One other piece of advice; when you're scouting one of the big rapids, pull your boat several feet above river level, and maybe even secure it with a bowline. I failed to take these precautions on one river and watched my boat run the very rapid I was scouting! The river had come up over a metre in 45 minutes. I didn't recover my boat, which had been hauled in by some local fisherman, until the next day. By then, the gear inside had travelled far and wide along local bartering routes. Don't under-estimate the great appetite of monsoon rivers (or the trading instincts of the locals).

You may ask, if it's so wet, why bother? First, it doesn't rain all the time. The rain generally comes in cloudbursts interspersed by bright sunshine. Occasionally, there is a dry day. Thus, there's sunshine enough to dry damp clothes and revive spirits. Second, the monsoon is one of the most beautiful times of year in Nepal's Middle Hills. The countryside takes on a lush, Bali-like character. The cloud formations and sunsets are spectacular, with the weather constantly changing. Finally, the monsoon water levels on these lower rivers offers some of the best 'big water' boating anywhere. Because of the consequences of a swim in these conditions, monsoon boating is recommended for experts only.

And what about the infamous leeches? Well, if you paddle hard enough they won't have a chance to attach to your boat, to slowly work their way through your sprayskirt, to squirm through the final defense of your thermals . . . arrrrgh!

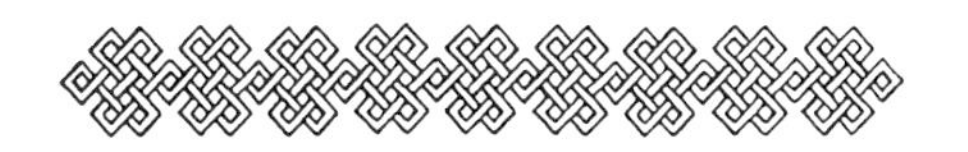

Key to sketch maps

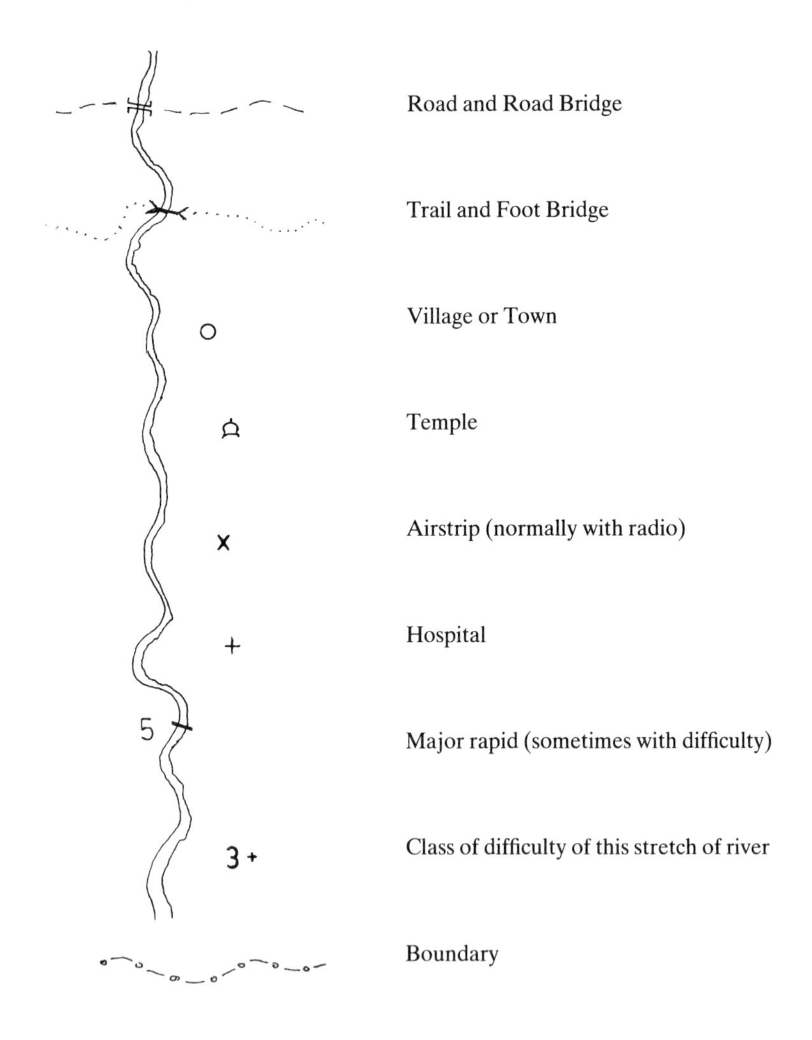
Road and Road Bridge
Trail and Foot Bridge
Village or Town
Temple
Airstrip (normally with radio)
Hospital
5
Major rapid (sometimes with difficulty)
3+
Class of difficulty of this stretch of river
Boundary

GOVERNMENT HEALTH WARNING: FAILURE TO READ THIS PAGE CAN SERIOUSLY DAMAGE YOUR HEALTH.

Using these river guides

Introduction

We have tried in the descriptions that follow to give you a 'feel' for each river and the important things that you would probably want to know if you were thinking of running it. What these river descriptions are not, is a blow by blow account of how to run each rapid. This would be totally inappropriate as Himalayan rivers change dramatically from year to year with each monsoon flood. We have normally noted major rapids or other hazards, but be warned – these often get washed away and new ones appear. Every time you run a river in Nepal – it's a first descent!

We have run most of these rivers ourselves; where we haven't, and have had to rely on others for information, then this is credited at the top. Most of our informants are personal friends whom we have paddled with and whose judgement we trust. Almost all the river descriptions have been checked out by several others who have have done the river and we hope you find the information useful and reasonably consistent. Nothing in the Himalaya and in a changing country like Nepal can ever said to be accurate, but if you do come across a really big 'whoopsie' please drop us a line – we welcome contributions to our next edition (Lots of brownie points and a free book!).

Suggested start and finish points are those we think will be best for most people – sometimes a difficult decision. Where there are alternatives, we have tried to make this clear in the text and we also usually include a little bit of information about the river above the recommended start point (just to excite the interest of our hair-boating friends).

'River days' is the length of time most groups would take to do the river, including rest. The lowest figure is how long most kayak groups would probably take, raft trips are normally slower and would therefore normally take the higher number of days.

How Difficult?

We have used the standard International Classification of Difficulty (see Appendix D) when grading the rivers. We haven't been super conservative just because we're writing a guide book – we've given the river the classification that we think most experienced river runners would agree with.

If you have rafted or kayaked in places like Canada, America or New Zealand you should have no problem relating to our classifications. If your experience is limited, then the power of Himalayan rivers may well make you think that what we call a class 4 is really what you think of as a class 5; well, be warned!

One of the problems of the International Classification is that the majority of white water is class 3 and 4 and in fact there is a vast difference between an easy grade 4 and a hard one. We have used + and – grades to be more definitive:

1	2	3	3+	4–	4	4+	5–	5	5+	6

Where we call a river class 4+ we mean that in our opinion this is the overall standard of the river – there may be long sections at a lower standard of difficulty, but to run the river safely you need to be 100% capable of paddling at this level.

GOVERNMENT HEALTH WARNING: FAILURE TO READ THIS PAGE CAN SERIOUSLY DAMAGE YOUR HEALTH.

Class 4– (5) means that in our opinion the overall standard of the river is Class 4-, but there are a few class 5 rapids that can be relatively easily portaged if required. Our opinion on the grade of difficulty is based on typical water volumes for the **stated month** only – normally November. If the monsoon is late then water volumes will be much higher and the river correspondingly more difficult, if not impossible.

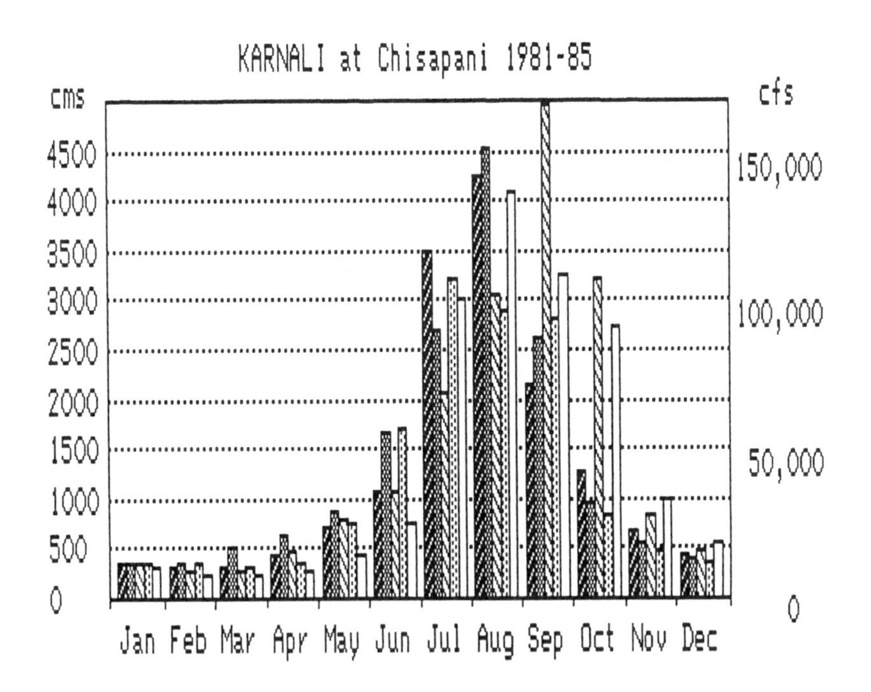

We have based our opinion on the class of difficulty of the river as it was when we, or our informants, ran it. Earthquakes, landslides, floods, etc. may completely change a river and make it easier or harder: thus you should note that these river descriptions are by definition out of date, and to a larger or smaller extent, misleading. Nepal is an exotic, adventurous third world country where communication is difficult and outside help or rescue may be impossible. Most of the rivers are remote and you will probably be paddling with loaded boats. **We have NOT taken these factors into account when grading a river for difficulty** – you must make your own allowances and we strongly advise you to be sensibly conservative when considering the difficulty of a proposed river journey.

Altitudes

Most altitudes are taken, by courtesy of the Topographic Surveys Branch, from the 1:63,360 series of Topographical maps produced for the Government of Nepal in the 1960's. These can normally be reckoned to be accurate to +/− 10 metres and were used to draw the river profiles that accompany most river descriptions. These profiles are drawn to different scales, but the ratio between the vertical and horizontal scale has been kept constant so that gradients can be compared between different rivers.

Water volumes and Hydrographs

Quoted figures and hydrographs are long term average flows, (usually over ten or more years). 100 cumecs (cubic metres per second) is aprox. 3500 cfs (cubic ft per second). Many of these river journeys see a huge increase in volume from the suggested start to the finish and it is difficult to choose a meaningful figure for the summary; when in doubt we have tried to select a figure for roughly half or two thirds down the river.

Sketch maps

The sketch maps that accompany the river descriptions are just that: they do not pretend to be accurate: they are merely a guide, drawn from many conflicting sources, as to the nature of things at the time of writing. We have tried to indicate all known bridges, and selected villages and trails, but these are fairly frequently washed away by the monsoon floods so that any map is out of date soon after it is drawn.

Names of rivers and villages

Many rivers have several different spellings; we don't profess to be an authority on this, but have attempted to use the spelling that appeared to us to be in most common use and/or would cause least confusion (we have used Tamba rather than Tama Kosi and Tamur rather than Tamar River). Village names can be particularly misleading: locals can have two different names for a village and then a government map gives it a third one; again we have tried to use the most common name – one that we hope local people will recognise!

River Descriptions

As is common practice, all directions are given as if going down the river; RIGHT always means river right; LEFT always means river left. Distances are in kilometres and heights in metres (5 miles = 8 kms and 3.281 ft = one metre).

RIVERS OF CENTRAL NEPAL

Introduction

A wide choice of fine rivers and relatively good access has made this a justly popular region with river runners. Two large and famous rivers, the Trisuli and the Kali Gandaki drain the watershed and join together to make up the mighty Narayani that flows out to the plains of India.

The relatively good network of roads makes access to the rivers fairly easy and cheap from Kathmandu. A new road is being built west from Pokhara and this will open up the Upper Kali Gandaki and Modi Khola, so that in the future we expect Pokhara to develop as a second centre for river runners.

Commercial Rafting

Traditionally the Trisuli has been the most popular river for rafting, with only a few rafting trips being arranged on other rivers. Though the Trisuli offers some great rafting, we think that its popularity and proximity to the main highway detract from the experience for many people. If you are looking for a rafting trip close to Kathmandu or Pokhara then we recommend that you consider the other rivers of the region – particularly the Kali Gandaki.

When planning your rafting trip, try to build this into your other holiday arrangements so that you minimise highway travel – for example fly to Pokhara, run the Kali Gandaki down to Chitwan National Park and then return by road to Kathmandu.

Self-sufficient Trips

The rivers of this region are ideal for self sufficiant trips – most are only a day's bus ride from Kathmandu and most are just a few days long. If you are new to Nepal, these rivers are good ones on which to gain experience. This region is well populated and it is normally possible to find food and basic accomodation in villages, so you can travel very light if you so wish.

Note that you don't have to be an expert boater to enjoy a self sufficient trip: there are relatively easy rivers like the Seti or lower Kali Gandaki that are quite suitable for inflatable 'duckies' or similar boats.

Guide Book Rivers

Trisuli
Impressive gorges and some exciting rapids. Popular for rafting and intermediate kayaking. Different start points offer trips of varying length and difficulty.

Modi Khola
A blue mountain stream and kayakers dream. Flows from the Annapurna Sanctuary, great paddling with a stunning mountain backdrop.

Kali Gandaki (Upper)
A beautiful unspoilt river with good white water, makes an ideal medium length raft or kayak trip.

Kali Gandaki (Lower)
A large volume river, but relatively easy and with unspoilt scenery. A beautiful, relaxing raft, kayak, or 'Duckie' trip.

Seti
A scenic, unspoilt and easy two day raft trip on a small volume, blue, warm and friendly river – a nice 'warm up' trip for kayakers.

Marsyandi
Continuous and exhilarating white water with magnificent mountain backdrops – one of the best class 4 kayaking rivers in the world! Also an exciting 2 day raft trip for experienced crews.

Buri Gandaki
A little travelled but easy river, requiring a pleasant trek to the put in, which makes an interesting alternative start to a Trisuli trip.

Other Rivers

Badi Gad – This is a long staight river that joins the Kali Gandaki just before it makes the big turn East. It appears to have an easy gradient, and to offer a few days of relatively easy boating – probably awaiting a first descent.

Myagdi Khola – Another tributary of the Kali Gandaki joining it at Beni. Probably offers some paddling for the expert kayaker.

Andhi Khola – A small volume river that can be seen from the Pokhara to Butawal road – easy access and probably a day or two of fun kayaking at the right level.

Madi River – Another small river and the main tributary of the Seti, joining that river at Damauli. A day's trek in from Pokhara and then...?

Darandi Khola – Just west of Gorkha and flowing south to join the Marsyandi below the dam. A possible day or two of kayaking?

Ankhu Khola – This flows in a valley between the Trisuli and the Buri Gandaki, and joins the latter river below Arughat – this again probably offers a few days of exploratory small volume kayaking.

Tadi Khola – This rises in the Gosai Khunda mountains to the north of Kathmandu and flows south west to join the Trisuli downstream of Trisuli Bazar. Relatively close to Kathmandu, but to our knowledge, no one has yet paddled it.

Mahesh Khola – Joins the Trisuli at Baireni. A small river followed by the main highway to Kathmandu. Has been kayaked in high water from near Dharke.

Rapti River – Flows through Chitwan National Park. 'Dungas', traditional dug-out canoes, can be hired to view the wildlife.

N.B. Most of the above rivers are small volume and probably need medium water flows to be runnable – late October?

Hospitality . . . *by Arlene Burns*

As a child I remember making the long journey to visit my grandparents in Alabama. As we drove through the early evenings, I would be attracted by the soft glow radiating from nearby farmhouses and wished that we could just stop there for the night. My mother dutifully informed me of the dangers of strangers and especially entering their houses. Perhaps that is why I find Nepal such a natural home: you can, and are expected, to invite yourself and your weary travelling companions into a friendly hearth for the night.

Trisuli

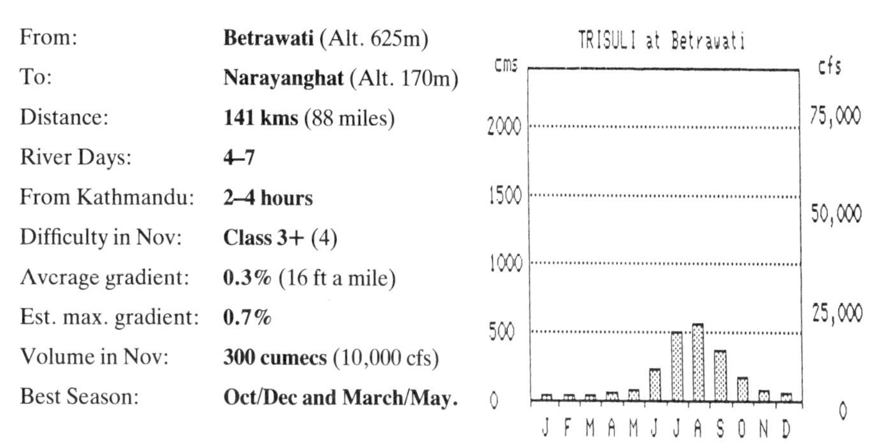

From:	**Betrawati** (Alt. 625m)
To:	**Narayanghat** (Alt. 170m)
Distance:	**141 kms** (88 miles)
River Days:	**4–7**
From Kathmandu:	**2–4 hours**
Difficulty in Nov:	**Class 3+** (4)
Average gradient:	**0.3%** (16 ft a mile)
Est. max. gradient:	**0.7%**
Volume in Nov:	**300 cumecs** (10,000 cfs)
Best Season:	**Oct/Dec and March/May.**

Summary

The Trisuli is Nepal's most popular rafting river. Impressive gorges, exciting rapids, some easier sections, and easily accessible from Kathmandu and Pokhara. Recommended for intermediate kayakers and those wanting a cheap white water rafting trip.

The River

Legend says that high in the Himalaya at Gosainkund the god Shiva drove his trident into the ground to create three springs – the source of the river and hence its name Trisuli.

Not far after this source the Trisuli joins the Bhote Kosi that flows from Tibet; the two rivers joining in some pretty fearsome looking gorges that are visible on the way up to the Langtang Trek. By Betrawati the gradient has eased and after this it becomes a more mature and powerful river which later adds many other major rivers to its flow – the Buri Gandaki, the Marsyandi, and the Seti. When the Kali Gandaki joins it, shortly before the plains, it changes its name to the Narayani. Here, it is a truly mighty river – peak flows in the Monsoon have been measured at 25,700 cu.mecs (extreme, instantaneous discharge); about 900,000 cubic feet per second (cfs) or fifty times the typical flow of the Colorado River through the Grand Canyon!

Normally the flow on the main rafting section of the Trisuli is about half that of the Grand Canyon, and in many ways the rapids are smaller scale versions of those on the Colorado; they are formed mainly by boulder outwash from tributary streams and are characterised by big green shoots, holes either side, and huge exploding waves down the bottom.

The river has carved some truly impressive gorges in its lower part as it cut its way through the 2000 metre high Mahabharat Range. These gorges are also the route followed by the Prithvi Highway, the main highway from India to Kathmandu, and the roar of diesel trucks undoubtedly detracts from a river trip – happily for much of the river the highway is some way from the river itself. The opposite side to the road is relatively wild and uninhabitated and you should see plenty of wildlife, a profusion of colourful birds, including eagles and vultures – especially true if you continue on down into Chitwan National Park where you may see crocodiles and rhino by the riverside.

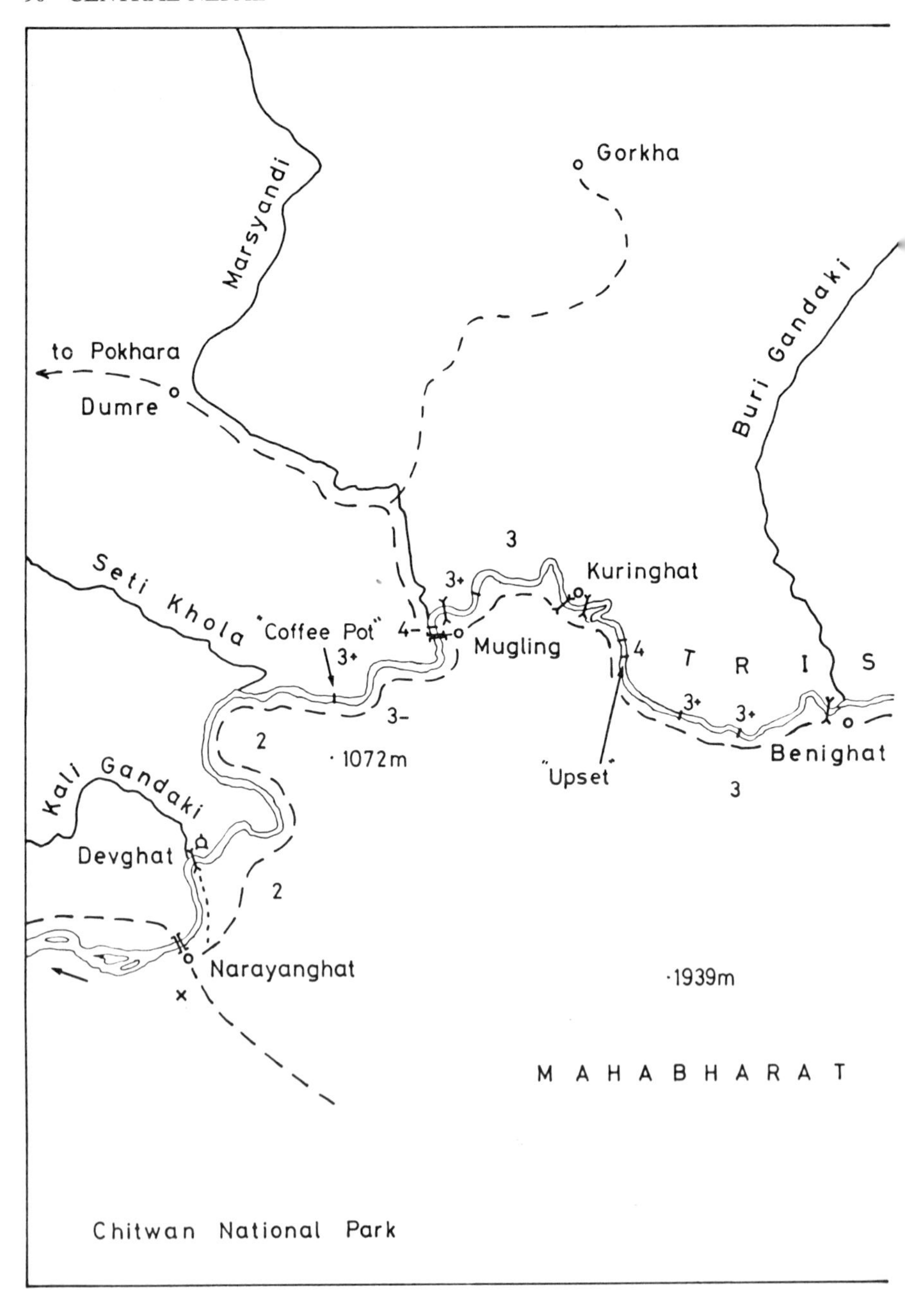

WARNING: Laser-phobic ink – do not photocopy.

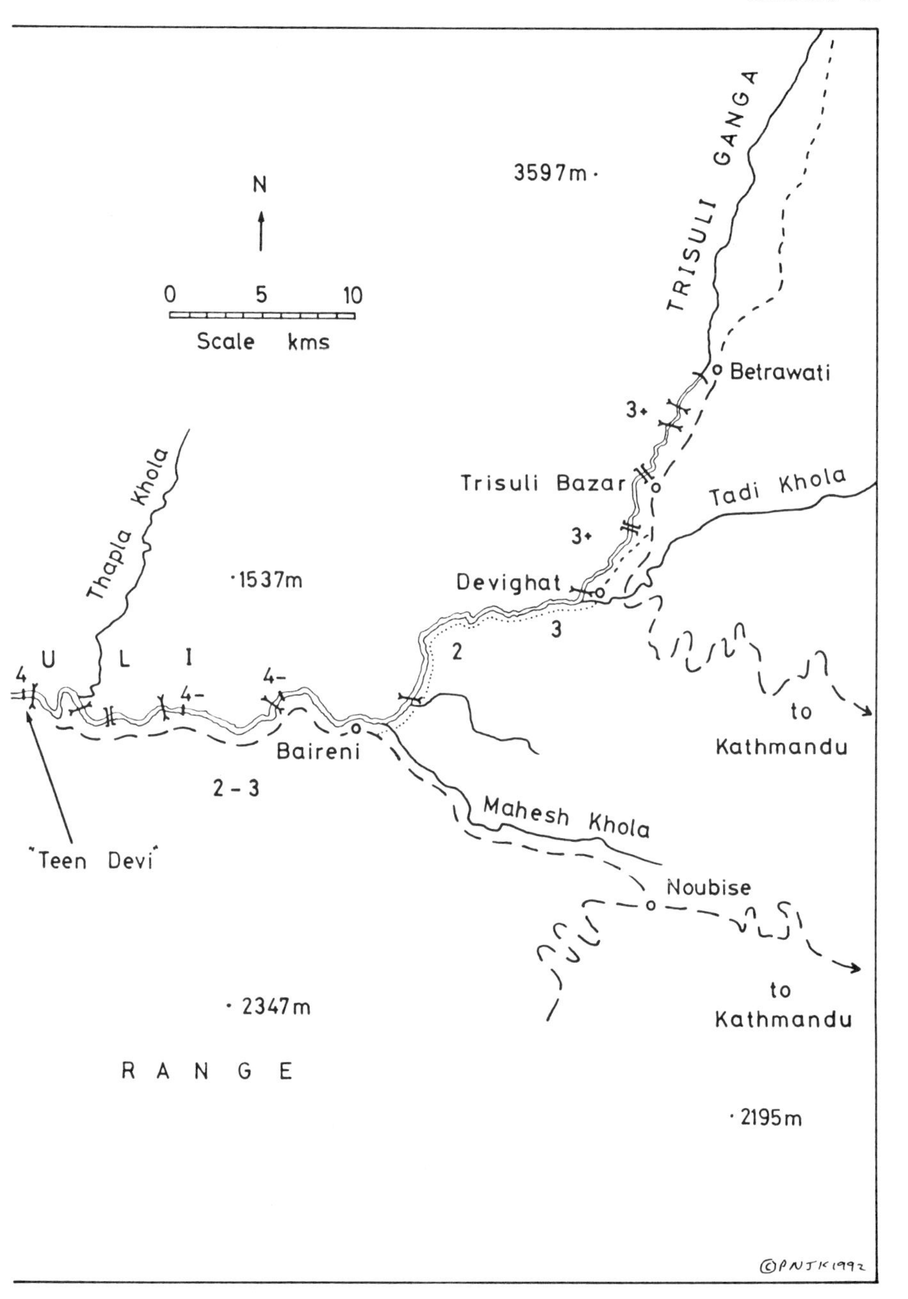

N
0 5 10
Scale kms
3597m
TRISULI GANGA
Betrawati
3+
Trisuli Bazar
Tadi Khola
3+
Devighat
3
2
Thapla Khola
1537m
4
U L I
4-
4-
Baireni
2-3
"Teen Devi"
to Kathmandu
Mahesh Khola
Noubise
to Kathmandu
2347m
R A N G E
2195m
©PNJK1992

Rafting

A rafting trip on the Trisuli needs no recommendation from us: thousands of thrilled rafters have written home and recommended the trip to their friends. For many people it represents the ideal compromise trip: just the right length of time, exhilarating rapids, but not too difficult, easily accessible from Kathmandu and at a cheap price.

If anything, we feel that it has been over-promoted by rafting companies because it is so convenient from Kathmandu. Certainly, if you're looking for more of a 'wilderness' experience, unsullied beaches, and unspoilt scenery then we suggest that you should consider one of the other rivers in this book.

The rapids on the Trisuli are mainly big, bouncy and relatively safe: 'flips' (where the raft capsizes) or other accidents are rare in normal water conditions, and if you wish, it is possible to walk around the few difficult rapids. If you have doubts about whether this is the river for you, please read our sections on choosing a river trip and safety.

There is a wide choice of different length trips on offer, from a one week relaxed trip all the way from Trisuli Bazar to Chitwan to half day 'tasters' specials. Trisuli Bazar is normally only a starting point in higher water conditions – Sept/Oct or April/May.

For many people the optimum length trip is three days, starting at or near **Baireni** and taking out at **Narayanghat**. This gives you a full and satisfying experience – you run all the major rapids, watch the river grow as its tributaries join, marvel as it cuts its way through impressive gorges, then leave it when it spreads out over the great plain of the Ganges.

If your time or budget is limited, then a one or two day trip is offered by many companies – these can also save travel time if scheduled as a break of the journey from Kathmandu to Pokhara, or Kathmandu to Chitwan. These short trips can vary from fairly relaxed float trips, avoiding the more difficult rapids, to one day 'roller coaster' specials. The latter can run some of the best of the white water but pose obvious dangers and can be a rather vicarious experience!

> **N.B.** *Before booking a trip, do read the section on 'Selecting a Company' in the chapter 'Rafting with a Commercial Operator' and check carefully what you are getting for your money. The Trisuli is popular with the 'cowboy' operators who appear to offer you a lot, but give you a really bad experience.*

Note that the cheaper outfitters like to camp on the highway side of the river – easy logistics, but usually the road makes it noisy and dirty.

Kayaking

The Trisuli is a popular river for kayakers and can be particularly recommended for training and familiarisation with 'big water'. Intermediate paddlers who are unfamiliar with relatively large volume rivers will find this a friendly initiation: expert paddlers will revel in honing their technical skills, playing and surfing the big rapids.

The river has been kayaked from near the Tibetan border down to Betrawadi by some of America's top expedition boaters. The Bhote Kosi from near the border to Syabru Bensi is described as Class 4 and 5; from there down are some pretty mean, inaccessible gorges that drop at 5.0% (250 ft a mile), definately Class 5 and 6, and that probably represent a nightmare for the average recreational kayaker.

The intermediate paddler will probably want to start at Betrawadi, where the river is relatively small – 85 cumecs as against 300 near Mugling. This gives a day or two to get used to the nature of the river before hitting the bigger rapids lower downstream. The more

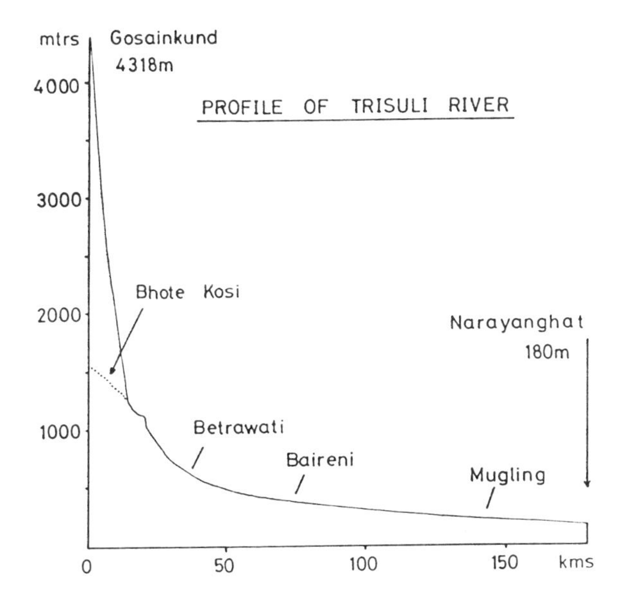

experienced paddler may prefer to concentate on playing the big rapids, putting in below Baireni and perhaps accompanying a raft group so that he has a light kayak.

Access and logistics

Betrawadi is 4-6 hours drive from Kathmandu by a pleasant and scenic road. There are plenty of local buses but these are usually crowded and it is sometimes a bit of a hassle to find one, especially if you have kayaks to transport. Alternatives are a private minibus which costs about $90 or a taxi costing about $40.

Baireni takes about 2-3 hours. Again there are lots of crowded local buses. One reasonably convenient option is to book a seat on the tourist bus to Pokhara, $4, and get dropped off at Baireni or the place you want. A private minibus to Baireni would cost about $60 and a taxi $25.

In high water conditions, expert kayakers have started at Dharke on the Mahesh Khola, the tributary followed by the main road from Kathmandu.

There are many take-outs on the Trisuli, but most people choose to finish at Mugling or Narayanghat which are major bus stops, or they continue down to Chitwan. The return trip to Kathmandu is usually fairly straight forward but sometimes you have to wait a few hours for a bus with space on the roof. Journey time back from Mugling should be about 3-4 hours.

We recommend camping on this river – there are lodges to stay in alongside the highway, but these are very noisy and unpleasant. Because there are so many raft trips, firewood may be scarce and a stove is recommended. Best map covering the whole of the Trisuli is probably that published by H.M.G. Ministry of Works and Transport, Suspension Bridge Division: 'Central Region – Main Trail Map' at a scale of 1:250,000.

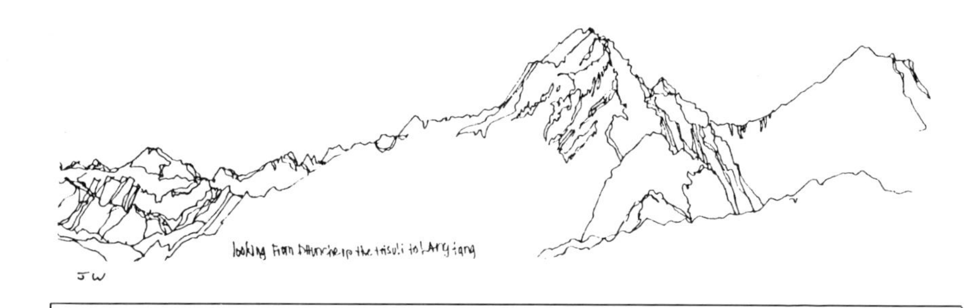

looking from Dhunche up the trisuli to Langtang
JW

The Upper Trisuli Gorges, 1987 . . . *by John Wasson*

This was an epic with many facets. We had a solid crew: John and Jocelyn Wasson, Bob McDougall, Phil DeRiemer, Bob Beazley and Arlene Burns. We got sort of talked into the trip by Don Weeden who bagged out at the last second.

We bussed, trekked and sweet talked our way to Timure, near the Tibet border and put in. A day of good paddling with a few portages brought us back to Syabru Bensi: plans changed here as Arlene and Jocelyn decided to pass on the canyon below and head for Kathmandu in the morning. Beez knew he should go back because his wife was arriving in two days and she was expecting to be met at the airport.

However, we convinced him that true first descent glory awaited us and that two or three days would be plenty to make the 40 kms to Trisuli Bazar. It took six. We named it the 'Na Ramro Gorge'. We were utterly spent but saved some face by getting back to Kathmandu on Christmas Eve. The ladies welcomed us back but it was a few days before any of us could speak in complete sentences. Jocelyn understood but I'm afraid it was the beginning of the end of Beez's marriage. These things happen.*

(= Nepali for No Good)*

Description

Betrawati to Trisuli Bazar 7 kms, Devighat 10, Baireni 18.

Recommended put-in for kayaks is aproximately 1 km before the Dam at **Betrawati**, at the bottom of the hill where the road comes close to the river. This does require a scramble down the bank, and rafts might prefer to put in further downstream. There is an alternative, but less pleasant, put-in at Trisuli Bazar on the left below the bridge.

From Betrawati to Devighat is class 3+ water. The river is steep, really fun kayaking, and quite friendly. Do take the time to look around you, especially behind for the views of the Ganesh Himal.

The Dam at Betrawati was built in the 70's and was one of Nepal's first Hydro Electric Power schemes. Normally the Dam diverts about half of the water flow so there is often too little for rafting in the winter months. In higher water or when the dam is not diverting water, the difficulty is greater – probably class 4. One of the local rafters describes it as 'a blast in high water'.

6 kms brings you to **Trisuli Bazar**, a fairly typical roadside market town. Note the local produce being loaded onto trucks – the flat river terraces of this area are fertile and lower than the Kathmandu Valley and this used to be the main supplier of sub tropical produce to the wealthy merchants of the Capital. If you have time here, the place to visit is Nuwakot an ancient fortress which sits imposingly on the ridge to the East. This is one of the most historic fortresses of Nepal guarding the important trade route to Tibet – worth the one hour walk for the view from the top.

Just below Trisuli Bazar on the right bank is a HEP station: it appears that this may have been superseded by a bigger one, another 4 kms further downstream just below a road bridge. In low water conditions, the outflow from this doubles the volume of the river. Another 4 kms of pleasant paddling brings you to **Devighat** and the confluence with the Tadi Khola. There is road access to Devighat and there appears to be a reasonable put-in for rafts and campsite about one kilometre upstream from the confluence.

Devighat is quite a picturesque spot with a temple by the confluence. You will come across several square piles of stones on the beach and if this is your first river trip in Nepal you may think what useful picnic tables these make. A word of warning: these contain bodies awaiting cremation or a water burial in the next monsoon.

Good class 3 water, with plenty of small play waves continues for the next two kms after which the valley widens. Look out for a couple of rickety aerial cableways that would fail any Boy Scout pioneering badge. Class 2 water gives a chance to drift along and enjoy the scenery. After several kilometres the Kalphu Khola comes in on the left followed after 2 kms by the Mahesh Khola. The roar of traffic warns of the approach of the highway again and the scruffy village of Baireni.

Baireni to Buri Gandaki 30 kms, Kuringhat 26, Mugling 12.

Class 2 water with a few 3 class rapids for the first few kms give those starting at **Baireni** a chance to get 'warmed up'. The first slightly harder rapid, probably a class 4– comes after about 5 kms – about an hour and a half in a raft? This rapid was named 'Snell's Nose' by Nepalese rafters in honour of Colonel John Blashford-Snell who was one of the first to run it and broke his nose so doing. No, the rapid isn't rugged and knarly – it's now a straight forward shoot with big bouncy waves and you are very unlikely to flip a raft or break your nose.

More mainly class 2 water brings you after another 5 kms to a longer more interesting class 4– rapid – on the left after a left hand bend. This requires some manoeuvring to avoid a small headwall and some ledges that follow. This is known by many as 'Monkey' rapid, no doubt after the mannerisms of the rafters after running it – leaping around, spitting, scratching with delight, grinning and chattering. the name has nothing to do with the troops of monkeys you will see on the right bank!

A new road bridge is being built to replace the interesting cable ferry at the confluence of the Thapla Khola. The river now does a big bend for 2 kms away from the road – a peaceful spot to lunch or camp. Shortly after meeting the highway again, there is a purpose-made rafters' put-in, restaurant and campsite; also a bridge which is warning of the approach to 'Teen Devi Rapid' on the left.

'Teen Devi' is class 4, and in most water conditions it is the most difficult rapid on the Trisuli, so many companies prefer to start their trips below here. It is usual practice to land above the rapid on a small beach on the left and to climb up and along the top of the rocky bank to scout. There are also some good spots along here for taking photos. This is a long rapid like a giant boulder field which needs some careful route finding and precise manoeuvring for rafts. Great fun and immensely satisfying to get a clean raft run – give yourselves a team cheer and a group hug at the bottom!

For kayaks, their greater manoeuvrability probably makes this an easier rapid, but it still requires skilful route finding and those not sure of their roll should consider the possible consequences of a long, rough swim.

Three kms later, and the blue waters of the **Buri Gandaki** enter on the right. The river now bends away from the road again; a peaceful section for relaxed drifting and a possible campsite or lunch stop. About 6 kms after the Buri Gandaki the left handside of the valley is blocked by a high, vertical cliff dropping spectacularly straight into the river. The road builders were forced to blast a rock gallery to traverse this. The river does a sharp right bend and runs along the base of the cliff with the dark crag overhanging above. This is an eerie place to be, with the roar of diesel engines echoing high overhead: paddle fast and don't think about the consequences of a truck coming off the road!

A long rapid follows shortly afterwards on the right. Known sometimes as 'Twin rocks', this is a class 3+ in low water. The river now relaxes for the next 4 kms – time to sit back and enjoy the scenery. Note the aerial cable cars that connect the villages on the right bank with the highway – a wooden box on two pulleys running on a steel cable stretched across the river, pulled across by a man or boy sitting in the box: drifting by in the middle of the river, and deep in thought, it's easy not to see the cable until a cheery 'Namaste' surpises you from a few feet above your head.

The valley narrows, becomes a gorge, and the rapid known as 'S Bends' or 'Ladies Delight' is on the left – class 3+ in low water. Another 3 kms through this gorge brings you to two rapids. The first (sometimes known as Gloria) is after a sharp left hand bend – this is a straight forward class 3, with big waves in high water. Make sure you break out on the right immediatly below this, and just before a slight right hand bend, to land and inspect the next rapid, 'Upset'.

'Upset' is infamous, and probably the most photographed rapid on the river. There is always a monstrous hole and a wave here that seem to dwarf a raft. Measure of size for this is how many Tata trucks you think would fit in the hole, on a scale of 1 – 5 ! Having said this, perhaps we should reassure you: like most big holes it's not as fearsome as it appears – most rafts bob out with most of their crew and right way up – but an excellent spot for action photos (a good excuse if you don't want to run this rapid).

One km after 'Upset' and immediately after a left hand bend is 'Surprise', a class 4–. There is a popular rafters' put-in just below and then shortly afterwards the river enters a deep awesome gorge, particlarly spectacular early or late in the day, when much of the

Trisuli above Mugling (Jock Montgomery)

chasm is in shadow but sunlight shines on vistas of distant hillsides. The gorge ends after about 2 kms and the river then curves away from the highway and there is a possible campsite on the bend where the Pasupati stream enters on the right.

Two kms further brings you to the picturesque village of **Kuringhat** built on a bluff on the right, with two suspension bridges swooping gracefully over the river to the left bank. The wide beach on the left is a favourite put-in and overnight camp for commercial raft groups.

The river again turns away from the highway and there is a dramatic landslip as the river curves around to the left. For several hundred metres high, the hillside has had its surface flesh stripped away to reveal the raw white bones of the underlying rocks. Drift by and marvel at the mighty forces that are uplifting these mountains and carving the valleys.

Back to the highway unfortunately, but the road now starts climbing gently away from the river and there are beaches on both sides of the river that would make possible campsites. After another kilometre the river enters a gorge again – warning of another rapid around the corner – called 'S' or 'M...F....' rapid.

Two kms on, and a cable car crosses the river and heralds the approach to **Mugling**. The town is on the left, some 70 metres above the river, which curves around it at some distance. An elegant new suspension bridge crosses just above the confluence of the Marsyandi. 'PinBall' rapid follows closely after the confluence, class 4–. This rapid is well named: you need to pick your route carefully as it has some potentially lethal 'pin' spots on the right. We recommend that you scout this before running it.

If you want to pull out or spend some time here, the best place to land is just upstream of the road bridge – it is usually possible to stop either above or below the rapid. A rafters' path zigzags steeply up the bank to the bridge and from here it is three minutes' walk into town for cold cokes.

Mugling to Seti Khola 15 kms, Devghat 17, Narayanghat 6.

Mugling is a favourite put-in for more relaxed float trips down to Narayanghat or Chitwan. One rafter says, 'I like this stretch – it feels more mellow and relaxed, the sun comes out, and the gorges are just beautiful'. 'Pin Ball' is the last serious rapid on the river – from here on down its mainly class 1 – 2, perhaps one or two of the rapids could be called 2+ or 3− in the right conditions and kayakers will still find a few waves to surf. This is a peaceful section: most of the time, the highway is high above the river

What is different about this stretch of river is the volume: below Mugling some 400 cumecs and by Narayanghat a mighty 790 cumecs or 28,000 cu ft sec. You have a feeling of being pushed along by this powerful giant. This power has been used by the river to carve its way right through the heart of the 2000 metre high Mahabharat Range of Mountains. These are some fairly impressive gorges!

The 15 kms to the confluence with the Seti Khola has several small rapids; the biggest might be a class 3+ and is called 'Coffee pot' – kayaks get swirled around like the grounds in the bottom of the pot! Most of the time you can just sit back, relax and enjoy the dramatic canyon. Note how the vegetation has changed as you have gone down the river and the banks are now thickly clothed in semi-tropical jungle. The junction with the **Seti** is a favourite rafters' campsite and lunch stop. Take a stroll here and have a look at the timber weirs that locals have built out into the Seti to trap fish.

Also take time to inspect the dugout canoes that are used as ferry boats about 2 kms below the Seti. Here, there is a wide beach on the left and the small village of Gai Ghat and the highway are close to the river. This is a good take-out if you do not want to continue

further. Below here there are only a few small, swirly rapids – the last one around the big bend is called 'Swimming' rapid – ask your rafter about this one. Perhaps we should mention that crocodiles have been seen quite high up the river, but relax, there have been no instances in Nepal where a crocodile has attacked a raft or kayak and to be honest you will be lucky to see one. Following this last rapid is 'Windy canyon' – Murphy's 5th River Law says that wind always blows up a river – certainly true in this case: smell the hot spicey aromas being wafted up from the Indian plain.

Devghat at the confluence of the two most holy rivers, the Trisuli and Kali Gandaki, is a special sacred spot where many Hindus come to die and be cremated. This is a peaceful, contemplative spot with small shrines and hospice homes in the shade of the trees. Dress with respect and be careful not to touch anything, or anyone, because many of the pilgrims here are high caste Brahmans who would be defiled by contact.

Most famous resident at Devghat is an old religious teacher, Guru Pagla Babu. Babu only has one arm, and the story goes that many years ago, as contrition for the state of world and as a sacrifice for peace, Babu chopped off his little finger. The following year, the world was in an even bigger mess so he chopped off another finger ...... etc.!

Probably the best time to come here is the Maghe Sankranti Jatra which is a religious festival to mark the passage of the Sun's course from the Tropic of Capricorn to the Northern Hemisphere, sometime in mid January. Several thousand people of diverse tribes and castes converge on Devghat to bathe in the holy waters of the river and to pray to the Sun God.

Back on the river, now called the **Narayani**, and a few kilometres brings you out of the foothills and onto the great Indian plain with the river disappearing into the heat and haze of a flat horizon. Well, not quite: it actually disappears under the long road bridge at **Narayanghat**. This is a large and rapidly growing town and what a contrast to the river, Ugh! The left side above the bridge is the most convenient take-out but is a 'really gross beach'. If you want to stay the night, there is a convenient hotel on the right bank above the bridge. Buses for Kathmandu leave from the main intersection which is only 100 metres from the bridge.

If you are continuing on the river to Royal **Chitwan** National Park we recommend that you make arrangements in advance in Kathmandu – camping inside the park is only allowed with a special permit and it is patrolled and guarded by army units. Probably the nicest way to end your trip is to paddle on down to one of the luxury safari camps e.g.Tiger Tops Tented Camp or Jungle Island Resort. Expensive but worth it; talk nicely to the Safari Companies and you might be able to negotiate a special deal. If you are very lucky, you may see one of the rare fresh water dolphins; these unfortunately are threatened by pollution from the new paper mills – sponsored by the Chinese.

There are some good islands on which to camp a few kms below Narayanghat and a few kms further will bring you to the Park Check Post on the right bank. It is about another 17 kms further to Jungle Island Resort. (The Narayani and Chitwan National Park are shown on the map of the lower Kali Gandaki).

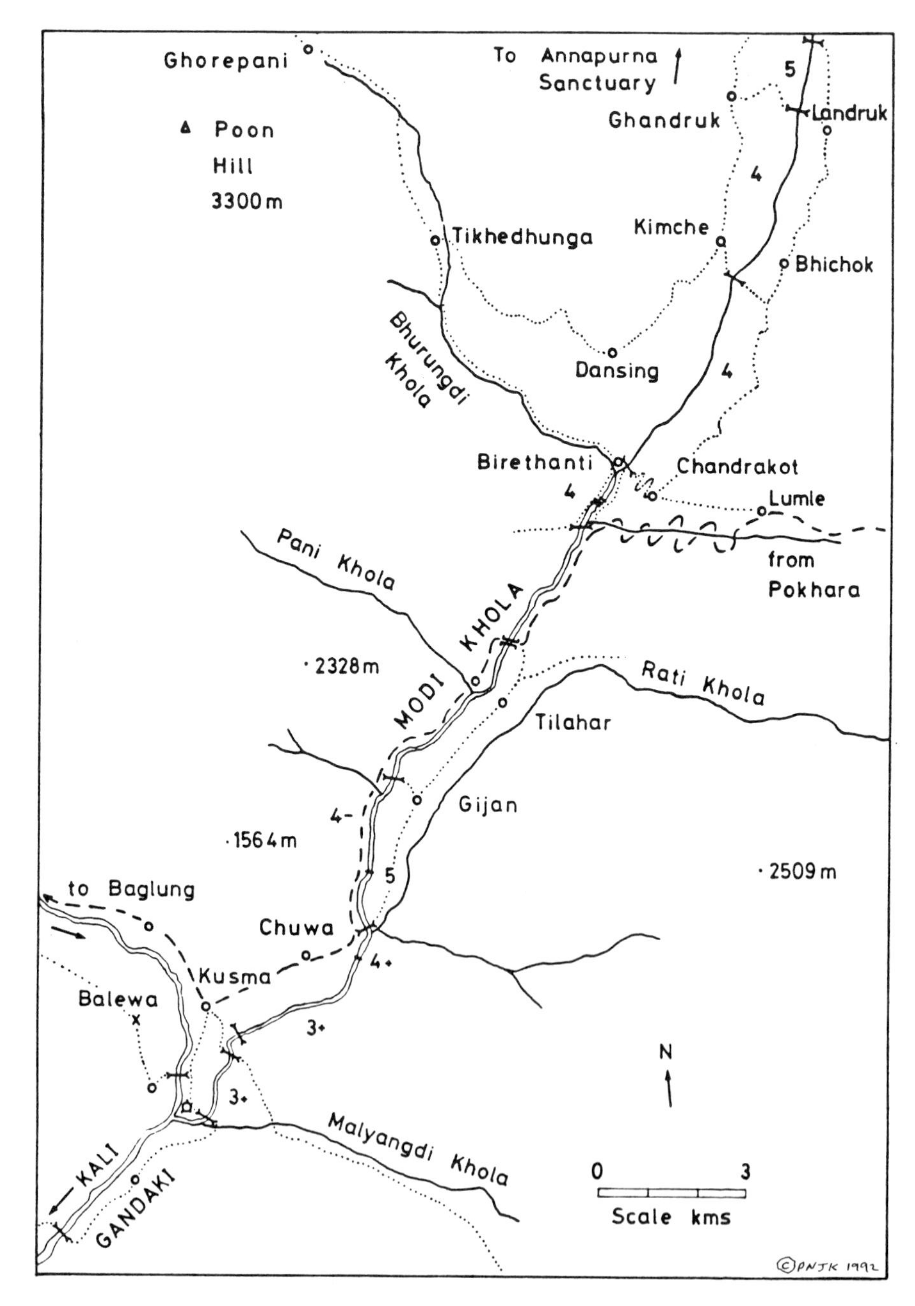

WARNING: Laser-phobic ink – do not photocopy.

Modi Khola

From: **Landruk** (Alt. 1290m)
To: **Kali Gandaki** (Alt. 690m)
Distance: **26 kms** (16 miles)
River Days: **2**
From Pokhara: **2 days**
Difficulty in Nov: **Class 4** (5)
Average gradient: **2.5%** (125 ft a mile)
Est. max. gradient: **4%**
Est. Volume in Nov: **20 cumecs** (700 cfs)
Best Season: **Nov/Dec and March/April**

Summary

A blue mountain stream for expert kayakers. Continuous class 4 white water with few portages and a spectacular mountain backdrop make this a kayaker's dream. Normally run as a lead in to the Kali Gandaki and often combined with a trek to Annapurna Sanctuary.

Probably the best kayaking river of its kind in Nepal and highly recommended by all who have done it.

The River

The Modi Khola was aptly described in one guide book as 'A mountain torrent spawned by the glaciers of Annapurna'. This is the river that flows from the Annapurna Sanctuary and drains the snows of that stupendous amphitheatre of Himalayan giants. The river is only some 40 kms long, but its flow comes from the snow melt of seven peaks over 7000 metres and of course the 8091 metres of Annapurna One. Our impression is that the volume will fluctuate more than most rivers because of this high and localised drainage area. Get a warm sunny day and the volume could double by the afternoon. The few tributary streams add little to its flow.

Rafting

This river is too small and technical for most rafts.

Kayaking

This is a small volume, fun river and everyone we know who has kayaked it has raved about it afterwards!
'The best river we did.'
'The most continuous river any of us have ever paddled.'
'Great class 4 eddy hopping.'
'I've never smoked so much in my life.'

The river is small, with technical paddling, lots of medium size boulders and house rocks. Very continuous and few big drops – only a few (if any) portages – quite unusual for this gradient. Experts will revel in eddy hopping and scouting most of the river from the boat 'It was all just runnable by eddy scouting – but every corner I came to, I thought: there's a class 5 around here – but there never was.....just wonderful!'. This is creek boating, but with a backdrop of the highest mountains in the world.

Ideal time to kayak this river is probably November. We paddled it over Christmas – still very runnable and great fun, but rather low, and cold! Because the river is tight and technical, it normally does take some time to run it, and it is one to savour and linger over: typical paddling time for the river is a day to Birethanti and a day from here.

At high water flows the river becomes a 'fearsome Bobsleigh run' and Gerry Moffat warns, 'Don't even think about doing it, if you're not sure'. Gerry and Guy Robbins did a run down it in early October and likened it, in high flow, to 'a mini North Fork' (North Fork of the Payette); they ran the whole 25 kms in 6 hours. Another group had 9 swims and an epic rescue.....!

If you have the time, trekking up to Annapurna Base Camp and then following the river from its source – first on foot and then by kayak – and onwards down the mighty Kali Gandaki to the jungle lowlands must be one of the journeys of a lifetime.

When we ran the river, we were very pressed for time, so we started at Birethanti. But we have very reliable reports from Bob McDougall, Sarah and Mike Brewer, and many others that the river from Landruk (the old bridge) is the same class as the river below Birethanti. Bob McDougall put in another 3 kms upstream at the New Bridge and reports that the river downstream from here is class 5, 'gorgey', a lot of scouting, several portages, and it took them half a day down to the to old bridge. All parties agree that further upstream, at Chhomrong, the river is, by most people's definition, unrunnable.

Modi Khola (Foxy)

Access and logistics

A new road is under construction from Pokhara to Baglung and goes down the valley of the Modi Khola. This should make the logistics of getting to the river a lot easier. When we went in, the road was supposedly only open to construction traffic; so it took us 2 taxis, 3 sets of porters, one dump truck, one jeep, a bit of carrying ourselves, a total of $60 and a lot of hassle to get the four of us plus kayaks from **Pokhara** to **Birethanti** in a day and a half.

If the new road is open, then you should be able to get to the river easily in a few hours' drive. A taxi is likely to cost about $20. The new road descends to the river about 2 kms below Birethanti and you could start here if your time was very limited – but you would be missing the best half of the river! If your time is too limited to start at Landruk, then do consider putting on at Birethanti – this is a really nice village with good lodges to stay in and is only an hour's walk from the new road.

Those who have done it agree that the old bridge at **Landruk** is the ideal place to start kayaking from. This is probably best reached by taking a taxi to Lumle, and hiring porters here to carry the boats to Landruk – a day's walk.

If you want to trek up to the Annapurna Sanctuary you could leave your kayaks and paddling gear with a lodge keeper in Landruk – you should allow about 6 days for the return trek from here.

Most kayakers will probably want to paddle this river with light boats and it should be possible to arrange for a porter to accompany you down the river. From below Bhirethanti, the road follows the river fairly closely for most of the way, so walking is easy.

There is a beautiful full colour detailed topographical map of the Annapurna National Park at a scale of 1:125,000 titled 'Annapurna Conservation Area' that costs about $5. This is a lovely map to own and study but unfortunately only covers the top portion of the river above Gijan. There are some useful trekking maps for the Annapurna Sanctuary and if you intend to continue on down the Kali Gandaki then you might like to consider the 1:125,000 H.M.G. Central Service Map for the Parbat District that covers both rivers.

Description

Landruk to Birethanti 8 kms, Rati Khola 12, Kali Gandaki 6.

Landruk (also called Landrung) is a large pleasant village with good views and several lodges in which to stay as it is on one of the main trekking trails to the Annapurna Sanctuary. The village is some 300 metres above the river and the 'Old Bridge' on the trail to Ghandruk (Ghandrung).

The 'Old Bridge' is the recommended starting point, and from here it is straight into continuous class 4. The first two kilometres of paddling sets the tone of the rest of the river. Unfortunately there is almost no time to warm up, but you do have the consoling thought that if you survive and enjoy this, then you will relish the rest of the river. This is tight, technical boating. Some scouting from the bank will be required, but it is mainly possible to scout the drops by eddy hopping. Depending on the water flow, a couple of portages may be required, but potential portages are all straight forward.

From the old bridge at Landruk to the next bridge below Kimche is about 4 kms, but this will probably take 2 – 3 hours to paddle because of the technical nature of the river. There are a few houses on the right bank – a settlement called Ghandruk Besi. A trail from here follows the right bank down to Birethanti – aprox. 4 kms. The river continues as class 4, 'with some excellent drops', but is described as easing off a little as it approaches Birethanti.

Birethanti is a pleasant village on one of the old main trails up to Tatopani and Tibet. It is on the main Annapurna Circuit trekking route so there is a good selection of comfortable lodges. Loxmi Lodge is a five star establishment with hot showers, soft beds, clean sheets and relaxing armchairs in a beautiful garden with a fine mountain view. Purists will say that this is no way to start a kayak trip! This can be highly recommended but does cost $7 a night: over the street is the Riverside Lodge where we paid 30 cents a night for a room – very clean despite the chickens that kept popping out of the roof! There is a good German bakery here and it is also possible to buy other basic trekking supplies like muesli, milk, chocolate, etc.

This is a mellow village to spend time in, to sit and watch the passing travellers on the stone flagged trail: colourful pony trains going up to Tibet, herds of sheep coming down from the hills, trekkers, traders, porters and officials of every kind of tribe and nation – all queueing to cross the chain suspension bridge over the river. However, the river beckons and you can be assured of some good spectator support as you set off again.

The river continues with more technical eddy hopping, fairly continuous class 4. About a kilometre down from Birethanti is a good spot for photographs with a view looking up the river at Machhapuchhre (Fish Tail) peak and a further km brings you to a footbridge, tea house and the new road.

A gorge starts about 1 km below the footbridge and a 2 metre drop here is quite photogenic and will probably need scouting. The gorge continues for about 3 kms with lots of little drops – great fun! The valley opens out a bit and the river eases for a kilometre or two where the Pani Khola (Pati on some maps) comes in from the right. The village of Tilahar is 300 metres up on top of the ridge on the left.

After the footbridge leading to Gijan (again on top of the ridge) the river gets a little harder again, climaxing with what might be a class 5 rapid close to the road (It's got to be 5, because we carried it!). There is a welcoming tea house at the suspension bridge just before the **Rati Khola**. After here, the road climbs up the hillside and is lost to sight from the river. There is a class 4+ rapid about a km below the bridge. There is now a marked change in the valley with very few houses, grassy banks and what look like sandstone or limestone cliffs. This is a beautiful stretch of open gorge with more wildlife than people – eagles following kayakers down the river. It looked a great place to camp – and if you are happy with the river, perhaps the place to pay off any porters?

A few kms bring you to a picturesque old chain suspension bridge. This appears to be now little used, having been replaced by a new one a little way downstream. Time for a rest and chat with other travellers at the Tea House at the end of the new bridge? **Kusma** is about 45 minutes walk from here, some 350 metres up on a high river terrace above the Kali Gandaki. The town is the administrative centre for the Parbat District and has some caves to explore.

A water-measuring station is below the bridge. The pleasant gorge continues with good camping possibilities and grade 3+ water to the **Kali Gandaki**. Another main trail crosses the river about a kilometre up from the confluence. Just below the bridge is a rapid, and then there is a temple and small beach on the right where the two rivers meet. This beach is not a pleasant spot – see the guide to the Kali Gandaki – and we suggest that you stop at the bridge, or above the rapid, rather than at the confluence itself.

Modi Khola and Machhapuchhre peak

Vultures . . . *by Foxy*

Drifting along, there was rarely a time when we were totally alone, for there was always some form of wildlife to keep us company. A remarkable variety of birdlife inhabited the river environment. Perhaps the most amazing of these was the vulture, a surprisingly huge, hunched-up, bundle of flesh and feathers. They perched on branches so thin, that it was hard to believe they wouldn't break under the weight. A thin bald neck and a long sharp beak protrude menacingly from the top of the body as it sits watching and waiting to see what the river will provide.

We drifted silently right through one squadron perched on riverside rocks and ran a gauntlet of hungry eyes and long necks. How many paddlers had lost their heads to a passing vulture? I tried not to think about it for there was always a first time. I started paddling swiftly through the colony. All their heads turned in unison as their eyes followed me, but their wings remained motionless and their claws stayed firmly clasped upon the rocks as I diminished into the distance – perhaps they didn't like the wrapping of plastic and neoprene?

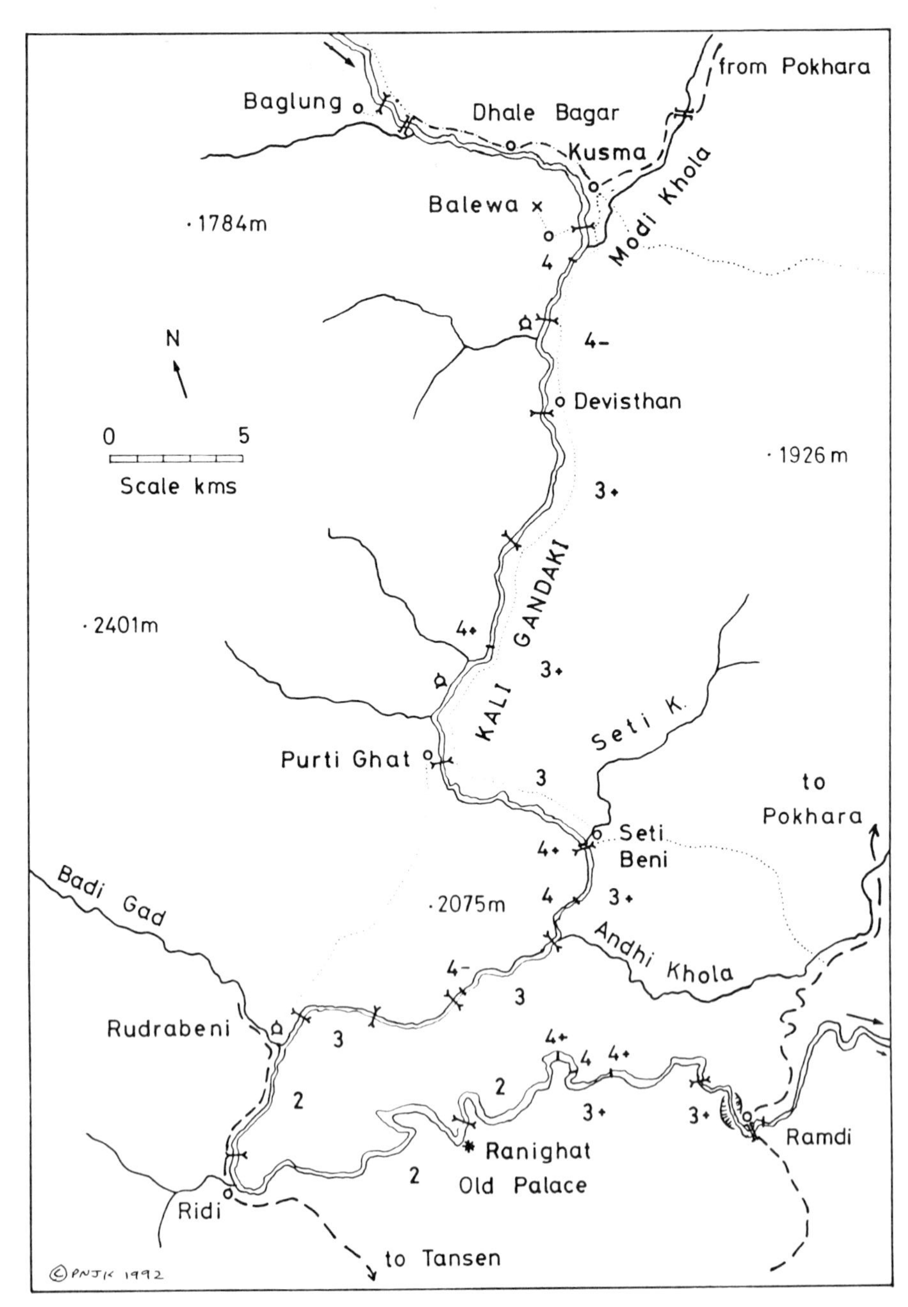

WARNING: Laser-phobic ink – do not photocopy.

Kali Gandaki (Upper)

[The Kali Gandaki (lower) from Ramdi is described separately]

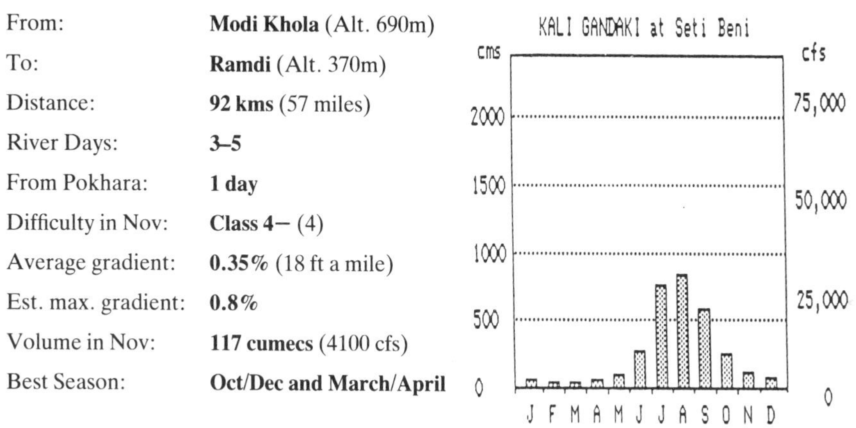

From:	**Modi Khola** (Alt. 690m)
To:	**Ramdi** (Alt. 370m)
Distance:	**92 kms** (57 miles)
River Days:	**3–5**
From Pokhara:	**1 day**
Difficulty in Nov:	**Class 4–** (4)
Average gradient:	**0.35%** (18 ft a mile)
Est. max. gradient:	**0.8%**
Volume in Nov:	**117 cumecs** (4100 cfs)
Best Season:	**Oct/Dec and March/April**

Summary

A beautiful unspoilt river with good white water, gorges, wildlife and a feeling of remoteness. Recommended for people wanting an exciting medium-length raft trip and as a self-sufficient kayak trip for intermediate and expert kayakers.

We recommend combining this river with a trek beforehand up into the mountains. Also consider continuing down the lower Kali Gandaki to Chitwan National Park.

The River

One of the famous names of Himalayan rivers, the Kali Gandaki rises in Mustang, an enclave of Nepal poking into Tibet on the other side of the Himalaya. Here, it is a flat and braided river, flowing in an arid open valley: the explorer Michael Peissel ran this stretch of the river in a small hovercraft in 1973.

At Kalopani the river drops off the roof of the World and cuts one of the deepest gorges in the world between Dhaulagiri, height 8167m to the west and Annapurna 8091m to the East. This gorge is one of the ancient trading routes through to Tibet and is now a favourite route for trekkers. Below Tatopani, the gradient eases and the river is probably runnable from upstream of Baglung.

After the confluence with the Modi Khola, the river swings south through an area where tourists are almost unknown. The only road access in the 214 kms of river is at two places, Ridi and Ramdi, and the river feels remote and wild. The few people you will see enthusiastically beckon you over so that they can meet you. There are few villages actually on the river – most are located on the river terraces some hundreds of metres above, where it is cooler and where there would be fewer mosquitoes in the monsoon.

The Kali Gandaki is named after the goddess Kali and is considered a particularly holy river; an auspicious place to be cremated. It is also a gold bearing river – we met several small groups who were sluicing and panning the gravels of the river bed for miniscule amounts of the metal.

There is abundant wildlife on the river: we saw small animals, quite close on the bank and unafraid, that were strange to all of us: enquiries back in Kathmandu make us think these were either civets or red pandas. We also saw signs of leopard and otters and this is a good river for the bird watcher.

Rafting

Not many groups have rafted the Kali Gandaki. This is probably because in the past it was a 2-3 day trek to get to the put-in. All who have rafted it speak highly of it, and would probably agree with our assessment that the new road to the put-in could make this the second most popular rafting trip in Nepal.

If we compare the Kali Gandaki with other popular rafting trips it could best be said to be something like a shorter Sun Kosi trip – perhaps slightly easier white water, fine scenery, wildlife and an unspoilt valley. It makes a pleasant alternative to a Trisuli trip.

The new road that is being built from Pokhara up to Baglung has dramatically improved access to this river. The put-in and take-out are roughly half a day from Pokhara, so a raft trip could leave Monday morning and be back Friday night. If you have more time, we recommend a trek beforehand, perhaps following the river down from Jomsom – a great combination of one of the world's best treks and one of Nepal's best rivers.

True connoisseurs of river exploration will want to extend the rafting trip and continue on below Ramdi down the lower part of the Kali Ganadki, into the Narayani and down to Chitwan National Park (because this lower section is easier and different in character, we have described it separately).

Confluence of Kali Gandaki and Modi Khola

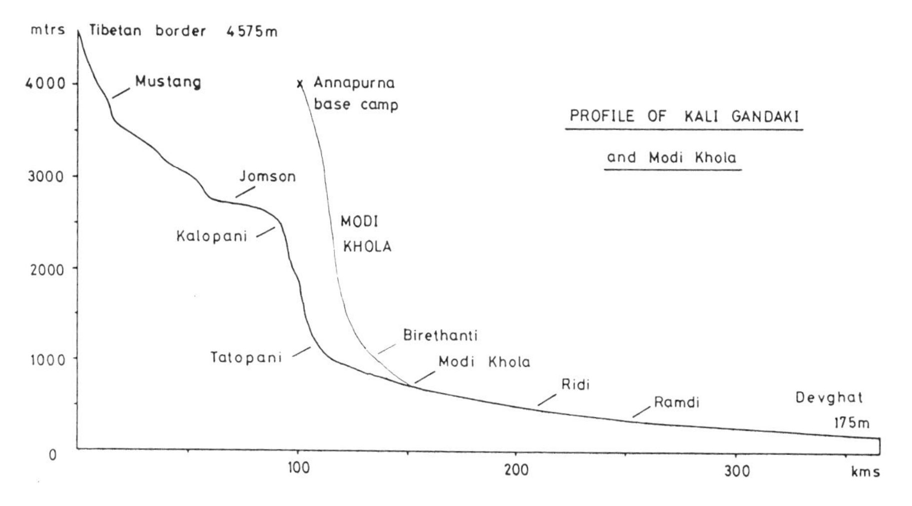

Kayaking

This is a beautiful river where you feel that you are really on an expedition and it is ideal length for a self sufficient trip. There are some holes on the river that you wouldn't want to play in, but by and large, the difficulties are obvious and the river is friendly. Also a lot of fun – there are play-waves to surf almost all the way down the river. Our impression was that there is as much white water and fun for the kayaker on this river as, say, the Trisuli.

Expert kayakers will be at home on this river and enjoy themselves; aspiring and confident intermediates would find this an enjoyable and fulfilling expedition, but we would recommend the support of more expert kayakers in the group. Many expert kayakers will probably choose to start on the Modi Khola and paddle down into the Kali Gandaki.

We ourselves have not paddled the Kali Gandaki above the confluence with the Modi Khola. However, this has been paddled by other people and we have walked and scouted this section. It is said that a group of German kayakers have put in below Tatopani and from what we could see from the trail, that closely follows the river, this looked mainly class 5, hard but not impossible. From Ghoreshar the river appears to be mainly class 4 and 4+.

Access and logistics

If the new road from Pokhara is open, then it should take 4-6 hours to drive to **Kusma** and there will be the usual Bus and Taxi service. It may take longer than expected to complete the road so do enquire when making your plans. If the road is open for only part of the way – then porters can be hired from the road head. If there are problems with the road, it may be worth flying into the STOL airstrip at Balewa, just on the other side of the river from Kusma.

An attractive option for a rafting group is to have the rafts and equipment sent separately with a Sirdar and for the rafting guests to fly to Jomson and trek down the famous gorge of the Kali Gandaki – a popular and comfortable trek taking about 4 days. Another trek/river combination is the Annapurna Sanctuary – this will particularly appeal to expert kayakers who can paddle down the Modi Khola.

In the past, the usual put-in has been either on the Modi Khola or at the confluence of this river with the Kali Gandaki. We cannot recommend the confluence because this only has a small beach which is slick with the human grease from cremations. Human bones crunch underfoot and ghouls in your party will love this spot!

The obvious start point in the future is where the new road bridge crosses just downstream from Baglung, or alternatively where the new road first comes close to the river, just beyond Armadi at a village called Dhale Bagar. However, whilst we have scouted this section of river from the trail, we haven't actually run it, so we suggest that you enquire of rafting or trekking companies in Pokhara for up-to-date information on the road and for the best put-in.

Recommended take-out is at Ramdi, where the main road from Pokhara to the Terai crosses the river. Local buses cost about $1 per person for the scenic 6 hour trip back to Pokhara. These leave around 8 or 9 a.m. and, be warned, there are often no afternoon or evening buses. A taxi might be worthwhile if your time is limited (3 hours back to Pokhara?), but this needs to be arranged in advance in Pokhara as there is no transport available for hire at Ramdi. It is possible to cut short this river trip by one day, by taking out at Ridi; however, we do not recommend this as you will be missing the best rapids on the river and the spooky memorable old palace at Rani Ghat.

If you have the time, then we suggest that you consider continuing on down the river, a pleasant, relaxed float trip, to Narayanghat, and perhaps Chitwan?

We recommend this river as a self-sufficient trip because of the unspoilt nature of the valley and the fine beaches for camping. Local people are very friendly but most of the villages are high above and some distance from the river. We found reasonable but limited, supplies of driftwood for fires. Most detailed map for the river is the 1:125,000 H.M.G. Central Service Map for Parbat District.

'Some holes you might not want to play in' (Jock Montgomery)

Description

Modi Khola to Purti Ghat 24 kms, Ridi 33, Ramdi 35.

The upper Kali Gandaki has carved a series of four river terraces and most of the villages are located on these some distance above the river. For most of its way the river is incised some 300 metres into these terraces as a narrow V-shaped valley, at times narrowing into a gorge.

From **Baglung**, the river appears to be class 4: we have scouted this section, but not run it. We started at confluence with the **Modi Khola**, and from here the river is a fairly continuous class 3+, perhaps 4−. The second big rapid is just 5 minutes down the river with a double drop, wave trains and holes quite big enough to flip a raft! – a class 4. The river keeps moving with plenty of white water interest.

After the first bridge, the valley becomes more of a gorge with green grass and mossy sides, few houses, and beautiful camping spots. Waterfalls come tumbling down from above – at one point straight into the river as a shower bath for passing rafters.

A large landslide on the right bank is just before a small village and the bridge to **Devisthan** (up on the river terrace). The left bank trail is close to the river for a while and then climbs diagonally up the hillside. Keep an eye out for the next bridge because about 1 km below here are some hotsprings on the left. 1 km downstream is a pretty waterfall on the right and a further km brings you to a rapid flowing hard left onto some sharp rocks – probably worth scouting.

The valley opens out after the bridge at **Purti Ghat** (Rani Pani on the left bank) and the river eases off a bit as far as the confluence with the Seti Khola which comes in from the left. There is a big rapid is just after the confluence and before the bridge. The cliffs close in and the river enters a dark sombre canyon with black rocks glistening evilly in the shadows. This sets you in nice mood for 'Gloria', the next rapid. The **Andi Khola** comes in left and after a few kms the valley opens out again and there is another rapid. There are bridges every few kms but few people or houses.

The Hindu temple at **Rudra Beni** is worth a visit, at the confluence of the Badi Gad right (a river waiting for someone to explore it). The road on the right bank is a rude warning that the town of **Ridi** is close and this soon appears. It looks a very picturesque town from the river with colourful houses climbing the two hillsides from a broad beach. For reasons that are hard to pin down, it looks a very Indian town, and you realise that we are now close to the Terai and out of the mountains. All basic supplies are available here – beer, rum, vegetables, etc.

The valley changes shape below Ridi, with low shingle banks and the river meandering on a wide valley floor between steep arid hillsides. The current drops, rapids are mere riffles, and you are perhaps wondering if you should have got out at Ridi. But, this is only a pause, a pleasant time in which to drift along and spend some time with the ferry men who use dug out canoes to cross the river.

Ranighat is about 13 kms below Ridi and marked by a bridge that was just being rebuilt when we were there in 1990. But much more noteworthy is the splendid derelict Palace that is built on a bluff overlooking the river. This has stone terraces and a flight of stairs descending to the river to welcome passing river runners. This is like something out of 'Indiana Jones'! It was built in the 19th century by a former government minister who was exiled to this distant spot for plotting a coup. Now it is a sad, empty and eerie shell, seemingly avoided by the locals – its only inhabitants spiders, mice, bats and snakes.

In the middle of this derelict palace is a small barred temple, and through the cracks you can glimpse a well-kept altar, votive offerings and a terrifying image of Bhairab the god of destruction. A true test of nerve would be to camp here and explore by candlelight on a moonless night.

A few kms below the old palace the river speeds up again. A class 3 rapid is warning that 5 minutes below is the biggest rapid on the river 'Shake, rattle and roll'. This is on a sharp right-hand bend and is marked by a landslide into the river on the left. Land on the right, well above, to scout. Five minutes below, again on a right-hand bend is a another big rapid, but slightly easier. A km of class 3+ brings you to the last of the big rapids: 'Jonah' looks innocent – a straight-forward shoot with a big wave train visible down the bottom. Hidden in the middle of the waves is a monster hole that will gobble the unwary.

Class 3+ water continues to a suspension bridge, and a km below, the river enters a narrow gorge, with sheer rock walls dropping straight into the water. The water is swirly and off-putting, but relax, there are no rapids in this short gorge. The road bridge at the end of the gorge is **Ramdi**. Best take-out is on the left, either above or below a class 4– rapid. A winding path brings you up to tea houses and the bus stop in this friendly village.

Old palace at Ranighat (Foxy)

Kali Gandaki (Lower)

From information supplied by Mike MacDonald, Mike Wood, Nick Williams and others.

From:	**Ramdi** (Alt. 370m)
To:	**Narayanghat** (Alt. 170m)
Distance:	**128 kms** (80 miles)
River Days:	**3–4**
From Pokhara:	**4 hours**
Difficulty in Nov:	**Class 2** (3)
Average gradient:	**0.15%** (7 ft a mile)
Est. max. gradient:	**0.25%**
Volume in Nov:	**250 cumecs** (8800 cfs)
Best Season:	**Oct/Dec and Feb/April**

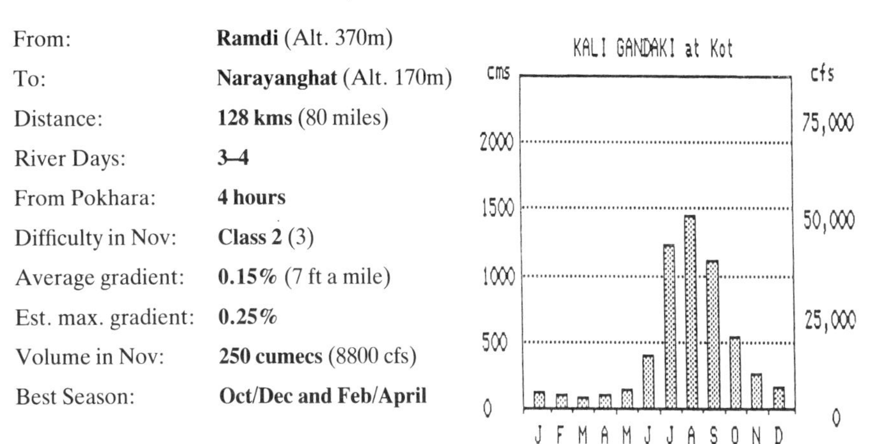

Summary

A big but relatively easy river, with beautiful, unspoilt scenery, small gorges, jungle and an abundance of wildlife.

Recommended as an easily accesible and relaxing river trip. A good river for small inflatable boats ('Duckies') or for kayakers with limited experience. A classic, best-of-its-kind, trip that deserves to be more popular.

The River

The upper part of the river above Ramdi, is described in the preceding section.

Below Ramdi, the river flows east in an open valley for approximately 100 kms between lines of hills before joining with the Trisuli river at Devghat to become the Narayani and to flow onwards to the Ganges and the Indian Ocean. There are no roads near the river, no tourists, and few other river runners: local people are natural, unspoilt and of course friendly.

The lower half of the river is relatively sparsely populated, with a jungle corridor and pristine white beaches. There is abundant wildlife along the river – including more than 250 species of bird. There are reports of people seeing the rare fresh water dolphin. Also rare, but occasionally seen, are crocodiles – the Gharial ones, mainly fish eaters, and the Muggers who will eat anything ....

This section of river has seen all kinds of craft on it from hovercraft to jet barges; happily the only craft that you are likely to see are the dug out canoes that are used by the local ferry men.

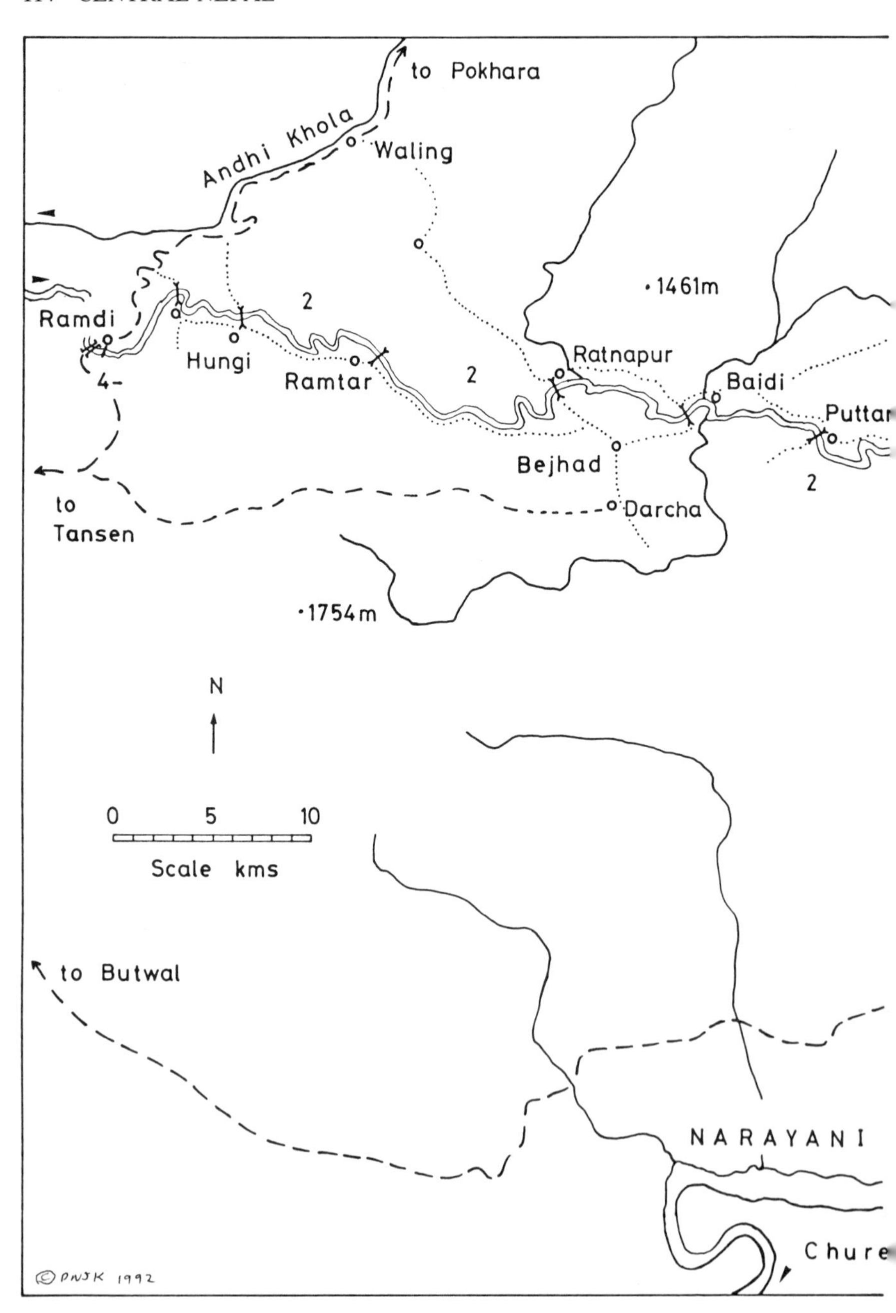

WARNING: Laser-phobic ink – do not photocopy.

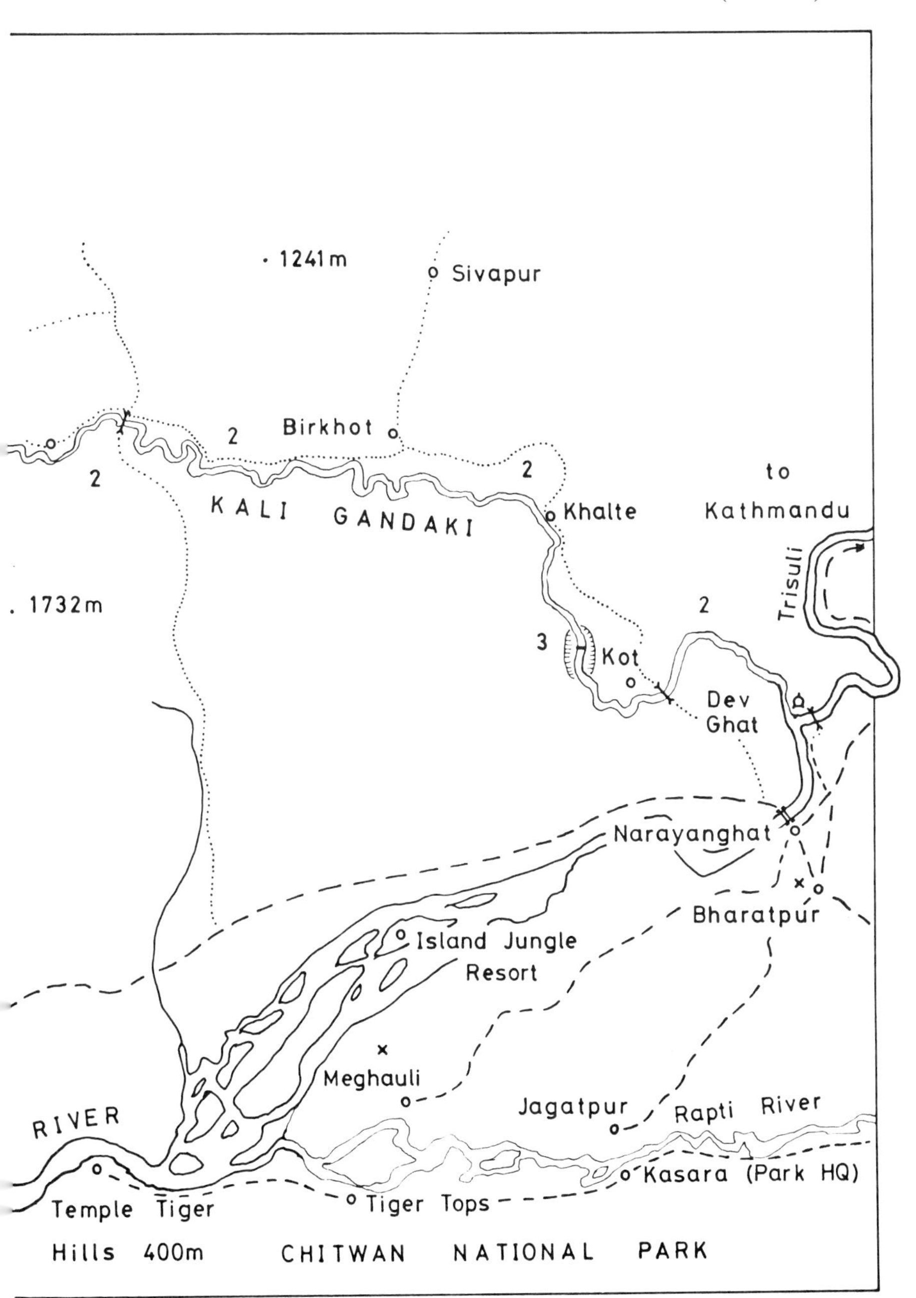

· 1241m
Sivapur
Birkhot
2
2
2
KALI GANDAKI
Khalte
to
Kathmandu
. 1732m
Trisuli
2
3
Kot
Dev
Ghat
Narayanghat
Bharatpur
Island Jungle
Resort
Meghauli
Jagatpur
Rapti River
RIVER
Kasara (Park HQ)
Temple Tiger
Tiger Tops
Hills 400m
CHITWAN NATIONAL PARK

Rafting

This is pleasant and relaxing 3-4 day float trip with a gentle but sufficient current. There are plenty of easy (class 2) rapids to add interest – but these are very safe. There is one class 3 rapid about half way down the river that can easily be portaged. If you're nervous about white water and don't want to get wet, but still want an interesting and pleasant river trip, then this is probably the one for you.

We think that this would be a good river for small inflatable canoes – 'duckies'. Also, perhaps a good choice for a family raft trip where some members want to try their hand at kayaking on easy water. Note that in high water, at the beginning and end of the monsoon, like most rivers, this then becomes much harder and could be dangerous to the inexperienced.

Many groups do this lower Kali Gandaki as part of a longer combined trip from the high Himalaya to the Plains. This is an immensely satisfying experience that we especially recommend – please see the previous section.

This river trip is offered by many rafting companies, but most do not actively promote it and you are unlikely to see any other rafts. We quite honestly think that, if you don't want big hairy rapids, this is a much nicer raft trip than the over-popular Trisuli (We're almost afraid to recommend it in case it does get spoilt!).

Kayaking

Kayakers normally do this trip for three reasons:

- as part of a longer trip down the upper river.
- to 'get get away from it all'
- as a first trip for a beginner.

Although it can be paddled in 2 days, most people would probably want to spend more time relaxing on the beaches in the jungle corridor. One rafter friend of ours did this trip with his girlfriend and it took the best part of a week ....

This is an excellent trip as a first river experience for beginners: rapids are easy, with obvious lines that introduce the idea of 'reading the water'. This is a friendly river and a great confidence booster for the more nervous.

This lower section of the Kali Gandaki compares to the lower section of the Seti Khola which runs parallel to it some 30 kms or so to the north (we have left it off the map to avoid confusing detail). Both are good rivers for the beginner/intermediate -the main difference is that the Seti is shorter, smaller and more accessible.

Access and logistics

It is only a few hours from Pokhara to the recommended put-in at **Ramdi**, or a day's journey from Kathmandu. Bus fare from Kathmandu would be about $3 or a private minibus would cost about $150. Some of the buses to Nepalgang or other towns in the far west go via this road so you can avoid a change in Pokhara if you are coming direct from Kathmandu.

There are few villages actually on the riverside: that, and the beautiful beaches for camping, make this an ideal river for a self- sufficient trip. There are limited supplies of driftwood for fires but these become more plentiful further down the river.

Normal take-out is **Narayanghat** – please see section on the Trisuli.

This is a 'get away from it all' river with few bridges, trails or villages so perhaps a detailed map is not going to be of much interest: however, if required, it is covered on the Syangja and Tanahun sheets of the H.M.G. Central Services Maps at a scale of 1:125,000.

Description

Ramdi to Baidi 43 kms, Khalte 57, Kot 11, Devghat 11, Narayanghat 6.

Best put-in is at **Ramdi** on the left bank below the bridge and below the big rapid. Ramdi is a pleasant and friendly village with the last cold cokes. For the first few kms the road is visible climbing up the hillside on the left hand side – your last sight and sound of motor engines for the next few days.

For the next twenty kms, the river flows in a wide open valley with quite a lot of villages on the terraced hillsides. Fairly frequent small rapids maintain interest, but all are easy and have obvious lines. There are lots of cairns on some beaches, marking where bodies have been buried awaiting the monsoon floods to carry them away down the holy river.

The bridge at **Baidi** marks a change in the valley: after this there are few villages and the valley sides close in and are covered in lush green vegetation. Mike MacDonald reported seeing four different types of monkey on this section, and more bird life than on any other river.

One of the few villages is **Khalte**, on the left bank and about 6 kms below here starts a rock gorge. The rock walls rise dramatically straight out of the water, a bit like the gorge above Ramdi. In normal water conditions, this gorge should pose no problems – there is a class 2 rapid at the start and a class 3 rapid in the middle of the gorge which can be portaged easily. Mike Wood reported though, that in high water when the Monsoon had started, this gorge was swirly class 4− water and the rapid in the middle was class 4+.

Somewhere below the gorge Mike had an encounter with a crocodile. 'Michelle suddenly turned around and yelled back 'crocodile' – there wasn't really much I could do except finish the rapid, close my eyes and paddle like hell!' (We should reassure you – we haven't heard of any rafter or kayaker being attacked by one in Nepal).

The spectacular and beautiful 'jungle corridor' continues down to the confluence with the Trisuli at **Devghat**. Please see the guide for the Trisuli for the description of the river, now called the **Narayani**, down to **Narayanghat**.

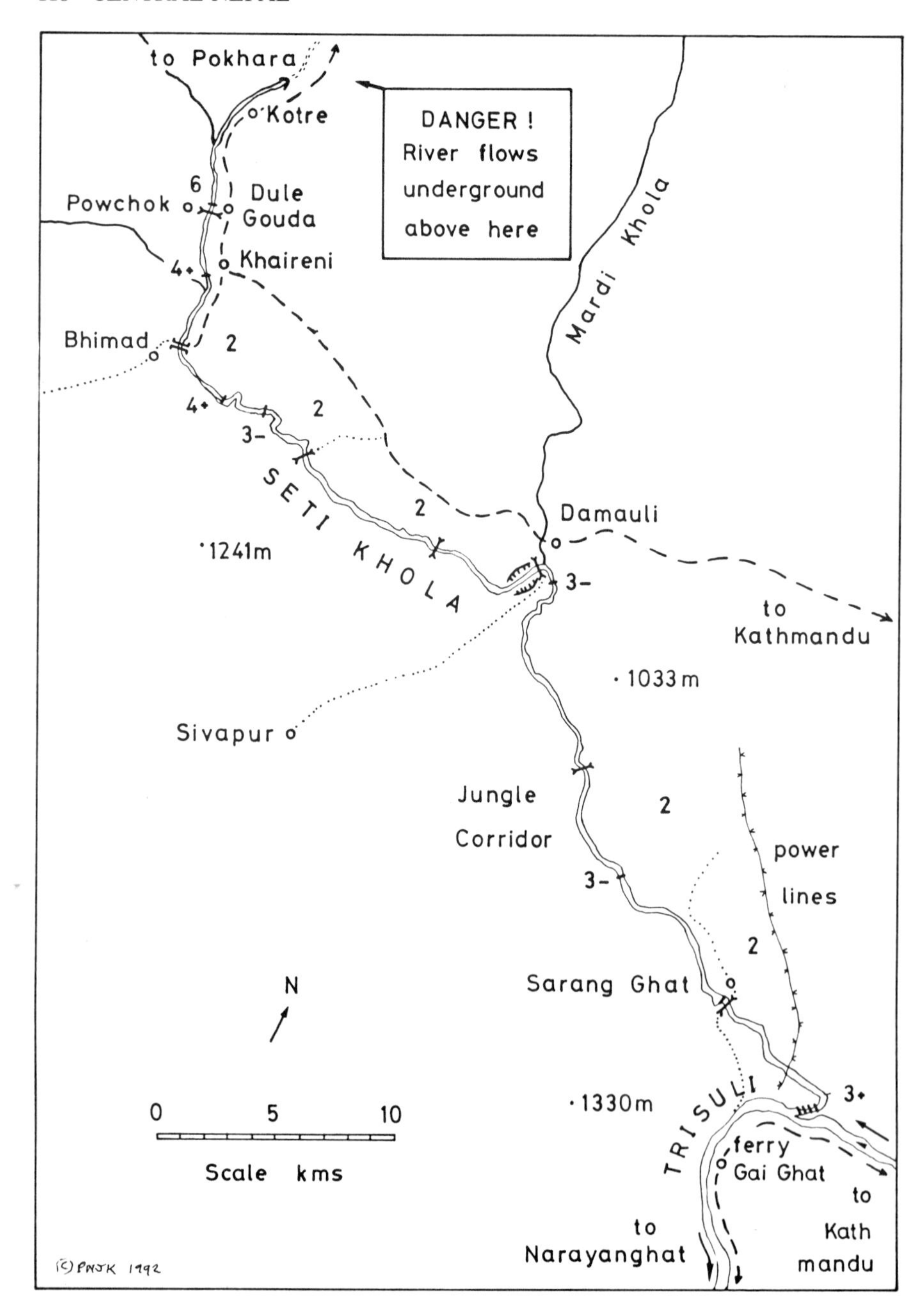

WARNING: Laser-phobic ink – do not photocopy.

Seti

From:	**Dule Gouda** (Alt. 480m)
To:	**Trisuli River** (Alt. 190m)
Distance:	**62 kms** (39 miles)
River Days:	**2–3**
From Pokhara:	**1 hour**
Difficulty in Nov:	**Class 3** (4+)
Average gradient:	**0.5%** (25ft a mile)
Est. max. gradient:	**0.8%**
Volume in Nov:	**40 cumecs** (1400 cfs)
Best Season:	**Oct–April.**

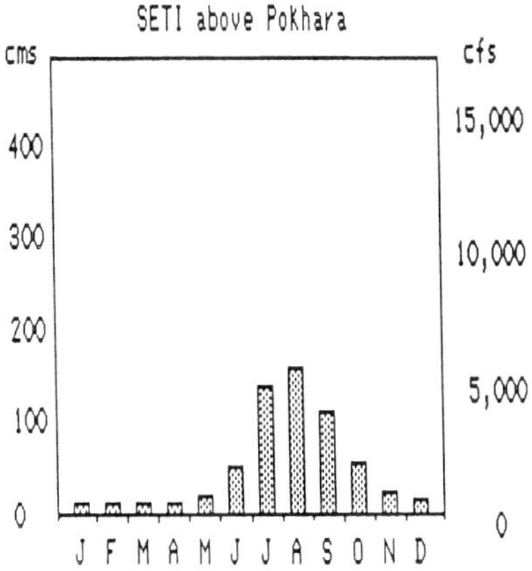

Summary

A unique river passing through two beautiful and contrasting scenic areas. Relatively small volume, blue and warm, we recommend this as a 'warm-up' river for intermediate kayakers. If started at Damauli, it makes an easy raft or kayak trip.

The River

The Seti Khola rises on the South East slopes of Machapuchare and then flows south, as a fairly typical Nepalese mountain river, It is dammed for Hydro Electric power just above Pokhara and then shortly afterwards it disappears into a deep and very narrow chasm to reappear again in a wide valley a few kilometres below Pokhara – be warned though, the river disappears underground yet again, about 16 kms below Pokhara – so be careful where you get in!

From the recommended put-in at Dule Gouda it flows through a spectacular, almost eerie, broad river plain, at times meandering in braided channels, at other times incising the plain, leaving 100 metre high river cliffs. The rock here is reminiscent of builders conglomerate – pebbles and small boulders embedded in a coarse sand matrix, but more resistant to erosion than it appears at first glance. The Annapurna massif forms a spectacular backdrop – the well-known Australian paddler, Mike Wood wrote, 'The mist cleared and we were greeted with the best views I have seen on any river'.

After Khaireni, the Seti enters a typical Nepali valley, initially passing through some small, narrow gorges. It then winds a lot between interlocking spurs of the high, green hills, before entering a straighter 'jungle corridor', with only a sparse local population. This corridor continues all the way to the Trisuli, interrupted only by a short, narrow section which precedes the wide Mardi Khola confluence at Dhaumali.

Features to note on the river include quite a range of birds, from many vultures on the upper section to Kingfishers on the lower section. The jungle corridor has a lot of hanging, green vegetation on all sides and has several narrow valleys which could be explored on foot.

There are many well made dug out canoes (dungas) – used mainly for ferrying people across the river. An alternative form of river crossing is fords – The Seti has a low enough volume of water to allow this; these fords are usually across shingle banks, with a route marked by cairns or sticks. They present a somewhat unique navigation hazard!

Other hazards to look out for are fish traps and weirs – It was on this river that we saw a 2 metre long catfish that had been caught by a local fishermen.

Rafting

From: **Damauli** (Alt. 345m)
To: **Trisuli River** (Alt. 190m)
Distance: **32 kms** (20 miles)
River Days: **1–2**
From Pokhara: **2 hours**
Difficulty in Nov: **Class 2** (3+)
Average gradient: **0.5%** (25ft a mile)
Est. max. gradient: **0.8%**

This is a really pleasant, picturesque one or two day trip – no horrendous big rapids but plenty of friendly small ones. It doesn't need two days, but the 'Jungle Corridor' is so beautiful, with white beaches by a warm blue river, that it makes a great place to laze or camp.

Comment from one woman rafter was : 'this is the place I would like to spend my honeymoon'!

Rafting above Dhaumali is probably not worthwhile in view of the narrow, steep falls and shallow shingle rapids.

Kayaking

The Seti Khola is an excellent warm-up river on which to hone skills and build up confidence. The rclatively small volume and noticeably warm blue water make the river appear more friendly than other Nepalese rivers. This is one of those few rivers which can be recommended to expert and beginner alike and we don't know anyone who has kayaked this river who has not enjoyed it.

The river is mainly class 2, with a little class 3. There are two harder rapids, class 4+, that can be easily portaged or enjoyed by the more expert. The river below Damauli would be good training and confidence boosting as a first river trip for a beginner (obviously not a raw novice).

We have looked at some of the river upstream of Pokhara and it LOOKS as if it is probably kayakable for a few kilometres. The underground sections under Pokhara would make a very unusual Himalayan Kayak expedition......

Access and logistics

We recommend that kayakers put in **below the underground section**, which is about 16 kms below Pokhara near Kotre Bazar, on the main Kathmandu Highway.

Coming from Kathmandu, the road passes through Khaireni, then joins the Seti valley – running along the top of the river cliffs through **Dule Gouda**, for 2 kms, before descending close to the river. Best access is near the 24 km marker on the main highway. Leave the main road by a narrow lane behind a large Pipal tree and follow this down steps to the base of the cliffs to put-in immediately below a serious, probably unrunnable fall. The trail leads on over a footbridge to the Tibetan village of Powchock on the far bank.

Recommended put-in for rafters is at **Damauli**. Coming from Kathmandu drive through the main bazar, and then turn left at the school arch to gain a flight of steps leading to the river.

The Tourist bus from Kathmandu to the put-in costs about $4 per person (kayaks free); a private minibus would cost about $120. take- out is either at Gai Ghat near the confluence with the Trisuli, or further down the Trisuli at Narayanghat.

In our opinion the river is best enjoyed as a self supported trip – there are plenty of beautiful campsites and no shortage of firewood below Khaireni. Having said this, there are several cheap lodges at Damauli if you prefer to travel light.

The most detailed map of the river is the H.M.G. Central Service Map for Tanahun District at a scale of 1:125,000.

Description

Dule Gouda to Bhimad 8 kms, Damauli 22, Trisuli 32.

At **Dule Gouda** a seal launch below the class 6 fall is an exhilarating start, or a more sedate embarkation further downstream is possible. The river runs a meandering, braided course through class 2 rapids and shingle banks, interupted after 5 km by a twisting class 4+ drop, easily portaged if wished (Phil Bibby reports this as unrunnable at low water levels). The river's easy course continues, with a small stream from **Khaireni** joining from the left just before the valley narrows appreciably – last chance for spectacular photos of the Annapurna massif.

Small gorges carry the river under an incomplete road bridge at 2 km below Khaireni. Two kilometres later, the second steep drop is reached, on a left hand bend. This comes in two parts, the first a hard 4+, the second a class 4, round the next corner after 150 metres. This is easily portaged on the right bank.

The gorge nature of the river continues for the next 2 km, becoming increasingly narrow, with two class 3− rapids, before widening out.

Below **Damauli** the river continues as predominantly class 2. There is a short section of easy class 3 below Daumali. Another easy class 3 rapid is about half way to the Trisuli – roughly level with a point where pylon lines are seen on a high ridge on the left. Immediately above the bridge at **Sarang Ghat** is a boulder field leading into a class 3 rapid. The river reaches an exhilarating climax just before the confluence with the Trisuli (the power cables cross the river 2 kms before and provide plenty of warning) – a series of four rapids, class 3 and 3+, with big bouncy waves. These can easily be portaged if wanted. The rapids bring you into the Trisuli and the end of a really fine river trip.

On arriving at the **Trisuli**, continue downstream to take out at the ferry crossing and village of Gai Ghat or continue down to Narayanghat (see section on the Trisuli).

Underground . . . *by Peter Knowles*

This was our first river trip in Nepal and our resident expert in Kathmandu, Mike Wood, had suggested the Seti as the perfect river to start on, but had warned: 'Make sure you put in after the underground bit below Pokhara!'

After some time reconnoitring we found the place where the river emerged from out of a dark cavern into a wide valley. We explored the cave and then confidently set off down the river – a swift conveyor belt flowing over gravel bars, narrow and with few eddies.

The river raced along at a great pace and as there was no real need to paddle, we sat back, enjoyed the scenery and waved at local people. On rounding one corner we saw a cliff face ahead, but drifted on, assuming that the river would bend around it, as rivers usually do. However, as we sped closer we realised to our amazement and horror that the whole river disappeared into a cleft at the base of the cliff – straight as an arrow, with the current increasing and no eddies or pools in which to stop! With heart-beats racing we desperately accelerated and rammed the shingle bank at its lowest point; the boats started to slide back into the water, we dropped our paddles and clawed wildly into the loose gravel. Jock made it out of his boat and grabbed our bow loops. We stood up on the bank panting: silly grins and loud talk didn't disguise our shaking limbs.

Closer examination of the cliff confirmed the nightmare: the current ripped and tore its way into a small cleft with a loud roar and disappeared underground. The river emerged a few hundred metres downstream, but at a lower level. It appeared, that in high water, all the flow wouldn't make it down the sump and the river backed up and formed a lake, whirlpool and waterfall.

Near the river was a small temple to Shiva the goddess of destruction . . .

Seti above Damauli

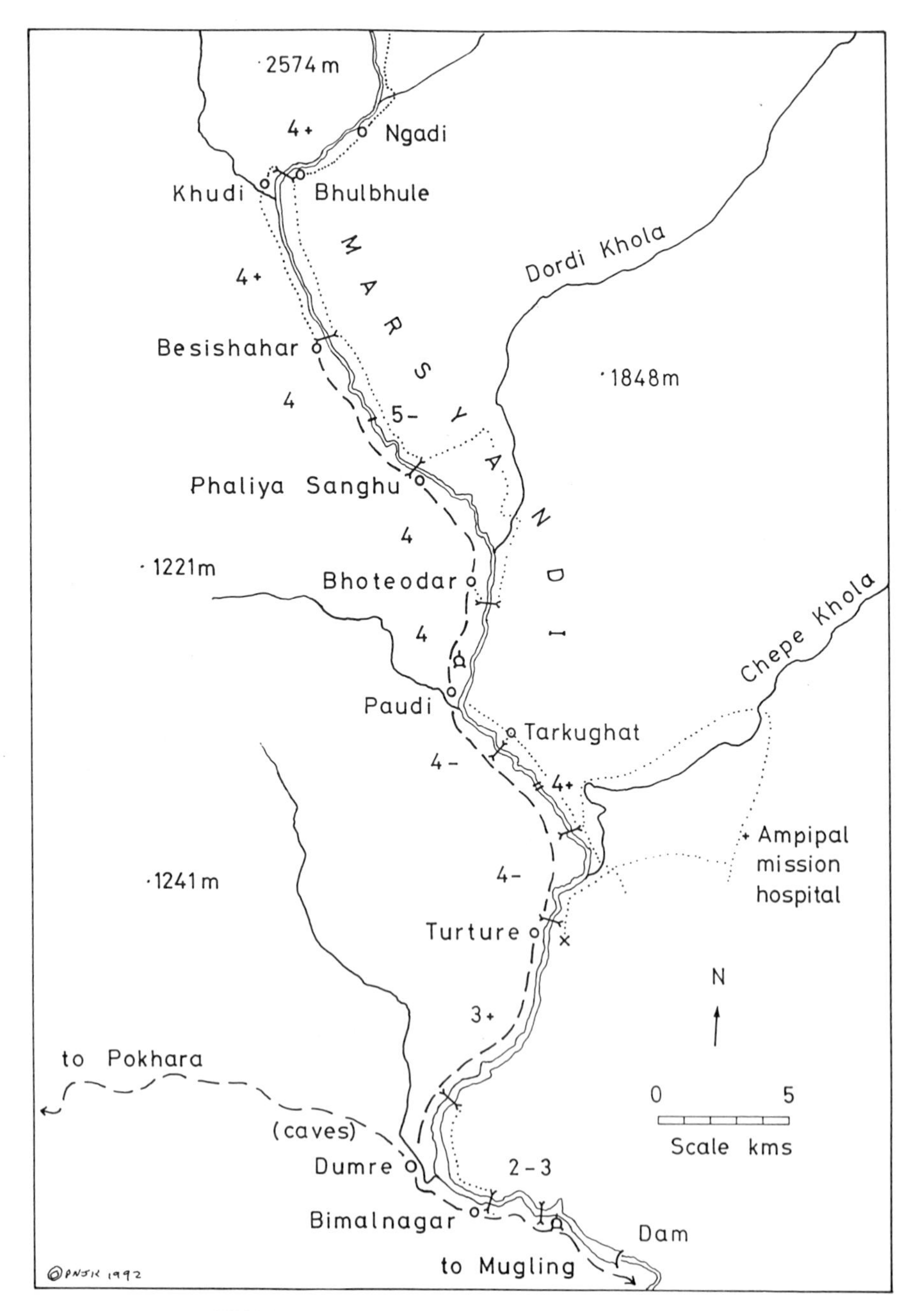

WARNING: Laser-phobic ink – do not photocopy.

Marsyandi

From: **Ngadi** (Alt. 850m)
To: **Bimalnagar** (Alt. 370m)
Distance: **52 Kms** (33 miles)
River Days: **3**
From Kathmandu: **2 days**
Difficulty in Nov: **Class 4+** (5−)
Average gradient: **1.0%** (50ft a mile)
Est. max. gradient: **2.0%**
Volume in Nov: **80 cumecs** (2800 cfs)
Best Season: **Nov/Dec, March/April**

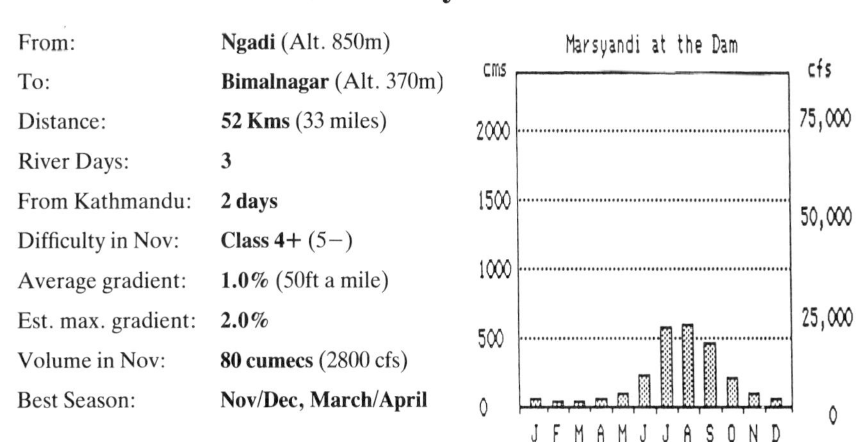

Summary

One of the most outstanding class 4 kayaking rivers in the World. Continuous, exhilarating white water with magnificent mountain backdrops.

Recommended for Expert Kayakers, and **rafters from Bhote Odar**.

The River

The Marsyandi rises on the northern slopes of the Annapurna Himal, flows east through an arid valley around Manang, and then swings south to join the Trisuli river at Mugling. Marsyandi means 'raging river' in local dialect,and this aptly describes it. Some of the river above Ngadi has been kayaked – The 1980 British Expedition started from Tilicho Lake at 4920m – but much of the upper river should probably be considered as unrunnable.

For most of the trip from Ngadi down to Bimalnagar the river is incised as a winding gorge into the valley floor, about 50 metres deep with sloping well-wooded sides. Only a few villages are visible from the river and at times you could almost be on a river in Idaho or British Columbia. As the river turns, fresh views unfold behind of the Manaslu and Annapurna ranges – a magnificent backdrop. There are beautiful campsites.

The lower Marsyandi gorges from Bimalnagar down to Mugling used to be an excellent river trip but a new dam has been built downstream of Bimalnagar to generate electrity for Kathmandu and so there is now almost no water left in this section of the river and it can no longer be recommended. Both the Dam and the power house are vital to the economy of Nepal and are sensitive security areas. Any incident could badly rebound on other river runners and you will appreciate why we ask you to stay away from this lower section of the river.

Rafting

From: **Bhote Odar** (Alt. 550m)
To: **Bimalnagar** (Alt. 370m)
Distance: **28 Kms** (17 miles)
River Days: **2**
From Kathmandu: **1 day**
Difficulty in Nov: **Class 4** (4+)
Average gradient: **0.6%** (30ft a mile)
Est. max. gradient: **1.0%**

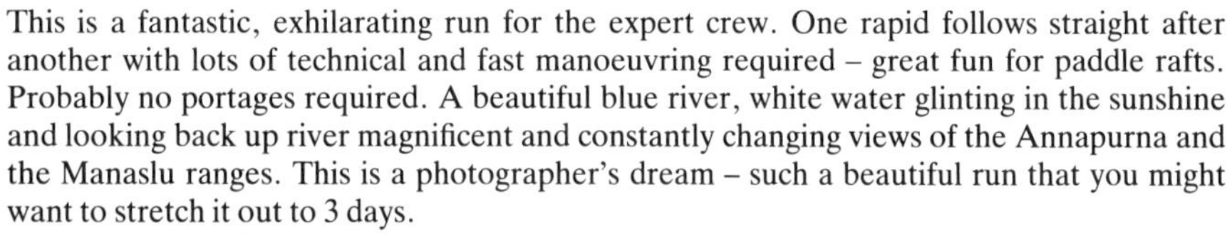

This is a fantastic, exhilarating run for the expert crew. One rapid follows straight after another with lots of technical and fast manoeuvring required – great fun for paddle rafts. Probably no portages required. A beautiful blue river, white water glinting in the sunshine and looking back up river magnificent and constantly changing views of the Annapurna and the Manaslu ranges. This is a photographer's dream – such a beautiful run that you might want to stretch it out to 3 days.

Comments we had on this run were:
'Most beautiful river I've done'
'My favourite river campsite'
'I couldn't believe how continuous it was – finish one rapid and you're looking straight DOWN the next one'

The river has been rafted from Phaliya Sanghu but Bhote Odar is probably the most convenient and usual starting point. In our opinion the river is too technical upstream to be rafted successfully – some really narrow gaps and tight manoeuvres through boulder fields.

In 1990 rafting permits were not available for the Marsyandi so no commercial trips were offered on this river at the time of writing. It seems however, that this restriction was instigated as a safety measure when the dam was being built, so this could well change – please enquire of one of the rafting operators to find out what the current position is.

Kayaking

Those who have done this river rate it as one of the best of its kind anywhere in the World. We couldn't think of another river that is so continuous, and consistently challenging over such a distance. When we did it in late November, we didn't need to portage once, and only had to scout from the bank a few times. But this is not a river to be undertaken lightly and a swim could be long and serious.

This is a great, exhilarating, white water challenge, that compares with the Tamba Kosi. The Marsyandi has less volume than the Tamba Kosi so is not quite as powerful and is perhaps slightly the easier river? – but has a longer length of more consistent white water.

Comments we received from paddlers were:
'My favourite best',
'A jewel of a river'
'Incredible! – such a high class continuous river without needing portaging or much scouting from the bank'.

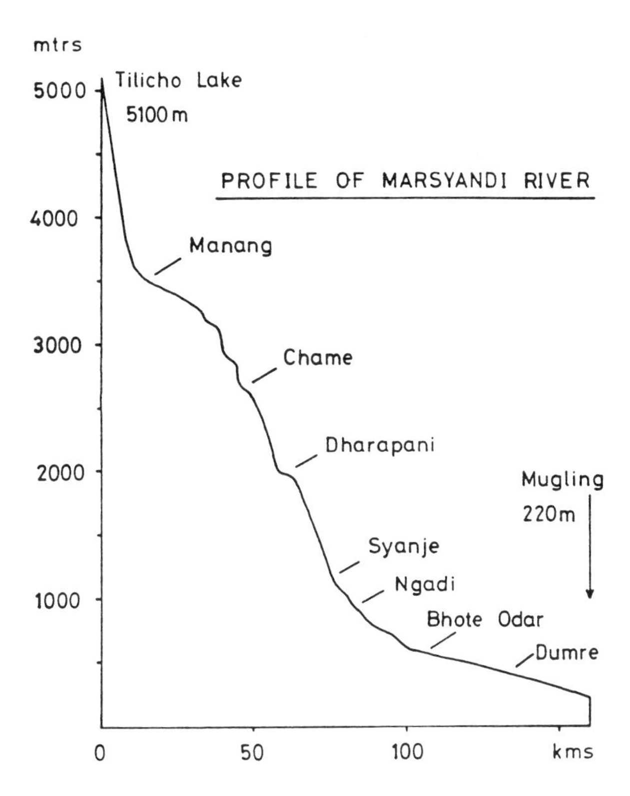

We recommend **Ngadi** as probably the best place from which to start kayaking. It could be started higher up: the river has been kayaked from Syange – the 12 kms to Ngadi described as a full day of class 4 & 5 paddling and bank scouting. Even higher up, from Jagot down, has been described by those who have scouted it as class 5 & 6 gorges and probably feasible in parts.

From Ngadi to Bimalnagar is a comfortable 3 days paddling – but it's such a beautiful river, and so photogenic, that you might want to make this 4 days.

Access and logistics

From Kathmandu to **Dumre** is 3 to 4 hours by bus, depending on the state of the road. The tourist bus to Pokhara can drop you off and costs about $4 – no charge for kayaks. The road from Dumre up the valley is unpaved and varies in standard from year to year – when it is in good condition buses can drive to **Bhote Odar** and trucks to **Besi Shahar**. When the road is bad, it's really bad – and only passable by ex-Russian 4 wheel drive assault trucks. Reckon on at least 5 hours by truck from Dumre to Besi Shahar – cost about $2 per person and the same for each kayak. A private minibus from Kathmandu to Bhote Odar would cost about $100.

The road and trail up the Marsyandi valley forms the first part of the popular trek, the 'Annapurna Circuit' and so there are plenty of lodges to eat or stay in. Also, no problems finding porters – they assailed our group even before we had got off the truck at Besishahar. We agreed on about $5 to carry each loaded boat in one day to **Ngadi** (longer than a normal porter day). If you're putting in at Bhote Odar, the river is about ten minutes walk from the village.

It would be very easy to stay and eat in lodges for this river trip, and have the pleasure of paddling light boats – but you'd miss out on some really fine campsites! Note that driftwood is limited and you would be wise to bring a stove if you intend to camp.

Recommended take-out is the small village just past Dumre called **Bimalnagar** – this brings you out on the main road from Pokhara to Kathmandu. It is possible to continue on a few extra kilometres to above the Dam but the river is no longer so beautiful, mainly class 2, and the take-out is not so easy to spot – also the dam site is a sensitive security area.....

Various trekking maps cover the river with dubious accuracy – nicest map to buy is the full colour official map of the 'Annapurna Conservation Area' at a scale of 1:125,000. – unfortunatly this only covers the river above Bhote Odar. H.M.G. Central service map for Gorkha District covers the whole river also at the large scale of 1:125,000. In the event of an accident, note the relatively well-equipped Mission Hospital at Ampipal.

Description

Ngadi to Besi Shahar 11kms, Bhote Odar 13, Chepe 13, Bimalnagar 15.

This is a very continuous run with lots and lots of class 4 rapids – mainly boulder fields that require technical manoeuvring and eddy scouting – exhilarating kayaking and rafting and great fun. Because the rapids are mainly boulder ones, you can expect them to change from year to year and what may be a class 4– this year may be a class 5 next year so beware!

From **Ngadi** to **Besi Shahar** is continuous class 4 and class 4+ and there is almost no respite – there are no sections at less than class 4. About 1km below the bridge at Behi Shahar is a good campsite next to some fine play waves, with early morning sun and a great view of Annapurna.

About 3 kms below Besi Shahar is a nasty rapid where the water is funnelled onto a big central rock guarded by shark teeth – this probably deserves a class 5 rating. The river eases off for a kilometre at **Phaliya Sanghu** through a narrow picturesque gorge with steep cliffs. The river then becomes class 4 and is not quite as continuous, but still lots of fun. **Bhote Odar** is some ten minutes walk away from the river, but there is a small village with tea houses on the opposite bank by the bridge called Bel Ghari Bazar – one of the few villages actually on the riverside.

A few kms further on, on the right bank is a Shiva temple with a lingam rock. The guru here welcomes respectful visitors and it's a beautiful place to camp.

Three kms past the next bridge are two rapids that are probably class 4+; the second of these has a house rock in the middle of the river that forms a 'terminal hole' in high water. The river eases a little after this, becomes more class 3+ and there are a few opportunities to relax!

Dumre is some distance from the river and the recommended take-out is about two kms below Dumre at the small village of **Bimalnagar**. You will recognise this by the suspension bidge across the river and the first sight of the main road. The village and main road are two minutes' walk up the path from the bridge. If you have time to spend, Don Weeden recommends that you round your trip off by a guided tour of the caverns just 2 kms west of Dumre – a spooky experience exploring these unusual caves by candlelight.

Marsyandi upstream from Ngadi

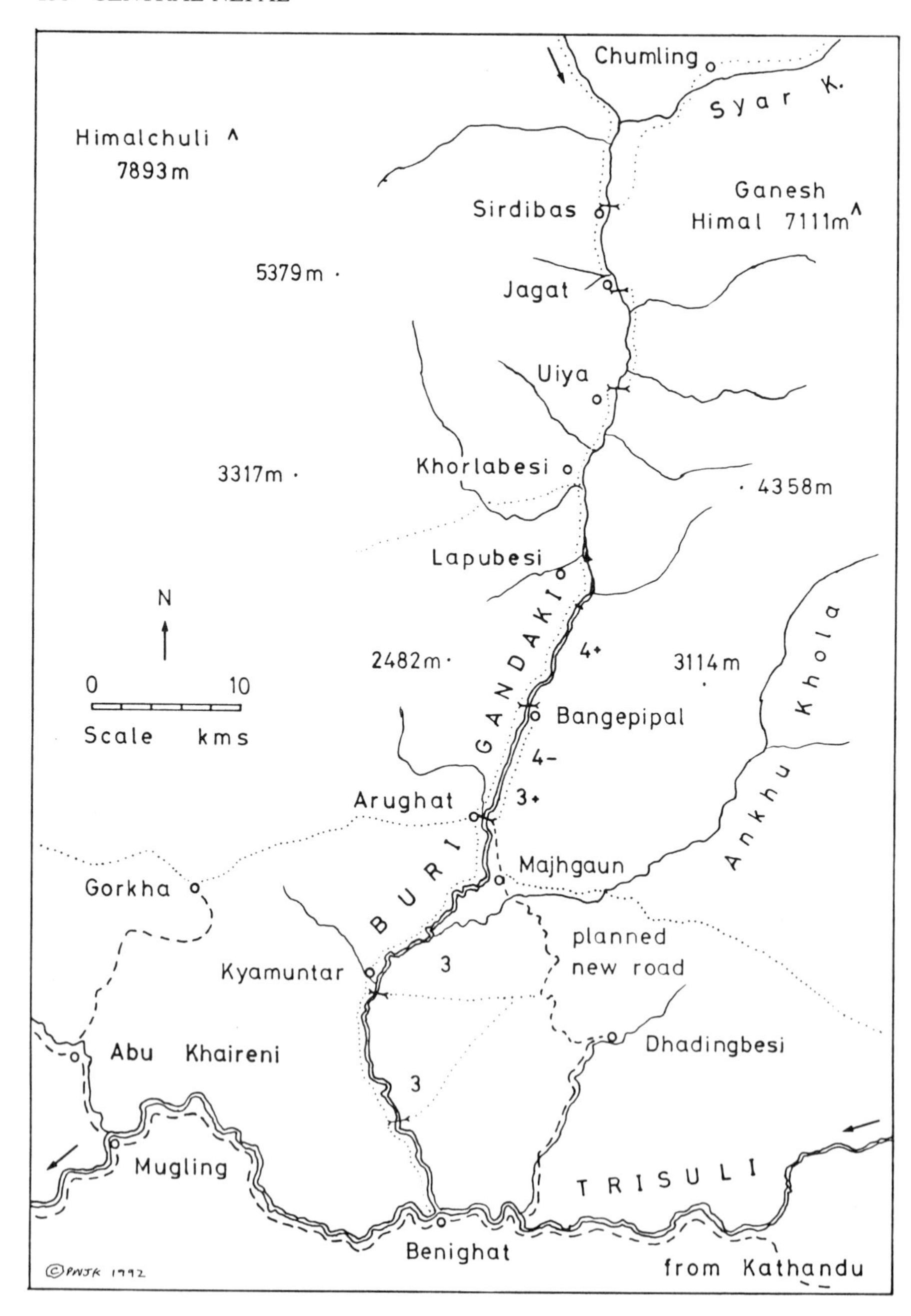

WARNING: Laser-phobic ink – do not photocopy.

Buri Gandaki

From:	**Arughat** (Alt. 480m)
To:	**Trisuli** (Alt. 330m)
Distance:	**34 kms** (21 miles)
River Days:	**1–2**
From Kathmandu:	**1 plus 2 days trek**
Difficulty in Nov:	**Class 3**
Average gradient:	**0.4%** (20 ft a mile)
Est. max. gradient:	**0.6%**
Volume in Nov:	**90 cumecs** (3200 cfs)
Best Season:	**Nov-Dec, Feb-April.**

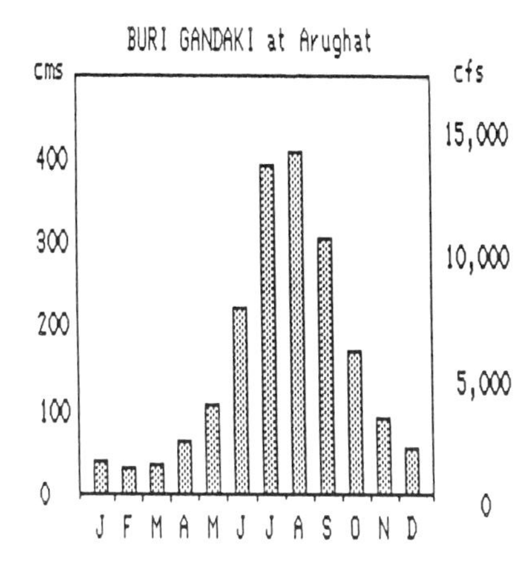

Summary

Combines a pleasant trek and short river descent – typical Nepali villages, good mountain views and a little-travelled, but easy river. There are several days of class 4 & 5 kayaking further up river.

The River

Lots of people know the Trisuli, Marsyandi and Kali Gandaki but mention the Buri Gandaki and few people know anything about it, few have trekked the valley, and hardly anyone has rafted or kayaked it. Half way between Kathmandu and Pokhara and yet it's a mystery river!

Like the Marsyandi, the Buri Gandaki rises wholly in Nepal and drains the Eastern slopes of Manaslu and the Ganesh Himal before flowing south through a steep-sided valley to join the Trisuli River upstream of Mugling. Many people have seen this confluence from the main highway to Kathmandu – they have seen the blue waters of the Buri Gandaki joining the usually more silty waters of the Trisuli and perhaps wondered what lies upstream. In fact, upstream is a river very similar in volume and characteristics to the Marsyandi but not as steep or as difficult in its lower portion. A glance at the river profile will show that the Buri Gandaki has a fairly easy gradient from downstream of Arughat Bazar. Upstream of here the gradient is still quite reasonable; it averages 2.3% (120ft a mile) from Sirdibas (Setibas on some maps) down to Arughat. This section of the river flows through a gorge-like valley, which gradually opens out above Arughat.

The 'Royal Trek', that used to be the main trail from Kathmandu to Gorkha, crosses the river at Arughat, but is not very popular. A few groups do trek up the valley of the Buri Gandaki to Manaslu and Himalchuli but the valley is still relatively unspoilt and a good introduction to Nepali villages and the friendly local people.

We were probably the first group to kayak the river in 1983 and we received a very friendly welcome. The Lodge keeper in Arughat insisted that we pay nothing for our rooms: he was so keen to have river runners as his customers and he looked forward to a whole new business as rafting came to the Buri Gandaki. One of our group, Mike

McDonald, trekked the royal route with his wife in 1990, so stayed at the lodge again: the lodge keeper remembered him and our group well, and sadly reported that river running on the Buri Gandaki hadn't taken off – in fact he hadn't seen another group since 1983!

Perhaps his hopes for a rafting boom might happen if, and when, the new road is built from Dhadingbesi and access becomes easier.

Rafting

From Arughat Bazar down to the Trisuli River is a pleasant trip of class 2 and 3 that offers an attractive alternative start to a Trisuli trip – particularly for a group that would enjoy the two day trek from Gorkha. The river is relatively small volume and should be friendly for first time rafters. The 34 kms from Arughat Bazar could be done in a day, but most groups would probably want to take longer in order to camp in this quiet scenic valley and to explore the unspoilt villages enroute.

The Buri Gandaki has only been rafted by a handful of trips, mainly we imagine because of the expense and hassle of having to carry in the rafts and gear. To our minds, this very fact that so few people have done the river must be one of the attractions of doing it – a unique rafting trip that few others will have done.

Kayaking

This river offers two levels of trip – an easy run down from Arughat, or a more difficult 'expedition' further up river.

The trip from **Arughat** down is very straight forward (well, it was when we did it ten years ago) and we think that this would probably be a suitable trip for people of limited experience who want to do their own thing – also probably quite a good river for inflatable kayaks. This would also be an excellent introduction to the pleasures and logistics of trekking into rivers.

Weir with fish traps

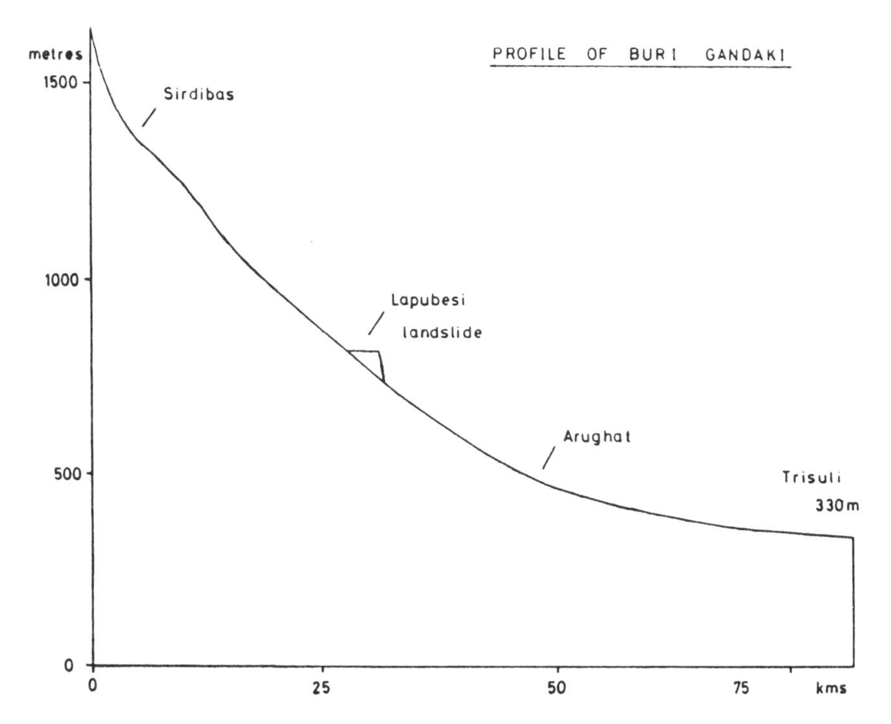

When we ran the river in 1983, our team started at **Lapubesi**, about 17 kms upstream of Arughat. A huge landslide had blocked the river here and created a lake going back for several kms upstream and out of sight. The river here was mainly class 4+, with a couple of slightly harder rapids, but eased off after a few kms to class 4− and then class 3 approaching Arughat. A particular and serious hazard was the risk of 'pinning' because of the sharp rocks washed down by the landslide. The river was a tight, boulder-strewn gorge, with some fun drops and beautiful water. Gerry Moffat compares it to the Marsyandi, but also warns 'note the nasty sharp rocks'.

The river profile, and our examination of 1″ to the mile topographical maps, makes us think that there is probably some good kayaking further upstream, waiting for an adventurous team ......

Access and logistics

At the present time the best approach to the Buri Gandaki is from **Gorkha** – this might change, if and when a the road is completed from Dhadingbesi. A private minibus would cost about $100. Local buses would involve a change at Mugling or at the village, Abu Khaireni, where the Gorkha road branches off from the Pokhara highway. If you had your own transport to Gorkha then you could be there by Midday, and could conceivably trek in to the river in a day and a half. But, the trek to **Arughat** Bazar is normally considered as a two day one, Gorkha is a really interesting town, and the trek very scenic and photogenic with excellent vistas of Manaslu and adjacent mountains, so it would be a shame to hurry.

Take-out can be at the confluence; a steep trail on the far side of the Trisuli, ascends to the road. Most groups would probably want to continue on down the Trisuli – please see the section on this river.

There are good campsites on the river but little driftwood for fires, so a stove is necessary. Best map covering the river is probably the 1;125,000 Central Service Map for the Gorkha District.

Description

Gorkha is an interesting historic town that is well worth exploring and we suggest you stay overnight: there is a good hotel, the Gorkha Bisauni, right by the bus terminus and the friendly Manager will help you hire porters. The town was the home of the founders of Nepal and has many temples and a particularly impressive old palace high on a ridge above the town, reached by a stone staircase that climbs up from the Bazar – some 300 metres.

This staircase is also the start of your trek into the river – normally about 8 hours of walking. This is a fairly easy trek that winds its way up and down small valleys, along ridges, through picturesque villages, and with fine views of terraced fields and the Manaslu and Ganesh Himalaya in the backgound.

Arughat Bazar is a large, pleasant village with stone-flagged main street and several shops and lodges. You can put on here, or if you are feeling more adventurous continue up the valley. It took us another day and a half to trek onwards up to Lapu Besi.

The big landslide at **Lapubesi** had formed a dam that was over 100 metres high in 1983, and the river tumbled down this in a cataract. Starting below here, technical class 4+ paddling takes you down for a few kms to a long 5+ rapid. Jock Montgomery remembers Mike MacDonald pinning on this rapid with a foam of water blasting over his head; 'somehow he managed to extricate himself and he even had the presence of mind to grab the bow loop and pull the boat loose . . . Gawd!' Class 4+ paddling continues down to the bridge at Bangepipal after which it progressively gets easier until the river becomes class 3 just above Arughat.

From **Arughat** down to the Trisuli is class 2 and 3. There is a fair gradient so there is a good current, but the river is friendly with obvious lines on the rapids. To be honest, when we did it, there was nothing that was noteworthy about this section – we bumbled down with a hang over from too many beers the night before! There is a fine beach for camping at the confluence, but it is probably better to plan on camping somewhere quieter before the Trisuli? – make the most of the fact that you're one of only a handful of people to run this river.

Trekking to the Buri Gandaki (Jock Montgomery)

Beware the GLOF!

Like most paddlers, we hadn't heard of GLOFs before we came to Nepal, but these large dangerous beasties can pose a special risk to the river runner. GLOFs occur in the high Himalaya and are most prevalent in the warmer months when the snow is melting. No, a GLOF isn't some form of Yeti, the letters stand for Glacial Lake Outburst Flood. The GLOF results from the sudden release of lake water which is pent up within a glacier or behind a moraine. This glacial dam suddenly gives way, or perhaps a large chunk of glacier or cliff falls into the lake, and a huge catastrophic flood wave sweeps down the valley.

GLOFs are capable of immense destruction: in August 1985 one occured on a tributary of the Dudh Kosi and sent a 10 metre high tidal wave of mud coursing down the valley. This washed away houses, fields, trails and most of the bridges. The only warning was a sound like thunder, or 'many helicopters'. So, if you hear this when by the river – run for your lives to higher ground!

Landslide dams are a similar natural hazard that again can cause immense destruction. Usually these give some warning because as the river dams up behind the landslide, the water levels downstream will drop abnormally, perhaps for several days, until the water level in the dam rises sufficiently to overtop the blockage and sweep it away in a matter of hours.

As in any country, flash floods caused by heavy rain in the mountains can also cause the river levels to rise suddenly and without warning – this may exceptionally case the river to rise metres within minutes.

For the river runner, these are very remote but real hazards, worthy of special note if you are running a river high in the mountains. Any flood wave will tend to dissipate as it sweeps down the valley, but even if you are running the lower reaches of a larger river, the most important point to remember is always to camp at a sensible height above river level.

The ultimate surf wave?

Bagmati

by Gerry Moffat

From:	**Min Bhawan** (Alt.1289m)
To:	**Chovar** (Alt. 1259m)
Distance:	**11 kms** (7 miles)
River Days:	**2 hours**
From Kathmandu:	**20 minutes!**
Difficulty in Sept:	**Class 3**
Average gradient:	**0.3%** (15ft a mile)
Est. max. gradient:	**0.6%**
Volume in Sept:	**35 cumecs** (1200 cfs)
Best Season:	**Sept**

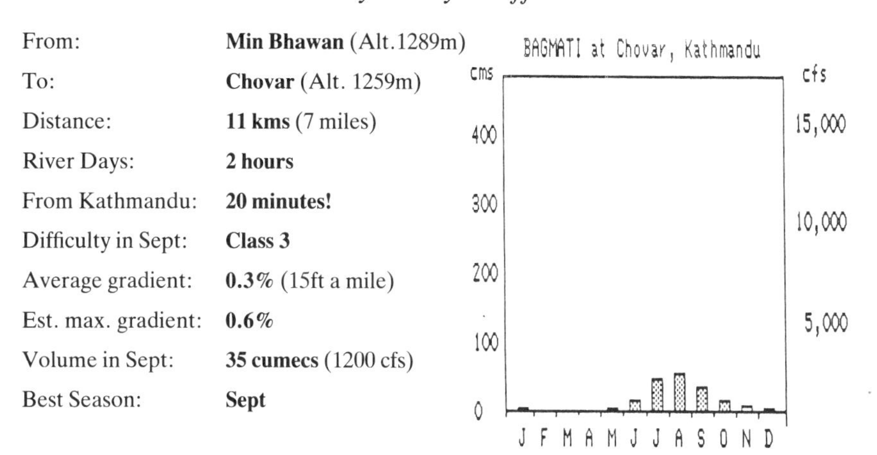

Summary

A unique cultural experience with some hidden dangers. Recommended only for the true enthusiast and a river not to be under-estimated.

The River

The Bagmati, although small, is probably the best-known river in Nepal. It rises in, and drains, the Kathmandu Valley. Flowing through several temple sites, this is a famous and holy river that is quite unique in Nepal in terms of its characteristics.

Rafting

You won't find this on the programme of most companies, but if you did want a trip, this could probably be arranged.

Kayaking

Some famous international kayakers have paddled this river, but it seems to have been largely avoided by the paddling fraternity in the last few years, perhaps on the advice of the early explorers.

Access and Logistics

The start of the trip at Min Bhawan is only a short taxi ride from Rum Doodle's Bar in Thamel, Kathmandu. Recommended take-out is at Chovar, but it would be possible to continue another 6 kms to take out at the Leprosy Hospital. It would be simple and reasonably cheap to have a taxi or mini bus meet you here.

Description

The monsoon raged on. News had just reached us that the main highway from Kathmandu to India had been closed, indefinitely: a small side stream had flooded and washed the road bridge into the Trisuli. This coincided with landslides on the roads to both the Sun Kosi and Trisuli Bazaar. All traffic in and out of Kathmandu had come to an abrupt halt.

For the company raft guides, assembled in Kathmandu's famous Rum Doodle's Bar, a double catastrophe was looming:

1. Kathmandu might run out of Kukuri Rum.

2. All guide training, play boating, and subsequent hammer ings would cease.

Yogi, the Head Barman, offered us the Nepalese sympathy vote – 'Kai Ga Nai' (what to do) and another round of drinks. Soon enough, old stories of how big the Trisuli would be, got bigger, and the usual 'true stories' grew wilder by the minute. The latest bigger and better river yarn was interupted in mid-flow by the River Leader, James Hogg, bursting in with a plan to continue the training programme.

We all looked up with eager eyes for our new quest: James enthusiatically announced: 'It's the Bagmati lads'. A state of awful shock descended on all those capable of grasping the concept of what we were about to be involved in. 'The Bagmati? Where's that?' called out the innocent newly-arrived first-year river guide. 'It's the sewer that runs through Kathmandu', was the reply. 'Oh, Shit.' 'Yes, exactly.'

But, James, as ever, had the answers, and after another round of rum and cokes we were almost enthusiastic. The rest of the night was spent scouring dimly lit bars for unsuspecting tourists – to be used for paddle power and training material .... And so, on the morning of the 25th September 1984, the Bagamati Rafting Expedition set off bravely to go where no living man had gone before.

It seemed a good idea to put in below, rather than above, the the burning ghats of Pashupatinath, where each year thousands of Sadhus and Sunyasins gather after their arduous pilgrimage from distant parts to celebrate Lord Shiva's birthday (Shivarati). It is here that the bodies of the dead are cremated and, in accordance with Hindu religion, the ashes are sprinkled on the waters of the Bagmati, to be carried to its confluence with the Holy Ganges and on to the holy city of Varanasi (sometimes known as Verynasty).

We put in below the ring-road bridge outside of Patan, sliding the raft into the water down a bank well greased by turds. The river proved to be predominantly class 2; however the challenge of trying to avoid all contact with the water added a new dimension to the sport of river running. We tried to avoid eddies – there's no telling what might have been floating there; and indeed a rafter from Liverpool claimed that he spotted some 'Mersey Gold Fish' swimming by.

Several kms drifted by and the scenery, if not the river, became quite pleasant with lush green terraces on either bank. A hill loomed up ahead and this was the approach to the legendary **Chovar Gorge**. The story goes that Manjushri took his sword and sliced Chovar hill in two, allowing the waters to drain out of the lake that once filled the valley and thus brought life to Kathmandu. This has not been technically denied by anyone, although some experts think that an earthquake might have helped! No matter, this natural wonder gave us an erie unwanted feeling once we entered it's depths.

It's probably worth mentioning that one should have a full set of inoculations before entering the gorge, as there are two class 3 rapids and you definitely will get wet. Both drops are technical, and the unwary may find themselves swimming in the pool at the bottom, as happened to our intrepid leader James Hogg – which goes to show that there is justice in the world; thank you Lord Shiva!

Take-out was at the Jal Binakak Temple immediately after the gorge on the right. Time for congratulations, a steam clean and preventative medicine back at Rum Doodle's.

N.B. Editors' note: We personally reckon this to be potentially one of the most dangerous rivers in Nepal and were concerned with the legal implications of including this in a Guide Book. However, Gerry Moffat's group wasn't the only trip to the river: do you remember the dramatic gorge sequence in the film 'Dudh Kosi: relentless river of Everest'? – actually filmed in the Chovar Gorge – there's a lovely photo in the book 'Canoeing Down Everest'. Mick Hopkinson always says that this was one of the most unpleasant if not quite the most dangerous rivers he has ever done!

RIVERS OF EASTERN NEPAL

Introduction

This is the Nepal that will be familiar to you from films and photographs – the World's highest mountains, steep sided valleys, roaring rivers, terraced hillsides, picturesque villages and hard-working Sherpas. These images are true, but only paint a partial picture of the region. Eastern Nepal is noted for the diversity it offers: here are terraced mountain valleys and rushing rivers, but also wide forested valleys, fertile lowlands, magnificent gorges, rolling verdant hills and luxuriant jungle. This diverse terain is watered by the abundant rainfall from the monsoons, and so supports a dense population of many different tribes.

This diversity is also true of the rivers – most paddler's concept of Nepalese rivers has been formed by images from 'Canoeing down Everest', and yes, the Dudh Kosi does represent your archetypal mountain river – but at the other extreme, in this same region, we have the Indrawati – a pleasant relaxing easy river meandering through a wide valley. The Sun Kosi is different again, in that it flows west to east for some 300 kms as a relatively mature, big volume river and at a low altitude; giving warm water and fine beaches for camping – a river runner's delight.

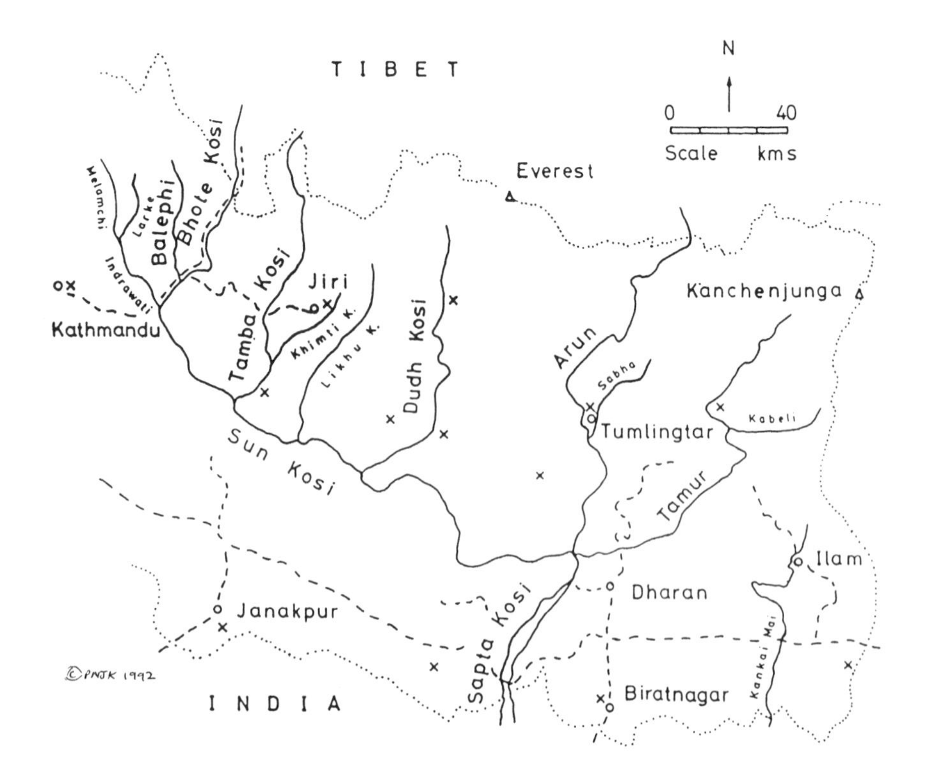

Commercial Rafting

The region offers some world class multi-day raft trips with excellent white water on unspoilt rivers. Road access is limited, thus heightening the experience and sensation of remoteness.

One day 'taster' raft trips are possible on the Upper Sun Kosi and the Indrawati rivers and are only a couple of hours from Kathmandu.

The Self-Sufficient Trip

The East of Nepal has some of the best long multi-day trips, for the white water enthusiast. A popular choice with expert kayakers is to run the Tamba Kosi and then the Sun Kosi followed by a trip down the Tamur. There are no easy multi-day trips in this region.

Logistics for most of the rivers are straight forward. Eastern Nepal is well populated and basic food supplies, if you run short, are available at many of the larger villages: however, if you have an accident, you are often at least two day's walk from the nearest road.

Guide Book Rivers

Sun Kosi
One of the ten best rafting trips in the world. Big rapids, warm water, no roads, continuous white water interest, beautiful scenery and great camping make this a classic ten day rafting trip. Also an excellent river for kayakers!

Bhote Kosi (upper Sun Kosi)
A beautiful mountain river only a few hours from Kathmandu. Offers 'taster' rafting days, or kayaking day trips at all levels of difficulty. Easy access and scouting from the highway.

Balephi Khola
A small, blue, mountain river, fun for kayaks, close to Kathmandu and with the feel of a 'mini expedition'.

Indrawati
An easy river only 3 hours from Kathmandu – yet unspoilt. A really pleasant day's float trip for rafts, kayaks or 'Duckies'.

Tamba Kosi
A great river for expert kayakers wanting a dramatic start to a Sun Kosi trip.

Dudh Kosi
Flying into Lamidanda, gives an alternative shorter start to a Sun Kosi trip. There is some steep and very difficult 'expedition' kayaking further upstream that requires expensive and time consuming logistics.

Arun
A shorter alternative to a Sun Kosi trip, but requires flying in to the start at Tumlingtar. Further upstream is some powerful, hard, big water 'expedition' boating through the impressive Arun Gorges.

Tamur
Another world classic! Five days of magnificent white water combined with a spectacular three day trek. An exhilarating and active raft or kayak trip.

Other Rivers

Melamchi and Larke Kholas – The two rivers that join to form the Indrawati. They probably offer one or two days of paddling for the kayaker in an exploratory mood -conveniently close to Kathmandu.

Khimti Khola – The main tributary of the Tamba Kosi, with a very steep but steady gradient of about 8% (400ft a mile) – most paddlers will want to leave this well alone, but it might appeal to real 'hair boaters'? (volume in November is 10 cumecs).

Likhu Khola – Next valley east and a higher volume river (33 cumecs in November). Stretches of this river are most probably runnable, but there are some steep sections and some nasty-looking gorges – comparable to the Dudh Kosi. We suspect that someone will have attempted it by the time you read this book!

Sabha Khola – This river joins the Arun near Tumlingtar, and appears to be the only tributary of the Arun that offers any potential for kayaking.

Kabeli Khola – Main tributary of the Tamur and probably offers a day or two of good paddling.

Kankai Mai Khola – In the far East of the country, this river drains the hill country around the tea growing centre of Ilam and looks as if it could be worth kayaking – volume in November is 23 cumecs. It descends from about 400m near Ilam to 100m at the Mahendra highway, about 70 kms – an average gradient of about 0.4% (20 ft a mile).

'High Anxiety' rapid, Sun Kosi

Sun Kosi

From: **Dolalghat** (Alt. 620m)
To: **Chatra** (Alt. 115m)
Distance: **272 kms** (170 miles)
River Days: **6–10**
Difficulty in Nov: **Class 4−** (5−)
From Kathmandu: **3 hours**
Average gradient: **0.2%** (10 ft a mile)
Est. max. gradient: **0.6%**
Volume in Nov: **400 cumecs** (14,000 cfs)
Best Season: **Oct-Dec, Mar-May.**

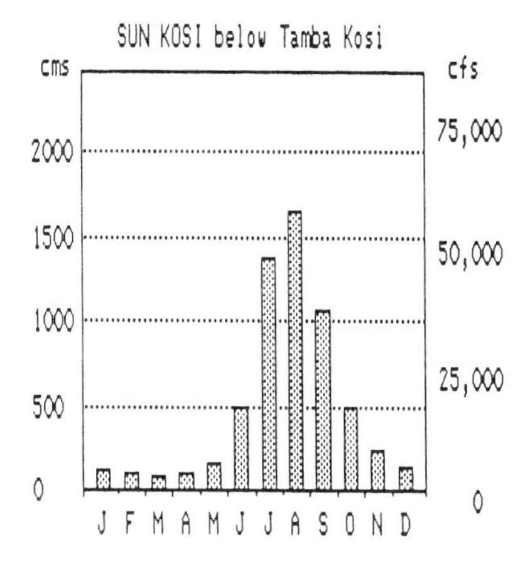

Summary

One of the ten best rafting trips in the world. Big rapids, warm water, no roads or towns, beautiful scenery and great camping make this a classic multi-day river trip. An excellent trip for intermediate and advanced kayakers. Rafters should be reasonably fit and comfortable on big water.

The River

Sun Kosi means 'River of Gold' – perhaps named after the gold that is sometimes panned from the river gravels, or alternatively it refers to the orange colour of the water in the Monsoon when it is thick with alluvial silt. The river rises near Tibet and is joined by the Bhote Kosi just downstream from Barabise. Most raft trips start at Dolalghat, so for convenience we have included the short length of the Sun Kosi above Dolalghat in with the description of the Bhote Kosi.

The Sun Kosi flows eastwards in Nepal through the great valley between the Mahabharat Lekh mountains and the Himalaya. It forms the watershed for most of eastern Nepal and gathering strength from tributaries draining the highest mountains in the world it emerges onto the northern plains of India where it joins the Ganges.

The volume increases considerably with the flow from these tributaries. In Novenber, the flow at Dolalghat is about 100 cumecs; lower down the river, through the big rapids of the 'Jungle Corridor', it would be about 400 cumecs which is aprox. 11,000 cfs – a typical low flow on the Grand Canyon of the Colorado. At the take-out, at Chatra, the flow is a mighty 800 cumecs (still only a fraction of monsoon levels) and you know that this is one of the major rivers of the World.

This is a large volume pool/drop river. Most of the major rapids are formed by monsoon debris brought in by side streams, and loose rockfall. These rapids change from year to year depending on the severity of the monsoon. A large monsoon in 1984 washed away Hakapur 3, which at the time was the hardest rapid, and created Meatgrinder and several new rapids.

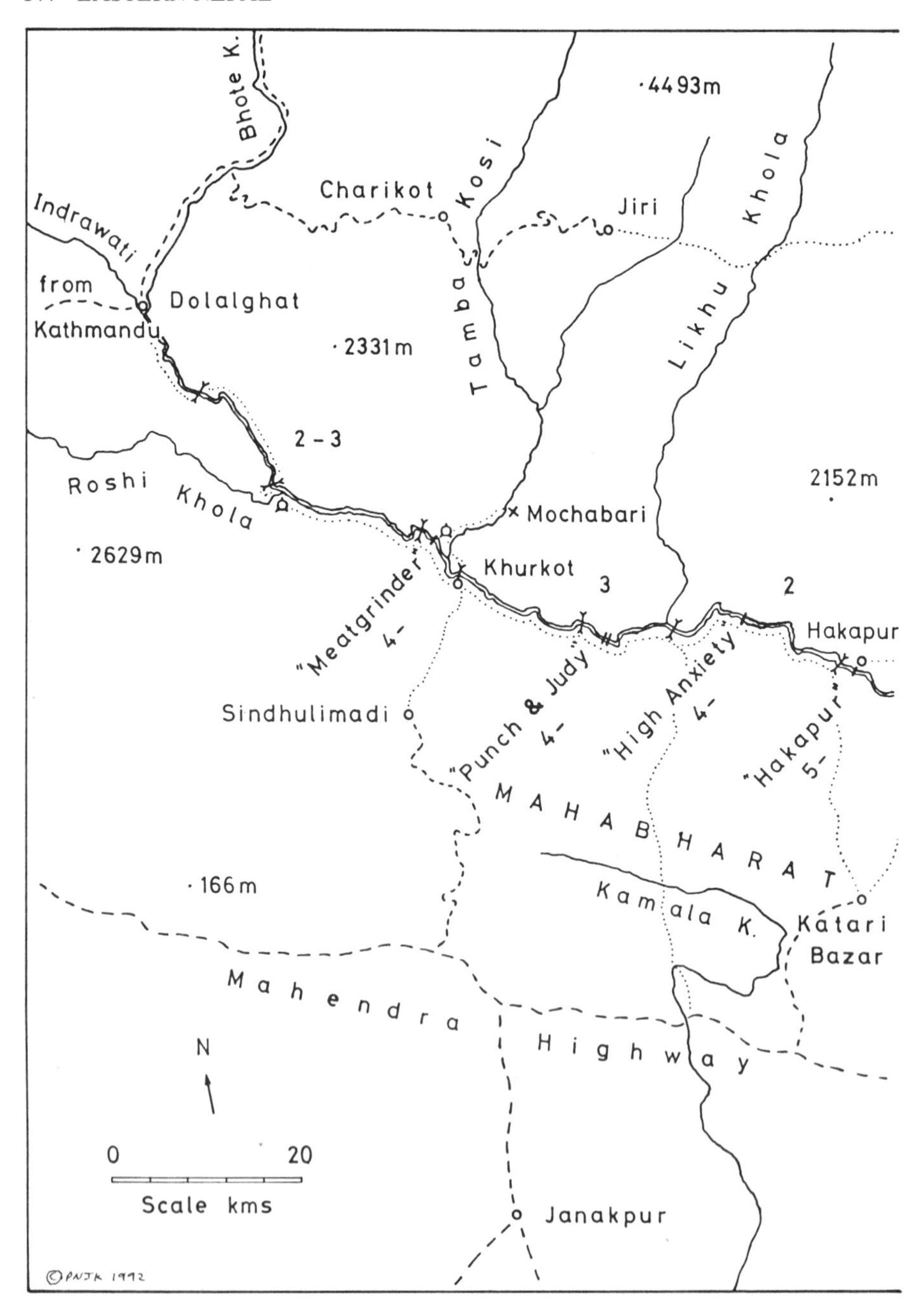

WARNING: Laser-phobic ink – do not photocopy.

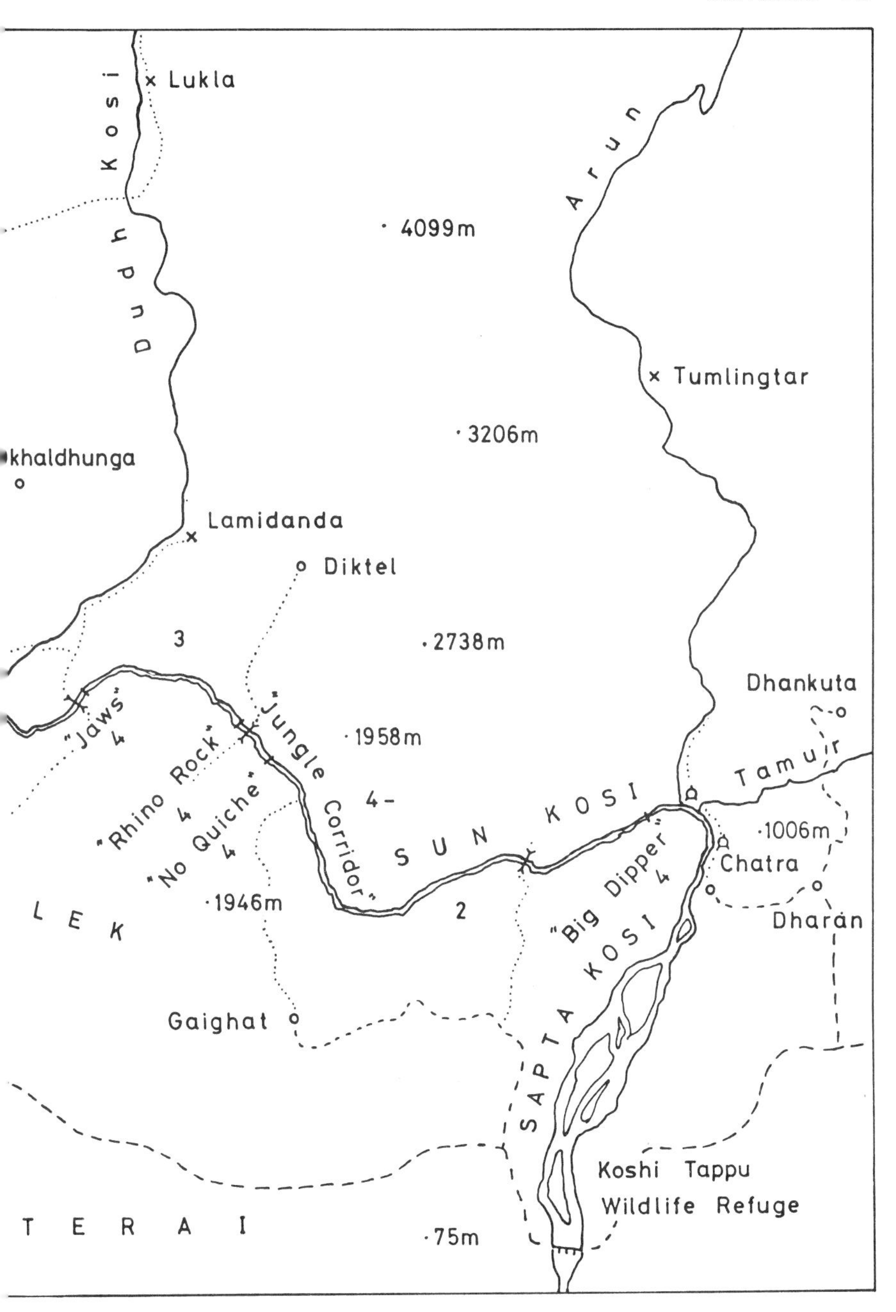

Dudh Kosi
Lukla
Arun
4099m
Tumlingtar
3206m
khaldhunga
Lamidanda
Diktel
3
2738m
Dhankuta
"Jaws"
4
"Jungle Corridor"
1958m
"Rhino Rock"
4
Tamur
4-
SUN KOSI
1006m
"No Quiche"
4
Chatra
"Big Dipper"
4
1946m
2
Dharan
LEK
SAPTA KOSI
Gaighat
Koshi Tappu
Wildlife Refuge
TERAI
75m

From the put-in at Dolalghat to the take-out at Chatra, 272 kms later, there are no roads or towns, just the occasional picturesque village and friendly shouts of 'Namaste' from the bank – this is unspoilt, rural Nepal at its best. All along the river are beautiful white sandy beaches for camping and the lower section of the river is heavily forested with troops of monkeys and an abundance of birdlife.

Rafting

Most raft groups start at Dolalghat, and from here the first few day's are relatively easy and are an excellent warm-up for the rapids below. From day three onwards, every day has at least one or two major rapids and lots of smaller fun ones. Most major rapids are pool/drop with huge bouncy pressure waves near the bottom – similar to the rapids of the Grand Canyon of the Colorado. 8-10 days running big rapids and floating through lush green countryside make this a truly memorable river experience.

It is possible in larger flows to extend a Sun Kosi rafting trip by starting higher up at Balephi or Khadichour – please see notes on the Bhote Kosi. For those with limited time, you could consider flying into Lamidanda on the Dudh Kosi, raft the last 30 kms of this famous river and then the bottom half of the Sun Kosi – this would make about a six day trip.

River flows vary immensely – from huge post-monsoon run-off in early October down to low winter flows in January and February, rising again in May with snowmelt and pre-monsoon rains. With the right group and experience it is possible to raft late Sept/Oct. At this time of year the river is high and wild and certainly not for the faint hearted.

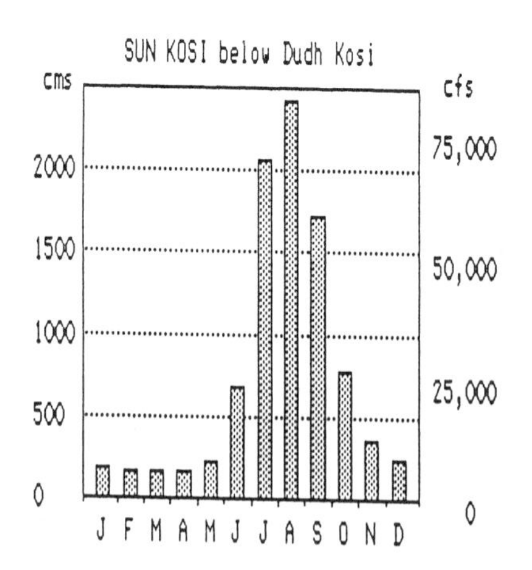

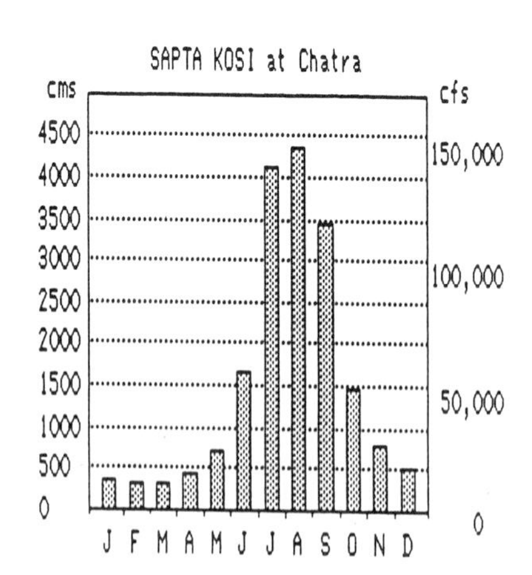

Kayaking

For intermediate and advanced kayakers this is a great river. Big bouncy grade 3-4 rapids with large surfing waves and lots of friendly holes make it 'like paddling on the Ocean with great waves crashing down on you'. The amazing thing is that, at almost any level, the whole river is runnable. Expert kayakers would only need to scout a few major rapids from the bank – all others could be done by 'eddy hopping'.

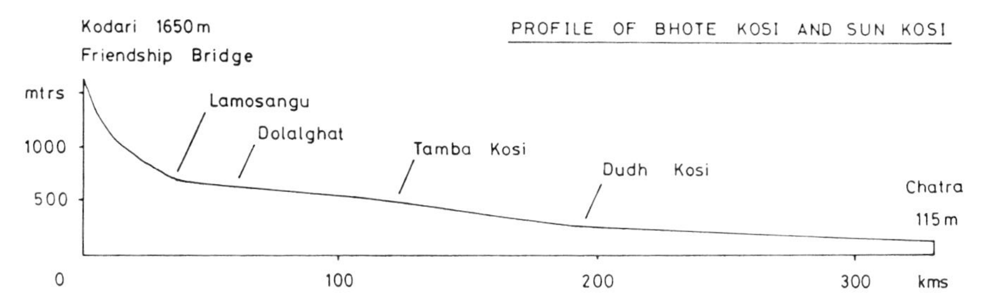

One of the nice things about the Sun Kosi is that, with the exception of a few big rapids like Hakapur that can be easily portaged, the general standard of the river gets progressively harder as you descend it so there is time to loosen up and practise your skills on easy water before you reach the more interesting, bigger and more continuous rapids lower down the river. If you are an intermediate paddler you will be pleasantly surprised and flattered by how much your skills improve by the end of the trip!

Most kayakers do this trip with raft support and benefit by being able to paddle empty boats, eat lots of good food and socialise. Of course they have to be prepared for constant abuse from the rafters who call kayakers 'river maggots' from their habit of infesting holes and eddies.

Expert kayakers often choose to start a Sun Kosi trip with a descent of the the Tamba Kosi – a much more difficult and demanding river (please see the notes for that river), and commonly arrange to meet up with a Sun Kosi raft trip on the third day.

Kayakers accompanying a rafting group may wish to take their minibus to Khadichour and start further up the river. This would give them 2-3 hours of good playing on grade 3 rapids before catching up with the rafting group late afternoon in time for a beer and food (please see notes on the Bhote Kosi).

Access and logistics

The usual starting point is just above the bridge at **Dolalghat** on the Indrawati. This is about 3 hours by road from Kathmandu and costs about $1 by bus, or $60 for a private minibus. The Sun Kosi normally takes about 8-9 days, but it's nice to add one day for a rest. This also gives you time to check out some of the small villages and temples along the way.

Most groups running the Sun Kosi camp each night on the beautiful beaches and there are usually adequate supplies of driftwood for cooking fires but kayakers wishing to do this river without support could probably do it by eating in small villages along the way. They would have to stock up in the village of **Hakapur** as there are not many villages lower down.

Best take-out is at **Chatra**. Keep close to the left bank and take out at the entrance to the irrigation canal. The village of Chatra is about half a km from the take-out point and you can hire ancient Landrovers for $15 to Dharan Baazar, about one hour's drive away. From here there are night coaches returning to Kathmandu. They leave in the late afternoon and take 16-18 hours to get to Kathmandu, Cost $5. Alternatively you can hire a vehicle to take you to the airstrip at Biratnagar (about 2 hours drive) where there are frequent flights back to Kathmandu. Biratnagar is the main city of the Eastern Region and there is a good bus service from here to other cities in Nepal and India (Darjeeling is a popular destination).

Chatra is the usual take-out point, but several groups have recommended continuing on through the **Koshi Tappu Wildlife Reserve**, to enjoy the very different wildlife of the Terai.

Note well that for the whole 272 kms from Dolalghat to Chatra, there are no roads and in the event of an accident, you are probably at least a day from help. There are several possibilities in the event of an emergency, depending where you are on the river:

- Walk to Mochabari Airstrip 10 kms up the Tamba Kosi.
- Trek south to the road at Sindhulimadi, aprox 20 kms.
- Trek south to the road at Katari bazar, aprox. 30 kms.
- Trek north to the airstrip at Lamidanda, aprox. 25 kms.
- Trek south to the road near Gaighat, aprox. 25 kms.

The Sun Kosi flows through such a long stretch of Eastern Nepal that you will need more than one map to cover it adequately. A general map of Nepal is good for its cover of the whole river and tributaries but for most detail we recommend the Government Central Services maps at a scale of 1:125,000 – you will need 3 sheets for the following Districts: Kabhre, Sindhuli, and Udayapur.

Description

Dolalghat to Tamba Kosi 63 kms, Dudh Kosi 74 kms, Chatra 135 kms.

From the put-in at **Dolaghat**, the first day or two is easy paddling. Below the first bridge at Dobhan Taar the river enters a beautiful small canyon with waterfalls and lush tropical growth. As the canyon opens up, note the large Bat cave on the right – but please do not disturb these sensitive animals. Some 10 kms or so below here is the first rapid of note: 'No Exit' is an easy class 3. Below the confluence of the Roshi Kosi on the right is a Shiva temple called Kuseshwar Mandir that is a great place to wander around. From the river it's recognisable by a large bunyan and a pipal tree.

About 5 km past the next bridge is the first major rapid – **'Meatgrinder'**. Class 4– it's a fairly straight run down the centre avoiding holes left and right. A few kms below here the **Tamba Kosi** joins the Sun Kosi on the left with a beach on the confluence. There is another beautiful Shiva temple overlooking the confluence of the two rivers. A few kms brings you to the next bridge and the large village of Khurkhot where it's possible to buy food, beer and cigarettes. Several more kms brings you to another bridge and 5 or 6 km below below here are **'Punch and Judy'** rapids – Punch is an easy class 4 and is shortly followed by Judy, a bouncy class 3.

A few kms below the confluence of the **Likhu Khola** is a short, class 3 rapid 'Pre-anxiety', and this is followed soon after by **'High Anxiety'** – a long class 4 rapid with a large hole on the left halfway down and a series of holes at the bottom. Tokshel **Hakapur** is a porter town at the next bridge on the trail to Okhaldunga. Several village stores stock such food staples as beer, and the very best brands of alcohol – have you ever tasted Cleopatra whiskey?

One km below here is the hardest rapid on the river, **'Hakapur 2'**, which should be carefully scouted. This was formed by a rockfall on the right and a massive mud slide constricting the river flow on the left. Boulders washed into the middle of this rapid form a large ledge with bad pour-overs and serious holes. This is not a nice rapid to swim and there have been several accidents here. There's still the best part of the Sun Kosi to be enjoyed so if you have any doubts, we suggest a portage on the left bank. If you do decide to run this, then you should have safety cover set up below with throw lines in position and ideally a rescue raft or kayaks to pick up swimmers – kayakers can earn their beers on this one!

'Hakapur' rapid, Sun Kosi

Some 5 kms below Hakapur, look out for the famous **Dudh Kosi** coming in as a narrow canyon from the left. Below here, the river valley widens into an arid area of gravel and rocks that is almost 2 km wide. Below the next bridge is a small rapid followed by 'Jaws' – quite a long rapid with a large ledge on the bottom right that forms a huge hole at certain levels. 'Dead man's eddy' below this has the dubious habit of collecting most things that float downstream.

Some 15 kms and a few small but fun rapids brings you to **'Rhino rock'**. This is just above the next bridge and marks the beginning of the **'jungle corridor'**. This section contains 6 rapids in about 10 km and is an exhilarating section of white water. At the end of the rapids a series of waterfalls cascades in from both banks and this is a great place for a wash and massage.

The rapids on the last few days are mainly wavetrains and these bring you down to the last major rapid on the river **'Big Dipper'**, which is a series of huge standing waves (that in low water hide some nasty holes) – an exciting climax. A few kms later and the mighty **Arun** river enters from a gorge on the left, almost immediately afterwards, the **Tamur** river also adds its waters and the combined river becomes the **Sapta Kosi** (Seven rivers). The confluence is called Tribeni Ghat and has an interesting temple to visit if you have time.

The river, now the Sapta Kosi, surges onwards, carving its way through its last obstacle, the foot hills. On the left bank after 5 kms is another larger Hindu Temple called Baraha Chhetra. On the day of the full moon in January every year, thousands of Hindu pilgrims throng here to pay homage to Lord Vishnu. Legend has it that once a demon god inhabited this area and troubled the holy men and pilgrims. Hearing of this, Lord Vishnu, preserver of the Universe, himself decided to kill the demon, and taking the form of a pig for the purpose, he slayed the demon in battle. The annual Baraha festival commemorates this victory and inside the Temple you will see a statue of Baraha, a pig-headed figure of Lord Vishnu.

Back on the river, you float along on the powerful current and then, rounding a corner, the hills dramatically give way to the totally flat Terai and the northern plains of India: you have reached the end of a classic and memorable river journey.

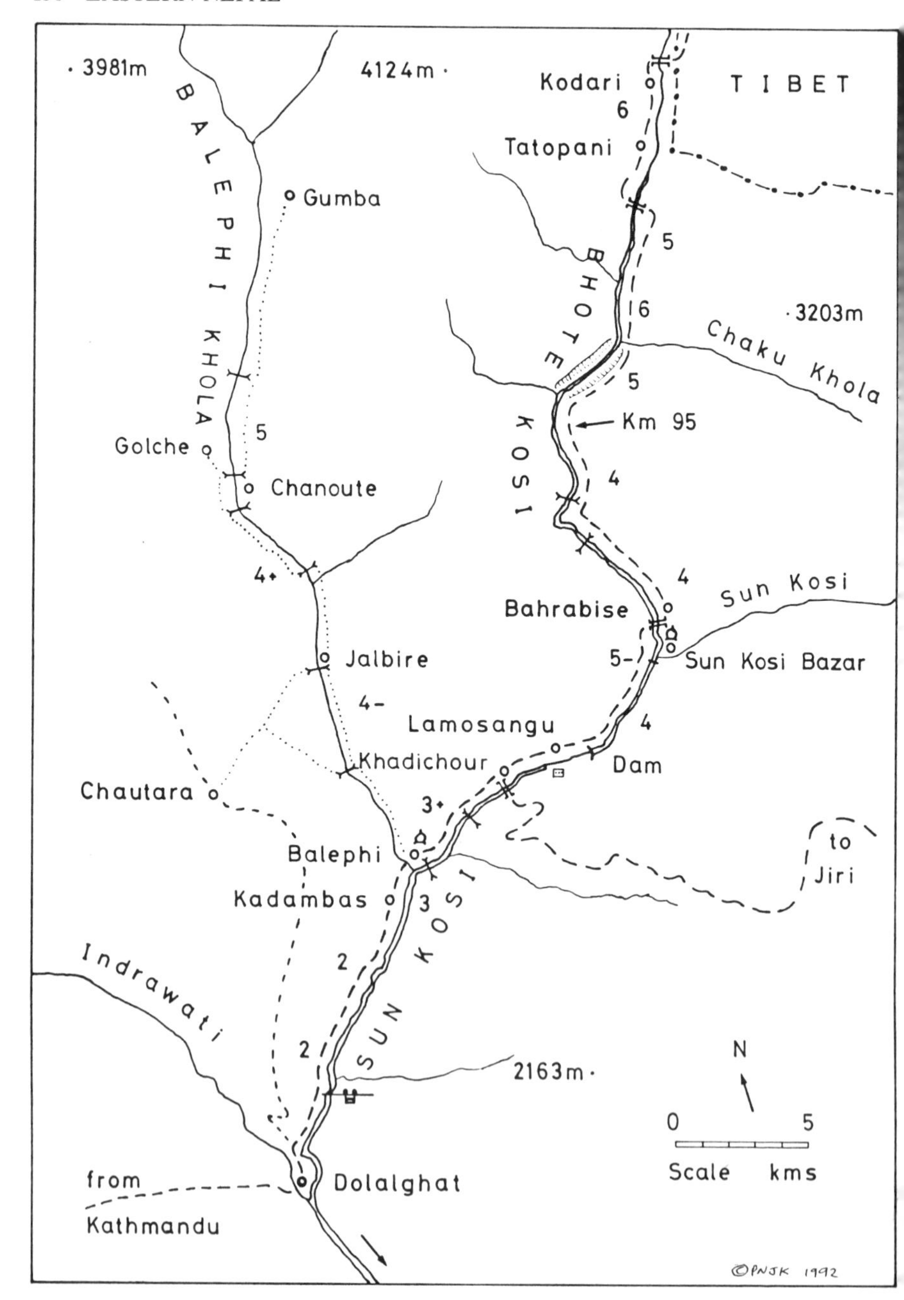

WARNING: Laser-phobic ink – do not photocopy.

Bhote Kosi

(includes the Upper Sun Kosi above Dolalghat)

Three separate and different day trips – see description section for summary of gradients etc.

Summary

A beautiful mountain river only a few hours from Kathmandu offering a relaxed day rafting or kayaking day trips at all classes of difficulty. Recommended for first time raft trips and all classes of Kayakers.

The River

'Bhote' roughly translates as 'river from Tibet' so there are quite a lot of rivers with this name in Nepal. This Bhote Kosi is the main branch of the Sun Kosi and it has been descended by kayak from near the Tibetan border at Kodari. The river is followed by the Arniko Highway from Kathmandu to Lhasa so access and scouting are relatively easy. The highway is normally blocked by landslides above Kodari so there is usually little traffic.

The river drops very steeply before Kodari as a youthful mountain torrent; then the gradient gradually eases off to become quite placid and relaxing before Dolalghat.

Technically, the Bhote Kosi ends just after Bahrabise where the **Sun Kosi** joins as a stream from the left: we have taken our description down to Dolalghat as this is where most Sun Kosi raft trips start.

The upper valley above Bahrabise is impressively steep and narrow, and there are some dramatic and scenic gorges down at river level. Just to drive up the highway and look at the the river is like reading an erotic novel – it quickens the blood and excites the mind!

A dam at Lamasangu takes water out of the river for a few kilometres but luckily has not spoilt the most beautiful sections of the river. The river below the dam is quite different – the section down to Dolalghat has well wooded sides and a wide blue river winding between white beaches.

Rafting

This is the river that rafting operators take VIP's on – it's a really pleasant half day trip, a blue river, a few small rapids and gleaming white beaches for barbecues. If you're not sure if you'd like rafting, this could be the ideal introductory trip for you. Many operators arrange an evening departure from Kathmandu, stay in one of the luxury lodges at **Dhulikhel** for a stunning view of sunrise over the Himalaya, then a relaxed morning's rafting on easy water – a few class 2 rapids to wet your appetite, then a gourmet barbecue and a couple of hours scenic drive back to Kathmandu.

In higher water, (Oct or May) Balephi or Khadichour become good starting points for an excellent class 3 day trip or as an extended start for a multi-day Sun Kosi trip.

Kayaking

The Bhote Kosi offers some great kayaking at most levels of difficulty – all very accessible from Kathmandu – this is the river that resident boaters hold their kayak clinics on. The river is relatively low volume and not too pushy, making for some fun kayaking – lots of boulder-garden type rapids, eddy moves, and play spots.

Further up the river, near Kodari, is water hard enough to challenge even the most masochistic of hair boaters. Most of the river can be relatively easily scouted from the highway that goes up the valley.

The river divides conveniently into four possible one day trips, that of course can easily be combined:

- Kodari to Lartza bridge – 6 kms, class 5 and 6.
- Lartza Bridge to highway km 95 – 11 kms, class 5.
- Highway Km 95 to Lamosangu – 18 kms, class 4 (5).
- Khadichour to Dolalghat – 20 kms, class 3.

These are summarised and detailed in the description section. Probably the most popular kayaking day trip is Khadichour to Dolalghat, but if you've got the necessary ability, Km 95 to Lamosangu is the most fun and would make a nice warm up on the way to the Tamba Kosi.

A particular hazard that we noticed were a few 'shark tooth' type rocks in the middle of wave trains at the bottom of rapids – so don't just gaily bounce down concentrating on the surfing potential!

Access and logistics

Dolalghat is about three hour's drive from Kathmandu, about another hour to Khadichour and a further two to Kodari. Bus to **Khadichour** would cost about $1 per head, private minibus about $70.

There are limited campsites on the upper river, but plenty of small lodges to stay or eat in at the towns along the highway. **Bahrabise** can be particularly recommended as a base for kayak trips. We have had two reports that some of the local people below Lamosangu are not as friendly as is normally the case in Nepal with minor incidents of stone throwing and petty thieving.

The upper river above Lamosangu is covered in fine detail on the Schneider 1:50,000 map, 'Lapchi Kang' or more cheaply on various trekking maps or the H.M.G. 1:125,000 Central Service Map for the Sindhupalchok District.

Description

From: **Kodari, Friendship Bridge** (Alt. 1650m)
To: **Lartza Bridge** (Alt. 1300m)
Distance: **6 kms** (4 miles)
River Days: **1**
From Kathmandu: 6 hours
Difficulty in Nov: **5–6**
Average gradient: **6%** (300 ft a mile)
Est. max. gradient: **10%**
Est. volume in Nov: 25 cumecs (900 cfs)
Best Season: **Nov-Dec, Mar-May.**

We have been told that the bottom 2 kms of this section have been kayaked, but we haven't managed to speak directly to anyone who has run it. If you're looking for some extremely steep and challenging 'hair-boating' reasonably close to Kathmandu, then this is it. May the Gods be with you!

From: **Lartza Bridge** (Alt. 1300m)
To: **Highway Km 95** (Alt. 960m)
Distance: **12 kms** (8 miles)
River Days: **1**
From Kathmandu: **6 hours**
Difficulty in Nov: **4–5** (6)
Average gradient: 3.0% (150 ft a mile)
Est. max. gradient: **6%**
Est. volume in Nov: **30 cumecs** (1000 cfs)
Best Season: **Nov-Dec, Mar-May.**

This section from Lartza Bridge has a slightly more reasonable gradient and has certainly been run – although we ourselves have not done it. The Australian Sun Kosi Expedition of 1981 ran the river from here. More recently, Guy Robbins also started from here and describes it as some fairly solid class 5 boating with one long class 6 rapid (portages) about 2 kms above the Chaku Khola. The road is fairly close to the river for the first 6 kms, up to where the Chaku Khola comes in on the left. Below here is a sheer-sided beautiful gorge of Mica-schist and limestone, with the road running along the top of the cliffs, a hundred metres or so above the river. Those who have done it describe it as 'a great paddle, hard and committing in a stupendous setting'. The road drops down to the river near km sign 95 and this makes a convenient and easy take-out.

From:	**Highway km 95** (Alt. 960m)
To:	**Lamosangu** (Alt. 700m)
Distance:	**18 kms** (11 miles)
River Days:	1
From Kathmandu:	**5 hours**
Difficulty in Nov:	**4** (5)
Average gradient:	**1.5%** (75 ft a mile)
Est. max. gradient:	**3%**
Est. volume in Nov:	**40 cumecs** (1200 cfs)
Best Season:	**Nov-Dec, Mar-May.**

Most of this paddling is class 4−; but there are several rapids before Bahrabise that merit scouting and possibly a 4+ rating. The rapids are mainly boulder gardens, some fun drops, and we managed to scout most of the rapids by careful eddy hopping. Guy Robbins ran this section in early October and reckoned that it was 'awesome boating' and one class harder.

Bahrabise is an interesting, friendly old village, of mainly Tibetan families. About a kilometre down stream from the bridge and town is a picturesque temple and pleasant grassy campsite on the left bank. Shortly after this is the confluence with the **Sun Kosi** and this has brought down a boulder flow that extends for at least a kilometre creating an interesting and testing series of rapids, mainly 4+ but one class 5. Sun Kosi Bazar, the village at the confluence, looks as if it would be an interesting old village to explore.

The river continues at class 4− level with some good play spots for surfing and rodeo artistes. At the Dam, take care to keep right (just in case the sluice gates are open – glug, glug, help!) and take out where the track comes down to the river. A minute's walk brings you out at the bus stop under a nice shady Banyan tree.

If you are continuing on past here, then the portage past the sluice gates will take about five minutes, but you may need to portage again because because most of the water has been taken by the diversion channel.

From:	**Khadichour** (Alt. 670m)
To:	**Dolalghat** (Alt. 620m)
Distance:	**20 kms** (13 miles)
River Days:	**1**
From Kathmandu:	**4 hours**
Difficulty in Nov:	**Class 3+** (lower section: class 2)
Average gradient:	**0.25%** (12ft a mile)
Est. max. gradient:	**1.0%**
Volume in Nov:	**90 cumecs** (3200 cfs)
Best Season:	**Nov-Dec, Feb-May.**

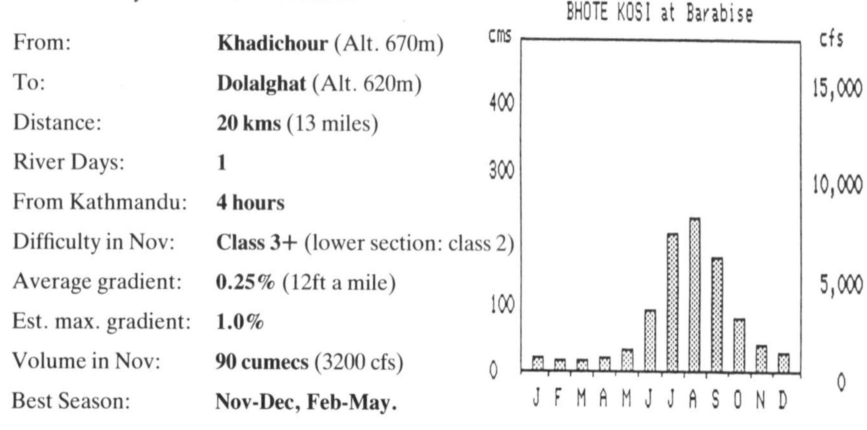

"...It looked a grade III from the bridge..."

This is a popular and fun section for everybody. The full section is best rafted in medium water flows. It's a blast of a trip in post- monsoon run-off (then class 4, for experts only). At low water levels it gets a bit too rocky for rafting so a start lower down below Balephi is better. Kayakers will enjoy this trip as a great warm-up day, lots of good play spots for practising technique and posing for the photographer.

Best put-in is on the left bank below the road bridge at **Khadichour**. A small gorge shortly after Khadichour adds scenic variety and whitewater interest (class 3+). There are several class 3 rapids down to **Balephi**, where it is worth a stop to look at the temple. The Balephi river adds a useful amount of water to the river and makes for some slightly bigger bouncy class 3 rapids down to below **Khadambas**. From here down there is time to to relax and admire the scenery – this bit of the river seems remarkably unspoilt with its steep forested banks and white beaches.

Don't relax too much so that you drift past the take-out on the right bank just at and above where the Indrawati river comes in – next road access 270 kms!

Marsyandi (Arlene Burns)

Balephi Khola

From information supplied by Guy Robins.

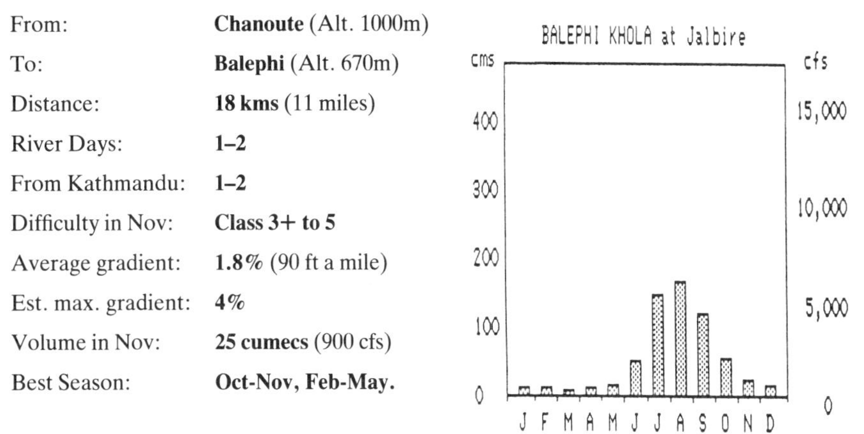

From: **Chanoute** (Alt. 1000m)
To: **Balephi** (Alt. 670m)
Distance: **18 kms** (11 miles)
River Days: **1–2**
From Kathmandu: **1–2**
Difficulty in Nov: **Class 3+ to 5**
Average gradient: **1.8%** (90 ft a mile)
Est. max. gradient: **4%**
Volume in Nov: **25 cumecs** (900 cfs)
Best Season: **Oct-Nov, Feb-May.**

Summary

A short, fun, kayaking trip, close to Kathmandu with the feel of a mini expedition: blue water, boulder-garden rapids, an unspoilt valley and good mountain views. A choice of starts gives different levels of difficulty.

The River

Please see the Bhote Kosi for a map of the river.

The Balephi Khola is one of the smaller tributaries of the Sun Kosi, joining that river a short distance upstream of Dolalghat and only 50 kms from Kathmandu. The river rises on the south ern slopes of Dorje Lakpa, 6990 metres, one of the mountains to the north east of Kathmandu and at the head of the Langtang Valley. It runs to the east of the Helambu region as a fairly typical, fast flowing Himalayan River, with steep valley sides.

The Balephi valley is off most trekking routes and ignored by guide books so is relatively unspoilt with picturesque villages and industrious, friendly people who call themselves Sherpas, but who in fact, are a separate tribe from those of the Khumbu region.

The river has a fairly typical longitudinal profile, very steep near its source, about 8.0% from Gumba, then 2.5% from Chanoute (class 4+), and finally easing off to 1.0% from Jalbire (class 3+).

Rafting

This cannot be recommended for rafting, being small volume, tight and technical.

Kayaking

Although the Balephi Khola is close to Kathmandu, to our knowledge only two groups have been on this river, but we think that it is bound to get more popular. Guy Robbins says, 'If you're up in the Bhote Khosi drainage, this is definitely worth the trip'. It combines some good paddling, a short trek and overnight stay, so offers a good introduction to self-sufficient kayaking in Nepal to anyone who is new to the country.

Guy Robbins and his partner Charlie Munsey put in a couple of kms above Chanoute just below a small village on the river left bank called Manghe. He says, 'You are immediately into class 4 to 5+ white water. It is a lot steeper up here and you will need to eddy hopp and scout well. There are some things you will want to check out and probably portage.'

The alternative starting point for a fine class 3+ (4−) run is at **Jalbire**. This is described as 'a boulder-garden type river with great playing'. As a general guide on river level, Guy says, 'If there looks like enough water at Balephi, then you'll be fine higher up'.

There is potential for some hard kayaking further up than Chanoute, but Guy reports a singularly unfriendly Police checkpost near the village of Pangtang, so make sure you have the right permits if you decide to go up this far.

Access and logistics

Balephi is about 4 hours by road from Kathmandu, about $1 by bus, or $30 for a taxi. Porters are readily available here for about $3 a day and there is a good trail up the valley (there used to be a jeep road). The trek to **Jalbire** should take about 3-4 hours depending on the enthusiasm of your porters. There are a couple of tea houses in the village for dal bhat and a roof for the night.

This river could be done as a two day trip from Kathmandu; travel from Kathmandu and trek into Jalbire on the first day, kayak down to Balephi the following morning and then return to Kathmandu in the late afternoon. This is probably best done by hiring a taxi for the two days and asking the driver to wait for you at Balephi.

Description

Chanoute to Jalbire 8 kms, Balephi 10.

The river can be scouted as you trek up the valley, so you can make your own decision about where to start kayaking.

Guy Robbins suggests that if you don't want to trek all the way to **Chanoute**, then a good place to put in would be the bridge some 3 kms above Jalbire. The District Medical Assistant lives in a blue house on the left of the trail after crossing the bridge and speaks excellent English. This would provide an exciting start to the run and probaby no portages.

Starting above Chanoute will give you harder kayaking and some portages will probably be required – a trip for the expert paddler.

Putting in at the bridge at **Jalbire** would give you a mainly class 3+ run, with a few rapids at a 4− level. Guy says to note 'the Room of Doom' on the left and just upstream of the old bridge below Jalbire. Just underneath this old bridge is a river gauge on the downstream side of a rock outcrop on the right – Guy reports that it was 1.0 metres when they ran the river in the first week of October.

Take-out is possible at **Balephi**, but if you have the time we suggest that you continue down the Sun Kosi for a little way to enjoy surfing the play waves on this bigger water – please see the 'Bhote Kosi' for a description of this run.

Indrawati

From:	**Sipaghat** (Alt. 730m)
To:	**Dolalghat** (Alt. 620m)
Distance:	**19 kms** (12 miles)
River Days:	**one** (4 hours)
From Kathmandu:	**2–3 hours**
Difficulty in Nov:	**Class 1-2**
Average gradient:	**0.6%** (30 ft a mile)
Est. max. gradient:	**0.8%**
Est. volume in Nov:	**40 cumecs** (1400 cfs)
Best Season:	**Oct-Dec, Feb-May.**

Summary

A small volume, easy river with unspoilt villages, warm water and easy access from Kathmandu. A pleasant float trip with numerous small rapids and a helpful current; this is an excellent river for beginner kayakers or for small inflatable 'Duckies'.

The River

The Indrawati drains the Helambu trekking region, the valleys to the north east of Kathmandu. Most of the rafting trips down the famous Sun Kosi actually put in on the Indrawati but in the past we have always ignored this river because it appeared flat and uninteresting at this point. Well, we were wrong! It actually has a surpising gradient and is an enjoyable and scenic river.

The river flows in a wide valley surrounded by small villages and fields of various crops. It meanders in a wide gravel bed, but has a surprisingly constant gradient which creates a series of small chutes and waves – straight forward, but lots of fun. The road leaves the valley and the river is peaceful and unspoilt. No trekkers or tourists have been here to teach the 'one pen' mantra to local children.

We have suggested **Sipaghat** as the starting point as this makes a convenient distance for a one day trip out from Kathmandu, but if you want a slightly longer trip then the road extends another 6 kms to Bahunepate and this section of the river has the same character as further downstream.

Rafting

Shallow braided rapids and ledges created for fishing make this unsuitable for rafting except at higher flows (e.g. in Sept/Oct) when it could make a good link up with a Helambu trek and or a continuation down the Sun Kosi.

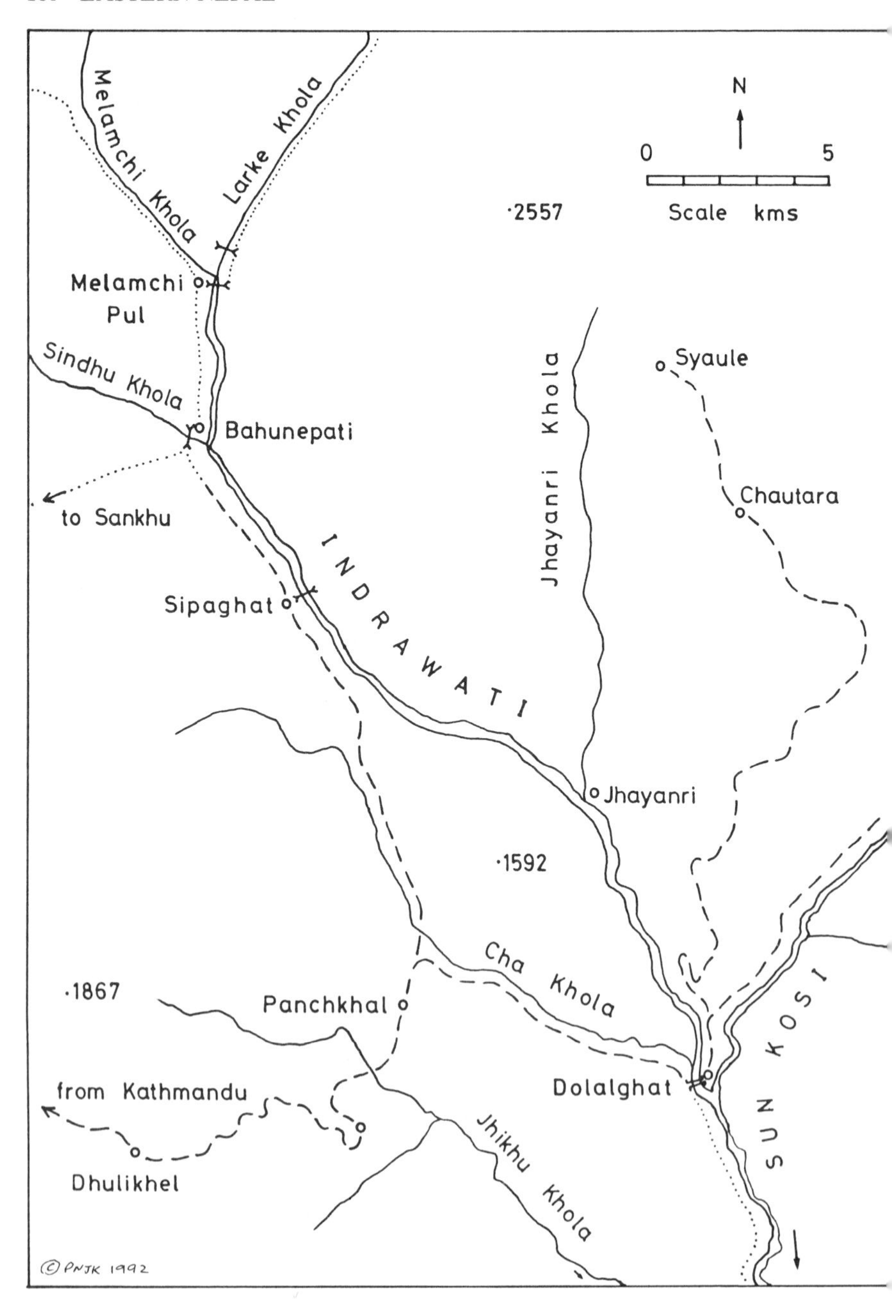

WARNING: Laser-phobic ink – do not photocopy.

Kayaking

We think that 'this is one of the best beginner rivers we have seen'. It has a helpful current, numerous small rapids, well-defined eddies and clean eddy lines. The lower volume of this river means that you don't get the pushy water and boiling eddy lines that you get on bigger rivers – a real confidence booster for the novice paddler.

This is the ideal 'first trip' for a beginner and could be combined with a next day trip on the Bhote Kosi.

For the more expert paddler, we believe that there is probably at least another day of more difficult kayaking upstream on both the Melamchi Khola and Larke Khola (both tributaries are probably waiting first descents.......). Although the road finishes at Bahunepati, Stephen Bezrucha suggests that jeeps have made it for some way up the Melamchi valley.

Access and logistics

Sipaghat, the suggested start point, is about two and a half hours taxi ride from Kathmandu; to hire a taxi for the day would cost about $35 and this would then meet you at Dolalghat (about 3 hours back to Kathmandu). A private minibus would cost about $60 – perhaps think about some mountain bikes for the exhilarating descent from **Dhulikhel**?

Most people would probably opt to make this a day trip from Kathmandu. We suggest an early start and breakfast at the 'Sun and Snow' lodge in Dhulikhel with its magnificent vista of the Himalaya. If you do want to make this an overnight trip there are plenty of scenic beaches for camping, but little firewood.

We mentioned the possibilty of linking this river trip in at the end of a Helambu trek: another option is a one day trek from the rim of the Kathmandu valley – either Sankhu or Nagarkhot – a potentially adventurous mountain bike ride?

Best map of the Indrawati is probably the Blue Central services map at a scale of 1:125,000 for either Sindhupalchok or Kabhrepalanchok the districts to the North and South of the river.

Description

The suspension bridge at **Sipaghat** makes an obvious put-in point. Below here the river leaves the road behind and is very peaceful. When we did this trip in early May there were lots of fisherman and children swimming in the warm water. No tourists come this way and the local boys must have the world record for waving and shouting 'namaste' as they run along the river bank leaping from rock to rock.

The river winds and braids on a wide gravel plain so you can play a betting game as to which is the best channel to take – when in doubt, to take the one with the most flow seems to work. There are several places where ledges or dams have been built across the river to channel the water into fish traps. These should be treated with respect and caution – It might make quite a good yarn 'when I was caught in this fish trap in the Himalaya'?

The Jhayanri Khola coming in on the left marks the half way point. Below here the river stays mainly in one channel, the gradient appears to ease a little and the rapids are further apart. The last few kms to **Dolalghat** are relatively flat. Best take-out is on the right before the bridge.

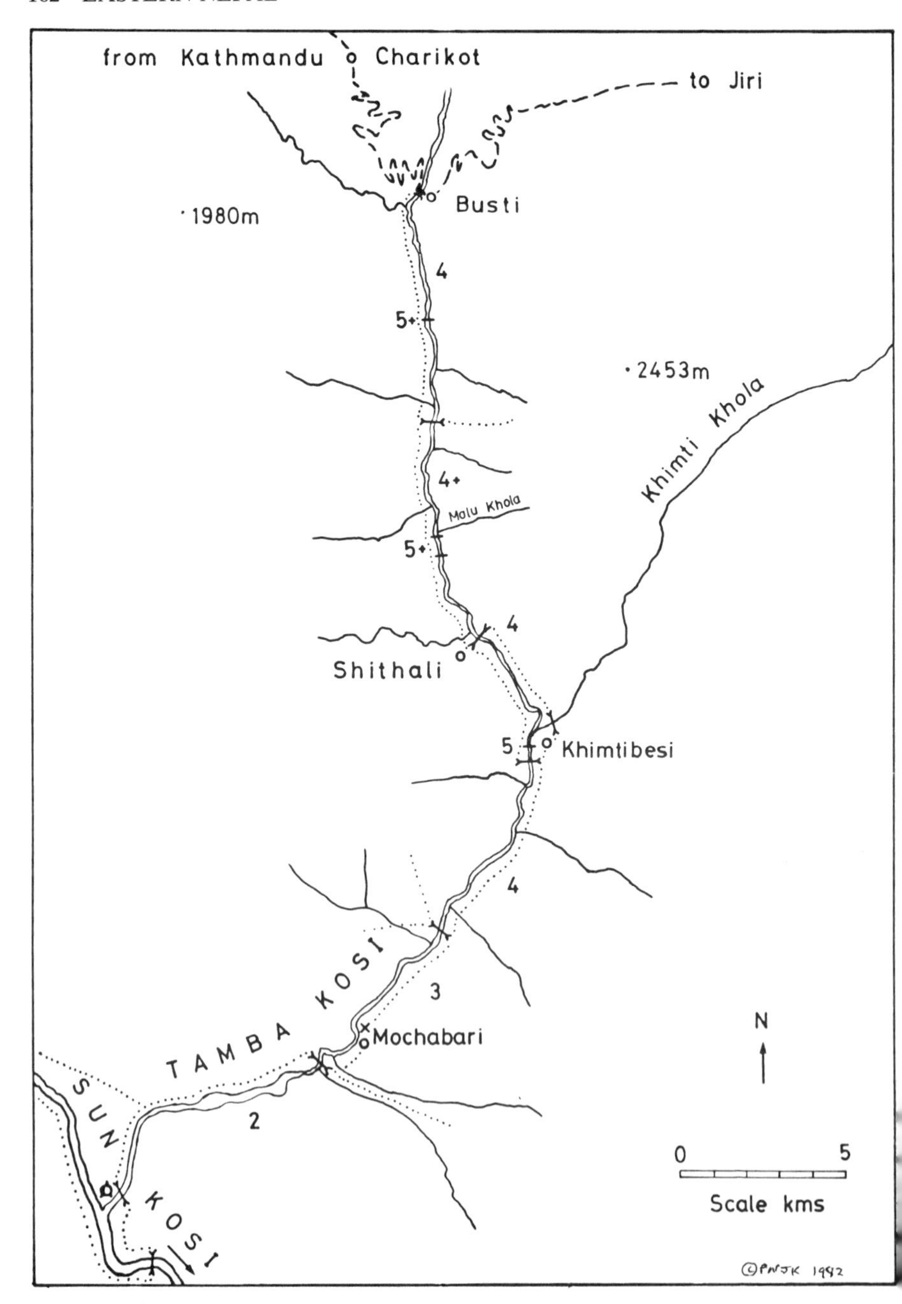

WARNING: Laser-phobic ink – do not photocopy.

Tamba Kosi

From:	**Busti** (Alt. 840m)
To:	**Sun Kosi** (Alt. 465m)
Distance:	**42 Kms** (26 miles)
River days:	**2**
Difficulty in Nov:	**Class 4+** (5+)
From Kathmandu:	**7 hours**
Average gradient:	**0.9%** (45ft a mile)
Est. max. gradient:	**4**.0%
Volume in Nov:	**80 cumecs** (2800 cfs)
Best Season:	**Nov/Dec or April/May**

Summary

An exhilarating white water challenge, fine scenery, away from main trekking routes yet easily accessible. Probably the best trip of this length and difficulty in Nepal – not to be undertaken lightly!

Recommended for Expert Kayakers.

The River

The Tamba Kosi is no mere side stream of the Sun Kosi – it's a substantial river with a volume twice that of its near neighbour the Bhote Kosi (the Upper Sun Kosi). The river rises in Tibet and flows for some 75 kms before meeting the road at Busti, the usual starting point.

The Tamba Kosi is usually run by expert kayakers looking for a more difficult and interesting alternative start to the Sun Kosi. Note that there is almost no warm up on this river – you are straight into class 4, continuous, powerful water. There are long rapids with some bad holes – only in the last few kilometres does the river ease off – this is probably NOT the river to do straight off the plane!

Tamba Kosi translates literally as 'River of Copper', but it is also known as 'the River of Sorrow'. During the reign of King Ranabahadur a smallpox epidemic led him to expel the common people from Kathmandu to the shores of this river. There remains in the local Newari language a lament called Sitalamaju which describes their arduous journey and their sorrow as their children died from the smallpox.

It has also been a river of sorrow for the few raft groups who have attempted it, having their own arduous journey carrying rafts and equipment around long stretches of rapids.

Rafting

This river could be rafted by an expert team at the right water level, but it would be a serious undertaking involving some hard portages – probably not most people's idea of an enjoyable trip. It might be suitable for an expert in a catamaran rig.

One of the few raft attempts was by an American team in October/November 1985. It is said that they had a major epic involving injury, loss of raft and equipment, and the curtailing of their Sun Kosi trip. A French team attempted a raft descent in late October 1990 and talked about 'Labours of Hercules' carrying the rafts and 'Mental exhaustion'.

Kayaking

For the expert Kayaker this is a great river: everyone I have spoken to comments on the river with enthusiasm and respect:

- *'A great paddle'*
- *'A lot of fun if you don't freak out'*
- *'The great thing (in low water) was scouting from the boat'*
- *'Like good sex' (this from a woman!)*
- *'A swim would be very serious – you'd be lucky to get the swimmer, let alone the boat'*

This is a river that is best done at low water levels – we ran the river in Early November and at this level the harder sections were daunting with few eddies and class 5 rapids leading staight into continuous class 4+ water. We had to do a lot of scouting from the bank and some longish portages. A month later and the river has more eddies – still hard enough to satisfy all but the most masochistic hair boater, but mainly scoutable from the eddies and only a few short portages. January to March would be too cold for most boaters, but local experts reckon that April or May would be 'perfectamundo'.

Most groups who do the river portage some of the rapids, but all the rapids have in fact been run – in the right conditions, and by some of the World's best boaters! Although Busti is the usual starting point, the river is probably feasible from some 40kms upstream, below the village of Lamabagar at an altitude of 1200 metres. People who have trekked up the river say that it looks pretty flat and class 2 or 3 for the first 20 kms or so above Charikot.

Access and logistics

The usual starting point is **Busti** bridge on the highway to Jiri, a few kms past **Charikot**. This is about 7 hour's bus ride from Kathmandu, cost about $2. A private minibus would cost about $150. Charikot has a reasonably-sized bazar for such staples as beer and glucose biscuits.

Most groups running the Tamba Kosi continue on down the Sun Kosi (see separate description) and arrange to meet a commercial raft trip so that they have light kayaks for playing the rapids on the Sun Kosi – not to mention the good food, and social pleasures of a raft trip! A fast lightweight kayak trip could probably continue down the rest of the Sun Kosi in about another 4-6 kayak days.

If your time is limited and you don't want to run the Sun Kosi then there are several options: to trek or paddle up the Sun Kosi to Dolalghat, 3 days? : trek back up the Tamba Kosi, 2 days?: or trek out south to Sindhulimadi, 1-2 days, and catch a night bus back to Kathmandu. Don Weeden, one of the pioneer kayakers in Nepal was working here on an Aid project and actually used a kayak to travel between the villages. He suggests the possibility of flying out from the airstrip at **Mochabari** (Akase) near the bottom of the river.

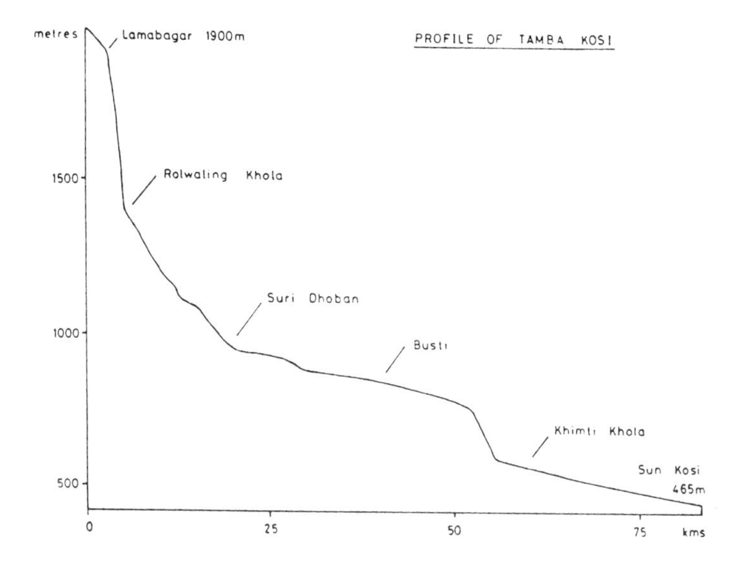

According to Don there are several interesting villages near the river and a small group should be able to eat and stay overnight in tea houses if they wished – some knowledge of Nepalese would be helpful!

Best map of this river is the Schneider 1:50,000 'Tamba Kosi'.

Description

Busti to Khimtibesi 19 kms, Mochabari 12, Sun Kosi 11.

Put in just over the bridge on the downstream left bank. If you have arrived late, there is a campsite about 1 km down on the right bank where the Charnawati comes in. 5 kms of continuous class 4 rapids lead to a harder class 4+ rapid on a left hand bend: this is warning of a class 5 rapid 'Seal Launch City' in the next kilometre – this can be portaged right if necessary, with a nice seal launch re-entry.

Another 6 or 7 kms of continuous class 4+ leads to two more class 5 rapids 'Hudson to the left' and 'Master Blaster' within a kilometre of each other – the first of these is where the Malu Khola comes in from the left, pre-warned by a steep hill close to the river also on the left. These can be portaged on the right if necessary.

Another 7 kms of magnificent class 4 water continues past Shithali bridge and to the confluence of the **Khimti Khola**. Very shortly after is the fourth big class 5 rapid 'Fatal Attraction'; again this can be portaged right if necessary.

Class 4 water continues, but now the rapids are more pressure orientated, with lots of fun haystacks and waves to play on. The water gradually becomes less difficult until it is class 3 down to **Mochabari** (Akase airstrip is close to the river on the left bank). Easy water and a scenic wooded gorge leads the last few kms to the Sun Kosi – don't miss the beach at the confluence on the right.

Time for congratulations and a beer!

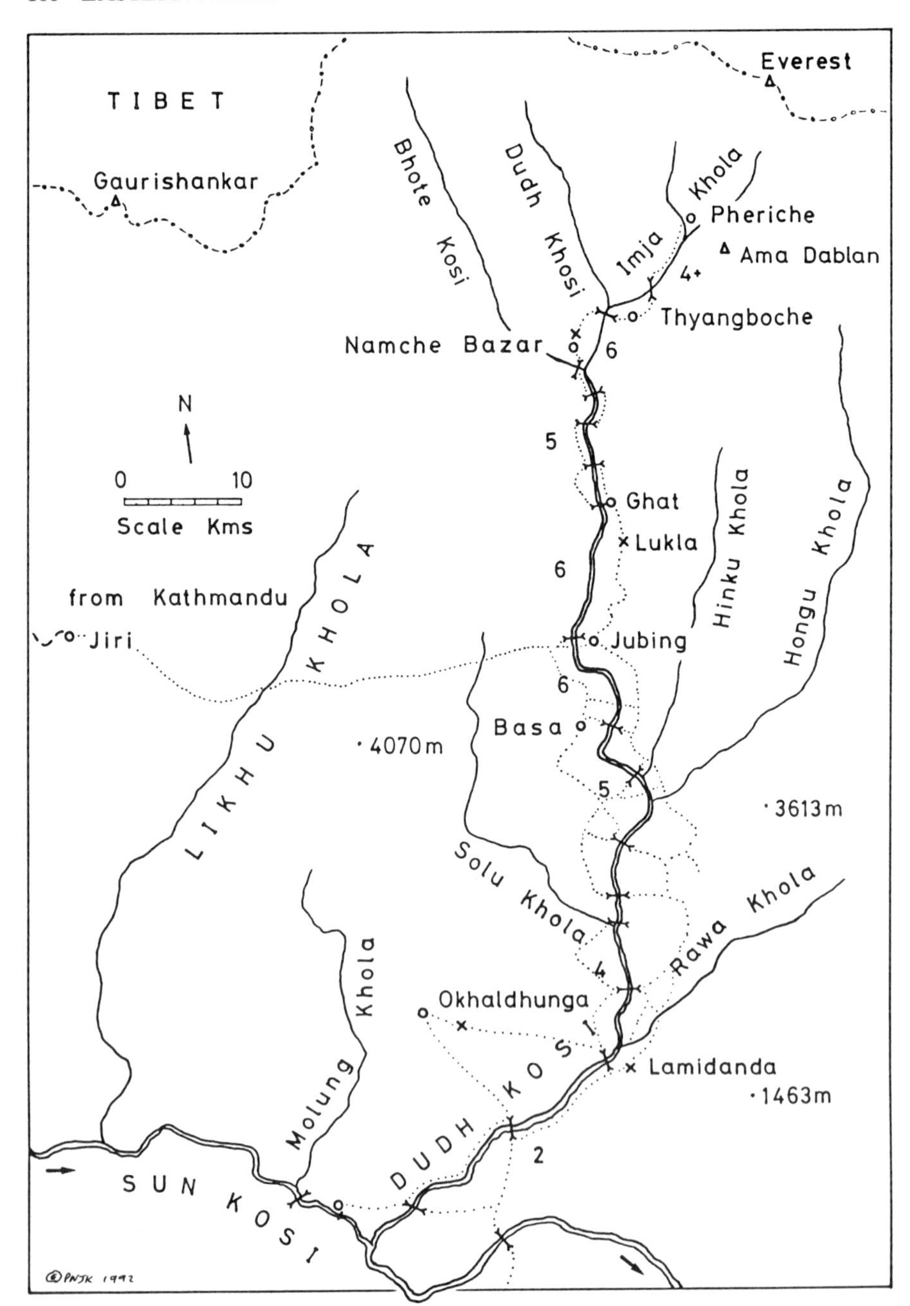

WARNING: Laser-phobic ink – do not photocopy.

Dudh Kosi

From information supplied by Roger Huyton, Mick Hopkinson, Mike Hewlett, Mick Coyne, John Taylor and others.

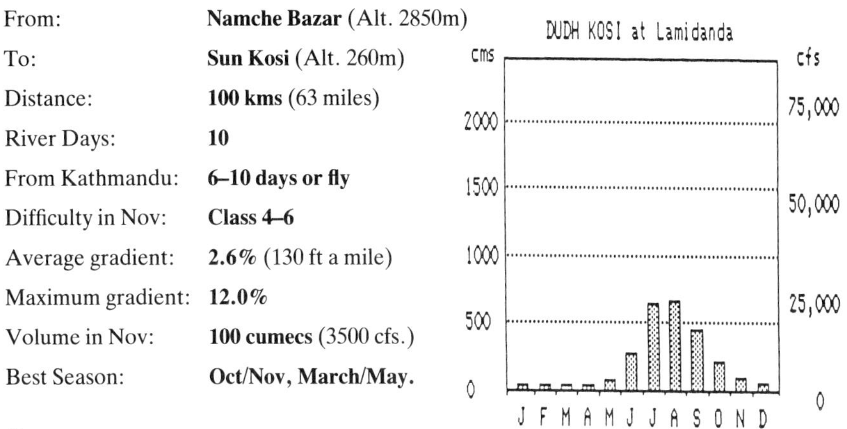

From:	**Namche Bazar** (Alt. 2850m)
To:	**Sun Kosi** (Alt. 260m)
Distance:	**100 kms** (63 miles)
River Days:	**10**
From Kathmandu:	**6–10 days or fly**
Difficulty in Nov:	**Class 4–6**
Average gradient:	**2.6%** (130 ft a mile)
Maximum gradient:	**12.0%**
Volume in Nov:	**100 cumecs** (3500 cfs.)
Best Season:	**Oct/Nov, March/May.**

Summary

A 'steep rock-infested ditch' with only fame to recommend it.

The River

The Dudh Kosi has been called the 'Relentless river of Everest', a convenient label, but not true. If you look on a school atlas, the river is shown as rising on Everest and draining south to the Sun Kosi. Unfortunately, it is not the Dudh Kosi itself, but one of its tributaries, the Imja Khola, that actually starts from the Khumbu Glacier. This is one of four glaciers that start on the mountain; the other three drain to tributaries of the Arun, a much more powerful river, that has an equal and argueably stronger claim to be the river of the mountain.

The Dudh Kosi has become well known as the river of Everest because it is on the main trail to Everest Base Camp and so tens of thousands of trekkers and mountaineers have walked along part of it and also, of course, because of kayaking films and books.

Where the trekking trail comes close to the river between Ghat and Namche Bazar the gradient is steep but reasonable. This is deceptive though; the majority of the upper river is very steep with a gradient of up to 12% (600 ft a mile) flowing in a deep gorge with the trail a long way above. If you take a glance at the river profile, you will see what we mean. Downstream from Basa (and south of the main trekking route) the gradient becomes more reasonable and just before Lamidanda the river becomes almost flat for the last 33 kms.

The Dudh Kosi has seen several huge floods that have scoured out the river bed and washed away the usual rounded, water-worn boulders; leaving instead jagged glacial debris all the way down the river – hence the derogatory but perhaps apt description 'rock-infested ditch' that has been coined by those who have kayaked it.

These floods have mainly been caused by **'GLOFs'** – glacial lake outburst floods. A fairly recent one in August 1985 had a flow of 11,600 cumecs, 17 times the average flow in August. A ten metre high tidal wave of water, mud and debris crushed houses, swept away bridges, removed whole fields, and gouged out a a new river channel: those who had kayaked the river in 1976 didn't recognise it when they returned ten years later.

Expeditions

The Dudh Kosi is famous for the several expeditions that have attempted it. Most famous of these, was a group of British Kayakers in 1976 led by **Dr Mike Jones**. The film, made by Leo Dickinson, has become an outdoor adventure classic that has thrilled and inspired people to try the sport of white water kayaking. In Britain, it changed the layman's image of kayaking and encouraged a whole new generation to take up the sport. It won several prestigious awards for adventure and sporting films and has been shown in most countries of the world – there can be few kayakers who have not seen it and been impressed by the skill, courage and humour of the kayaking team. This film also did a great deal to open people's eyes to the potential and excitement of Himalayan river running. Mike Jone's book about the expedition 'Canoeing down Everest' went to two editions, was translated to German, and has sold 10,000 copies todate.

This 1976 expedition wasn't in fact the first one: a Czechoslavakian team put in at Pheriche (on the the Imje Khola) in April 1973. They ran some of the river down to Ghat and the lower river from Lamidanda. The 1976 expedition was primarily to make a film and constrained by time: they ran a very short section above Namche Bazar (perhaps one km?), most of the section from Namche to Ghat (say another 8 kms) and another two kms at Jubing. Mike Jones and Mick Hopkinson kayaked the last 32 kms of flat water down to the Sun Kosi.

Several attempts have been made on the river since 1976 by different teams, all successful in their own measure. One of the more interesting attempts was a French man who swam down part of the river.

Ten years after the 1976 expedition, Mick Coyne led another British team on a return attempt. The object was to run as much of the river as was feasible, and again to make a film. The team also took microlights for aerial views of Everest and the river: the film was aptly titled 'Thin air, white water' (affectionately nicknamed by friends as 'Thin hair, white knuckles'). For kayakers, it is interesting to see the advances in equipment and technique that had occurred in ten years – the 1976 team used long, fibreglass slalom boats: the 1986 team had short polyethylene rotobats. It was nice to see that one of the stars of the 1986 team, Roger Huyton, was a veteran from the the earlier trip.

Roger recounts how on this more recent trip 'Our Sirdar told me he was talking to the owner of a tea house who said that ten years ago 'other people came down the river – they were like gods – they had big muscles and nothing could kill them'. Maybe I looked too decrepit for Lakpa, our Sirdar, to point out that I was one of them!' The 1986 expedition paddled the 12 kms of the Imja Khola and then the Dudh Kosi from Namche to Ghat. After an abortive attempt below Jubing the team of six put in near Basa and did the remaining 86 kms of the river without shore support – most of this section is deep in a gorge and as Roger Huyton puts it 'there wasn't anyone to hear our screams'!

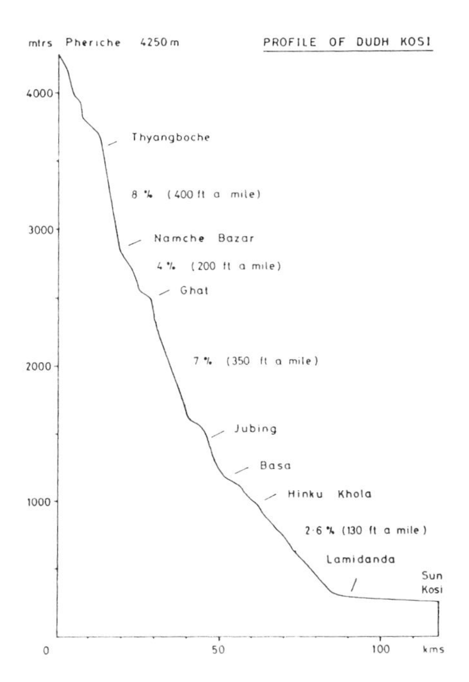

Rafting

Only the bottom 32 kms of the Dudh Kosi **from Lamidanda** can be recommended for recreational rafting.

Above Lamidanda, small rafts have made it down some sections of the river, but portages are reported as extremely difficult and note that people have all commented about the sharp and jagged rocks and generally unpleasant nature of the actual river bed.

It seems quite a reasonable idea to start a Sun Kosi trip by flying into Lamidanda, rafting the bottom 32 kms of the Dudh Kosi and so to then continue down the last half of the Sun Kosi. This would give something like a 6 day raft trip instead of the usual 9 day Sun Kosi trip – however you would miss out some of the best rapids on the Sun Kosi that are above the Dudh Kosi confluence.

Kayaking

No one, who has run this river and to whom we have spoken, recommends it! It could be that they want to maintain a certain mystique about the river – but read on ......

If your interest is recreational paddling, then this is probably the last river you should select; the message from every one we have spoken to is that this river is difficult and expensive to get to, and isn't either satisfying or much fun to paddle – Nepal has many, many challenging rivers that you should first consider. If you have the time, money, experience, and enthusiasm for 'an expedition' why not do a river that is still awaiting a first descent? or one of the more remote longer rivers like the Karnali? If you are wanting to test your paddling skills to the technical limit – why not choose a river nearer home, hospital and undertaker?

On the positive side: this is a wonderful area with beautiful scenery; as one person put it: 'I was besotted with the valley – I yearn to go back'. We can see the appeal of being able to say that you have trekked into Everest and then kayaked down the river, but in terms of paddling, scenery and logistics the trek into Annapurna Sanctuary and down the Modi Khola is a much better trip. If you do decide to combine a trek with a kayak trip on the Dudh Kosi, we think you need to be quite realistic about the difficulty, dangers, logistical problems and substantial costs.

The first problem is where to start kayaking: The majority of the upper river is extremely steep and hasn't been paddled – remember that almost all the impressive sequences you see on the films were shot on 'easier' sections. Even these easier sections have a lot of class 5 and 6 rapids and portages. This is also high altitude where every move is more tiring and difficult. If you put in at **Namche** there is only some 10 kms of enjoyable paddling 'a real buzz' down to Ghat. After that, its 7% gradient, class 5, 6 and impossible and at the bottom of deep awesome gorges.

A reasonable option might be to leave the boats at Jubing on the trek in; then to collect them here on the way down the valley and start kayaking near **Basa**. From here to Lamidanda is an average gradient of 2.6% (130 ft a mile) and is reported by those who have done it as class 4 and 5 with difficult portages – demanding and committing (at the bottom of a 500m gorge) but feasible.

Best time to do this river is debateable: normally a steep and medium volume river like this would be better in low water levels. However those who have done the river reckon that in low water it would be 'bloody awful – just chockful of sharp rocks'; so you are probably better with a reasonable flow, ideally the end of October?

Mike couldn't understand why they had run short of food, but John had his suspicions.

Access and logistics

It is normally reckoned that the trek into **Namche Bazar** takes 9 days from Kathmandu (allow half a day for a porter 'strike' at Khari Khola!). Flying into Lukla is the other alternative, but either way of transporting boats and equipment to the river is expensive.

If you are intending to kayak parts of the upper river, then you will almost certainly want a team of porters to carry your equipment and perhaps boats. You will perhaps also feel that this river merits a shore support group with climbing and rescue skills? You should consider and plan for the effects of altitude.

Probably most paddlers would view the upper river as 'an expedition' and we would recommend that you contract the logistics out to a reliable trekking agency. You will almost certainly need a special expedition permit and Liaison Officer if you are attempting this upper river – more cost to be budgetted for.

A trip starting near **Basa**, should logistically be easier and cheaper – this is only about 6 days from Kathmandu. An experienced group of expert kayakers could be self-supporting from here, although it might be tempting to try to arrange a food and spares dump further down the river. Until Lamidanda, there are almost no paths or villages near the river because it runs in a deep gorge although paths do drop down to cross the river every few kms. This is best planned as a self-contained trip.

We recommend that you carry on down the Sun Kosi, a 3 or 4 day trip that can easily be done as a self-supported trip. Most paddlers though, after an arduous trip down the Dudh Kosi, would probably prefer to have a raft meet them at the confluence with good food, beer and other comforts and then to holiday and relax down the last half of the Sun Kosi.

If you are planning a trip then we recommend that you buy the three Schneider maps that cover the river above Lamidanda at a scale of 1:50,000 : Khumbu Himal, Shorung/Hinku and Dudh Kosi. The river below Lamidanda is covered at a scale of 1:125,000 on the HMG Central Service Map of Okhaldhunga District.

Description

Namche to Ghat 10 kms, Basa 24, Lamidanda 34, Sun Kosi 32.

Pheriche to Pangboche is about 6 kms and is described as mainly class 4+ with a few class 5 drops and portages. In 1986 there was even a small lake on this section, where the Nare Khola comes in off Ama Dablan. Below Pangboche there is a class 5-6 gorge down to Thyangboche bridge and another gorge at the same standard down to Namche Bazar. Mike Hewlett ran the first bit of this solo: described as 'a brilliant paddle' by Mick Coyne but Mike says 'I hated it'!

From **'Namche Steps'** down to Ghat is described as an enjoyable and challenging class 4-5 paddle, with a few portages, much scouting, and probably taking about 3 days to paddle the 10 kms. The main trekking trail is reasonably close to the river and there are plenty of tea houses.

After **Ghat** the gradient steepens, the trail leaves the river which drops into an awesome gorge with at least one 30 metre waterfall – Mike Hewlett says 'nothing would tempt me there'. The valley opens out a little upstream of **Jubing**, but the gorge starts again shortly after the village. The 1986 trip put in again here, but had an 'epic' doing one kilometre in two days and sensibly hired porters to carry the boats further down the valley. Mick Coyne says 'We were lucky we didn't lose anyone'; Roger Huyton summed it up as 'Bloody awful'. Any reader fancy a first descent of this bit?

Some 5 or 6 kms below Jubing the trail to **Basa** crosses the river and below here the gradient eases to a slightly more reasonable 2.6% (130 ft a mile). This is where the 1986 team put back onto the river. This section was not filmed but proved to be some good class 4-5 kayaking with loaded boats. Mick Coyne wrote about it: 'Four of us swam and the portages were often as intense as the kayaking. On several occasions it took two hours, much climbing skill, blood and sweat to move twenty metres'. Roger Huyton described it: ' We were deep in this gorge, exhilarating but risky paddling and I was thinking 'There's no one to hear us scream!'.

Unfortunately there are few views of the mountains because you are in such a deep valley. This lower part of the Dudh Kosi is off the main trekking route and villages are friendly and unspoilt.

It took the group 3 long hard days to paddle down to Lamidanda – Roger Huyton describes the last stretch as 'ten kms of stonking white water'. **Lamidanda** is a village and airstrip some 3 kms from the river. The small picturesque town by the bridge is called Rabuwa and sells basic supplies.

The last 32 kms from Rabuwa is flat, but with a good flow (3-4 hours to the Sun Kosi) and pleasant scenery. The river goes into a narrow gorge just before the confluence with the Sun Kosi.

Comment from Mick Coyne: 'We really appreciated the Sun Kosi after the Dudh Kosi'.

Dudh Kosi (Kites and Kayaks)

A Tale of Two Kayaks . . . *as told to Peter Knowles*

Don Weeden described how, on a kayak trip down the Sun Kosi in 1980 and cruising some way behind the rest of the group, he came to the confluence with the Dudh Kosi.

Don looked with amazement, because there on the beach at the confluence, were two villagers washing and polishing two fibreglass kayaks. he landed alongside the men and after the usual friendly greetings, he asked them what they were doing (Don has worked as an aid worker in Nepal so speaks the language). The villagers explained that some years previously two men in strange clothes had come down the Dudh Kosi and landed on this same beach. The villagers had given them tea, and although these strange men spoke very little Nepali they managed to communicate something about a helicopter. A little while later, the helicopter arrived and the Nepalese pilot explained that he had come to collect the men, and he sternly commanded the villagers 'to take very special care of these wonderful boats, because these important men will return some day and their lives will depend on it.'

The villagers proudly said that ever since they had been looking after the boats, washing and polishing them every two weeks and keeping them in their houses out of the sun and the rain. Don realised that these were the two remaining 'Everest' kayaks that Mike Jones and Mick Hopkinson had used on their famous descent of the Dudh Kosi. Don explained to the villagers that sadly one of the men (Mike Jones) had since died, kayaking on another river, so they would not be coming back. The villagers were saddened, but Don suggested that he take the boats off their hands. They agreed, and he gave them some money for taking such good care of the boats. Don towed the boats down to where the rafting group was camped and in due course the kayaks were transported back to Kathmandu.

One of the kayaks didn't look to good because it had been hung in the best place in the house – over the fire! The other one was in fair condition so Don decided to try it out on a short river trip: 'A disaster,' says Don; 'I was amazed that those guys got down the Dudh Kosi in those long boats'.

Some years later, in 1986, Don Weeden was having a drink in a Kathmandu Bar with Mick Coyne who had just returned from the second Dudh Kosi Expedition and casually mentioned that he had one of the original Everest kayaks: a hush of awe quietened the room as the paddlers realised that this was Mike Jone's famous boat. Don told his tale, and after discussion, Mick suggested and it was agreed that the boat should be returned to Britain. Mick duly arranged this so that now the boat is in the Pyranha Museum back in the North of England where it was originally made.

And the second boat? In the following year, 1987, another American paddler, Dan Dixon, was looking for an old kayak to take on an adventurous 'bandit' trip to Tibet: he wanted an old boat because there was a strong chance that the kayak would either be confiscated or never make it back. Somehow, Dan ended up with Mick Hopkinson's old boat, and after smuggling it across the border and hitch hiking up to near the source, Dan Dixon and Arlene Burns ran much of the upper Tsampo (the Brahmaputra) down to Shigatse.

Arlene had important deadlines back in civilisation, but Dan carried on down the river solo, through unrun gorges, finishing near Lhasa. He hitched up to Lhasa to resupply, but whilst he was away the boat was stolen, so, a little sad, but knowing that he had achieved an impressive 'first descent', Dan made his way back to the comforts of Kathmandu. Presumably, somewhere, high on the Tibetan Plateau, north of Everest remains this second fibreglass kayak.

Dr. Mike Jones remembered . . . *by Dave Manby*

'Mike Jones whose good friends call Rupert for an unknown reason performed the job of tea boy with alarming vigour' was the introduction that Chris Bonnington gave the 16 year old Mike when covering the 1968 British trip down the river Inn in Austria for the Daily Telegraph Magazine. Mike maintained that Chris Bonnington was only filling column inches and there was no truth in the statement but from then on the name stuck and so Mike reckoned that Chris owed him several favours.

It took four years for Mike to start pulling in these favours. Chris had been the journalist on Blashford-Snell's attempted descent of the Blue Nile in Avon Redshanks and he remarked that kayaks might have been a better craft to have used. That was enough for Mike to go ahead on and he immediately started extracting his pound of flesh. This was the first trip that Mike led and it became typical of his trips: conceived in a bar, planned on a beer mat and organised whilst in the middle of something else (this time his medical degree course at Birmingham university). As was often the case with Mike's escapades a lot depended on all trafic lights being green – or at least amber.

The river lived up to it's reputation: half way through the trip Mike had his 21st birthday and Mick Hopkinson was the only member of the team left on the river to share the celebration. That night they were camped above a serious stretch of white water. In the middle of the night Mike woke Mick up saying that he was sure that he had heard bandits in the bushes; they drew their World War One revolvers and sat back to back hoping that their sodden ammunition had dried out sufficiently to work. The following morning Mick opened his eyes to find Mike fast asleep and that he was staring down the barrel of Mike's loaded cocked revolver with his finger still around the trigger! Four days later the two of them, having no real idea of where they were rounded a bend to see the Portugese Bridge and the Reuter's reporter – by coincidence, they were exactly on schedule.

I met up with Mike in 1975 when I got invited on a trip round the Austrian Alps and Mike came out to join us after the first week. He was literally in the middle of his final university exams and we had to get Mike back to Birmingham a fortnight later in time for his last psychology paper. It was a typical Mike Jones trip: in one day it was not unusual to run three sections of serious white water, rush back to the campsite, cook a curry that included everything that was to hand, and then down to the bar for some serious drinking. We got reprimanded for leading the British Youth Team astray at Lofer slalom, destroyed the Swedish and Dutch teams at Augsburg in back to back boat races, got Slime to pay the bar bill at Landeck to cover his embarassment, and still managed to paddle all the top runs of the time. At this time the Everest trip was being talked about and this I suppose was the start of the '18 months of planning'. The Everest story is well known, if not, buy the book or rent the video.

Two years later Mike decided to head for K2 and the Braldu river in the Karakorum. He drowned whilst rescueing a friend. He was 25.

Life around Mike could only be described as 'hectic', but he also had the charisma and basic common sense which enabled him to persuade all but the most staid of institutions that his idea was not only feasible, but also worth backing. He had millions of acquaintances and many friends: I think I was friend of his – he certainly was a good friend of mine. I owe him a great deal.

Porters, lower Arun (Jock Montgomery)

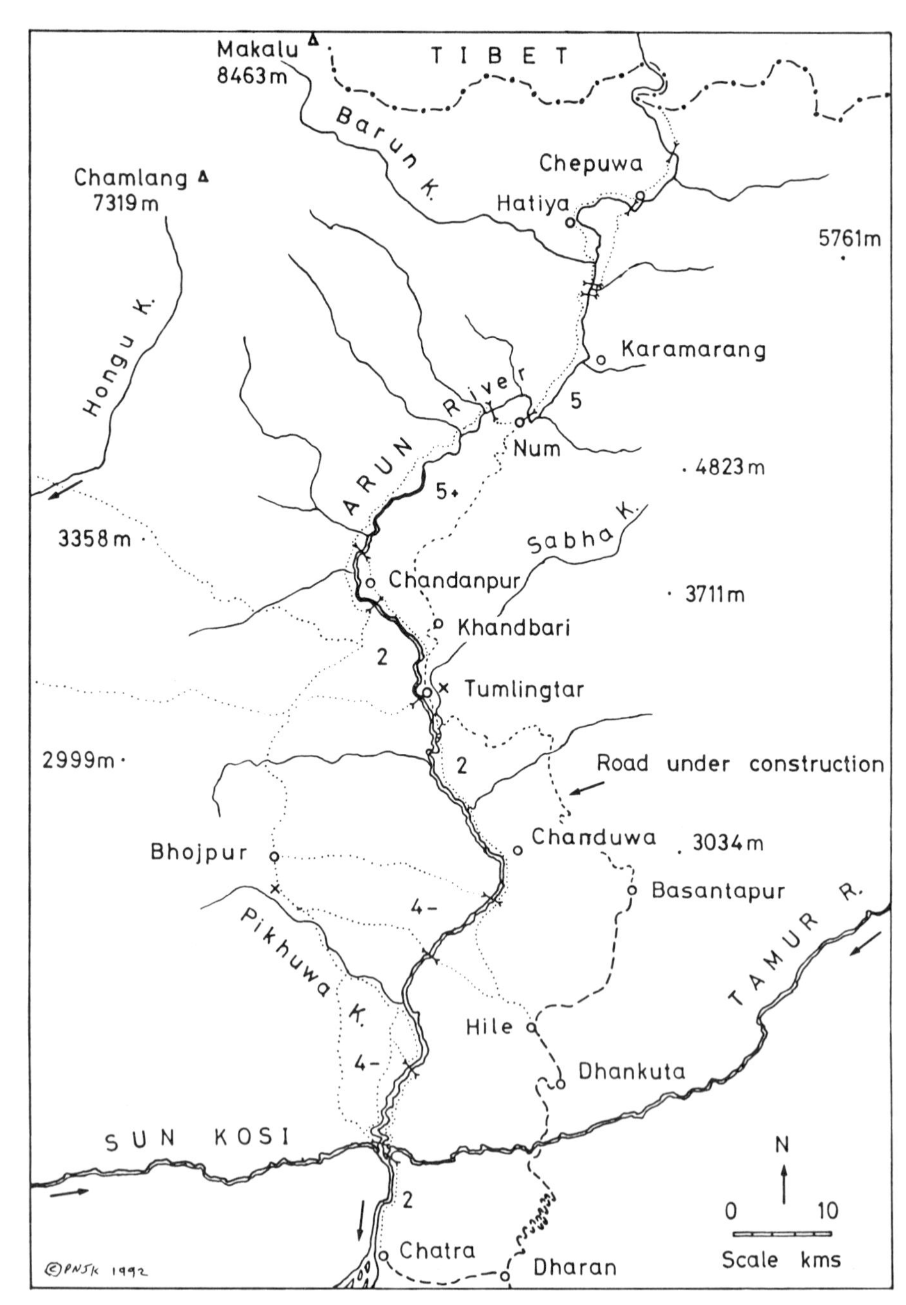

WARNING: Laser-phobic ink – do not photocopy.

Arun

From information supplied by Arlene Burns, Wolfgang Haibach, Shyam Piya, Al Read and John Wasson.

From:	**Tumlingtar** (Alt. 290m)
To:	**Chatra** (Alt. 115m)
Distance:	**70 kms** (44 miles)
River Days:	**3**
From Kathmandu:	**1 day fly in**
Difficulty in Nov:	**Class 4–**
Average gradient:	**0.25%** (12 ft a mile)
Est. max. gradient:	**0.4%**
Volume in Nov:	**215 cumecs** (7500 cfs)
Best Season:	**Nov-April.**

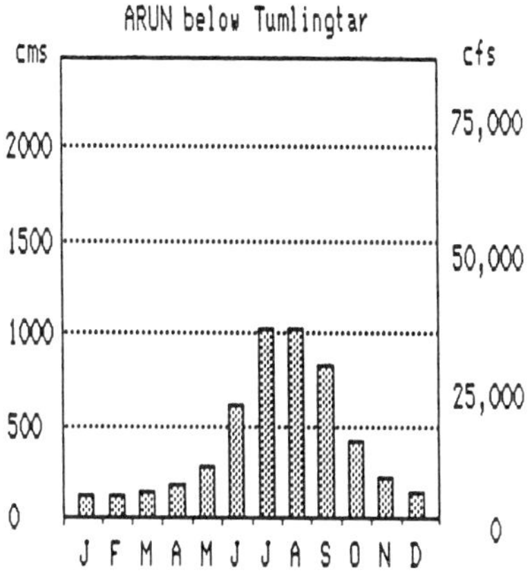

ARUN below Tumlingtar
cms
cfs
2000
1500
1000
500
0
75,000
50,000
25,000
0
J F M A M J J A S O N D

Summary

A powerful and famous river: big rapids, good scenery, unspoilt and little-travelled. The lower half of the river compares to the bottom part of the Sun Kosi and we recommend it as a similar but shorter rafting trip.

The River

The Arun is respected as one of the most mighty and powerful rivers of Nepal. Its source is on the Tibetan Plateau, to the north of Kathmandu and it then swings in an easterly arc for some 200 kms, draining the Northern slopes of Everest and Makalu before cutting south through the Himalaya and into Nepal. It cuts through the Himalaya in some deep and awesome gorges that have fascinated explorers, travellers, geographers and river runners, and then flows almost directly south to join the Sun Kosi shortly before the Indian plain. The gorges and gradient ease off near Chandanpur as the valley opens out and the hills get lower.

L. R. Wager, a mountaineer and geographer, explored these gorges on the upper Arun and as a result, in an article in the Geographical Journal in 1937, he suggested the now accepted theory of antecedant drainage – that these major rivers had developed before the Himalaya and that they had maintained their courses by cutting progressively deeper gorges as the mountains were uplifted.

In more recent years the river has been the subject of detailed Hydro Electic feasibility studies. The Arun III is a huge project that envisages a dam near Num and a 10 km long tunnel; however, it seems unlikely that this one billion dollar scheme will be completed before the year 2005. The project is dependent on a road that is being built from Basantapur to Num – of interest to the river runner in that it may give cheaper and easier access to the river. The river and its tributaries drain a huge watershed and the river carries a high load of sediment and glacial silt – colour varies between a milky brown to a greeny-grey.

Volume above Num has been estimated as about half that at Tumlingtar. Below here, tributaries add only a small flow.

The deep gorges of the upper river are thickly forested, with a wide variety of plant and animal life – very beautiful, but at times dark, damp and gloomy. This upper valley north of Num is sparsely inhabited, mainly by Bhotia people, many of whom still practise the old Bon Po religion. Lower down, the valley becomes well populated with a wide variety of different tribes. The whole area is relatively unspoilt, and sees only a few trekking groups, mainly taking the Eastern approach to Everest.

Expeditions

This mighty river has tempted and challenged river runners. Al Read writes of the first reconnaissance in 1977: 'Mike Yager, Lopsang Gyalpo, Jo Sanders and Andy Harvard put in the Arun at Num bridge: In short order they were in horrendous water and flipped the boat, an Avon Professional, losing everything – sleeping bags, clothes and shoes. All the group made it to the two banks but Sanders and Gyalpo were trapped on a narrow beach under a cliff and had to spend the night without fire or shelter (in February). The next morning they had to get back into the freezing cold river and swim downstream to a place where they could climb out of the gorge. The group then walked – in their underwear – to be picked up at Tumlingtar. The raft was hung on a rock in the middle of the river and disappeared the first night – never to be seen again.'

A team of American kayakers, John Wasson, Cully Erdman and Tom Ruwitch, ran much of the upper river in 1979 and made a dramatic film for the ABC 'American Sportsman' programme.

This upper river was then left alone until April 1986 when a German team of kayakers from the Alpina Kayak Club put in near Karamarang. They likwise ran almost all of the gorge, with only a few portages, but were impressed by the difficulty and power of the river. Wolfgang Haibach reckons that it took them 9 days to cover the 60 kms down to Tumlingtar – this gives an idea of the difficulty. The Germans were a very strong, experienced team and they had porters to carry their equipment and food and to meet them each night. This makes the next attempt on the Arun Gorges even more noteworthy – two lone unsupported kayakers.

Arlene Burns and friend Karen were experienced expedition kayakers, who had heard enough about the Arun to decide that it sounded interesting. They were trekking into Makalu base Camp in November 1989, and on a flip of the coin, decided to take kayaks and paddle back down the Arun. Arlene's tale is told on the adjoining page.

Rafting

Several companies offer commercial rafting trips on the lower half of the Arun **from Tumlingtar**, but it is one of the less popular rivers and only sees a few trips each year. However, the rafters who have done it and talked to us, recommend it as the ideal trip for someone who wants to run a big white water river but hasn't got the time to raft the Sun Kosi or the Karnali. They say that the river is, in all ways, better than than the Trisuli and should perhaps best be compared with the bottom half of the Sun Kosi – excellent big rapids, fine beaches for camping, a beautiful unspoilt valley, picturesque villages and a wooded gorge – the 'jungle corridor' – with its associated wildlife. 'We passed scores of birds; herons, egrets, storks, brahmini ducks – all celebrating the sunshine and the river'.

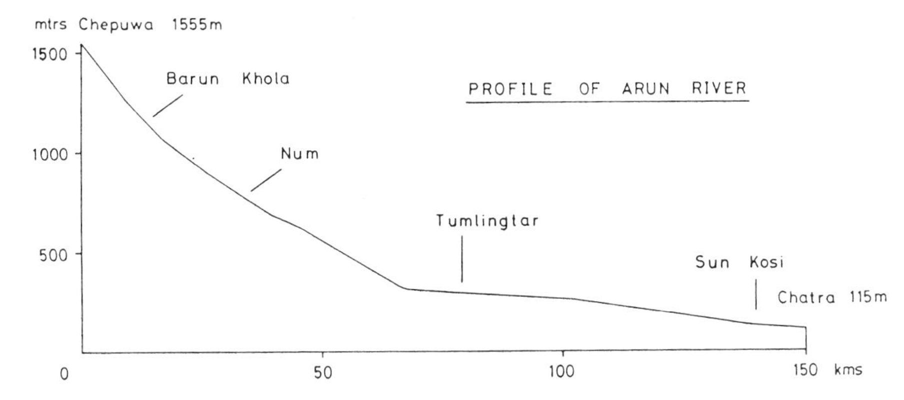

Tumlingtar is the obvious and most convenient starting point and everyone recommends that you fly into here as it is only a short direct flight from Kathmandu and only forty minute's walk from the river. The 70 kms down to Chatra has been kayaked in a day, but normally makes a relaxed 3 day raft trip and you can then fly back to Kathmandu if you wish.

Kayaking

We have yet to speak to a kayaker who is wildly enthusiastic about this river. The lower half of the river is obviously still a fine kayaking trip, with plenty of good rapids for playing, but logistics and expense probably make it a second choice when compared with other rivers.

Those who have done the upper river, all seem to agree that it is beautiful, but very serious, committing and hard work – an expedition! Arlene Burns says, 'The gorges are so deep that they get little sunlight – banks are covered in big, black, slimey rocks that make scouting and portaging difficult and dangerous.' Wolgang Haibach led a trip in April 1986 and says that it was 'one of the most beautiful rivers I have paddled' but warns that 'whenever sidestreams join the Arun, heavy rapids can be expected. Big boulders combined with heavy water pressure make this an extreme and expert-only experience. Scout ing is always required and is very tiring and time-consuming; several portages can be expected....' This upper river may appeal to expedition kayakers with suitable big water experience who are looking for a fresh challenge.

Access and logistics

Most groups fly in to **Tumlingtar**. The alternative is to trek in from Basantapur, about two days to the south, but even the trekking guide books do not speak highly of this, describing the lower Arun Valley as hot and torrid, and recommending a flight to Tumlingtar as a better start. If you are thinking of trekking, please see the section on the Tamur for a detailed description on how to get to Basantapur.

Best take-out is at **Chatra**. Most commercial raft groups arrange to have a night bus meet them here to take them back to Kathmandu, or alternatively arrange for a minibus to drive them two hours to the airport at Biratnagar for the convenient flight back to Kathmandu. Please see the 'Tamur' section for alternative travel arrangements.

Campsites along the river are described by everyone as excellent and we are told that there is plentiful driftwood for fires. Best map is the 1:125,000 H.M.G. Central Service Map for 'Dhankuta District' which covers the lower river from Tumlingtar down.

Description

Num to Chandanpur 35 kms, Tumlingtar 12 kms, Sun Kosi 60, Chatra 10.

Wolfgang describes the section from Karamarang to Num as mainly class 3-4 with one section of 5. (He says that there was an impossible section further upstream). Downstream from Num is a very difficult, deep, canyon of class 4 to 6. 'Rock formation is granite, which is beautifully shaped in various colours – There are almost no villages, the banks are heavily forested with fine waterfalls and there are many beautiful spots to camp'. These gorges finish near Chandanpur; the valley then opens out and the river becomes class 2 for a while down to Tumlingtar.

Below **Tumlingtar** the valley is open with many villages and cultivated terraces. The river is class 1-2 and, for those starting here, this makes a peaceful and leisurely introduction to rafting. Below Chanduwa the ridges begin to close in and the vegetation becomes thicker. The current picks up and the rapids become more interesting. The river is now flowing through a forested canyon similar to the 'Jungle Corridor' on the Sun Kosi, with luxuriant vegetation, remnant of the vast forest that once covered the middle hills of Nepal; broad-leaved trees, bamboo, creepers, ferns and mosses form a thick canopy on the river banks.

This 'Jungle Corridor' continues down to Tribeni at the confluence with the **Sun Kosi**. Rapids on this section are described as 'big and bouncy – like the Sun Kosi' and the difficulty as class 4−. In 1987 a jet cargo boat was succesfully driven up to Tumlingtar to demonstrate the potential for this means of transport (They also attempted the Sun Kosi, but didn't get beyond 'Big Dipper').

Tribeni is a holy and unique spot at the confluence of the Tamur, Arun and Sun Kosi rivers. The combined rivers now become the **Sapta Kosi** and this surges onwards to Ganges and the Indian Ocean. Please see the 'Sun Kosi' section for a description of this stretch. Note to keep close to the left bank so that you do not miss the take-out at **Chatra**.

The Arun Gorges . . . *by Arlene Burns*

'I planned to head into the mountains of Eastern Nepal with a few good friends: should we take kayaks and paddle the Arun? Our fate was decided by the toss of a coin . . . Yes!

When we arrived at the river the local villagers tried to dissuade us from doing the river: it is always a tricky thing trying to interpret the descriptions of whitewater from locals – how could they discern what was 'runnable' when to them, a mere slip into flatwater was most often fatal? But, we could not ignore the disconcerting roar of the river from 1500ft below, nor were the thunderous blasts of dynamite from somewhere downstream any comfort (testing for a future hydroelectric scheme).

I woke up in the middle of the night and wandered out of the Seduwa schoolhouse for a wee pee, and was instantly invigorated by the sight . . . the storm had finally broken and full moonlight shimmered through the crystal sky onto a freshly-whitened Himalaya. I remained outside through the approaching dawn, an auspicious day to begin our descent down the Arun river. We descended to the river and enjoyed our last moments with Hedy, A.D. and our porters. One of the porters was begging me not to go, and after

He realised our intent, he elaborately caressed each kayak with an urn of sacred water. Another blast of dynamite echoed through the canyon to remind us of what awaited us . . .

Karen and I crammed our warm clothes, five days of food, pots, tent, first-aid kit, spare paddle, camera, etc. into our kayaks as a crowd of locals gathered around us and observed every move. It was a lot of gear to fit into two small boats, and I was again reminded of our vulnerability in being just two (and girls at that!) on such an isolated and formidable river. We launched into the icy water and waved goodbye to our companions.

Some way down the river and deep in the gorge, we stopped for our third scout of a rapid. I returned from looking at the rapid to a horrifying sight – my kayak and all my gear, was heading down the rapid without me! Our situation had changed dramatically and instantly . . .

Karen quickly jumped into her boat and headed downstream; I scrambled over slimy boulders along the shore as far as possible and then climbed the cliffs into dense jungle, though roots and rocks, stinging nettles and thorns, thinking of my shoes that were conveniently stored inside my boat. I eventually came to a large tributary of turquoise waterfalls and granite slides and followed this down to the main river. No sign of Karen and with dusk approaching I contemplated our situation: was Karen O.K.? – would she be forced to solo this mighty river? At least she had her gear, I had just the little that I was wearing and contemplated bare-footed hiking out of one of the world's deepest gorges . . .'

(Arlene perseveres with her scramble along the bank and links up with Karen, who had searched downstream and luckily spotted the missing boat pinned above an undercut.)

. . . 'We freed the boat, just at dark, with a trusty 'Z drag', but everything in the front of the boat was gone, while everything in the back remained in a newly soaked form. We slid and scrambled back in the dark to the one and only tiny beach for miles and by 11 p.m. we had built a fire, eaten our noodle soup and were snuggled together under one dry bag. Thus the first day of our trip came to a close: it could easily have ended very, very differently.

Our trip down the mighty Arun continued next day. It greeted us with five days of continuous, steep and nasty rapids which required long scouts, several 'Wrath of God' portages, nerve-wracking sneaks, and (alas!) some brilliant white water. Time after time we rounded the next corner hoping for flat water ahead, only to find another horrendous rapid. But, eventually, we emerged from the gorge, the river changed character dramatically and we cruised downstream in the bliss of having survived.'

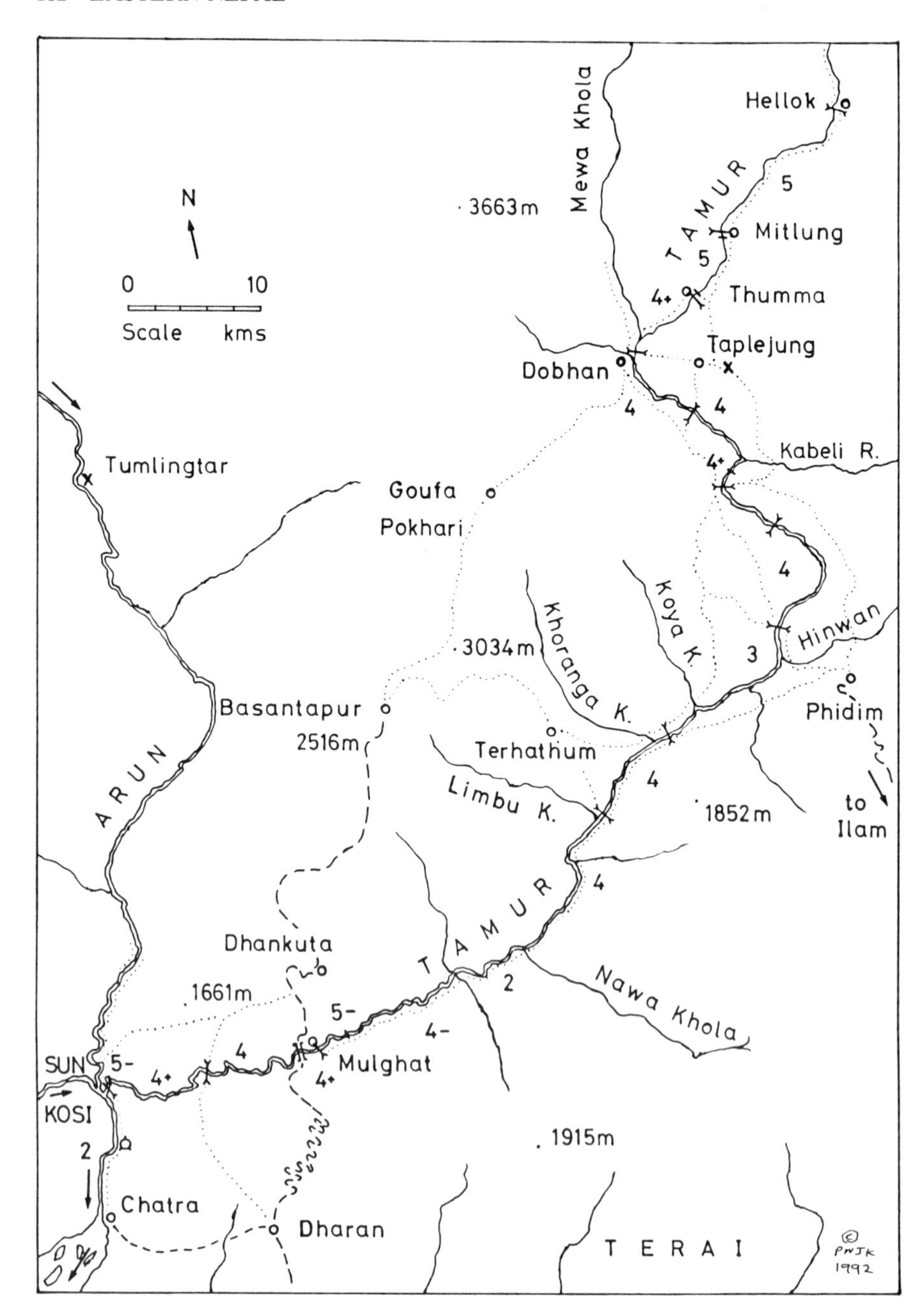

WARNING: Laser-phobic ink – do not photocopy.

Tamur

From:	**Dobhan** (Alt. 630m)
To:	**Chatra** (Alt. 115m)
Distance:	**120 kms** (75 miles)
River Days:	**4–6**
From Kathmandu:	**3–4 days, or fly**
Difficulty in Nov:	**Class 4** (5−)
Average gradient:	**0.4%** (20 ft a mile)
Est. max. gradient:	**1.0%**
Volume in Nov:	**150 cumecs** (5250 cfs)
Best Season:	**Oct-Dec, Feb-April**

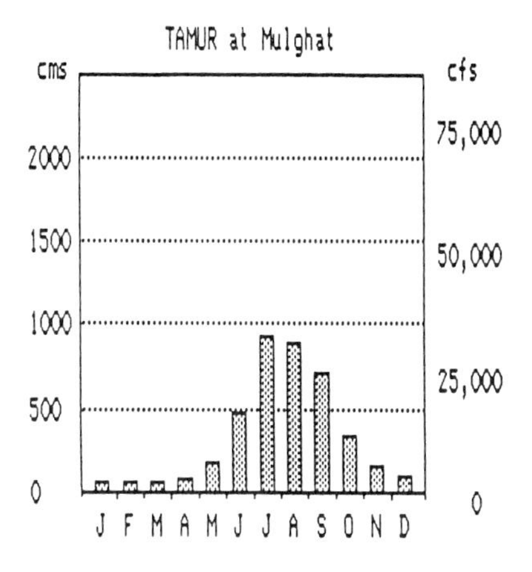

Summary

A magnificent white water trip, one of the best in the World, with aproximately 130 rapids in 120 kms. The river flows through a beautiful and unspoilt valley and the trek to the start is one of the most scenic in Nepal.

Highly recommended as an exhilarating, active, white water rafting or kayak trip and well worth the journey from Kathmandu.

The River

The Tamur and its tributaries drain the snows of Kanchenjunga, third highest peak in the world. The river is the sixth largest river in Nepal and seems to have a feeling of thrusting power and of being constrained by its valley sides.

Above Dobhan, the Tamur and its tributaries have a steep gradient and are probably only of interest to expedition kayakers. Downstream from Dobhan the gradient is more reasonable, but the river profile is unusual in that the river steepens in the last 40 kms before its confluence with the Sun Kosi. The Kabelli river adds about a quarter to the volume of the river, but from here down there are no substantial tributaries.

The valley itself is beautiful and unspoilt with relatively few villages and little agriculture. Valley sides are well wooded, there are good beaches for camping and plentiful signs of wild life. The river has much more of a feeling of being a 'wilderness' rafting trip than many of the other more popular rafting rivers.

Local people are a fascinating collage of tribes and castes (one of my reference sources quotes 27 different languages and dialects being spoken in one local district). Locals have seen few westerners and are very welcoming, pressing you to sample their Tungba, a delicious and reviving drink made by pouring hot water over fermented millet.

Rafting

The Tamur was one of those rivers which several people we spoke to had rafted but about which they were strangely reticent – 'yes, a fine river' they would say – 'but a long way from Kathmandu', and then change the subject. Well, in October 1991 I made a special visit to Nepal to run this river, and it was worth every penny! I can see why people were reticent about it – this is the kind of river that you feel is too good to put in a guide book, but should be reserved for a select few!

On our trip down the river we counted about 130 rapids in 120 kms. The Tamur probably has more white water interest on it than any other rafting river in Nepal and in our opinion it is one of the best white water trips in the world. The first section of the river below Dobhan is very continuous, but almost all the rapids are runnable on sight. On the middle part of the river the rapids are more well-defined with pools and flat sections between. Rapids are fast and powerful, often with breaking waves and sometimes with serious holes and pour-overs, but all rapids are easy to scout. This is an active, white water raft trip where you'll get wet and stay wet!

Cam MacLeay, one of the world's best rafters, summed this river up as 'Outstanding . . . a fantastic run for a good team'. This comment perhaps gives a warning – we think you should be doubly careful when checking out the experience of your proposed rafting company. We would recommend this particularly as an exciting paddle trip for fit and active rafters looking for a second time trip.

Most rafting trips start at **Dobhan** and from here it is a 4 to 6 day journey down to Chatra. Whilst it is possible to fly into Taplejung, we especially recommend the trek in from Basantapur. This trek takes you along the top of a 3000 metre ridge through beautiful woods and meadows with magnificent views of Kanchenjunga, Makalu and the Everest Massif in the far distance. A Trekking leader described this to us as 'the most scenic trek in Nepal' and we feel that you would find it hard to disagree – a great way to start a river trip! Lazy people please note (aren't all boaters lazy?) that this trek is not too arduous as it goes along the top of the ridge and then drops down to the river.

The best white water section on the river is the last 40 kms down to the confluence with the Sun Kosi. Rafters who enjoy asset stripping rivers could put in at **Mulghat**, where the road crosses, for a one or two day trip (A finale to a Sun Kosi trip?).

Kayaking

We ran this river as a self-supported kayak trip in October 1991 in high water conditions, with a team of pretty experienced boaters from Britain, Idaho, California, Washington, Colorado and New Zealand. The almost unanimous opinion was 'this is the best river I've done'! Other comments were: 'chunky', 'Gutsy', 'A blast', 'great playing potential – you could have caught a million waves'; 'like high water on the Lochsa – but 70 miles of it'.

In October this was a very pushy, big water river, continuous, hard class 4+ boating – mostly scoutable from surging eddies and the tops of waves, but with BAD consequences if you got the lines wrong. Demanding kayaking – that, and a lot of playing left us pretty bushed by the end of the day. In November, the volume is a lot less and we reckon the river would be less committing – however, people who have done it then, reckon the river is just as difficult; rapids are steeper and more technical, holes are mean, and there are some nasty pour-overs. In lower water levels rapids are more well defined with pools and flat sections between, and you have time to catch your breath – also better eddies to catch the play waves, weh, hey!.

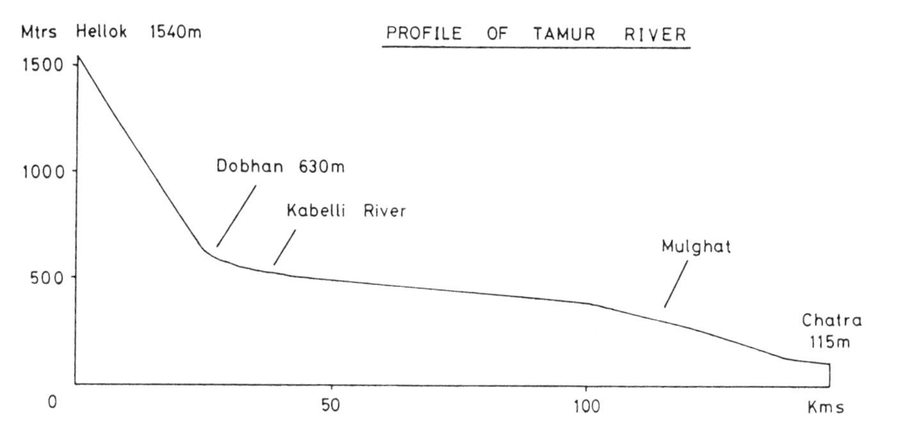

As has been mentioned, this river has great play potential, so it would be nice to do this with raft support and empty kayaks. However, it is a really good length for a self-sufficient trip and the river has this nice remote, 'wilderness' feel about it, better appreciated in a small self-sufficient group. We rushed down the river in 3 days, but 4 would have been much better.

The river upstream of **Dobhan** has been kayaked by a group of German paddlers from the Alpina Kayak Club in 1984. They started from Hellok and reported some hard class 5+ boating with 3 major portages (Gradient on this stretch is 4.0% – 200 ft a mile). Just after I wrote this I had a letter from Gudmund Host in Norway to say that they also kayaked some of this section in 1987, starting at Mitlung. He says, 'The continuous character of this section (above Dobhan) makes it rather serious; we had a near fatal swimmming incident in the middle part. The section below Dobhan is well suited for rafting and related vulgarities'!

We should just mention that the last 30 kms of the river from **Mulghat** downstream makes a great day or two's paddle for a suitably experienced group – perhaps as a superb finale to the Sun Kosi? Reckon on about 5-6 hours of paddling to do the 45 or so rapids.

Access and logistics

Dobhan, the usual start point for the Tamur is only a couple of hours walk from **Taplejung** Airstrip, so in theory you could be on the river the same day as leaving Kathmandu. However, flying is expensive and you would miss the trek in, which for this river can be particularly recommended.

A night bus to **Dharan** cost us about $4 and took 16 hours. After breakfast and a freshen up, we then hired a pick up truck for $50 to take the six of us up to **Basantapur** where we arrived in mid-afternoon. Basantapur is a fascinating hill top town with a thriving bazar for buying all the things you have forgotten. The town is an important staging point for trails into Eastern Nepal so there should be no problems finding porters. We negotiated a deal: $7 per porter to Dobhan, to be paid $1 up front, $2 at Goufa Pokhari, and $4 at Dobhan. We also made it clear that there would be a bonus if we got there fast with no problems (and duly paid a bonus of $2). This worked well: our porters, although carrying awkward kayaks, seemed to overtake everyone else on the trail; we raced along behind trying to keep up

(Some roughty toughty climbing expedition was not too pleased to be overtaken by these river bums wearing shorts and sandals! It took us two and a half days, but three would be more reasonable.

As has been said earlier, this trek along the top of the ridge can be highly recommended – the path winds gently up and down through ancient moss-covered trees and sunlit meadows. We caught fleeting and tantalisingly magnificent views of the Kanchenjunga Massif through fleecy clouds. Goufa Pokhari at the top of the ridge is a holy lake and favourite overnight rest stop. Soon after this, the trail drops steeply through sinuous waves of rice terraces sprinkled with little toy houses. This is one of the most interesting and scenic treks that we have done. There are plenty of lodges and tea houses to stay in, as this is the main trekking route to Kanchenjunga.

We think that the river is probably best planned as a 4 day kayak trip, or a 6 day rafting trip. There are plenty of fine beaches for camping and we found ample driftwood for fires. Note that it is possible to buy basic supplies in Mulghat if you run short. Phidim is a possible emergency evacuation route, but you should check on the current state of the road from here to Ilam (the road is planned to continue to Taplejung and this may offer an alternative access in the future).

Finish point is at **Chatra**, some 10 kms below the confluence with the Sun Kosi – the combined river now becomes the Sapta Kosi. Keep close to the left bank as the river comes out onto the plain and take out just past the entrance to the irrigation canal. Ancient landrovers can be hired here for about $15 to take you back to Dhahran.

Best maps covering the river are the H.M.G. Central Service Maps for Taplejung and Dhankuta Districts at a scale of 1:125,000. It would also be nice to have with you, a more general topographic map covering the whole of Eastern Nepal, so that you can have fun trying to identify distant peaks, including Makalu and Kanchenjunga.

Tributary of Tamur near Dobhan

Description

Dobhan to Kabelli Khola 11 kms, Mulgat 77, Sun Kosi 22, Chatra 10.

The section above Dobhan is described as having 'a much more serious and continuous character' by Gudmund Host who ran the river in October 1987: 'At Mitlung a difficult class 5/6 rapid is followed by a nasty waterfall then flat down to one km above the suspension bridge at Thumma where there are three more class 5 and 6 rapids (one probably lethal). From Thumma to Dobhan is very continuous class 4+; the river eases gradually down to Dobhan.' (Gudmund reckoned the rapids below Dobhan as class 4).

Dobhan is a small village with a thriving bazar, where the Siwa Khola joins the Tamur. There is almost no time to warm up before you are into some class 4 rapids and for the next few hours there is almost no respite – just continuous class 3 and 4 boating!

There are a couple of bigger rapids about 5 kms below Dobhan. A bridge comes up at 7 kms, and 4 kms further the **Kabelli river** comes in on the left. This adds about a quarter to the volume. The second rapid after the confluence is about 1 km downstream on a left-hand bend. This is probably a class 4+ and might be an awkward one for rafts – our team christened it 'Hudson's last rite'.

Another 3 big rapids in 2 kms brings you to the bridge and another 7 rapids and 7 kms to another bridge that is not marked on official maps. 3 kms further is a long rapid with big boulders at the top and excellent surfing potential – promptly dubbed 'Hudson reborn'! Rapids continue at the rate of about one every km, but the river flattens out for a while a few kms before the Hinwan Khola.

The valley widens out a bit, with wooded sides, good beaches and a few villages. The river seems to have a pattern: it goes round a bend, flattens out and then you think, 'Phew, that must be the last of the white water for a bit', then, round the next bend is a nice class 4 with a super play wave.

Shortly below the Nawa Khola is a big bouncy class 4 rapid followed by three smaller ones: the river then flattens out with some 5 kms of 'dog water' and a dugout canoe operating a ferry service. Flat water continues with the Teliya Khola coming in from the right and Chharuwa Khola from the left. (Note that all these side streams are rain-fed and have very little water in the dry season). The valley here is about 1 km wide, with cattle grazing on the flood plain and gravel islands in the river.

An easy class 4 rapid, big and bouncy, follows the confluence. 2 kms further is another ferry and then 1 km past here a rocky ridge pokes out into the valley from the left and constrains the river against the right-hand side of the valley. This marks the point where the river gradient steepens and white water becomes more continuous and interesting!

About 9 roller coaster rapids (clas 4−) follow one after the other in the next 7 kms. This is followed by a small stream on the left (the Kami Khola) and a prominent landslide on the right. This is the marker for 'Don McKecknie', a big class 5− rapid that we would advise scouting. Three more big bouncy rapids and the suspension bridge at **Mulghat** comes in sight; keep your eyes on the river though for a big rapid we called 'Pariah Dog' with a tasty hole at the bottom waiting for someone to enjoy it.

Mainly easy class 4 rapids continue on, one after the other, past the road bridge and on for the next 9 kms to the suspension bridge at Chimraha – about 25 rapids in all, but we lost count! We needed a rest after this and found a beautiful and quiet campsite on the right bank 1 to 2 kms below the bridge.

We were glad we stopped where we did, as first thing next morning we were into two big class 4+ rapids and this was followed by a non stop helter skelter of rapids – about ten in the next 3 kms. The last couple of these were only class three and coincided with the valley widening, and the river appearing to leave the hills. Appearances were deceptive: the next rapid looked innocent – big and bouncy, but the waves hid a truly horrifying hole at the bottom, probably deserving a 4+ rating (our friend Bill checked this out for us in late November and had an interesting swim – he agrees with our rating and says that it might be helpful to mention that this is about rapid number 34 after the road bridge) Six more easy class 4 rapids came in little more than a km, followed by 4 class 3+ rapids in the next km. A sharp left hand bend marks 'Bat Below', a class 5− that we scouted and ran right. This takes you into a short but impressive narrow gorge with sheer rock walls – the scenic climax to a magnificent river.

At the end of this short gorge is the suspension bridge, confluence with the **Sun Kosi** and trail to Tribeni. If you're not in a rush, this is a good place for a rest and to take a ten minute hike upstream to the temple that overlooks the confluence with the Arun River; there can be few places in the world where three mighty rivers meet within such close proximity.

The combined rivers, now called the Sapta Kosi, after the seven main rivers that form it, surge onward to the Ganges and the Indian Plain. There is still plenty of current and a couple of small rapids to carry you on past another large temple complex where the Kokaha Khola comes in on the left after 5 kms. A few more kms brings you out of the Gorge and onto the great plain of the Ganges – a stunningly flat vista. Keep close to the left bank to take out just past the entrance to the irrigation canal at Chatra.

Rivers as a water resource

Considerable research has been done into the potential of Nepal's rivers as a resource for hydro-electric power, irrigation,and flood control. Some twenty large and medium size schemes have been suggested and if these were all put into effect there would be sufficient power to supply much of the Indian Sub Continent. This sounds too good to be true, and of course it is – most of these HEP sites are inaccessible, deep in the Himalaya, and the infrastructure costs are huge. Most of the sites are also far removed from the major customers in the large industrial centres of population.

One of the most promising HEP projects was a proposed massive dam at Chisapani where the **Karnali** *river breaks through the Chure Hills. This would have provided flood control, irrigation, and generated huge amounts of electricity (3600 megawatts) for sale to India, which has a critical daily peak demand. From a global viewpoint this made real sense and came out high on any environmental analysis. The World Bank were keen to lend the money for the project on a long term loan. But, from Nepal's viewpoint the scheme had few advantages: there was no big demand for electricity in the Far West, any profits from the sale of electricity would mainly go to pay off the loan. More worrying were the political implications: imagine that Nepal's big meighbour, India, becomes dependent on the dam for power; then some friction develops and by co-incidence one of the turbines breaks down: India could interpret the breakdown as sabotage and send troops over the border to secure its power supply .....*

Other schemes have been suggested that divert the Sun Kosi and Karnali through tunnels under the Mahabharat Range: these are only long-term possibilities, but we hope they will never come to reality in that they could devastate these world class rivers. At the time of writing there are a few small and medium size schemes in service, feeding electricity to Kathmandu and other Nepalese cities and towns. These are on the Marsyandi, Trisuli, upper Sun Kosi, Sapta Kosi and Seti.

To meet future demand Nepal has put its eggs in one large basket called the **Arun III** *project; a series of dams on the Arun gorges above Tumlingtar. This is estimated to cost one billion dollars and take some ten years to build. In theory it will generate cheap power, some for use in Nepal's large Eastern cities, and the rest for sale to India or Bangladesh. Critics of the scheme argue that it is just too big, costs have been underestimated, the project will take much longer than scheduled, and that it is totally dependent on a new road that has to be built for 100 kms over the mountains. If this project is delayed (as seems likely) then it may be necessary to go ahead with a smaller project as a stop-gap measure – projects on the Kali Gandaki and Bhote Kosi have been suggested as likely schemes – bad news for river runners.*

Larger schemes satisfy the demand for electricity for towns and industry. In the countryside, various micro-hydro projects have been quite successful, providing electricity to villages – tourist lodges, shops and wealthier householders. However, it should be noted that the average poor Nepali could never afford to use electricity for cooking; therefore HEP projects, large or small, are unlikely to reduce deforestation – in fact, some studies suggest the reverse: if you give people electric light then they stay up later and burn firewood to keep warm!

(For those interested further in development problems we recommend the section in David Reed's Rough/Real Guide to Nepal)

The Shangra Khola

by Whit Deshner

As for THE RUN in not just Nepal, but the whole world, the Shangra Khola surpasses all others. First reportedly run by a couple of Australians in Dahl Bats (a Down Under rip off of the Mountain Bat), only a few groups have been lucky enough to run this river since. This 150 km classic transgresses from alpine to tropical, small and technical rapids to giant delightful water. Its consistencies are warm water the entire length, and with the exception of a 15 metre harmlessly runnable drop, the river's gradient deviates little from 2% (100 ft a mile).

The closest village, **Cayganay**, is still a two day hike from the put-in. Not only are this village's people extremely friendly, the women are exceptionally beautiful . . . but I digress. Follow the trail due east; don't worry about getting lost, if in doubt just point and ask 'this way?' You'll know you are at the put-in by two unmistakable features: the water is pleasantly warm and the rapids are runnable. Just upstream neither of these two things are apparent. Don't look for the hot springs, the 'tatopani' issues from large fissures in the river bed.

The run starts as nothing more than a tight creek with all the eddy-hopping you can handle, each turn rewarded by a magnificent backdrop of the Himalaya – all minor peaks, but I've yet to see a river view that surpasses this one. Two or three days can easily be spent on this upper section. Campsites are plentiful as is firewood. Very few people inhabit this valley, but those who do spend a great deal of their time perfecting their 'rackshi' brewing techniques. Sip with caution: nothing I tried rated under a class 5!

Approximately 40 kms down, the river's character changes abruptly as it enters a sheer-walled white marble gorge. This gorge is sombre and suspicious, the sense of doom heightened by a slackening current foretelling of something horrible downstream; definitely a place which common sense would say to avoid. But fortunately commom sense has never been a river runner's attribute. There's really no way to scout this one, but don't worry, the **15 metre drop** the river delivers you into is harmless, it's not a waterfall but a 45 degree, smooth-channelled slide. Tke next 15 kms are nothing but slides and ledges, the highest about 4 metres, and all runnable. There is ample slack water between each to collect any flotsam and to marvel at the river-sculpted marble. Note that there are no campsites on this section.

As the river leaves the gorge, it quickly picks up numerous side drainages and the run takes on its third and final character; big water of the pool/drop species. Since the river still maintains its 2% gradient, many of the rapids are steep and will require a scout. However, at up to medium high flows all are runnable, and none are pegged at higher than a 4+ rating. In this section you'll also begin noticing palm and banana trees and also that the river, due to the lower elevation, is just as warm as it was rendered at the put-in. Wildlife is abundant; if you're a bird watcher, this valley has one of the highest concentrations of different species of birds in the world. One group spotted a rhinosorearse; unfortunately the rhino also spotted them and flattened their tents.

There are ample campsites in this lower section, but choose carefully for you can get one with both a mountain view and a river playspot. As for playing, about 40 kms below the gorge, and at almost all water levels is the most amazing surf wave any river has yet produced. Nothing really marks the wave but you'll know when you see it – it's river-wide, glass-smooth, fast, sometimes up to four metres tall, and really easy to catch. Don't miss it, because, unfortunately, eddies do not flank the wave and the only way back up is a long carry.

As for the rest of the run, there is nothing else to say but incredible; the run is fast action right to the end. Take out at the road bridge, the only one to cross the river before the Terai, as everything downstream of here is anticlimatic. At the bridge you can catch a bus back to Pokhara or Kathmandu.

The fifteen metre fall, Shangra Khola

The only drawback the Shangra Khola has is access. The headwaters lie in a politically sensitive area and the nearest road is often washed out by landslides, leaving the river more often closed than open. There is the possibility of trekking in from the west, but your best bet is to get up to date information on access from one of the more reliable rafting companies such as Himalayan Encounters in the courtyard of the Kathmandu Guest House.

RIVERS OF WESTERN NEPAL

Introduction

This is the most remote and wildest part of Nepal – often called the 'Wild West' – unspoilt, committing and with very few roads.

A glance at a map of Nepal will show that this Far West is very remote, but also the country is much wider here, and so the region is more vast and the main rivers are the longest in Nepal. The region receives less rainfall than areas further east, so supports a smaller population than the more fertile areas of Central and Eastern Nepal – this smaller population has had a lesser effect on the ecology of the region; there are still large tracts of coniferous forest on north-facing slopes, and on the lower reaches of the Karnali and its main tributaries are vast verdant stretches of pristine jungle and dependent wildlife – the kind of jungle that you used to read about in childrens story books, and that has all but disappeared from most other areas of the Himalaya.

Only in recent years have a few roads started to snake in from the Terai, but you will see from the map that these only touch the southern edge of the region. This area still has some of the most remote and unspoilt valleys, not just in Nepal, but anywhere in the Himalaya. It is a poor and undeveloped region that sees few foreigners or experiences much outside influence: the way of life remains little changed.

Commercial rafting

The lower Karnali, Bheri, Seti, Mahakali and the Babai Nadi are all offered as commercial rafting trips and offer a wide variety – from world class white water on the Karnali to a relaxing flatwater float on the Babai. What they have in common is unspoilt rivers, beautiful 'wilderness', jungle and exceptional wildlife. If these are the prime qualities that you are looking for in a river trip, then this is the region for you!

The disadvantage of the region is that because it is remote, the rafting trips on these rivers will cost you a premium. Note that if you fly to and from the river then there is no reason why a trip on one of these rivers need take any longer than one nearer to Kathmandu.

The Self-Sufficient Trip

For the adventurous river runner this is an exciting area. Even now in the 1990's, only the main rivers have been run, and then only a handful of times. This is not the area for a first-time trip to the Himalaya – we recommend that you gain experience on other rivers in Nepal before undertaking an expedition out West. Barry Miller has built up an enviable experience of running the rivers of the Far West, and he advises: 'You've got to get to grips with just how remote this area is . . . and something will come up that will make you realise this'!

The logistics of getting your boats and gear to the river can be expensive and need to be planned carefully. The region is quite well served for airstrips and it is well worth investigat ing the possibility of flying in to your river. Nepalganj acts as the hub for flights in the Far West.

Note that the Far West is a very poor area and a 'food deprivation zone' in international aid parlance. Villages have little if any food to be purchased and you should plan on being completely self-sufficient.

Guidebook Rivers

Karnali Lower
A world classic combination of BIG white water, wilderness, wildlife and a fine two day trek to the put-in. Probably 'best of its kind' in the Himalaya and a magnificent commercial raft trip.

Seti
Gives an alternative start to a Lower Karnali trip for 'softies' – avoids the trek and the big rapids, but still includes the unspoilt jungle and abundant wildlife.

Humla Karnali and the Upper Karnali
Long and committing, but a fantastic trip for expedition kayakers.

Bheri
An easy raft trip with excellent fishing and wildlife.

Babai Nadi
A short float trip entirely within the Royal Bardiya Wildlife Reserve – Magnificent wildlife.

Mahakali
The least travelled major river of Nepal. A good choice for a raft or kayak group looking for a wild and remote river, like the Karnali but not so difficult. Phenomenal bird life.

Other Rivers

Chamliya river – This is a tributary of the Mahakali, joining that river near Baitadi. Est. volume 30 cumecs in November. This looks like an interesting proposition for a short kayak expedition.

Budhi Ganga – Main tributary of the Seti, this is also probably waiting for a first descent . . .

Tila River – This is the river that flows from Jumla down to join the Karnali. It looks an obvious one to do on the map. It's a fairly small volume river (about 35 cumecs in November) and is about 70 kms long from Jumla to the confluence. The first 30 kms are at a reasonable gradient and then it drops at about 4% (200 ft a mile) for the next 40 kms. Chris Sladden and a British kayak team ran the bottom 12 kms and brought back a spectacular video of hard class 5 boating. It took them 3 days to cover these bottom 12 kms – a great deal of scouting and portaging.

Mugu Karnali and Langu Khola – The Mugu Karnali has been run from Gamgadhi but upstream of here are over 150 kms of river that flows through remote and forbidden Dolpo. How much of the river is runnable.....? This is one of the rivers that old hands to Nepal talk about over a rum and coke back in Kathmandu, but balk at the awesome logistical problems and commitment. One of the last long kayak adventures awaits some well-funded and experienced team.....

Thuli and Sani Bheri – These two main branches of the Bheri river offer more scope for would-be expeditions. These are both very remote and committing rivers, but the logistics would appear a bit less daunting than the Mugu as there are convenient airstrips. The Thula Bheri has the greater volume and appears to have a more consistent gradient.

Madi Khola and Rapti River – This is a relatively small volume river (35 cumecs in November) with what looks like an easy gradient and reasonable road access near Liban. As far as we know no one has run this to date.

Humla Karnali

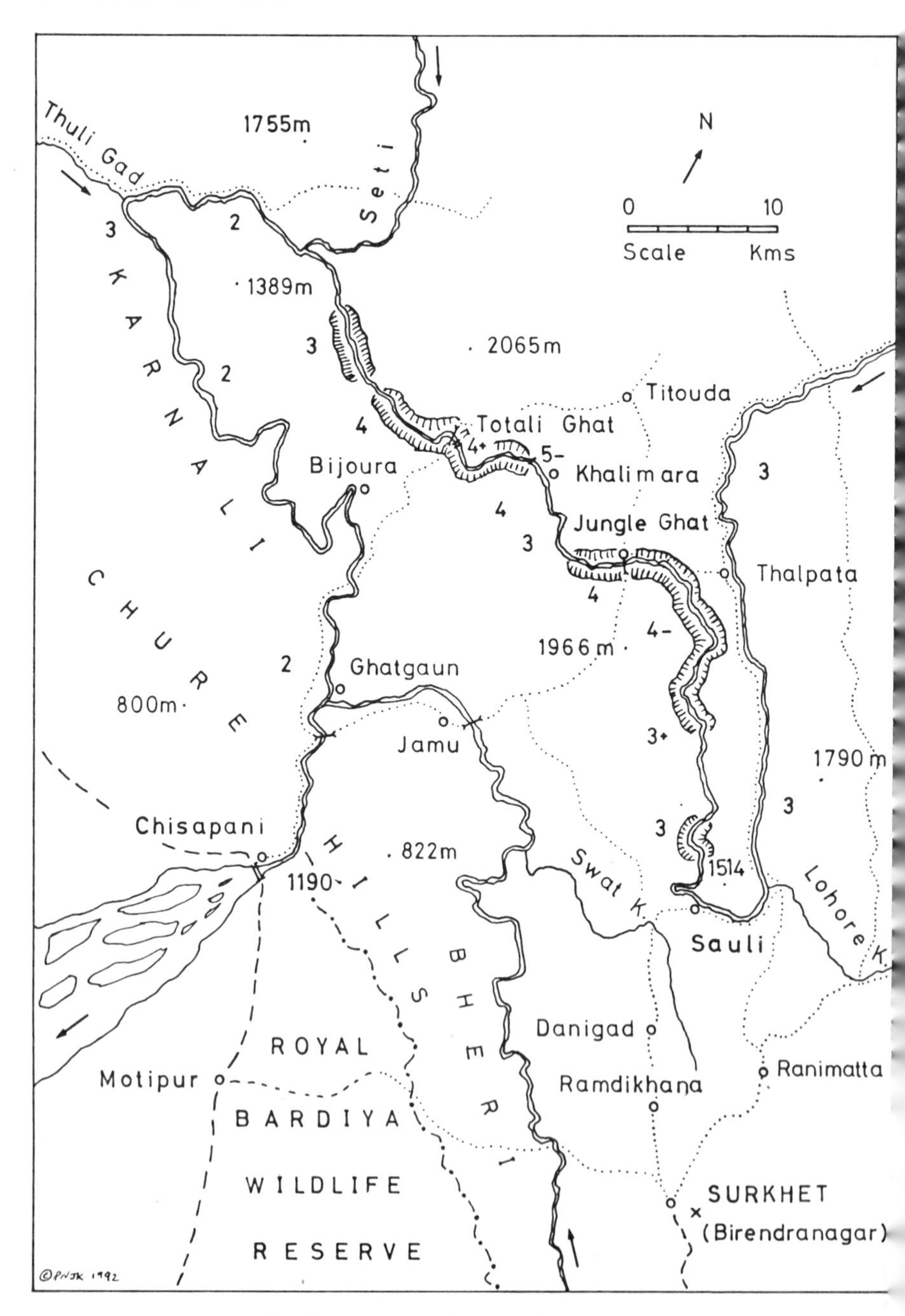

WARNING: Laser-phobic ink – do not photocopy.

Karnali lower

From: **Sauli** (Alt. 560m)
To: **Chisapani** (Alt. 195m)
Distance: **180 kms** (113 miles)
River Days: **5–7**
From Kathmandu: **1 plus 2 day trek**
Difficulty in Nov: **Class 4** (5)
Average gradient: **0.2%** (10 ft a mile)
Est. max. gradient: **0.5%**
Volume in Nov: **300 cumecs** (10,500 cfs)
Best Season: **Nov/Dec, March/April.**

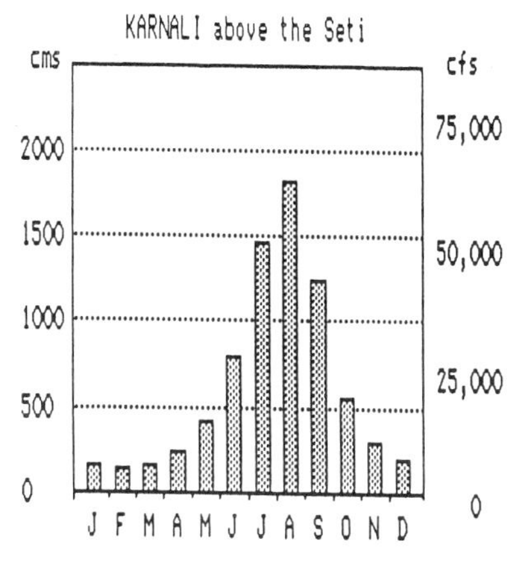

Summary

One of finest big volume rafting and kayaking trips in Nepal, and definitely the best combination trip: for trekking, white water rafting and wilderness – a World Classic!. Spectacular jungle-clad canyons, BIG white water and abundant wildlife – We recommend this as one of the ultimate trips for adventurous rafters and kayakers seeking excitement and wilderness.

The river

The Karnali is Nepal's longest and largest river and with its tributaries, it drains most of the Far West of Nepal – the 'Wild West' as many people call it. This bottom section of the river definitely lives up to that name – the area that it flows through is wild and unpopulated with some of the most pristine jungle scenery in Nepal, and abundant wildlife.

The rapids are also pretty wild, with the river building to its climax in these lower canyons. Shortly after the sharp bend in the river 'the elbow' by the Lohore Khola, the valley narrows into a series of canyons, the river speeds up, and there are big rapids, one leading into another, almost continously down to the Seti River. From the 'Elbow' down to the Seti the gradient is 3.0% (15 ft a mile), but after here, the gradient eases, as the river winds through some magnificent unspoilt scenery, eventually emerging onto the plains and flowing through the Royal Bardiya Wildlife Reserve to join the Ganges.

In terms of volume, the rivers is comparable to the Sun Kosi, but the Karnali is more constrained by its Canyon walls; giving bigger, more continuous and serious rapids. This constrained nature of the river means that any increase in volume has a more pronounced effect on the difficulty of the rapids and this makes it a river that is best run at low flows – November through to April. Highest extreme instantaneous discharge measured at Chisapani was an incredible 21,700 cumecs (760,000 cfs).

The high flows and gradient of this lower river has made it a prime contender for Hydro Electric Power Schemes. Three projects have been proposed: A tunnel through the elbow near Thalpata, a tunnel south from Sauli to the Swat Khola, and a large dam at Chisapani. At the time of writing, none of these projects has been approved or looks likely in the near future. From an ecological viewpoint we hope that these schemes will never get the go-ahead: this must be the largest and most unspoilt 'wilderness' area of its kind in Nepal. Wildlife is abundant: we saw lots of tracks and animal scat from bears, leopards, jackals, etc. We were sceptical when local people warned us that we shouldn't camp by the river and that if we did, we should keep a fire going all night. Later we were staying in a construction camp at Chisapani, and we were told that a local villager had just been killed by a tiger. The following morning we were woken early by Phil who heard something moving under his camp bed: this turned out to be a three-metre long python!

Fishing is also abundant in the river and the Karnali must compete with its tributary the Bheri for the title 'best fishing river' – please see fishing notes in the 'Bheri' section.

The trek to the start of the river trip is pleasant and highly scenic. It climbs through mixed Sal (hardwood) forest, and then traverses two ridge tops with excellent panoramic views of the Bheri forests. This river has seen so few descents that local people have met few westerners, and it is up to you to make sure that the contact they have is positive.

Rafting

In 1987 Pete Knowles, Mick Hopkinson and a team of international kayakers were asked by the Nepalese Ministry of Tourism to survey the Karnali and report on the potential for commercial rafting. In their report to the government, they said, 'It is the unanimous view of this team that this is one of the finest rafting rivers in the world'.

Since then, Pete has wondered whether this was an exaggerated view, but there have been several more kayaking trips, the first commercial raft groups, and all who have done the river seem to have been just as enthusiastic, if not more so – a lot of experienced rafters have said, 'This is the best river I've ever done'. It's a subject of debate amongst rafters as to whether the Karnali really is a better rafting trip than the Sun Kosi or Tamur; this depends on water levels, how you rate white water, wilderness and scenery and your own personal experience.

The rapids on the top half of the run start fairly easily, but then as you come into the Main Canyon it becomes a 'thrill-a-minute roller-coaster' with rapids on every bend. It is unlikely that you will need to portage or line more than one or two rapids, but this is just as well because some sections are so continuous that portaging is not an option – this is a trip for expert rafters and considering the wilderness nature of the terrain, it should not be under-estimated. If you are booking with a commercial company then you should thoroughly check out their experience on the river. (Note that if you would prefer to miss out this first section, then a start on the Seti River offers an easier and safer option).

The second half of the Karnali has little white water and to some people this is a real anti-climax; to others this is more than made up by incredible jungle, wilderness and wildlife – also some bigger fish!

Chisapani is the usual point to finish a trip – Chisapani means cold water, and this is a warning that the Karnali is a bit cooler than the Sun Kosi or Trisuli, and some thermal/shell clothing would be a good idea. Rather than rushing straight back to Kathmandu, we strongly recommend that you consider staying at the **Royal Bardiya Wildlife Reserve** for a couple of days. Someone said that this reserve 'Makes Chitwan look like London Zoo' – a bit exagerated perhaps, but it is certainly one of the best National Wildlife Parks in Asia. At the time of writing, only 'Tiger Tops' had a camp here and their safari lodge is understandably expensive – but you get what you pay for, and after 8 days of roughing it, how nice to splurge out on a bit of luxury!

Note that because of its remoteness and difficulty, the Karnali works out as a relatively expensive rafting trip, not one to cut corners on, but a premier trip that commands a premier

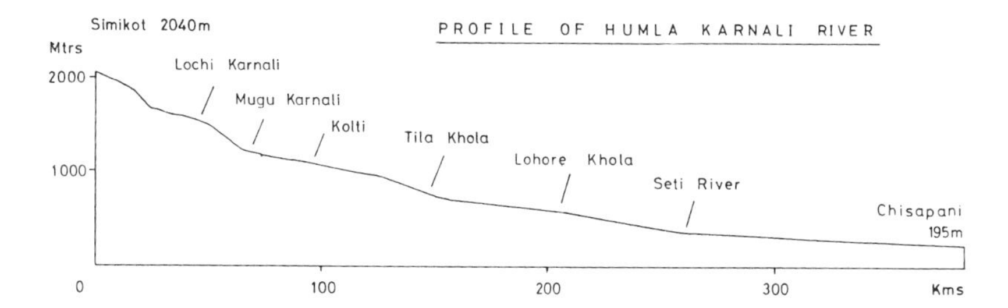

price. It should also be said that the Karnali isn't a trip for softies: the two day trek to the start is not hard but neither is it a Sunday afternoon walk, and the 3 days of class 4 big white water rapids will work you hard and have you pleasantly tired by the end of each day. Dave Allardice says 'This is not a river to be underated – this is a remote region – a swim in the middle canyon could have serious consequences – as one huge powerful rapid leads straight into the next'. For the rafter with previous experience, looking for a classic river trip, we think this is it – probably the best combination raft trip in the World. Go try it – measure it up against the Bio Bio, the Grand Canyon of the Colorado, the Landsborough, the Zambezi, the Tatshenshini, the Zanskar, or the Apurimac, and then come and tell us what you think!

Kayaking

Most of the comments on the Karnali as a rafting trip also apply to the kayaker – this has some of the best big water rapids in Nepal. The only disadvantage to the kayaker is that these are all condensed into the first few days and not nicely spread out for more play days. This is an incredible river for the expert paddler or the advanced intermediate who is happy on big water. Big rapid follows big rapid, with lots and lots of play potential, great surfing and some well defined eddies for such a big river – just super fun!

We are undecided whether this is best done with raft support or as a self-sufficient trip. There is some superb playing – better with light boats, but on the other hand this is such a magnificent wilderness trip that it is better experienced as a small tight group. We think that the smaller your group, the more you will be awed by the immensity of the jungle, this great river, and your own insignificance – especially so in the dark of night, surrounded by strange rustlings, howls and roars from the all-surrounding jungle!

Probably the main advantage to having raft support is to take longer over the the Canyon section, spliting it over several more days; giving more play time and more time to relish the magnificent scenery. However, the remoteness and difficulty makes raft support relatively expensive and this will persuade many people to go self-supported. It's also a good length so you don't have to carry too much food – most kayak groups will probably take about 4 days. If you prefer to play with an empty kayak, then have a talk to any company that may be running a raft trip – you may be able to negotiate a special rate as this a river where raft groups really like to have a couple of expert kayakers along as safety boaters.

We recommend Sauli as the best starting point, but if wanted it is possible for kayaks to put in on the Lohore Khola where the main trail from Surkhet to Dailekh crosses. Note that for several days upstream of the Lohore Khola, the Karnali is relatively flat and uninteresting – we think it is a waste of time and effort to start higher up, unless you are going to start a lot higher up on the Mugu or Humla Karnali (see separate description).

Access and logistics

We recommend **Sauli** as the best start point for this trip, reached by a 2 day trek in from Surkhet. **Surkhet** is called Birendranager on government maps and is reached, either by flying in (about $100 from Kathmandu) or by overnight bus via Butwhal, about 17 hours and costing $6. Larger groups might hire their own bus or minibus – around $300. The last section of the road from the Terai to Surkhet is quite beautiful and crosses first the Babai Nadu and then the Bheri rivers – see notes.

An alternative route is via **Nepalganj**, the largest city of the Far West and about 6 hour's bus ride to Surkhet. Nepalganj is almost half way between Kathmandu and Delhi, so if you are arriving from or travelling on to Delhi, then we suggest that you should consider travelling direct to this city (no convenient or comfortable routes other than by Taxi – about a 14 hour drive and at aprox. $200, surprisingly cost-effective. The snag with this might be arranging for raft and trekking permits.

Surkhet is a reasonably-sized town and all basic supplies can be purchased here. It is an expanding and relatively pleasant town that is the new government headquarters for the Mid Western region of Nepal. Only simple hotels are available at the moment, but your Hotel Manager will usually help arrange porters for you – readily available for about $3 a day.

There are two trekking routes north to the Karnali: we recommend the route via Danigad as the pleasanter and shorter. This trail to Sauli first heads west out of Surket and then climbs through mixed Sal forest to the ridge top village of Bayal Kanda and then passes through Ramdikhana – the school children here welcomed us with a special display of local dances. People here have seen very few Westerners and are very friendly – please observe the Himalayan Tourist Code so that they remain unspoilt.

Make sure you fill your water bottles because it is dry for the next 2-3 hours as you walk along the top of the ridge. This is a very old trail: inscribed pillars at Ramdikhana and Danigad date back to the 10th Century when this whole region was relatively unpopulated. There are wonderful views of terraced rice fields as you descend from Danigad to the Swat Khola, passing through the village of Sirichour, 30 minutes before the river. There is a good campsite where the trail crosses the Swat Khola and then the trail climbs steeply on the left of a wash to the top of the pass, where there is a small and welcome tea house.

If you are feeling energetic the trail off to the left climbs the ridge, the Malka Danda, from where there are sweeping views of the Karnali. From the tea house on the saddle you traverse around to the small village of **Sauli**, on a small ridge, and then drop down 200m to the river. We couldn't find any convenient beaches that were large enough for our group on this bank – you can either walk upstream for about an hour to where a small stream, the Khali Khola joins the Karnali and camp and start here; or alternatively, if you get here early enough, ferry the gear across to camp on a beach on the far side.

The usual finish point for the trip is the village of **Chisapani** where the river emerges onto the plains. The Mahendra Highway, the main East-west road along the southern borders of Nepal crosses the Karnali on a spectacular new single-strut bridge* that is being built. At the time of writing, the best take out was on the left by the ferry point and upstream of the new bridge. When the new bridge and new road is open, then this may be a better place to get out and it may be possible to catch a night bus straight through to Kathmandu.

Recommended options at the end of the Karnali trip are:

- Spend a couple of nights in Royal Bardiya Wildlife Reserve. (consider a take-out at their tented camp near the river.)

- Catch a local bus to Nepalganj and stay the night in comfort here before returning to Pokhara, Kathmandu or Delhi.
- Catch a local bus to Kohalpur (the junction where the road from Nepalganj joins the Mahendra Highway) to connect with a night bus back to Pokhara or Kathmandu. A local bus to Nepalganj will cost about $1 and take two hours.

Like all river trips in the 'Wild West', you need to be totally self sufficient on the Karnali. There are very few villages near the river and those that there are, will have little spare food to sell you. It is a fine river for camping, but note that on some sections, as detailed later, there are only a few beaches suitable for campsites; however, there is abundant driftwood for fires. Our own sketch map of the river is probably as good as any map as you can buy – the HMG Central Service Map for Surkhet District, at a scale of 1:125,000, shows the side streams in more detail, but misses off many of the trails and villages.

In the case of an emergency on the first half of the river, the trail crossings at Jungle Ghat and Totali Ghat are the only two practical egress routes. Below the confluence with the Seti, an evacuation down river would probably be the best option.

** Back in 1987 I talked to some of the engineers working on this bridge and being curious and naive I asked them why a sophisticated single-strut design had been chosen rather than a suspension bridge. 'Was it cheaper'? I asked. They laughed. 'Of course not – it just looked more impressive.' Still being curious I dumbly asked 'But don't you need solid foundations in the middle of the river for the single-strut design'? The atmosphere suddenly grew heavy, teeth knashed, tired eyes looked at me angrily and I desperately tried to change the subject. Well, the bridge is almost finished and time will tell . . .*

'A thrill-a-minute roller-coaster'

Description

Sauli to Jungle Ghat 39 kms, Seti 36 kms, Chisapani 105 kms.

From the put-in near the village of Sauli, the river begins gently with many class 2 and 3 rapids, an easy roller-coaster rider with rapids at every bend. In this first few kms there are some great beaches for camping. Valley sides are steep, heavily forested and shoot up over 500 metres. There is one short canyon about 7 kms after the start, then the valley opens up slightly for 7 kms before narrowing into a much larger and longer canyon (18 kms) all the way down to Jungle Ghat. There are very few beaches on this latter canyon, but one after about 8 kms on a left hand corner makes a reasonable campsite. Streams coming in from both sides create beautiful waterfalls. The roller-coaster ride continues and the rapids get bigger and harder, class 4, just before Jungle Ghat.

Jungle Ghat has a few tea houses on both sides of the bridge, and not much else, but offers a chance to stop and meet all the interesting local people on the trail. Below here, the river becomes more serious with many large holes in the rapids. 2 kms downstream of the bridge are two large class 4 rapids; the valley then widens, there are good beaches for camping and rapids are class 3 for 7 kms down to the village of Khalimara. The village is on the right bank with a cable crossing just upstream.

Three kms below here you enter another steep and high canyon with very few beaches or camp sites for the next 17 kms. The first rapid is possibly a 5− with all the river feeding into a monstrous hole in the centre that we called 'Captivity' – worth a scout. Below here, the river is continuous class 3 and 4 BIG rapids, many large holes, and one rapid leading straight into the next – incredible rafting and kayaking and the ultimate fun! Just before the bridge at **Totali Ghat** are two class 4+ rapids, the first called 'Flip and strip' – these have some nasty holes lurking for the unwary, and you would be wise to scout them. Immediately under the bridge is a class 4 rapid, 'Lost Mutt', entertainment for bemused locals crossing the bridge.

The canyon continues for the next 6 kms with good class 3-4 white water. The last exit rapid is straight forward, big and bouncy, with huge waves constrained by sheer rock walls. Below here, there are several possible camping beaches in the next 4 kms as the valley opens out and the river quietens down to class 2-3 for a while.

'Red rock Canyon' now follows – lots of surfing and playing in a really beautiful Canyon with layers of red rock pushed into strange contorted shapes. This is a really fun section; rapids every few minutes, but all pretty straight forward class 3, and a relief after the main canyon. Just after Red Rock Canyon is a gauging station and wire across the river and 6 km further is the **Seti** confluence.

The Seti River adds about another 20-40% to the volume of the Karnali, but from here the gradient eases and now there is time to relax. There is still a powerful current, so you don't have to work hard and there is the occasional class 2 or 3 rapid to stop you falling asleep. This lower river has some magnificent jungle scenery, strange rock formations, beautiful large beaches for stunning campsites and an abundance of wildlife and fish. We are still debating whether the large foot prints we saw one morning were leopard or tiger. Most nights we saw cat prints; heard animal noises, rustlings, howls – jackals? – and one night a large animal crashing around – a bear? The famous explorer John Bashford Snell led a scientific expedition for Operation Raleigh down the lower Karnali in 1992 and reported capturing and measuring a five metre long python, and also observing crocodiles and freshwater dolphins. Birdlife is plentiful, over 200 species!

There are very few villages or signs of people. Until malaria was brought under control in the 1970's, this whole area was little populated. You may see a few fishermen, and we were lucky to come across a local craftsman carving a dugout canoe out of a massive Simal tree. If you are lucky you may meet some of the Raute (or Ragi) tribe, shy forest folk who used to live by gathering fruits and hunting monkeys with nets. Bashford-Snell talked to some of them in 1992 and they told him that there were none left in the forest and that they have been forced to abandon their nomadic way of life and traditional taboos against planting crops.

The first major settlement on the river is the village of Ghatgaun, a km or two above the confluence with the **Bheri**. This is an important ferry point, serviced by two huge dugout canoes, expertly paddled by the ferrymen. Shortly after the Bheri river a long suspension bridge swoops gracefully over the river and this marks the start of the final bedrock canyon where the river cuts its way through the Chure Hills. This is a beautiful canyon with dramatic rock formations. A water-gauging cable crosses the river just upstream of Chisapani. The main village is on the right, but for most groups it is better to take out on the left bank at the ferry or by the new bridge when it is open.

Downstream are the plains of India, the Ganges River and Indian Ocean.

'Ambush' . . . *by Ben Willems*

'The last two days were pretty flat water, but they weren't without excitement. Craig and I were paddling through the last gorge when suddenly a splash on my right by the bank broke the silence. I turned but saw only the ripples of some thing which had entered the water. And then I heard the splash of something on my left directly across the other side of the gorge, and my worst thoughts were confirmed, for there on the left bank was the third Marsh Mugger Crocodile, the size of our boats, slinking into the water exactly as they do on television. It was a planned ambush and we were easy targets; no antlers, fur or claws – just soft and pink. Well, I thought I was tired, but muscles weary from three months of paddling weren't given a second thought as we tore off downstream. We never did sight them again – polyethylene can't have been on their menu that day.....'

Dutch womens kayak expedition . . . *by Mieke de Moor and Gabrielle Marges*

One sunny day in spring 1987, while the men were canoeing in Turkey, we suddenly looked at ourselves taking care of their kids and thought how we were depriving ourselves of the same kind of pleasure. So, we took a decision; we planned our own expedition to the Karnali river in the Far West of Nepal, and even before the men had returned, we had broadcast our plans for the 'First Dutch Women's Kayak Expedition'.

Training courses followed and a lot of writing to make all the arrangements and get the necessary permits. Then, in November 1989, we set out walking from the Terai, the flat southern part of Nepal, up to the mountains, to reach the Karnali river. We were accompanied by twenty 'fans' carrying lots of food and three kayaks. Hard to please as women are, we not only wanted to go kayaking in Nepal, but also wanted to walk the side routes and watch the world change as we traversed valleys and mountain ranges on our way to the start of the river.

Suddenly, we came to a checkpost underneath a steep mountain at the beginning of one of the river's canyons. 'Papers, please, Memsahib'. How grateful we were for the safe feeling of being registered in the middle of nowhere; at least they would know where we were if anything happened! In broken English (just like us), the man in uniform told us how he had explained to the local people what country we had come from: that these ladies came from a totally flat country, so low that the birds above the land fly lower than the fishes swim in the sea . . . Incredulously they stared at us, at our red, pink and green dungas and our space age tents. They had never seen things like these before and they had to touch everything just to be sure; they will have some stories to tell in the next few years.

After two weeks of trekking through this wonderful country, we (Selien, Mieke and Gabrielle) started kayaking. How do you describe such a marvellous, exciting, dazzling trip? Everyone seems to use the same superlatives, so we won't try to surpass our male colleagues. And of course, when women paddle a river like this, it can't have been as rough as they told you, it must have been very low water, they must have carried over the difficult parts . . . so we won't try!

After a few days' paddling we said goodbye to the rest of our new family. Marloes, our Guide, and our porters would walk down to Chisapani, our take-out. The three of us put everything we would need for the next week in our kayaks and started paddling down the Himalaya. We got our orientation from a rough map, using the sun and our watches as a compass, and counting the curves of the meandering river.

We couldn't tell exactly where we were, when one day we camped on a beautiful little beach facing a water curtain sprinkling down a green wall of climbing plants. The evening sun sparkled off the water droplets and highlighted the hand marks of apes in the white sand. We felt far from any sign of human activity, but how wrong we were: when we woke up next morning we were staring at a huge rifle carried by a little man with a bivouac cap! Not knowing what to make of it, we tried to forget about the rifle and offered the man a cup of tea. Immediately he took off his cap, smiled a big smile and made the traditional 'Namaste' greeting. The ice was broken. He must have been as much impressed by us, three western women with strange colourful dungas, as we were by him with his ancient rifle.

Of course, we have many more tales to tell about our trip to this Far Western part of Nepal, but you will have to come to Holland to hear them! We only want to say that Nepal has become a very special country to us. Travelling as women has never been a problem. Nepal is a very tolerant country, not only so far as religion is concerned, but in every respect, inhabited by very friendly people with a fine sense of humour. We simply could be as we are, without first being regarded as women. Westerners can learn a lot from these people.

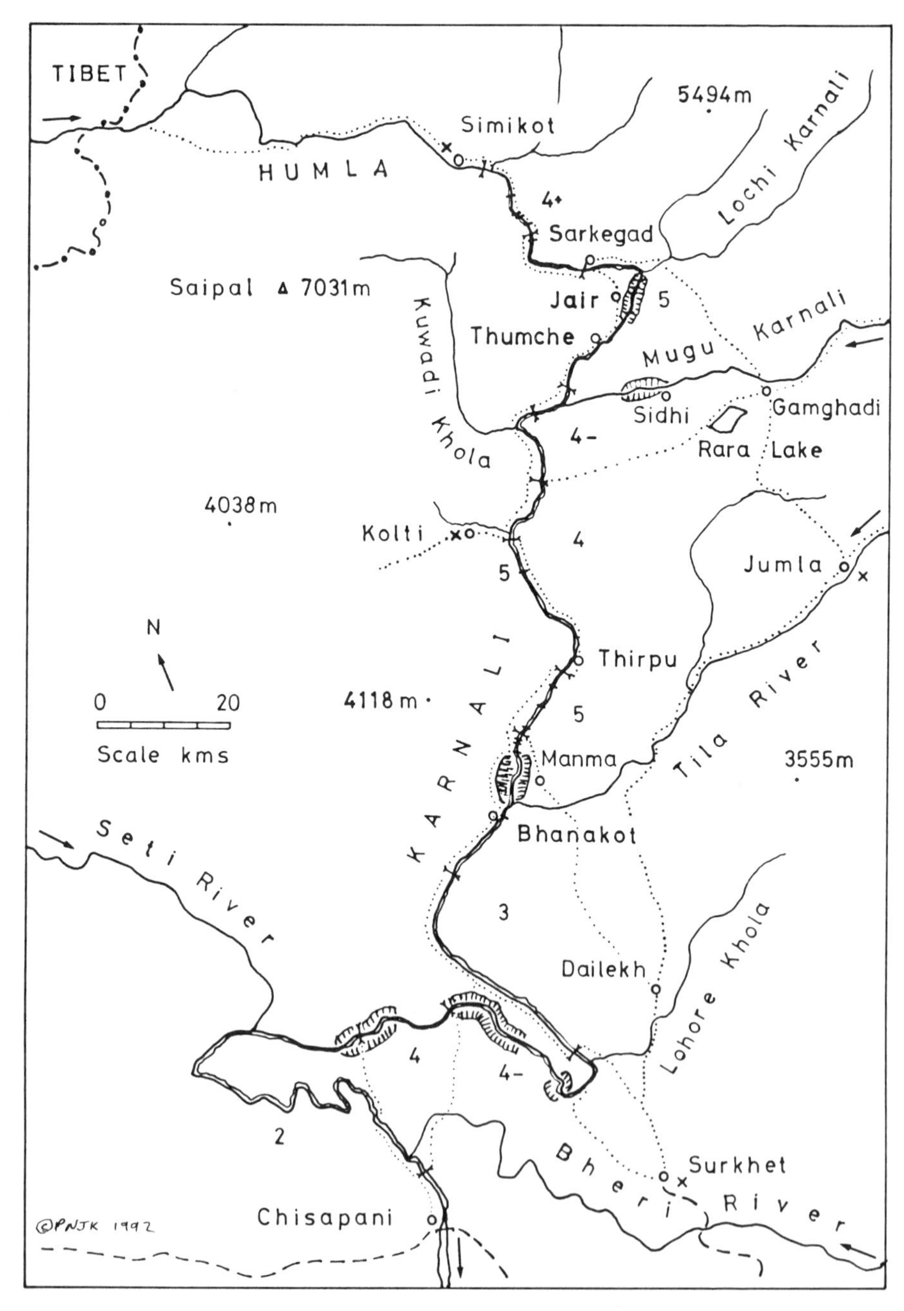

WARNING: Laser-phobic ink – do not photocopy.

Humla Karnali and the upper Karnali

(The lower Karnali below the Lohore Khola is described separately.)

From:	**Simikot** (Alt. 2040m)
To:	**Chisapani** (Alt. 195m)
Distance:	**385 kms** (241 miles)
River Days:	**16–20**
From Kathmandu:	**2 days fly in**
Difficulty in Nov:	**Class 5–** (6)
Average gradient:	**0.5%** (25 ft a mile)
Est. max. gradient:	**4.0%**
Volume in Nov:	**200 cumecs** (7,000 cfs)
Best Season:	**Nov-Dec, March-April.**

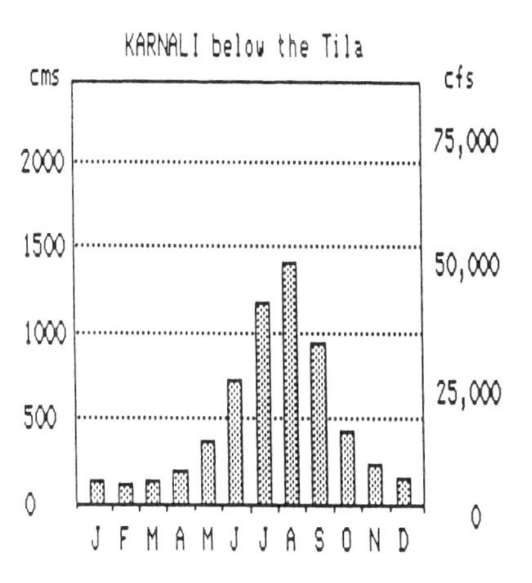

Summary

One of the finest white water kayaking trips of its length in the world – nearly 400 kms, most of it class 3 to 5, with only a few kms to portage. In the heart of the 'Wild West' of Nepal – no roads, remote, unspoilt and committing.

Only recommended for experienced expedition kayakers.

The river

The Karnali rises in Tibet near **Mount Kailas** – holy to Budhists and Hindus as the four-sided mountain that is the centre of the world and from which four major rivers flow – the Karnali, Indus, Sutlej, and Brahmaputra (Tsangpo). The Karnali has a total length of about 500 kms and a glance at a map of Nepal will show that the river flows roughly North to south and drains the heart of the remote Far West Region.

What makes this river particularly interesting to the river runner is the surprisingly steady gradient as it descends from the Himalaya to the Indian Plains. This gives some very continuous and exhilarating white water, with only a few relatively flat sections and only a few kms that are unrunnable – quite exceptional in our experience for a river of this length and gradient.

The Humla Karnali is particularly beautiful, with pine forests and high mountain peaks (many still unclimbed) bordering a blue alpine river. A deep and pathless gorge, just after the Lochi Karnali, forms a natural barrier that isolates this upper valley of the Humla Karnali. Below here, the landscape is more arid, the valley is wider and in the distance are the long, high ridges (the 'Leks') that are a feature of the Far West. This type of scenery continues to 'the elbow' where the Lohore Khola joins. The bottom section of the river, below here, is different again – deep canyons, wild and little populated, some of the most pristine jungle scenery in Nepal, and abundant wildlife. We think that this bottom section of the river is so distinctive, and is such a special raft trip, that we have described this separately – please see 'Lower Karnali'.

The valley of the Karnali is one of the historic trade routes between the plains of India and Tibet. The Chinese invasion of Tibet and subsequent closure of the frontier caused considerable hardship to the Nepalese Traders and villagers on this old trade route. We were pleased to see that in 1987 the trade had to some extent revived and were amazed to discover that the main pack animals were still sheep, each beast carrying a small home-spun pack bag filled with rice on the way up the valley and salt on the return. Half way down the Humla valley, whilst portaging a rapid, we got caught up in a massive traffic jam as 100 sheep coming up the valley met a similar flock going the other way! At night, the accompanying drovers built individual fires to sleep by – to surround the herd and keep the wolves away.

The Humla Karnali below Simikot drops at about 2.0% and with a volume in November of something like 80 cumecs (2600 cfs), it has very much the feel of a narrow mountain river. The river gets bigger all the time; the Lochi and Mugu Karnali add maybe another 35 cumecs each, so that near Kolti the river has grown to about 180 cumecs. Below the Tila the river has a volume of 240 cumecs and then, swelled by the waters of the Seti and Bheri rivers, it has a mighty volume of 630 cumecs where it breaks out onto the Plains at Chisapani.

Rafting

The lower section of the Karnali below the Lohore Khola makes an excellent, world class raft trip – this is written up separately – please see 'Lower Karnali'.

We do not recommend rafting above the Lohore Khola. The Humla Karnali is too small and difficult and would require many difficult portages. Below the confluence of the Mugu Karnali is some excellent rafting and some fine white water; however, this is spoilt by a long section of difficult rapids above the Tila that would require lengthy and difficult portages.

We used kayaks when we ran the river in 1987, but two groups have rafted it in higher water conditions and both confirm our assessment. Bruce Mason led a large American expedition down the Upper Karnali in early November 1981, putting in near Gamghadi on the Mugu, and took 10 days down to the confluence with the Humla and then another 10 days down to the Tila. Barry Miller and Malcolm Ulrich flew into Simikot in late October 1990 with two cat-a-rafts and it took them 20 days to do the Humla Karnali with a lot of portaging and a further 19 days to cover the rest of the river down to Chisapani.

One rafting possiblity is to fly into Jumla, trek down the Tila valley and then start from below the Tila confluence. However, from here to the Lohore Khola is fairly uninteresting and doesn't seem to us, worth the extra time and expense when compared with access from Surkhet.

Kayaking

This is a superb river trip for the white water kayaker looking for a major expedition – This is like the Marsyandi, Trisuli and Sun Kosi rivers all put together: every kind of rapid, spectacular gorges, magnificent scenery and unspoilt wilderness. Mick Hopkinson probably summed up this trip for most paddlers when he called it 'the most committing river I've ever done'.

This is also an immensely satisfying trip to do: you fly into **Simikot** at over 3000 metres, right in the High Himalaya with unclimbed peaks all around and then kayak down through three separate and diverse ecological regions to emerge in the heat and the dust of the

Indian Plains. (The flight is quite spectacular: you fly up the river so get a good view; Simikot is the most remote airstrip in Nepal and you land on a terrace on the valley side by flying directly at the mountain – no second chances! A ramp assists subsequent take off.)

The Humla and upper Karnali are difficult to grade, in that this does depend just how many rapids you portage. We feel that to run the river in a reasonable time frame and to avoid undue portages it should be rated a class 5−. This is a river that is best paddled in really low water conditions: we would suggest April as the best month, in that it should be warmer than December.

Above Simikot the river steepens considerably – about 4.0% for 50 kms, and then flattens off on the Tibetan Plateau at around 3700 metres. Whilst not impossible, this section above Simikot would need shore support, and much scouting and portaging. If border politics ever allowed it, it would be great to take kayaks by road through Tibet to Lake Manasarowar, undertake a pilgrimage around Mount Kailas, and then do a complete descent of the Karnali from the Tibetan Plateau, down through Nepal to the plains of India, Wow!

Karnali above the Tila confluence

We recommend this as a self-supported trip, but suggest that you consider employing porters for the first few days on the Humla Karnali, down to just below the first gorge. From here on, a kayak group would be twice as fast as the porters and it would be frustrating waiting for them. Assuming all runs to plan, you can probably reckon on about 5 days to below the first gorge, 6 days to the Lohore Khola and 4 days to Chisapani – this makes no allowance for rest days, etc.

Access and logistics

Simikot, the starting point, is best reached by flying in from Nepalganj, the hub for flights in the Far West of Nepal. You will probably need to make your flight reservations actually in **Nepalganj** (Don't believe what they tell you in Kathmandu, Nepalganj is the other end of the country and a rule to itself!), so it's probably wise to send an advance party to make any arrangements. Night bus to Nepalganj takes about 18 hours and costs about $6.

We chartered a twin otter to take our group of six kayaks, gear and people into Simikot; this cost about $1700 in 1987 and RNAC in Nepalganj could not have been more helpful. If you are a small team, then the alternative would be to fly in on the scheduled daily service, approx $120 per person. To trek in up the river would take about three weeks, and probably wouldn't work out that much cheaper.

Bruce Mason started on the **Mugu Karnali** near Gamghadi in 1981, having trekked in from Jumla. We talked to Barry Miller, who was on this trip (and who also ran the Humla in 1990). He described the Mugu as smaller volume than the Humla, generally easier, still great class 3-5 white water, but the Sidhi Gorge was unrunnable and had to be portaged.

Whether you fly, or trek into the river, you should plan to be totally self-sufficient – there is very little food to be purchased, in aid parlance this is a 'food deprivation zone' and in 1987 the United Nations were flying in loads of rice to feed the poor. If you do fly into Simikot, you should have no problem in hiring porters to carry your boats and gear down to the river, about 1000 metres below the town. Some of our best porters were Bhotia women, cheerfully making light of their awkward loads, laughing and making fun of these strange foreigners. It might be worth considering a support group meeting you further down the river at the Lohore Khola; either a Sirdar with food supplies, or perhaps raft support, friends and beer for the lower river.

Don't believe all that you read about the Far West: the villagers we met down the river were very welcoming – a view shared by other groups. Despite the general food shortage, we were offered special treats of wild honey, eggs and fish. There are many beautiful campsites and no shortage of driftwood for fires.

In the event of an emergency, you are a long, long way from Kathmandu, even when you do reach somewhere to send a message. Note the airstrip at Kolti; that has radio facilities and in 1987 there was also a radio transmitter at Manma. Best map covering the upper river is the 1:250,000 H.M.G. Main Trail Map for the Karnali Zone. Two trekking/rafting agencies have built up good experience of the Upper Karnali and can be especially recommended: Shyam Piya of 'Karnali Tours and Expeditions' and Mrs Renchin Yonjan of 'Treks and Expedition Services'.

Description

Simikot – Mugu Karnali 70 kms Lohore Khola 135, Chisapani 180.

Simikot is a large village on a terrace high above the river, rather spoilt by being the District headquarters. The surrounding country, villages, and people are beautiful, fascinating and highly photogenic. ('Hidden Himalaya', by T.Kelly & V.Dunhan illustrates this area). We really wished that we had had more time to spend here and explore. It will take about half a day to move your gear and boats down the steep track to the river some 1000 metres below. The track descends into a side valley, the Ghat Khola, and there is a reasonable campsite and put-in just downstream of the confluence.

The river starts out as class 3 for the first 6 kms, then there is a lethal-looking class 6 with a portage left for 600 metres. Solid class 4 for 4 kms leads to a pool and beach as the river

Trekking down to the river from Simikot (Phil Bibby)

obviously narrows. The river drops into a huge hole and then disappears under a boulder about the size of an office block, followed by a series of class 5 and 6 rapids: The track on the left bank makes a convenient but long portage of 1.5 kms.

Class 2 for 2 kms leads into a scenic canyon. A class 6 rapid at the end of this, where the canyon narrows, needs a 400m portage left. From here a few kms of class 4+ water brings you down to the suspension bridge. Just after the bridge the river disappears under a huge house rock and is followed by some tricky rapids. Portage left or right – about 200m?

A few more kms of class 4 and 4+ will probably require some scouting from the bank and then the valley swings east; a rapid on the bend might be a class 5 and is worth a scout. The river bumbles on, nice continuous class 3 and 4 down to the next suspension bridge at **Sarkegad**. Below the bridge, up on the left bank, is the local High School and you can be sure of a delighted welcome. 10 kms of relatively relaxed and scenic class 3 and 4 brings you to the confluence with the Lochi Karnali and the first big gorge.

This gorge is the climax of the upper section: pathless, and with 500m cliffs. Until we ran it in 1987, it was unsurveyed and untrodden. We were naturally apprehensive, especially since the Hydro Surveyors in Kathmandu had told us that they couldn't get their helicopter in, and would we do a rough survey for them? (nice to know kayaks have their uses!). The gorge proved to be like some lost world with exotic fauna. Paddling (class 5) and portaging was tough, but O.K. and thankfully not as serious as we had feared. About 4 portages, 2 short ones, and two 300m long 'up and over' ones will probably be required and ropes (throw ropes) will probably be useful. The main part of the gorge only extends some 5 kms down to where the Nehar Khola comes in on the left. There is a rope bridge here and a rough path leads up to the the village of **Jair**.

Below the Nehar Khola, two big class 5 rapids follow in the next 2 kms. The river now eases and 3 kms of class 4– bring you to where the main trail rejoins the river, above Thumche. Note that the main trail bypasses the gorge by cutting around the shoulder of the mountain at some 1000 metres above the river and through the village of Jair. This is not shown correctly on most maps. All being well, you can plan on leaving your porters at Sarkegad in the morning and rejoining them at Thumche that evening.

Easy water and a scenic gorge lead down to the **Mugu Karnali**. From here it is mainly class 3 with a couple of 4– rapids, down past the Khatyar Khola (that drains Rara lake), past the suspension bridge where one of the main East/West trail crosses, and finally ends in a long class 5 rapid some 5 kms beyond where the trail turns off to Kolti Airstrip. The locals tried to persuade us from running this by trying to carry our boats around for us – we put on heroic faces and nonchantly refused their kind persuasions, but only to completely lose face when we all had minor epics, and had the stuffing knocked out of us! We hadn't appreciated just how the river had grown so much bigger and more powerful.

Some 20 kms of Class 3-4 leads on down past **Thirpu** – Barry Miller warns not to camp here as 'It's a town of robbers'. A few kms beyond here the river starts getting more interesting with some chunky class 4+, continuous big water for the next 12 kms; we made two short portages before stopping for the night. The next 8 kms are one of the hardest sections of the river and will require careful scouting and probably several portages (we made 3; 2 short ones and one of 500m). It took us a day to run this 8 kms. After the suspension bridge, the main trail is close on the right bank, which makes scouting and portaging easy. The Sani Gad comes in from the right, just after the bridge and marks the biggest rapids.

At the end of this section, the trail climbs and leaves the river as it enters a gorge; fear not, this is only class 3 for 5 kms down to the **Tila Khola** – time for congratulations and a beer (if you have one). The river continues as class 3+ for the next 3kms and then there is a big class 5 rapid that may need portaging.

Below here, the valley widens out and there are many villages for the next 20 kms. The river flattens out and meanders and braids in the wide gravel floor of the valley. There is still a powerful current, so you can just sit there, drift along, and admire the scenery all the way to the Lohore Khola – just the occasional class 3 shoot to wake you up. As the river bends around to the south east, the valley narrows, the sides become steeper and forested and of course there are fewer villages. The river still keeps as class 3 though, all the way to the **Lohore Khola**, which is marked by a temple at the confluence.

Perhaps the best part of the river is still to come, but we have described this separately in the previous section on the 'Karnali – lower'.

'Chicken shoot', Karnali

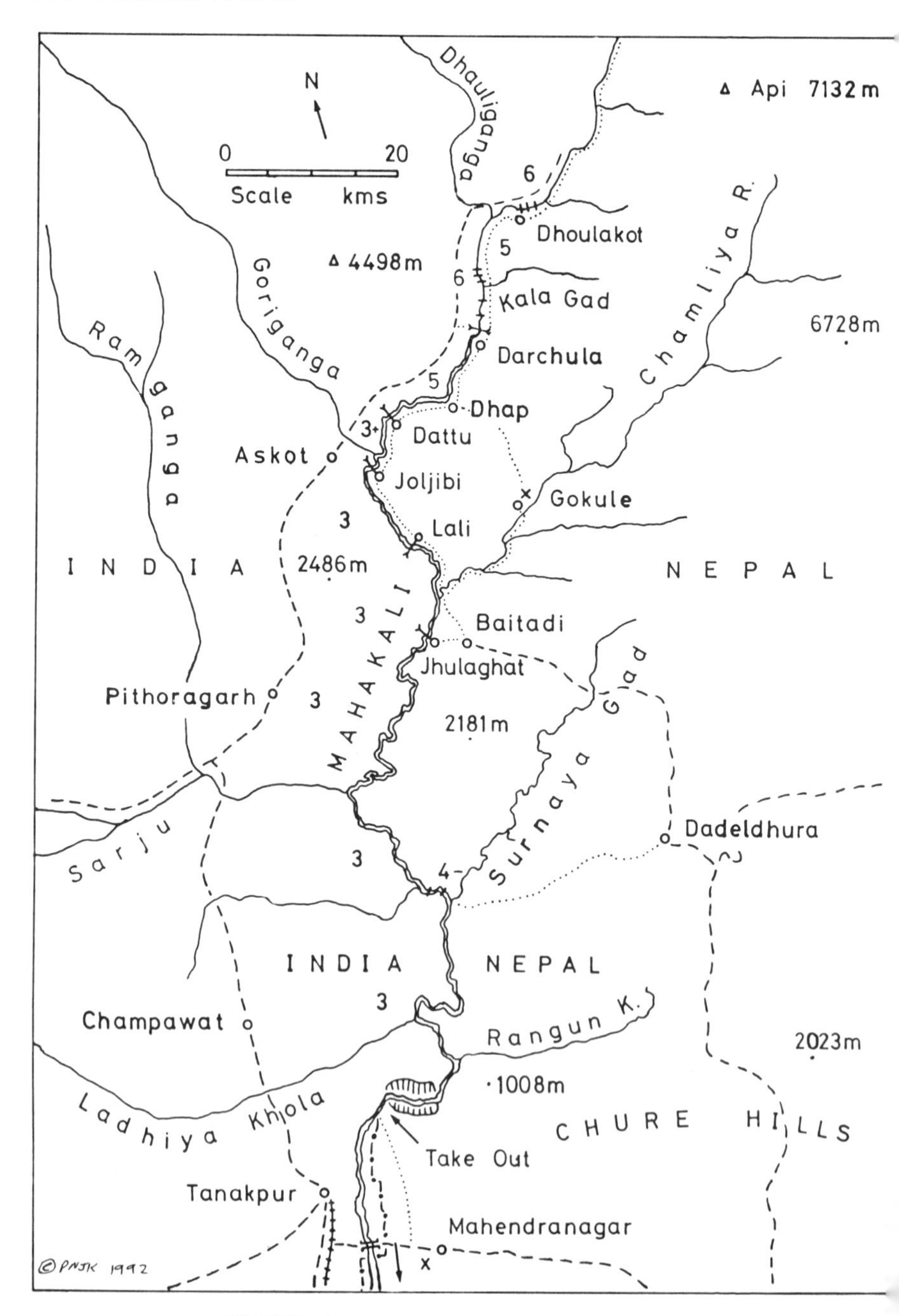

WARNING: Laser-phobic ink – do not photocopy.

Mahakali

by Chris Dickinson

From:	**Dattu** (Alt. 630m)
To:	**Indian Border** (Alt. 250m)
Distance:	**135 kms** (84 miles)
River Days:	**4–6**
From Kathmandu:	**2–4 days**
Difficulty in Nov:	**Class 3** (4−)
Average gradient:	**0.3%** (15 ft a mile)
Est. max. gradient:	**0.6%**
Volume in Nov:	**300 cumecs** (10,000 cfs)
Best Season:	**Oct-Dec, Feb-April.**

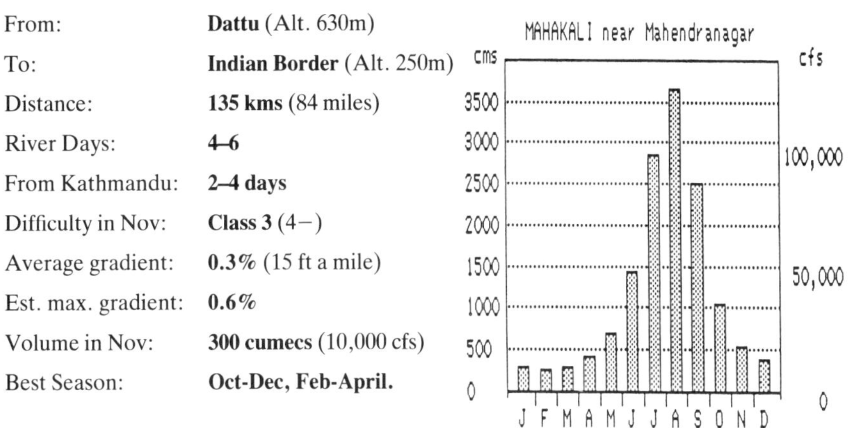

Summary

The least-travelled major river of Nepal; remote, unspoilt, good white water, excellent scenery, and phenomenal bird life; but far from Kathmandu. A good choice for a kayak or raft group looking for a wild and remote river that isn't too difficult. Some challenging kayaking further upstream above Dattu.

The river

The Mahakali is one of the great rivers of the Himalaya, rising on the slopes of Api (7132 metres), the highest peak in the Far West of Nepal. For most of its length the river demarcates the Western boundary with India.

The valley of the Mahakali (called the **Kali** on the Indian side) has always been a major trading route up to Tibet and also the main route for Indian 'yatris' on their pigrimage to Mount Kailas. They are helped these days by the road on the Indian side that goes up most of the way to the border with Tibet at the Lepu Lekh pass.

The river has a classic profile, steepening up very considerably above Darchula. The Goriganga river, which rises on the slopes of Nanda Devi, doubles the flow and below here the river changes character as it glides into a mature valley and easy gorges. There are few villages below the confluence of the Chamliya river, the Mahakali winds, serpent-like, into a jungle fringed wonderland of monkeys and colourful birds. Canyon walls alternate with pristine beaches. Trails are few and people are scarce. The scenery on this stretch is some of the best I have seen in Nepal.

Border politics mean that you either have to run the river from the Indian side staying on the right bank, or from the Nepalese side staying on the left bank and taking out before the river enters Indian territory. Just when the river flows out on to the Terai, it enters Indian Territory; some 20kms of bank were swapped by the British in 1927 so that they could build the Sarda Barrage and irrigation canal near Tanakpur. The road on the Indian side, and the fact that the river is much nearer to Delhi than Kathmandu, makes it more logical to run the river from the Indian side; however, the upper valley is closed to foreigners.

Rafting

The Mahakali is a fine big water rafting trip that compares favourably with the Seti/Karnali. This is a shorter trip and the white water is easier, but unlike the Karnali, there is white water interest all the way down the river. The scenery, jungle and wildlife are as good as any in Nepal and the bird life is exceptional.

Dattu is probably the best starting point for rafting as below here the river is mainly 2 and 3 – just a few more difficult rapids near the start and one long class 4– rapid (easily portaged if necessary) just above the Surnayad Gad. Expert teams could perhaps consider a put-in near Darchula. The alternative start, for a slightly shorter raft trip, would be to start near the confluence with the Chamliya River (aprox. 3 hours walk from Baitadi) – this would save a day or two of trekking (over a 1000m pass). Most groups would probably be best flying in to Gokule whilst the rafting gear is taken by road to Darchula. Consider running the river from the Indian side, putting in near Askot.

If you are thinking of a raft trip on the Mahakali then consider combining this with a trek further up the valley, perhaps to Api base camp if permitted. This, combined with a short luxury safari in **Sukla Phanta Wildlife Reserve** would make a great three week vacation. The reserve is just to the south of Mahendranagar and famous for its swamp deer and herd of wild elephant.

Note that the take-out on the Nepal side necessitates a 20km walk out to the Mahendra Highway. Start and take-outs are easier on the Indian side: teams from India have put in near the confluence with the Goriganga and taken out near Tanakpur.

Two rafting operators with experience of the Mahakali are 'Victoria Travels and Tours', and Shyam Piya of 'Karnali tours and Expeditions'.

Kayaking

We kayaked the river in relatively low water conditions in December 1991, starting upstream of **Dhoulakot**. We had a special permit to explore the river and were keen to run as much as possible. This upper stretch is steep, over 4 % (200 ft a mile) and it sticks in my memory, not so much for the quality of the white water paddling, for indeed there was some, but more for the constant stench of danger. Danger seemed to lurk around every corner, below every drop, and most intimidating of all in the many evil boulder chokes. This upper river appeared littered by a maelstrom of sharp angular boulders designed to pin and sieve kayaks; perhaps brought down by some glacial flood.

I would recommend a put-in below the **Kala Gad**, from here down to the **Dattu** the river is more friendly, still challenging class 3 to 5, but with more rounded boulders and a better choice of lines. You might want to consider employing porters to give bank support on this upper river but these can probably be dispensed with and you can go self-supported after Dattu. From here it is about 4 days paddling down to the take-out (allow 6 days in all from the Kala Gad).

This bottom stretch of river, from Dattu down, is a magnificent trip and ideal for any group looking for a really wild and remote river that isn't too difficult.

Access and logistics

The road on the Indian side of the valley makes it more logical to do the river from this bank provided you do not want to paddle the upper river above the Goriganga, which we are told is the limit for foreigners. If you are thinking of doing this then you should check out the current situation on restricted zones and the 'Inner Line' well in advance with the

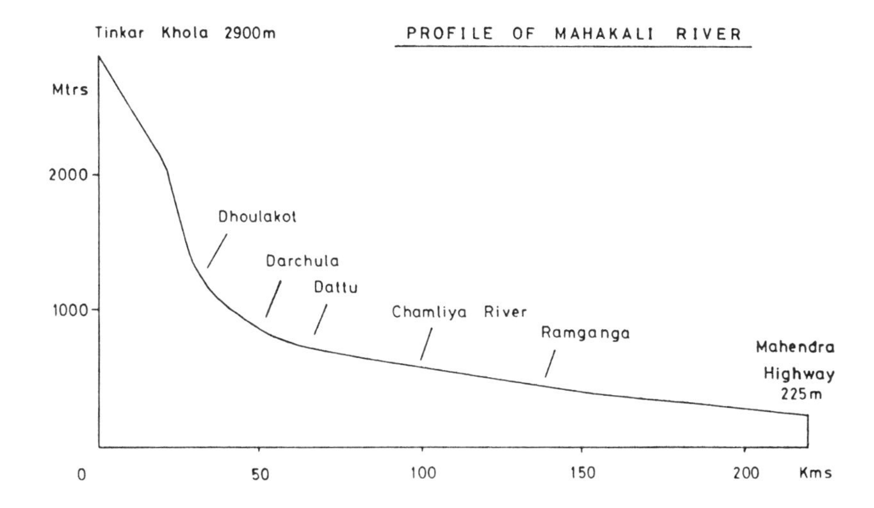

appropriate Indian authorities. There are no restrictions on the Nepalese side and improved communications have made the logistics of a Nepalese trip a lot easier than they might at first appear.

The new road into **Baitadi** means that if you are an impecunious kayaker you can hope to be here in two day's bus ride from Kathmandu at a cost of something less than $20; but note that this is a mountain road and may be blocked by landslides. This road is being extended to **Gokule** and on up to **Darchula**. The alternative is to fly in to Gokule (identified as 'Darchula' in the RNAC flight schedules) from Nepalganj at a cost of about $90 (Kathmandu to Nepalganj is aprox. $100). Porters should be obtainable in either place for the trek to the river, reckon about one long day from Gokule to Dhap. Basic supplies are available in Baitadi and Darchula, both places are even on the phone! We found adequate firewood supplies all the way down the river.

If you are running the river from the Nepal side, note well that you need to take out immediately the river comes out of the Chure Hills. Don't be tempted to continue on into Indian territory for an easier take out: this section of the river is a sensitive security zone with a powerhouse and two barrages, and you risk imprisonment and substantial fines. There are a few habitations in the jungle near this take-out and it may be possible for a small group to hire local people as porters, but I recommend that if possible you arrange for a reliable Sirdar and porters to meet you for the four hour walk out to **Mahendranagar**. This is a fairly tawdry border town, but there are several buses a day to Nepalgang and Kathmandu and also daily flights to these places.

Probably the nicest way to finish your trip would be a luxury safari in the **Sukla Phanta Wildlife Reserve** that is just to the south of Mahendranagar; the firm to talk to are 'Silent Safari' and they have an office in Kathmandu (tel 418755). Talk nicely to them and they could probably meet you at the take-out?

The H.M.G. Main Trail Map of the Far Western Region of Nepal covers the river in reasonable detail at a scale of 1:250,000 but shows nothing of the Indian side of the valley. The Indian Government are incredibly protective about restricting maps so no adequate ones are available for their side of the border.

Description

Dhoulakot to Dattu 35 kms, Chamliya 30, Sarju 40, Take out 65.

We put in about 5 kms above **Dhoulakot**. From here, the 14 kms down to the Kala Gad is mainly class 4 to 6 with much scouting. There is no path next to the river, only steep cliffs and little of the river can be seen from the trail which is 400m above. The Dhauliganga adds some 40% to the flow. The last 2kms is mainly unrunnable and has many epic portages – one of our porters was injured by a rock fall on this section. It would be a lot easier portaging on the Indian side if this were permissible, using the road in places: but I still do not recommend this section, much better to put in at the confluence of the Kala Gad.

After the **Kala Gad** the river is a lively class 3 to 5, with frequent technical rapids of rounded boulders. There was one very dangerous rapid above the Nijang Gad which we portaged in the interests of longevity. Just before Dhap at the confluence of the Thuli Gad is a beautiful class 5− rapid which extends for over a km and which we christened 'Christmas Cracker' as we ate our Christmas lunch under a huge boulder at the top. The rapids kept coming as far as the bridge at Joljibi where the **Goriganga** all but doubles the flow of the Mahakali; a neat town called Askot marks the confluence on the Indian side.

Below the Goriganga the character of the river changes significantly as the river glides into a mature valley and gorge. Flat, reflective passages are interspersed with rapids and the river bounces from rock bluff to rock bluff. The main trail leaves the river at the confluence of the **Chamliya** and some 5 kms further is the last bridge for over 100 kms, at Jhulaghat where the mighty Mahakali squeezes through a 5 metre wide cleft.

Downstream is relatively sparsely populated with only a few isolated villages. The river winds into a jungle-fringed wonderland of monkeys and colourful birds. A couple of kms before the confluence of the **Surnaya Gad** some large boulders signal a thundering great rapid, class 4−, with huge standing waves slapping you about. Playing here I had an anxious moment with a high volume pin on a vicious rock which was hidden behind a tempting surfing wave. Another big bouncy rapid follows and takes you down to the confluence where we pulled over to camp. Some grass-carrying girls fled in abject terror: the river here has no trails along its its course and the local people are genuinely isolated from outside influences.

More beautiful scenery and a series of relatively easy rapids (class 3) brought us to the Rangun Khola. A few kms later and the Mahakali took an abrupt turn to the west and plunged into the gloomy recesses of a sandstone gorge where the river carves a route through the last barrier of the **Chure Hills**. On an isolated beach, below rock walls, we made our last camp and in the morning woke to a fog hanging over the river. We set off, and after a few kms we could see the sun beckoning at the next corner and within minutes we emerged from the fog, the gorge, and the Himalaya into the bright sunshine of the Terai.

The **take-out** is at the end of this gorge, the edge of the hills and the end of the last rapid. Take out on the left bank exactly at the spot where the steep ground on this bank ceases. Immediately after here, in Indian territory, the river spreads out and braids with many dry channels. Please note well that there is nothing to mark the actual border. The end of a fine trip!

Catfish

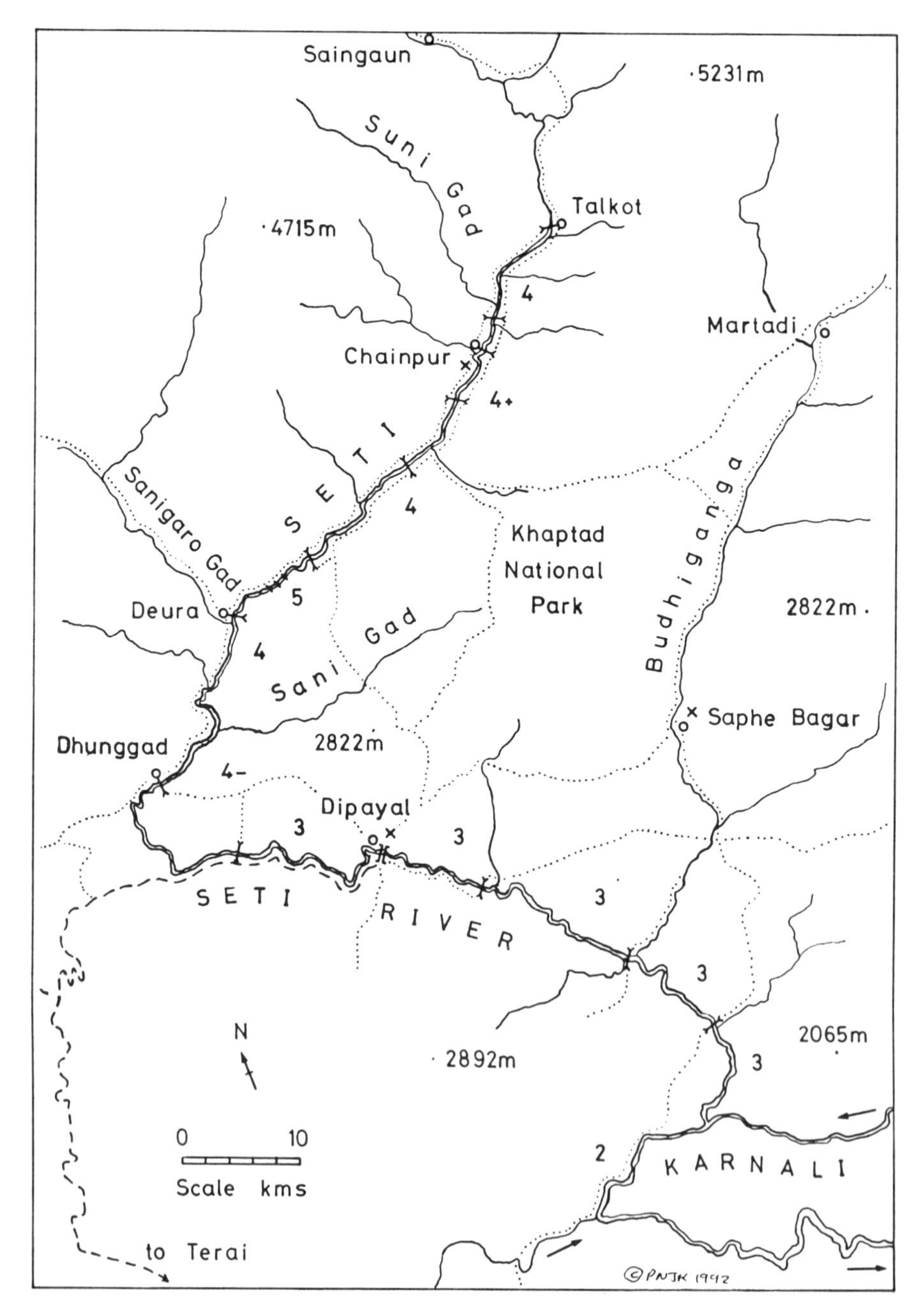

WARNING: Laser-phobic ink – do not photocopy.

Seti / Karnali

From information suppied by Frank Meyer and others.

From:	**Dipayal** (Alt. 490m)
To:	**Chisapani** (Alt. 195m)
Distance:	**155 kms** (97 miles)
River Days:	**4–7**
From Kathmandu:	**2 days or fly in**
Difficulty in Nov:	**Class 3**
Average gradient:	**0.2%** (10ft a mile)
Est. max. gradient:	**0.5%**
Volume in Nov:	**130 cumecs** (4500 cfs)
Best Season:	**Oct-Dec, Feb-May.**

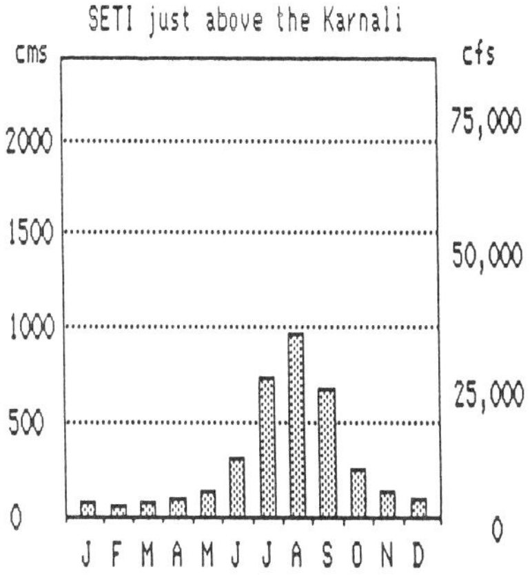

Summary

A remote, beautiful, and little-travelled river that offers the same jungle wilderness and abundant wildlife as the Lower Karnali but with an easier start. Further upstream is some excellent class 4+ 'expedition' kayaking.

The river

The Seti river rises wholly in Nepal on the flanks of the highest mountains in the Far West; Api 7132m, and Saipal 7031m, and then flows south and south east to join the Lower Karnali. This is a remote valley, far from Kathmandu, that sees very few foreigners and has only had a few river descents. Although remote from Kathmandu, there is road access to the middle part of the valley and there are two airstrips at Dipayal and Chainpur and a good number of villages up the valley. Local people follow an unchanged lifestyle as subsistence farmers, and are naturally curious and friendly.

The river has a typical longitudinal profile, very steep in its upper stretches above Talkot and with a reasonable gradient of 0.6% (30 ft a mile) downstream from Deura. The many tributaries increase the volume considerably from perhaps 14 cumecs (500 cfs) above Talkot, to some 130 cumecs just before the confluence with the Karnali.

Only a few groups have run this river. Frank Meyer and a team of American kayakers ran the river from Talkot in 1986. A year or two later, Barry Miller ran the river in a cat rig from near Chainpur. A few other groups have started from near Dipayal. They report that the upper river has some steep-sided valley sides and two gorges, but below Deura the valley opens up with a wide valley floor in many places. There are plenty of excellent beaches for camping, and on the upper river there are distant views of the snow-covered Himalaya.

The upper river has the usual pattern of boulder-garden rapids familiar to Himalayan river runners and giving some fun kayaking. As it approaches the confluence with the Karnali, the Seti takes on a 'Big Water' nature similar to the easier rapids on the Karnali,

Sun Kosi or Trisuli. This lower section of the river has many of the attributes of the Karnali, which it joins – beautiful scenery and abundant wildlife – please read the section on the Lower Karnali.

Rafting

This is not one of your main-line raft trips – in fact you can pretty well guarantee that you will be the only group on the river – probably that season! To many people this is a very good reason for running the river. To our minds this is a quality trip, better scenery, wildlife and 'wilderness' than many other rafting rivers, but it is a long way from Kathmandu, and that has to be paid for in time and cost.

We think this river is perhaps best considered as an alternative start to the Lower Karnali. If you like the sound of the Karnali – it's jungle, wilderness and abundant wildlife; but are put off by the idea of the trek to the start and the class 4 white water; then here is a more mellow alternative. Starting on the Seti will give you another 50kms on this river and then a full 105 kms on the Karnali down to Chisapani – all the bottom section of the river that is best for jungle, scenery and wildlife.

Those who have done the river talk about blue-green water, gleaming white beaches, green jungle-clad valley sides – just superb scenery, beautiful campsites and an excellent 'away from all' river trip. Rapids are described as relatively easy class 3 – straight forward shoots with some medium-sized bouncy waves.

Probably the best way to do this trip is to fly into the river at **Dipayal** and start here – a trip of around 6 days. Putting on from where the road meets the river would give you another 20 kms and an extra day's rafting. Below Dipayal you will be on your own, with no villages for the next 195 kms down to Chisapani – a memorable wilderness trip! We recommend that you spend a couple of days at the end of the river trip on a safari in the Royal Bardiya Wildlife Reserve near Chisapani.

Kayaking

From:	**Talkot** (Alt. 1380m)
To:	**Chisapani** (Alt 195m)
Distance:	**255 kms** (160 miles)
River Days:	**10**
From Kathmandu:	**2 plus 8 days trek** – or fly
Difficulty in Nov:	**Class 4** (5)
Average gradient:	0.5% (25 ft a mile)
Est. max. gradient:	**2.0%**
Volume in Nov:	**130 cumecs** (4500 cfs)
Best Season:	**Oct-Dec, Feb-May.**

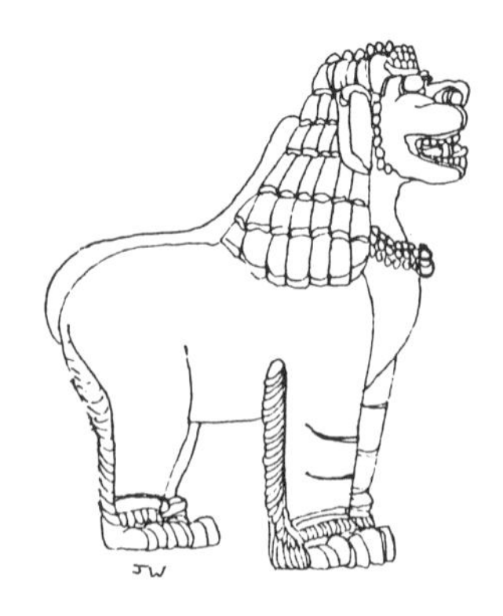

This is one of those rivers that offers a choice of two or three levels of kayaking depending on where you start. The higher you go up the river, the longer it will take to trek in, the steeper the gradient, the harder the paddling, and the more time you will spend scouting and portaging.

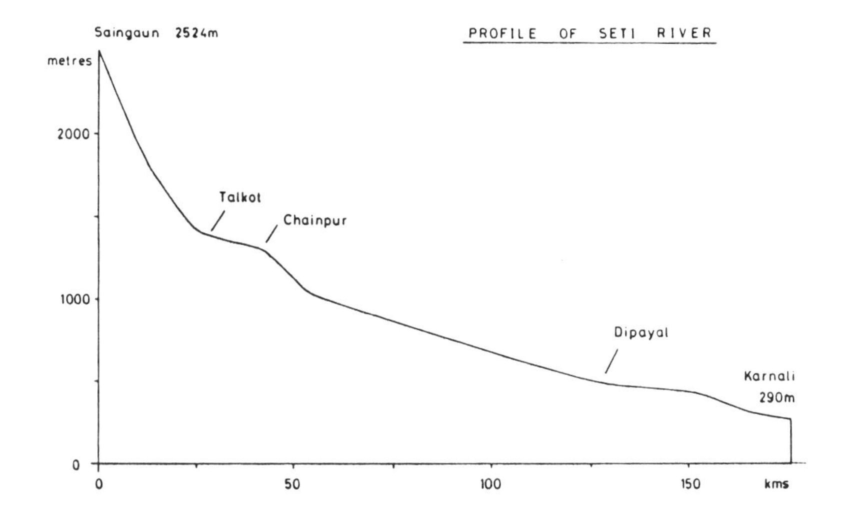

Where the highway first meets the river is the obvious starting point if you want least hassle and easy paddling. The trip from there downstream might be suitable for inflatable or folding kayaks in competent hands, and would suit an adventurous group with good outdoor experience, intermediate paddling skills, looking for a self-sufficient, remote wilderness experience.

The river becomes noticeably harder just upstream from **Deura**, so a start near here avoids any major problems and yet gives 205 kms of class 3 and 4 boating – an attractive option for many groups, but this would require a trek in for 2 or 3 days.

Upstream of **Talkot**, the river gradient steepens sharply and the river is almost certainly class 5 and 6, requiring shore support, and considerable scouting and portaging, so Talkot seems to be the natural starting point. The 1986 American Kayak Team put on here and it took them ten days down to Chisapani. They reported blue-green sections of class 3 and 4 water down to near Chainpur, and then some harder sections down to near Deura. It took this group ten days to trek in to Talkot from Dadeldhura (just off the left edge of our map). An attractive alternative for a small group would be to fly in to Chainpur.

Access and logistics

Flying in to the Seti seems to make a lot of logistical sense, if you can afford it – reckon on about $80 from **Nepalganj**, the air-hub of the Far West, plus excess baggage. Please see the Karnali sections for more travel details.

Now that the new East-West road along the Terai, the Mahendra Highway, is almost complete, the road option is worth considering. However, the road over to Dipayal and Dadaldhura is rough and like all mountain roads, may be blocked by landslides, particularly after the monsoon. You won't be able to find out about about local road conditions until you get to the Far West so if you plan to travel this way, then you should allow plenty of time and flexibility in your plans. To travel by bus from Kathmandu would mean an 18 hour night bus to Nepalganj; then if you're lucky, perhaps another 8 hour one to the river – total cost less than $10.

Note that this is a remote river and you should be totally self-sufficient for all supplies. You may wish to use porters to accompany you if you decide to paddle the upper river, but for most of the lower river there are no trails alongside and no villages, so you need to be entirely self-contained. Dipayal could be used for emergency evacuation, and some fresh supplies could be purchased here, but from here on down, you are on your own for some 155 kms to the first feasible take-out at Chisapani.

The most detailed maps covering the river are the 1:125,000 Central Service Maps for Bajhang, Dolti, and Surkhet Districts. The H.M.G. Main Trail Map for the 'Far Western Region' covers the whole of the Seti and lower Karnali on one sheet, and has most of the same information, but on a scale of 1:250,000.

Description

Talkot – Deura 45 kms, Dipayal 55, Karnali 50, Chisapani 105.

Frank Meyer ran the river in late October: he describes the first day's paddling from **Talkot** to Chainpur as enjoyable class 3 and 4, aprox 14 kms with a nice canyon at the start. After Chainpur, the first few kms are steep, 'a continuous maze of boulders and holes tilted at a frightening angle', giving some good class 4+ boating. About 14 kms down the river is a second gorge, class 4, and then the class 4 water continues for another few kms to the start of 'The Landslides'. These are three landslides located a few kms upstream from **Deura** and each has formed quite a big class 5 rapid.

From here on, we are told that the river is mainly class 3 with an occasional class 4 drop. This continues down to where the road meets the river and then below here the river is 'class 3, but very scenic'.

Below **Dipayal**, the river continues as class 3, but as the river approaches the Karnali, the rapids take on 'big water' characteristics, becoming big and bouncy class 3 with some nice surfing waves. The largest tributary of the Seti, the **Budhi Ganga**, comes in on the left about 28 kms below Dipayal and adds considerably to the flow (This is another of the smaller rivers of Nepal that is probably still waiting a first descent . . .). The scenery gets better as you go down the river, habitations get less, the jungle gets thicker on either side, and then you're into the mighty **Karnali** – and the scenery gets even finer!

Please read the write up on the Lower Karnali for details about the river down to the take-out at **Chisapani**.

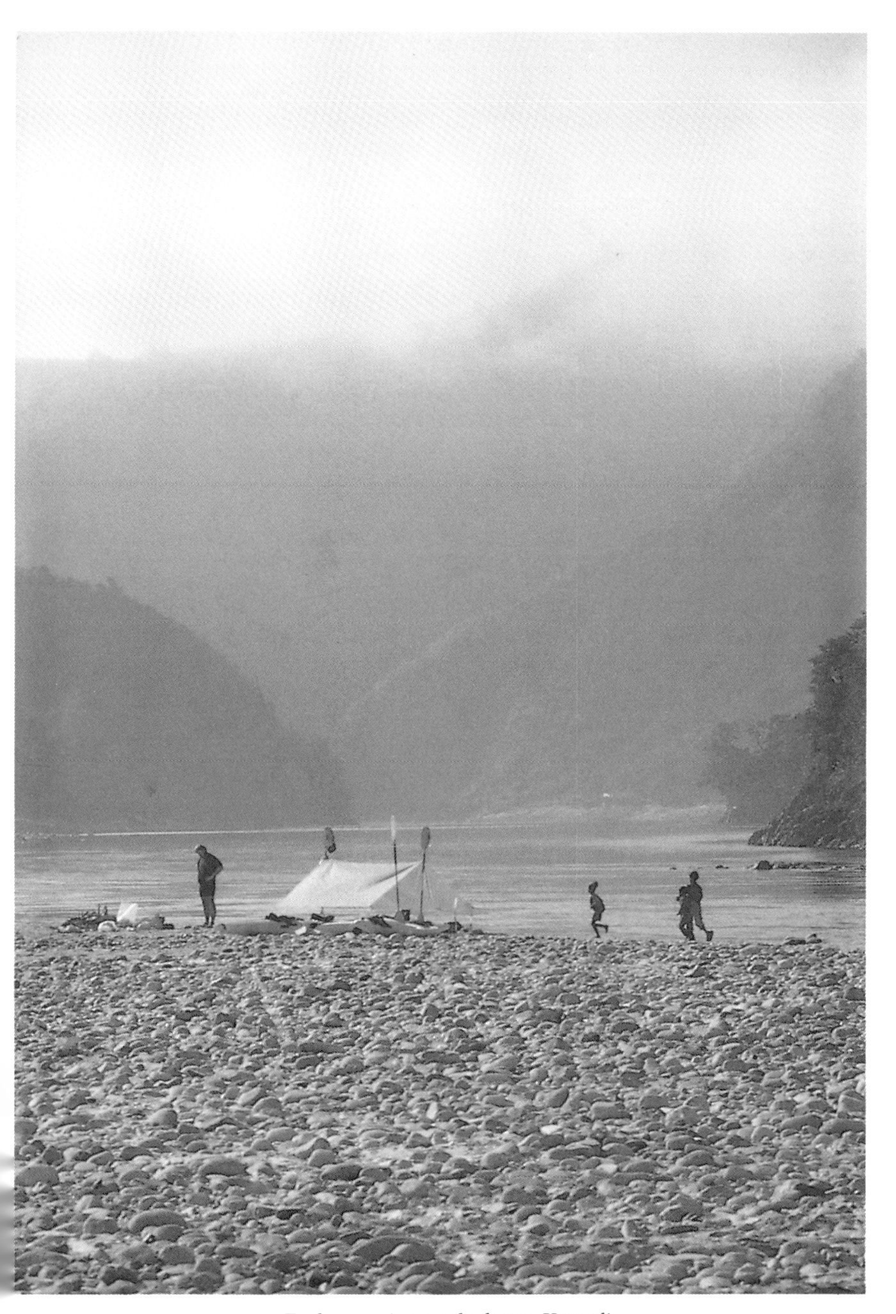

Early morning on the lower Karnali

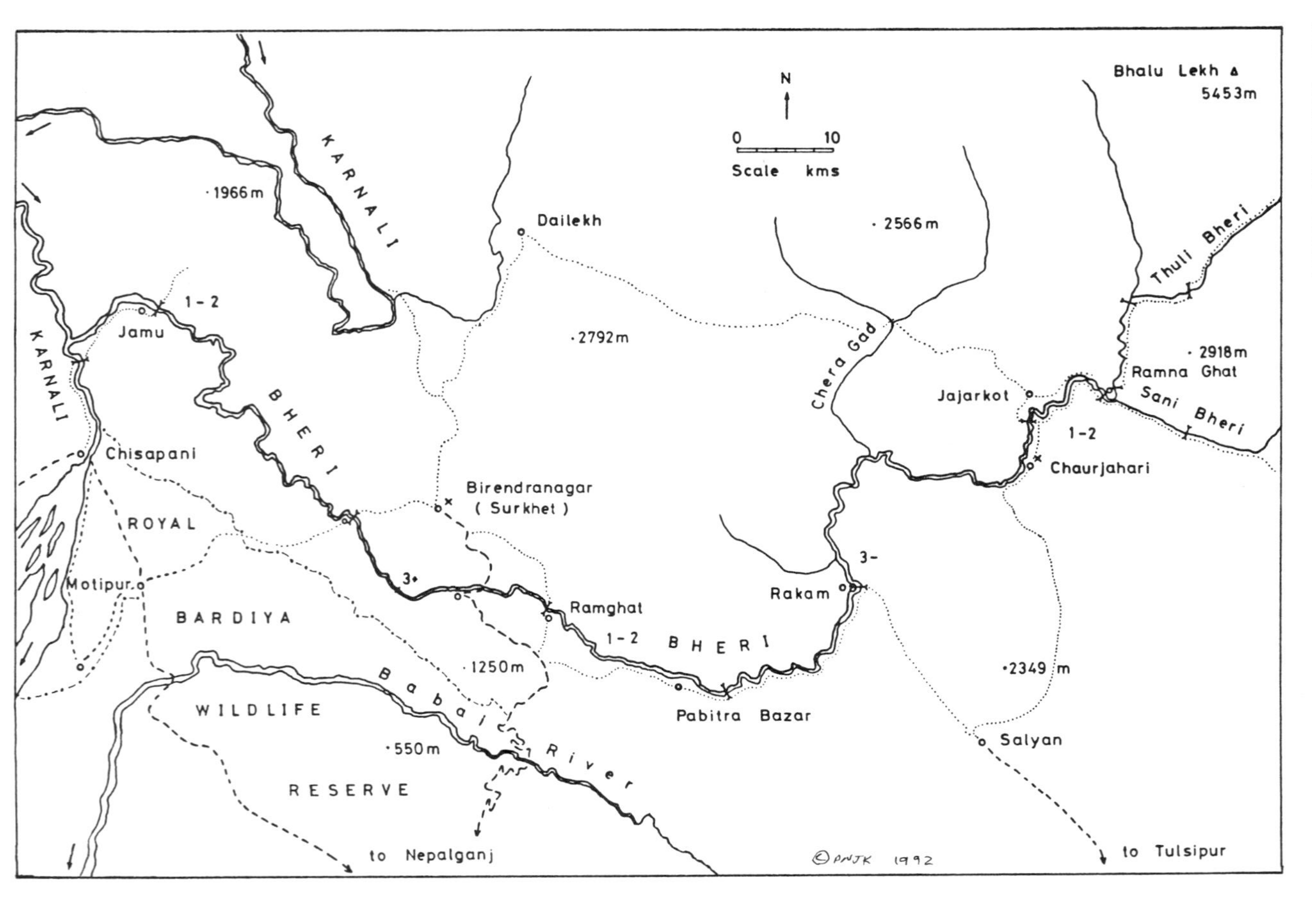

WARNING: Laser-phobic ink – do not photocopy.

Bheri

by Jock Montgomery

From:	**Ramnaghat** (Alt. 770m)
To:	**Chisapani** (Alt. 195m)
Distance:	**200 kms** (125 miles)
River Days:	**6–10**
From Kathmandu:	**6 days** (or fly in)
Difficulty in Nov:	**Class 2** (3+)
Average gradient:	**0.3%** (15 ft a mile)
Est. max. gradient:	**0.5 %**
Volume in Nov:	**170 cumecs** (6000 cfs)
Best Season:	**Oct-Dec, Feb-March.**

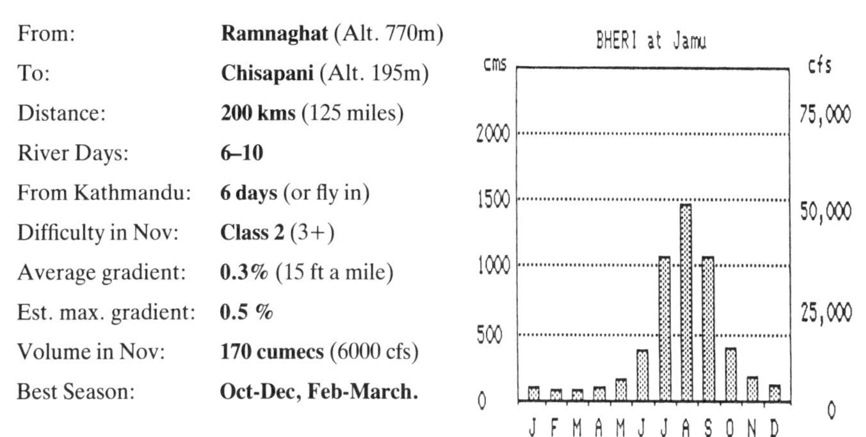

Summary

A remote and easy river; beautiful scenery, good fishing, unspoilt villages, interesting local peoples. Blue water, white beaches and fine campsites.

The river

Two large tributaries, the Thuli (meaning big) and Sani (small!) join at Ramnaghat to form the main Bheri river with the village and airstrip of Chaujahari half a day's walk downstream of the confluence.

Further upstream of this confluence, there is challenging water as the gradient becomes much steeper (1400m in 100kms). The river rises in Dolpo and when we ran the river in 1985 this region was closed to tourists. It is now open to organised groups, so it should now be possible to get permission for this upper section .... but this would certainly be a serious river expedition.

We put in just upstream of the confluence in Febuary 1985. The water was crystal clear with visibility of 20-25 ft, of a clarity that none of us had ever seen in any river in Nepal. There are plenty of remote campsites and big beaches on this river.

Peter Byrne led the only other two trips before ours and had told us tales of class 4 and 5 'killer' rapids. The gradient and big volume seemed to confirm this and we were hoping for white knuckle fever rapids around each bend in the river, but never found any. At high, post-monsoon levels there probably are some class 4 rapids.....or who knows what?

We spent a leisurely ten days on the river. It was quite wide for the first three days, then on the fourth day there was a series of easy class 3 rapids. On the sixth day we reached the ferry and road to Surkhet. A few miles below here is the hardest rapid of the trip – a short class 3+ drop (a class 4 at higher levels). Local people are interesting and unusual; many have never seen a westerner before and you will be greeted with wide-eyed wonder. One of the last nomadic hunting tribes in Nepal, the Raute, roam the forests south of the Bheri.

We reached the confluence with the Karnali on the ninth day and could easily have made it to Chisapani the same day, but the gorge is spectacular and well worth an overnight stay.

At Chisapani the the Karnali bursts out into what is geologically the Indian/Gangetic plain. You enter an entirely new ecosystem full of herds of deer, gaur, wild elephants, etc. The game viewing in **Royal Bardiya Wildlife Reserve** surpasses that of Chitwan and, if possible, I recommend that you continue with a float through the Reserve and a stay at Tiger Tops Camp (see section on the Karnali).

Rafting

This must be one of the premier float trips in Nepal: it has some of the best fishing in Nepal, beautiful and diverse scenery, lots of wildlife and unspoilt villages. Himalayan River Explorations offer commercial rafting trips on the lower part of the Bheri starting near Surkhet and finishing at Tiger Tops Camp – about 80 kms and a 4-6 day trip. Other rafting companies also have experience of the river.

Kayaking

Easy whitewater makes this an interesting trip for the novice boater wanting to do an 'expedition' on a remote river, but because of this remoteness any group should have previous experience of the country. The river should be suitable for inflatable 'duckies' or folding boats.

Fishing

The Bheri is renowned as one of the best rivers in Nepal for fishing – particularly Masheer. Unfortunately we ran the Bheri in early February which is a little too early for Masheer but we still managed to catch two small ones – one of 5 pounds, one of 8 pounds.

These are tremendous fighting fish that are a type of carp. They feed mainly on algae, minnows and fresh water molluscs and in Nepal they are called 'Sahar'. The cartilage on the back of the mouth can crush freshwater clam shells or fishing lures! There are two species found in Nepal and a third (the largest) is found in India. They can grow up to 45 kilos in Nepal.

Best fishing season is said to be from November through to mid-December and mid-Febuary to April – also the best months for a raft trip!

Access and logistics

There is an airstrip at **Chaujahari** and this is only a short flying time from **Nepalganj**, so if you are a group it is worth considering a charter flight (see notes on air transport).

A bus from Kathmandu to **Tulsipur** will take about 16 hours and from here a rough road continues to Salyan. From Salyan, it is about 3 porter days to Chaujahari.

There are several Foreign Aid Projects in this area and we recommend that you make contact and try to hire your porters with their help. This entire region is quite remote in terms of western visitors and if you do hire porters on your own, and problems develop, word will be passed back and the aid projects blamed because locals believe that all Westerners are related. The Aid projects will appreciate your concern for their reputation and will usually willingly give you help in arranging porters and somewhere to stay. You should get excellent porters (as we did) and your good will to your porters will bolster the project's delicate balance in the community.

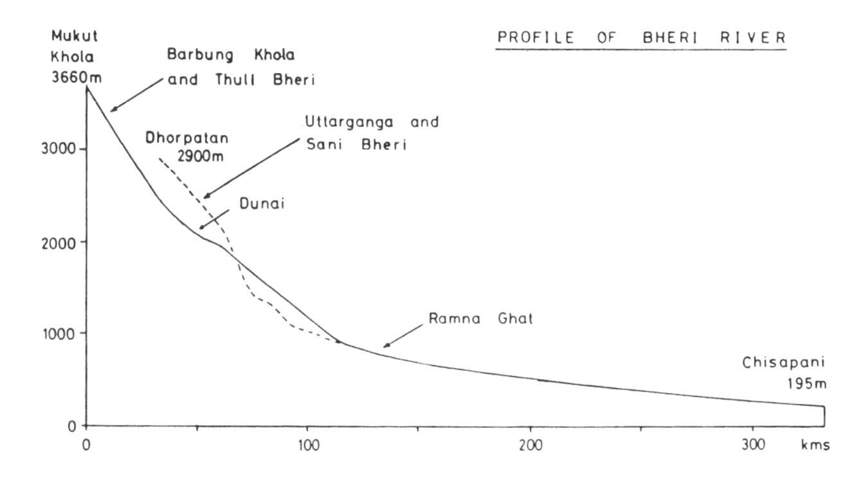

Food can be a bit of a problem. Although Tulsipur, Salyan and Charjahari are major trade centres, fresh vegies can be hard to find in the winter and spring. We found only eggs, garlic, potatoes and the like, but also found the same in villages along the river.

Please see the section on the Karnali for notes about the take-out at **Chisapani**. Be sure to take out here unless you have already pre-arranged transport back through the park – it's a long carry back to the road! At least one previous trip has floated through the park and then on into India without realising it – you can imagine the problems they must have had trying to get back into Nepal!

Best maps covering the river, at a scale of 1:125,000, are the blue Central Service Maps for Surkhet and Jajarkot Districts; the walk in is covered on the map of the Salyan District.

The Royal Bardia National Park

by Steve Webster

The Royal Bardia National Park lies approximately 400kms west of Kathmandu. It covers an area of over 1000 square kilometres and is bounded on the west by the great Karnali river and to the east by part of the Nepalganj-Birendranagar highway. Much of the park is hill country and the northern border is made up of the Siwalik Hills.

Between 1850 and 1950 the area was set aside as a royal hunting reserve and in the mid seventies it was declared a wildlife reserve with an area of only 350 square kilometres. The Nepalese authorities seeing the need to preserve the ever shrinking habitat of the area have gradually reclaimed much of the land inhabited by 'landless' villagers and now the park extends over 1000 sq kms. The park was recently given National Park status together with the translocation of some 20 or so rhinoceros. The park is dominated by sal forests but also consists of riverine forest and some fine grass land areas known locally as phantas. These areas provide superb habitat for an abundance of wildlife including spotted deer, barking deer, sambar, swamp deer, black buck, sloth bear, wild boar, and numerous others.

The general area is occasionally referred to as 'Karnali' after the great river which forms the western boundary. The deep blue waters (in season!) of the Karnali emerge from a narrow gorge at Chisapani. The gorge itself is home to both the gharial and marsh mugger crocodiles, which in this area have been known to grow upto extraordinary sizes. The river widens as it meets the lowland plains and slows down to a sluggish pace. Islands of gravel and sand emerge and these are frequented by by the blue bull or Nilgai.

The park is also home to the Royal Bengal tiger, leopard and is one of the few areas of Nepal where wild elephant still roam freely.

In the early 1980's Tiger Tops Nepal pioneered tourism in this remote and beautiful area and to date it is the only private tourist facility available; offering a lodge situated on the southern borders of the park and a tented camp situated on the banks of the Karnali towards the gorge at Chisapani – a convenient and welcome take-out after a raft trip.

Babai Nadi

From information supplied by Megh Ale

From: **Surkhet Highway** (Alt. 320m)
To: **Mahendra Highway** (Alt. 180m)
Distance: **50 kms** (31 miles)
River Days: **2–3**
From Kathmandu: **1 day**
Difficulty in Nov: **Class 1**
Average gradient: **0.3%** (15 ft a mile)
Volume in Nov: **36 cumecs** (1300 cfs)
Best Season: **Oct-Nov.**

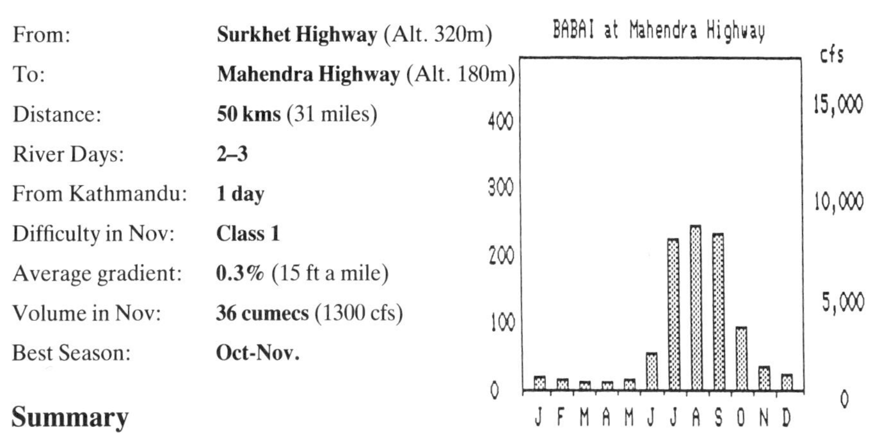

Summary

A float trip through, and entirely within, **Royal Bardiya Wildlife Reserve**. Pristine 'jungle' with incredible wildlife. Probably the best wildlife raft trip in Nepal with excellent fishing.

The river

Please see the section on the Bheri river for a map.

The Babai flows through the heart of the Royal Bardiya Wildlife Reserve – one of the most impressive reserves in Asia. This is a total wilderness trip with beautiful scenery in a completely unspoilt and unpopulated valley. You will see lots and lots of wildlife – tigers and game are in the whole area. There are rhinos and wild elephants in the reserve and many crocodiles – both muggers and gharial. What better way to see wildlife than drifting quietly along in your own boat?

Fishing is reported as excellent, with lots of Masheer, the famous fighting fish (see section on the Bheri River).

The highway to **Surkhet** forms the Eastern boundary to the reserve and forms a natural starting point where it crosses the river. The Mahendra Highway marks the western boundary and makes a natural and convenient finishing point. There is no other access within the Park. You need a camping permit for the Park and should take advice from the staff of the reserve to minimise any dangers from wildlife. The Babai is of small volume and has a gentle gradient; it meanders and braids through gravel bars and there are plenty of pleasant beaches for camping.

The river actually starts near **Tulsipur** and flows west along the line of the Chure Hills and then turns south to cross the main East-West Highway (the Mahendra Highway). It could probably be run in kayaks from near Tulsipur.

Rafting

This is an easy float trip. We suggest allowing 3 days to give plenty of time to see the wildlife. Most people will probably want to do this as a commercial trip accompanied by a specialist guide familiar with the wildlife. October and early November give the best water conditions – after this the many gravel bars would make it too shallow for rafting.

Kayaking

This would be an exciting and very different kayak trip – but don't blame us if you end up savaged by a Rhino! The river is probably still kayakable in low water conditions but will be harder work and you may have to drag your boat over gravel bars.

Access and logistics

The start point at Babai Bridge on the **Surkhet Highway** is about two hour's drive from Nepalganj and you could drop off from one of the Surkhet buses. Nepalganj is about 18 hours by night bus from Kathmandu and there are frequent flights if you wish to fly. There are few taxis in Nepalganj, but you should be able to hire something to get you to the river.

Note that you need a special camping permit for the Reserve. If you are with a commercial company they will arrange this, otherwise one of your group will almost certainly have to visit the Park Headquarters at **Motipur** (Thakurdwara).

This section of the Mahendra Highway is now complete and the drive back to Nepalganj should take about 2 hours. This is the main East-West highway, but be warned there isn't much traffic and only a few buses each day. It might be wise to arrange to hire some transport to meet you?

Note well that there is no habitation or access points other than at the start and finish of this trip and you need to be completely self-sufficient.

Medical problems — Appendix A

by Doctor Andy Watt

Introduction

As we said in the earlier section on staying healthy, you are unlikely to to suffer anything worse than a stomach upset – BUT, if you do have more serious problems, these may well be on the river, many miles from any road, hospital or telephone, hence this detailed section which is written primarily for the First Aider in your group. It doesn't attempt to cover all serious injuries (he/she should have some knowledge of these) but rather those problems that we feel are particularly relevant to river running in Nepal.

The common problems are accidents (particularly around the fire and kitchen area) and diarrhoea.

Diarrhoea, Dysentry and Food Poisoning

Definitions:

- **Diarrhoea:** loose bowels due to simple gut infection not requiring treatment beyond fluid replacement.
- **Dysentry:** a more severe infection with an ill patient, a temperature, and blood and slime in the stool.
- **Food poisoning:** acute, often severe, episode of vomiting and diarrhoea starting and finishing within a day or two.

Diarrhoea is a fear of many first timers, but this fear is usually exagerated and the diarrhoea is just a minor inconvenience needing only fluid replacement. Again, we emphasise the importance of good hygiene being your best protection.

Types

- **Viral:** this is the commonest and usually self-limiting. The body restores order after one to several days – just as well, because antibiotics are no use against viruses. Treatment is simple fluid replacement – see later.
- **Bacterial:** often self-limiting as well. The severe, sudden onset diarrhoeas and those that occur within the first ten days of arrival in Nepal are usually bacterial.
- **Amoeba/Giardia:** these usually cause more chronic diarrhoea with a slower onset and lasting for days or weeks.
- **Food poisoning:** this is caused by bacterial toxins, not the bacteria themselves; they are thus usually short, self-limiting illnesses. Within 2-6 hours of consumption of food sudden onset of vomiting, abdominal pain and diarhoea leaves an exhausted, unwell patient. Recovery is often rapid: full recovery often takes place within two days. Fluid should be taken if possible, and anti-vomiting medication may be useful but antibiotics are of no benefit. (Note that the first day of Bacterial dysentry is often similar so any antibiotics should be delayed for at least a day.)

Treatment

Oral Rehydration Therapy (ORT) is your most important remedy. The discovery and promotion of ORT has saved millions of third world children from death. Even in the most severe form of diarrhoea – Cholera – it is the fluid replacement that saves the lives – not any drugs.

A much simplified sum shows why this can be important. 10% dehydration will make you very unwell. 50%–60% of your body weight is water. Therefore, in a 65 kg person, a fluid loss of 3.5 litres brings them CLOSE TO THE EDGE.

The aim of fluid replacement is the ability to produce a dilute (pale yellow) urine. Any CLEAN fluid will do in the early stages, but after a while, salt and glucose replacement become important (N.B. Rafters rum punch is NOT recommended). If you have Jeevan Jel, Diorylate, or similar rehydration powders then use these (they taste a lot nicer – which makes it easier to persuade the patient do drink the quantity of fluid that is needed). A makeshift solution can be made from 2 level teaspoons of sugar and a good pinch of salt in a glass of clean water. Potassium can be gained from bananas or fruit juice.

Severe Diarrhoea

This requires treatment which should be aimed at the appropriate bug. However, no matter which bug causes diarrhoea; your stool looks the same to you, me, or even an experienced Doctor without his microscope. Therefore, some rules of thumb are required for those wilderness consultations halfway down the Sun Kosi:

1. **Simple diarrhoea** with none of the associated symptoms above only needs simple fluid replacement. Carefully review your hygiene practices to try to identify any lapses. Both sufferer and the group should reinforce their hygiene to prevent further spread.

2. **Consider antibiotics if:**

   a) After 3-5 days the diarrhoea persists and the patient is tired and unwell. (If you are a self-sufficient group facing some hard paddling, with only limited time and supplies, then you may decide to take antibiotics before 3-5 days are up).

   b) If the diarrhoea had a sudden onset, with blood, slime, very frequent stools, and a temperature, then it is probably bacterial dysentry (but see the note above about food poisoning) and should be treated with Norfloxacin or Nalidixic acid – bugs in Nepal are becoming increasingly resistant to the old favorite of Bactrim /Septrin.

   c) If the diarrhoea has had a gradual onset there are two possibilities:

   - Eggy burps, excess farts, abdominal distention, intermittent diarrhoea, with no temperature; this is probably Giardia.

   - The above plus abdominal cramps, weight loss, and blood in the later stages; probably Amoeba.

Treatment in both cases is Tinadazole or Flagyl. N.B. NO ALCOHOL. (Follow up treatment with Diloxanide for Amoebic dysentry is recommended).

Anti-diarrhoeal agents: Lomotil/Imodium and Kaolin/Morphine.

These work by paralysing the bowel and therefore reduce the body's ability to flush out the infection. It is obviously better to flush out the infection and replace the fluid loss with ORT but these drugs are useful as temporary expedients to stop your bowels up whilst on extended bus or plane journeys, or if you get severe gut cramps.

Should I eat anything?

Obviously keep taking fluids. You won't starve the bugs by not eating (as they have a 25ft tube of rich juices to thrive on) but you will provide further material for your gut to have diarrhoea with. The best rule is to follow your appetite – or lack of it! You should obviously avoid alcohol and spicy foods and in some long-term diarrhoeas it is better to avoid dairy products.

Why not take antibiotics preventatively or before the 3-5 days is up?

- All viral, and some bacterial diarrhoeas are self-limiting.
- All antibiotics have side effects.
- Antibiotics change the natural bugs in your gut, killing off good bacteria as well as harmful ones.
- Bugs get resistant to frequently used drugs.

Note that many Americans take Pepto Bismal to prevent and treat diarrhoea.

Simple Cuts

River water is fairly dirty, so at the end of the days paddling, or for an extended lunch break, wash the cut and apply povidone iodine. If possible allow the cut to dry out and only apply a dressing to protect the cut when you are doing something dirty, or perhaps going on the water again. This daily routine of washing, iodine, and fresh dressings is important if you are to avoid infection – we all get minor cuts, and experienced groups almost make a group therapy of this! So called waterproof dressings are not, but note that finger tubigrip is excellent for bandaging fingers.

Hand Blisters

These are fairly common on multi-day trips, even amongst experienced paddlers who perhaps have not been paddling recently. If you feel a faint soreness then it is worthwhile trying some 'moleskin' or 'second skin' strapped over the friction point before a blister is formed. Blisters usually de-roof with further paddling and treatment is then as for a simple cut: see above.

Larger Wounds

Check the patient is fully immunised against Tetanus. Remove dirt and dead tissue and clean the wound with antiseptic solution, or if none available, lots of iodine water. Remember to apply direct pressure, not a tourniquet, if there is excessive bleeding.

Currently, First Aiders are taught to leave a wound open and apply Povidone iodine, a dressing and elevate. However on the river, providing a waterproof dressing that will keep the wound dry and clean can be difficult, if not impossible, so there is a strong case for closing the wound if it is clean, not too deep, and not too contaminated. These cautions apply particularly to the legs. Closure is best done with steri-strips or butterfly sutures; remember to first shave either side of the wound. Tincture of benzoin ('Friars's Balsam) applied to the skin makes the steri strips stick better. Sutures are an alternative, but require prior training and knowledge of local anaesthetics.

The wound will be sealed and waterproof within 24 hours, but it must be kept dry and clean during his time – a rest day?

The danger of a closed wound is that any infection can be hidden. If the wound has been properly cleansed then the risk is low. Signs of infection include a reddening of the skin surrounding the wound and increased tenderness. Clear or blood stained fluid coming from the wound is normal, but cloudy fluid or pus indicates infection. If this happens, open the wound, wash, apply Povidone iodine again and a dressing; repeat this daily until the infection has been resolved. Antibiotics (Sporidex, Augmentin, or Erythromycin) are not needed unless the infection spreads beyond the stage mentioned, or if the patient has a temperature.

Burns

Wood fires are used a lot on river trips and burn injuries are fairly common. Even with removal of the heat source, the flesh will still be very hot and the burn should **immediately be immersed in any cold water** for a reasonable period of time. The key thing here is fast decisive action to prevent serious flesh injury – we've seen rafters taking a running jump straight into the river!

If the burn has not broken the skin, then simple washing and a dry dressing will be adequate. Blisters should not usually be pricked. With more serious burns, give pain killers, wash with an antiseptic solution and dry with sterile gauze. Apply Silver Sulphadiazine or Flamazine with a non-adhesive dressing on top, bandage and elevate. As bandages for the hands are obviously a problem, simply put cream on, then put the hand in a plastic bag and tie at the wrist.

The problem with burns is not the initial injury, but infection of the damaged tissue: Silver Sulphadiazine is probably the best protection against this although Povidone iodine cream can be used. Try to keep the dressing dry and check for infection by changing the dressing and washing the wound in antiseptic solution every day or two. If infection starts then do daily dressings and consider antibiotics.

Any burn involving more than 10% of the body area is serious. Pain killers and fluid replacement in small frequent amounts are important and evacuation should be considered.

Tenosynovitis ('Tendonitis')

Definition:

Inflamation of the synovium (part of the sheath surrounding some muscle tendons) usually at the wrist. This is fairly common amongst kayakers doing continuous days of paddling.

Diagnosis:

Moderate to severe pain on slight wrist movement, sometimes with creaking felt over the wrist. One point is very tender to touch – usually on the thumb side of the back of the wrist.

This area may be swollen. Point tenderness distinguishes tenosynovitis from other vague wrist pains incurred after sprains.

Treatment:
This is an 'over-use' injury and the only cure is complete rest in a splint and sling, sometimes for weeks – time to go trekking? If you have to continue paddling then we recommend that you splint (from forearm to knuckles) and elevate the arm in a sling when you are not actually paddling. Use a supportive wrist bandage whilst on the water and consider using a paddle with a different control (feather). It is worth taking an anti-inflammatory drug.

Piles (Haemorrhoids)

These are common in rafters, kayakers and mountaineers; no-one knows why. Symptoms are pain, bright red bleeding on defecation, or a lump sticking out. Treatment is purely symptomatic – careful washing and application of a local anaesthetic cream. Paradoxically, both diarrhoea and constipation can make them worse.

Colds and Ear problems

Colds and sore throats are fairly common on multi-day trips. Treatment is symptomatic but do remember to keep up your fluid intake. If the infection moves down to your chest, a dirty spit, sometimes green, can result. Anything worse than this should probably be treated with antibiotics, especially if the patient has a temperature.

Kayakers sometimes complain of 'water in the ear' – often when they have a cold and have been rolling. The sensation is in fact not caused by water in the external ear but is due to a blockage of the very narrow tube that joins the inner ear to the throat and this can cause a painful inbalance of pressure. This may be eased by exhaling against a closed mouth and pinched nose, or swallowing – however don't do this if you've got a really snotty nose as this may spread infection. Inhaling steam helps and decongestants such as actifed or ephedrine nose drops may also help. It is good idea to wait until any colds have cleared before you spend a lot of time rolling around in holes.

External ear infections should be mopped out 4 times a day with cotton wool and ear drops applied. Try an earplug made with cotton wool smeared with vaseline when on the water.

Animal Bites

The best prevention is to avoid dogs and monkeys altogether. If bitten, then **clean the wound IMMEDIATELY** with anything, but preferably soap and water, followed by antiseptic solution and treat as a cut. Check if the patient has been immunised against tetanus.

Rabies does exist in Nepal but your chances of getting it are very low. However, it is invariably fatal if not treated. So if you have not been immunised against it and are bitten by a mammal (including a bat), you must assume the worst.

The incubation period for the disease is 10 to 90 days so you have two alternate courses of action:

Your most practical course is to take a post exposure immunisation as soon as possible – this consists of one dose of rabies antibodies and six doses of vaccine and takes ten days to act. Current cost in Kathmandu is $700 (probably covered by your Medical Insurance?).

Theoretically you could have the dog kept under observation for seven days and if it hasn't died by then, then neither will you. If it does die you should still have time to start a post exposure course. But how do you keep a rabid dog in a kayak?

Note that even if before your trip, you were immunised against Rabies, you will still need one or two further injections if bitten.

Although there are 46 different species of snakes in Nepal, including some poisonous ones, snakebite in tourists is almost unknown.

Major allergic reaction

These are rare but can be fatal. Symptons are collapse, throat swelling, and severe wheeze, especially after certain foods or insect bites. Treatment is 0.5 ml adrenaline injection under the skin, and, if the patient can swallow, antihistamine and steroid/cortisone tablets.

Dentistry

Broken or lost fillings can be replaced by temporary fillings such as gutta percha (heat until soft and insert a plug in the cavity) or 'Cavit'. Remember to dry out the cavity thoroughly first with cotton wool. Oil of cloves may deaden any pain.

Abscesses can be very painful and treatment with antibiotics should be considered (Sporidex, Augmentin, or Erythromycin). Anti-imflammatory drugs are good dental pain killers. Any treatment is just a temporary measure until you can see a dentist – your Embassy in Kathmandu will be able to recommend one.

Sunburn

Treat symptoms with bland ointment or calomine lotion. Some authorities recommend an anti-inflamatory drug for more serious cases.

Skin Rashes

Rashes are difficult to diagnose and usually treated syptomatically with a bland cream. If persistent, try Hydrocortisone creams so long as you are sure that it is not a fungal infection (in which case try Canesten cream first). Anti-histamine pills or cream are useful for severe itch and for persistent insect bites.

Infestations

You are unlikely to aquire **fleas** on a river trip unless you are staying at local lodges. If these critters have befriended you then the best remedy is an extended lunch time to air your bedding and clothing in the heat of the midday sun. Flea powders are a good fall back.

Scabies can be picked up by walking barefoot near local vllages although it is more common in the hands. These small mites burrow in the web space between the fingers and toes. There will be a severe itch and close inspection will reveal 'burrow holes'. Treatment is by applying lotion or cream (e.g. Scabex) over the whole body from neck down for 24 hours.

Hair or pubic **lice** are picked up from staying in local lodges/houses or from very close contact with infected people. You will be very unlucky to become infected, but if this does happen try Malathion as there is some resistance to Scabex..

Worms have a long incubation period, and won't pop out until you get home ......

Headaches

These are usually due to a combination of bright sun, exercise and dehydration: treatment is shade, rest and lots to drink.

Female medical problems

Gut infections and antibiotics interfere with the oral contraceptive pill – see the 'Medical advice' section.

Cystitis is indicated by a 'burning' pain whilst passing urine, frequent small trips to the toilet and cloudy or smelly urine. If mild just increase fluid intake. If it persists after one day then start antibiotics (Augmentin, Norfloxacin, or erythromtcin)

Thrush can be precipitated by antibiotics given for other reasons. Symptoms include itchy white discharge and a red rash. Treat with Canesten and remember to treat any partners as well, to prevent reinfection.

Fever Management

As you may be several days away from medical advice, you may be faced with the problem of a high fever, which may worsen if you don't treat it. Ensure adequate fluids are taken and give Paracetamol or Aspirin for the fever.

The main possibilities are:

- **Viral:** usually with a flu-like feeling – sore eyes, headache and muscle aches. No specific treatment required; just fluids, paracetamol or aspirin. – Chest Infection: a productive spit, often green, occasionally chest pain. Treat with Amoxycillin or Erythromycin.
- **Cystitis:** see above.
- **Bacterial Dysentery:** see text.
- **Malaria:** high fevers, chills, and headaches. Although the patient may have mild diarrhoea, there is no other source of infection identifiable. If patient has been in a risk area and hasn't been taking anti-malarial medicines, consider treatment with Chloroquine (not always effective), Mefloquine or Fansidar. This will need a review by a Doctor in Kathmandu.
- **Meningitis:** severe headache with temperature, neck stiffness and severe eye pain with bright lights. Treat with a high dose of Amoxycillin, or Erythromycin and evacuate.
- **Hepatitis:** itch, appetite loss and nausea. Diagnosis confirmed after 5 days when the patient turns yellow. Keep drinking fluids and use Aspirin (NOT Paracetamol).

Sprains

Ankle and knee sprains are common. Immerse in cold water for at least half an hour, then bandage firmly, elevate and rest – the more you walk, the slower the recovery.

Fractures

We cannot cover all fractures in this appendix. Basically the best pain relief is to splint the joint, immobilising joints above and below the fracture – give pain killers before you do this. Pad any parts of the limb that touch the splint and any bony parts, e.g. wrist, and elevate. If there is broken skin, then treat as for a cut but do not attempt to close any wound. If bone is visible then start treatment with antibiotics (Augmentin, Sporidex). Check finger/toe circulation after putting on the splint and loosen strapping if white or painful.

Shoulder Dislocation

Shoulder dislocations are relatively common amongst river runners and especially amongst intermediate kayakers who are often unfamiliar with the power of big water rivers. Prevention is better than cure: as a kayaker or paddle rafter you should never let your hands go above the level of your shoulders – forget those well-posed photos of boy racers desperately reaching over the top of a wave.

In the wilderness situation, it is reasonable for you to try and reduce a dislocated shoulder – the technique is simple, you are unlikely to cause more damage than has already been caused, the healing process can start sooner, there is likely to be less damage to the shoulder in the long term, and the patient will be more comfortable during the evacuation. We know of many instances where shoulders have been reduced on the river bank by people with little medical training – in all the instances known to us, the technique has been successful, but of couse it should always be the patient's decision whether to attempt reduction.

Action must be swift. Relocation can easily be done in the first few minutes, but becomes progressively more difficult as muscle spasm sets in. In a very muscular person you have only a couple of hours, in a thinner person, maybe 4-6 hours.

If you suspect a dislocated shoulder then:

1. Give your strongest painkiller and also, if you have it, 5 mg of valium to suck – absorbed faster than by swallowing (valium is a muscle as well as a brain relaxant).

2. Gently remove bouyancy aid and paddle jacket and carefully examine the arm and shoulder: check if the patient can move his fingers, hand and wrist. Also check and record the pulse at the wrist.

Diagnosis is usually obvious. The patient realises his shoulder is out, the elbow will lie away from his trunk and he will be quite unable to move his arm. The change in contour of his shoulder will be obvious. The head of the upper arm bone (humerus) lies outside and in almost all kayaking dislocations, in front of the cup of the joint where it can usually be felt.

Complications are unusual but should be checked for:

- Fracture of the upper humerus is rare and indicated by severe pain, excessive swelling, and grating of the arm with movement. The elbow may touch the trunk. Strap up and evacuate.

- Common, but not serious, is numbness in a small area of the outer upper arm. This indicates bruising of a small nerve close to the shoulder joint and should be just noted (subsequent physiotherapy will be delayed).

- Very uncommon is paralysis of the fingers with definite numbness. This may indicate major nerve damage. This will recover slowly in the weeks after reduction, but it should be the patient's decision when reduction should be done; now or later. Gentle reduction now is probably still the best course, as it is likely that the most damage will already have been done and as early reduction will allow the nerves to heal sooner.

The principle of Good Reduction is:
--- a very slow continuous pull --- to tease out the muscle spasm. When the humerus head comes to the edge of the cup, it will 'clunk' into place. If you pull too hard or too sharply, muscle spasm will worsen and keep the humerus head more firmly outside the cup. There are several techniques and we particularly recommend two:

- Lie the victim face down on a flat boulder, rock ledge, etc. with a table-like edge, so that his arm hangs freely down. Attach a weight to his wrist with a bandage, scarf, or similar – a helmet or bucket is ideal. Start with a weight of around 2 kg (3kg for a large patient) and very slowly increase this to double; if the patient has pain then decrease the weight. Leave the patient alone so that gravity does the work as the patient's muscles relax. The patient should feel a 'clunk' which will indicate relocation.

- The older technique has the patient on his back and you sit with legs extended, facing his head, holding his wrist between your thighs. If his right shoulder is dislocated, place the arch of your right foot (not the toes) in his armpit. Keeping you arms straight (less tiring), very, very slowly lean back. (Don't press too hard with your foot as it is resting close to nerves in the armpit). Up to 5 minutes later, a clunk will indicate relocation.

After treatment, whether relocated or not, check and record the wrist pulse again and strap the arm to the front of the chest with the hand level with the other shoulder. On reaching civilisation, you should of course consult a doctor. We also strongly recommend that you consult a good physiotherapist as soon as possible, so that you can minimise long-term damage; you are best returning home for this.

Medical Facilities

There are two well-established medical clinics in Kathmandu that are used by the expatriate community and knowledgeable tourists: The Ciwec Clinic and the New Nepal International Clinic. Both are staffed by western Doctors, charge western prices, and have 24 hour cover. In almost any medical situation you would be well advised to consult them first. If you have no money or insurance, then try the queues at Patan Mission Hospital or Tribhuwan University.

Outside of Kathmandu, facilities are poor to non-existent by our western standards There are government hospitals near most of the major rivers, but many lack even basic drugs (but note the Mission Hospital at Ampipal near the Marsyandi is well staffed and equipped). You may be better off with self-treatment until you can get back to Kathmandu.

Suggested further reading

Dr Dave Schlim's chapter in Lonely Planet's book 'Trekking in Nepal'. 'Medicine for Mountaineering', by J.Wilkerson; published by the Mountaineers, Seattle.

For information on our
complete line of technical
clothing, layering systems
and sportswear,
please call or write:
patagonia
UK: (44) 71.924-2155
USA: 1-800-336-9090
Patagonia U.K. Ltd.
24 Wilkinson St.
Sheffield, S10 2GB
South Yorkshire, U.K.
Photo: NICOLAS BROWN
©Patagonia, Inc.,1992

Medical Kit

Appendix B

By Dr Andy Watt

Introduction

In the wilderness situation, where there is no doctor, I think there is a case for an informed person with first aid training to prescribe drugs or to try other paramedic skills. This can save a trip and relieve discomfort, or convert a more serious problem into a manageable one.

All of the items and drugs listed here are usually available without prescription in Kathmandu (except for: suppositories, Cavit and gutta percha, finger tubigrip, local anaesthetic cream or lozenges for the mouth). However you should have some knowledge before you buy them and an idea of what conditions you might be dealing with. Most of the drugs have some side effects and you should enquire about allergies and previous medical trouble before prescribing. Women in early pregnancy should be especially careful.

Make sure people know where the first aid kit is carried. Also think about a small back up medical kit in case you lose the main one.

Basic Medical Kit – checklist

Elastoplast or Leukoplast.
Antiseptic cream – Povidone iodine/savlon.
Iodine for water sterilisation.
Sterile needles and syringe – every traveller should carry these.
Triangular bandage.
Safety Pins.
Gauze swabs – sterile and non-sterile.
Steri-strips or butterfly sutures.
Crepe bandage – one, 7.5 or 10 cms wide.
Cotton or open wove bandage – one, 5 or 7.5 cms wide.
Scissors.
Sterile scalpel or razor blade.
Band aids – assorted sizes.
Paper and pencil.
Burn ointment.
Eye ointment.
Throat lozenges, boiled sweets, or strepsils.
Sunscreen.
Antacid.
Aspirin – for pain, fever and inflamation (alternatives are Paracetamol and Ibuprofen).
Lomotil/Imodium – for diarrhoea.
Norfloxacin/Nalidixic acid – for bacterial dysentry.
Tinidazole – for Giardia or amoebic dysentry.
Sporidex or Augmentin – antibiotics for most infections.
Temgesic – for severe pain: reasonably safe and strongly advised.
List of contents (waterproofed) – with doses of drugs & side effects.

Supplementary – checklist

This is just a check list to remind you of other items that you may wish to take. It is not intended that you take all of them: it was not written for you to go blindly through ticking off your purchases, but for you to consider the need for each item, based on your group size, the trip you are doing, the known and likely problems in your group, your own experience, and the existing contents of your first aid box.

Finger tubigrip and applicator.
Non-adherent dressings, e.g. Melolin.
Thermometer.
Forceps or tweezers ('Splinter' forceps are recommended).
Candle and matches.
Oral rehydration powders – e.g. Jeevan Jel.
Temporary dental fillings – Cavit or Gutta percha.
Local anaesthetic cream or lozenges for the mouth (e.g. Bonjela).
Hydrocortisone cream – for itching skin or rashes.
Piles ointment Tincture of Benzoin – 'Friar's Balsam' (only a few mls needed).
Ear drops.
Moleskin/Second skin.
Alcohol wipes.
Adrenaline injection.
Antihistamine.
Antibiotic for anyone allergic to Peniccillin.
Antifungal cream.
Codeine – mild to moderate pain and cough.
Anti-inflamatory, e.g. Ibuprofen.
Decongestant, e.g. Actifed.
Paracetamol – for pain and fever.
Anti-Vomiting – Stemetil or Promethazine suppositories.
Valium.

Back up kit (or a really basic one) – checklist

Duct tape, tincture of iodine, sterile needle, sterile gauze swabs, eye ointment, Sporidex or Augmentin, Tinidazole, Norfloxacin, Temgesic, Aspirin, Promethazine suppository, Ant-acid, Imodium.

Bring out waterproof containers and re-sealable plastic bags for the kit, also plastic dropper bottles for tincture of iodine.

Notes on Medical Drugs — Appendix C

By Dr Andy Watt

The best name known of the drug is in capitals, the first name is the generic or 'proper' one, i.e. not the company or brand name. The only injectable drug listed here is Adrenaline. S/E = side effects. (Again we don't expect you to buy everything: this list is large in order to give you flexibility in deciding what to include in your own list).

ACTIFED (Pseudoephedrine 60mg/ and Triprolidine)
A decongestant and antihistamine that reduces that 'bunged up' feeling in colds, sinus and ear infections. It does not alter the underlying illness. Side effects are nervousness and possibly sedation. Dose: one tablet every 8 hours.

Adrenaline injection = Epinephrine 1:1000
For collapse, throat swelling and wheeze due to major allergic reaction. S/E fast pulse, nervousness. Dose 0.5 ml subcutaneously.

Ampicillin / Amoxycillin
Penicillin antibiotic drugs for chest, ear, throat and urinary tract infections. Side effects are diarrhoea and occasionally a rash. Check the patient is not allergic to penicillin. Dose 250-500 mg, every 8 hours, for 5 days.

ANTACID / Gelusil / many other names
For indigestion and gastritis. Side effects: aluminium based preparations can cause constipation, magnesium ones diarrrhoea. Sensible antacids are a mixture of both. Dose 1-2 tablets or teaspoons up to every 3 hours.

Anti-diarrhoeals: Loperamide = IMODIUM / Diphenoxylate = LOMOTIL
See note in Appendix A. Recommended only as a temporary expedient when on bus or plane rides, or for severe gut cramps. Dose: 2 tablets or capsules initially, then one with each bowel movement, up to a maximum of 8 tablets in 24 hours.

Anti-inflammatories IBUPROFEN is good but ASPIRIN is stronger. Not for stomach ulcers.

ANTIHISTAMINES: Chlorpheniramine = PIRITON / Diphenhydramine = BENADRYL / Terfenadine
Drugs for skin rashes and severe itching. Also used for travel motion sickness. Side effects are sedation. Piriton dose: 4 mg up to 6 hourly. Benadryl 50 mg up to 6 hourly. Terfenadine has recently become available and is less sedating; dose: 60 mg twice daily. (Creams can be useful for itching rashes).

Anti-vomiting: Prochlorperazine = STEMETIL / Promethazine = PHENERGAN / Avomine

ASPIRIN
For mild pain relief, fever treatment, and anti inflamatory. This flexibility however must be balanced against the gastritis it can cause. Not for those with ulcers, severe indigestion, or kidney disease. Other S/E (rarely) allergic reaction. Doseage 300-600 mg up to 6 hourly after food. Can be combined with Codeine or Paracetamol for moderate pain.

AUGMENTIN
As for Amoxycillin, but can also be used for skin infections. Doseage 1 tablet 8 hourly.

Bonjela
Local anaesthetic for the mouth.

Buprenorphine: TEMGESIC = TEDGESIC
For moderate to severe pain. NOT SWALLOWED, but held under the tongue. This is a relative of the opium pain killers but is not so powerful and not so addictive. Side effects are nausea and feeling 'spaced out'. Dose: 0.2-0.4 mg, every 8 hours. Not usually advised for head injuries.

Cephalexin: SPORIDEX = Keflex
Antibiotic for skin wound and other infections. A relative of penicillin therefore not for those sensitive to penicillin. Side effects are a rash and unusually, a severe allergic reaction. Dose: 250-500 mg every 6 hours for 5 days.

CHLOROQUINE: Nivaquine = Avlocor = Resochin
See 'Malaria precautions' section. An anti-malarial medicine. S/E mild stomach upset, itch. Anti-malarial dose is two tablets weekly. Treatment dose (not always effective); initially 6-7 tablets depending on patient's weight, then 3 tablets 6 hours later.

Clotrimazole = CANESTEN cream
Cream for both skin fungal infections and the treatment of Thrush. S/E are local irritation. Skin dose; one application per day for 1-2 weeks. Thrush dose; 2 applications per day for 3 days (an applicator is useful and remember to treat the male partner). If not available, try Miconazole (DAKTARIN) for skin or iodine pessaries for thrush.

Codeine
A multi-purpose drug for mild to moderate pain relief, diarrhoea and cough. Side effects are indigestion, sedation and constipation. Dose: pain 30-60 mg up to 4 hourly; 15-30 mg up to 4 hourly for cough and diarrhoea. Can be combined with Aspirin or Paracetamol for moderate pain.

Diazepam = VALIUM
Anti-anxiety agent, sleeping pill and muscle relaxant. Useful in shoulder dislocation. Side effects are sleepiness. Dose: 5 mg up to 3 times daily. Dose may be higher if little response.

DILOXANIDE FUROATE
Follow up treatment for amoeba cysts in the gut fluid (The other antibiotics only kil amoeba in the gut wall). S/E; gas and itch. Dose: 500 mg 8 hourly for 10 days.

Ear drops: Neosporin or Otosporin
For external ear infections. S/E occasional local sensitivity. Dose every 6 hours afte mopping out the ear. (Also see note after eye drops)

EPHEDRINE NOSE DROPS 1%
For persistent congestion (see text). Not for those on blood pressure treatment. S/E nervousness in high doses. Dose: 1 or 2 drops up to 4 times a day. Do not use for more tha 5 days.

Erythromycin
An alternative antibiotic for people sensitive to penicillin; for chest, ear, skin, throat an urinary infections – but not as good as the first line antibiotics. Side effects are a rash an nausea. Dose: 250-500 mg, every 6 hours for 5 days.

Eye ointment: Sodium sulphacetamide = LOCULA / Chlortetracycline / Chloramphenicol
For eye infections with discharge, or after injury. (DO NOT BUY eye drops containing STEROIDS or cortisone ingredients as these can worsen viral eye infections). Side effects are occasional local allergy, Locula is not for those allergic to sulpha drugs. Dose: 6 hourly, or 3 hourly if severe. (Neosporin 0.5% ointment can be used for both eyes and ears.)

FANSIDAR (Pyrimethamine 25mg, Sulphadoxine 500mg)
For treatment of malaria (not for use as a prophylaxis). S/E rashes and (rarely) blood problems. Not for sulpha-allergic people. Dose 2-3 tablets depending on patient's size.

Gamma benzene hexachloride: = Lindane = SCABEX
Treatment for Scabies. S/E skin irritation. Apply to whole body from neck down. Leave for 24 hours. May need second application.

Hydrocortisone cream 1%
For persistent rashes, insect bites and severe itch. Not for fungal infections. Do not use on the face unless there is a severe condition. Do not use for more than two weeks without medical advice.

Ibuprofen = BRUFEN
Anti-inflamatory drug and good substitute for aspirin. Not for people with kidney disase or stomach ulcers. Side effects are indigestion. Dose: 400-800 mg every 8 hours.

MEFLOQUINE = Lariam
Anti-malarial. See 'Malaria precautions' section. Expensive. S/E vomiting, faints and (rarely) behaviour changes. Anti-malaria dose; 250mg weekly and 2 weeks after leaving affected area (U.K. doctors advise a maximum of 6 weeks). Treatment dose 1 gram then 500mg 6 hours later.

Metronidazole = FLAGYL
For suspected Giardia or Amoebic dysentry. Side effects with high doses are an 'unwell feeling' and a metallic taste. Do not take alcohol. Dose for Giardia 400mgs 3 times a day for 3 days. Dose for Amoeba 800mgs 3 times a day for 5 days (follow up with Diloxanide).

Miconaxole = DAKTARIN cream
For suspected skin fungal infections. Side effects are occasional local allergy. Dosage as for Clotrimazole.

NALIDIXIC ACID
For bacterial dysentery. S/E (unusually) skin rash in strong sunlight. Dose: 500mg 6 hourly for 5 days.

NORFLOXACIN
For suspected bacterial dysentry. Side effects are nausea, abdominal cramps and diarrhoea. Dose: 400 mg twice daily for 5 days.

PARACETAMOL = Acetaminophen = Tylenol
For mild pain relief and fever. A good substitute for aspirin. Dose: 0.5-1.0 grams up to 4 hourly up to a maximum of 4 grams every 24 hours – DO NOT EXCEDE THIS DOSE.

Pile ointment: Ultaproct / Anusol
Side efects are (occasionally) local reaction with a rash and itching. Dose: as indicated.

Povidone Iodine = BETADINE cream or solution
For treating cuts etc. Not for people sensitive to iodine. Cream can be used as a burns dressing. Solution can be used in emergency for water sterilisation, 8 drops per litre.

Prochlorperazine = STEMETIL
Anti-vomiting. S/E (unusually) spasms of hand, eye, or head. Dose 25 mg suppository once, or 10mg tablet 6 hourly.

Proguamil = PALUDRINE
Anti-malarial, see 'Malaria precautions' section. S/E mild stomach upset, occasionally mouth ulcers. Dose 200mg daily.

Promethazine = PHENERGAN = Avomine
Anti-vomiting, an anti-histamine and for travel sickness. S/E drowsiness and occasionally dry mouth and blurred vision. Dose 25mg up to 8 hourly.

SILVER SULPHADIAZINE = Flamazine
For burns, see text. Not for sulpha-allergic people.

Tinidazole = TINIBA = Fasigyn
For suspected Giardia or amoebic dysentry. Not available in the U.S.A. DO NOT TAKE ALCOHOL. Side effects are a metallic taste and nausea, severe hangover with alcohol Dose for Giardia 2 gms once; for Amoeba 2 gms daily for 3 days (follow up with Diloxanide).

With thanks to Dr D.R.Shlim, Kathmandu; and Dr G.Irvine.

Wilderness medicine is as much a product of experience as any known facts. You may have different experience, and your comments will be welcomed by Dr Andy Watt, c/o the publishers.

International river classification of difficulty

Appendix D

Class 1: Easy
Moving water with occasonal small rapids. Few or no obstacles.

Class 2: Moderate
Small rapids with regular waves. Some manoeuvring required but easy to navigate.

Class 3: Difficult
Rapids with irregular waves and hazards that need avoiding. More difficult manoeuvring required but routes are normally obvious. Scouting from the shore is occasionally necessary.

Class 4: Very difficult
Large rapids that require careful manoeuvring. Dangerous hazards. Scouting from the shore is often necessary and rescue is usually difficult. Kayakers should be able to roll. Turbulent water and large irregular waves may flip rafts. In the event of a mishap there is significant risk of loss, damage and/or injury.

Class 5: Extremely difficult
Long and very violent rapids with severe hazards. Continuous, powerful, confused water makes route-finding difficult and scouting from the shore is essential. Precise manoevreing is critical and for kayakers, rolling ability needs to be 100%. Rescue is very difficult or impossible and in the event of a mishap there is a significant hazard to life.

Class 6: Nearly impossible
Difficulties of class 5 carried to the extreme of navigability. Might possibly (but not probably) be run by a team of experts at the right water level, in the right conditions, with all possible safety precautions, but still with considerable hazard to life.

Notes on contributors

Appendix E

Many, many, thanks to all the people who contributed material to this book. If we haven't mentioned you, our apologies, but then you should probably be grateful that we haven't had the chance to tell pernicious lies about you!

Megh Ale is an enthusiastic raft guide who enjoys exploring new rivers and places. In the off season he works in other countries and is becoming something of a tourist attraction in Europe for his culinary skills. People sample his special curry at peril to themselves and the raft.

Phil Bibby became an adrenalin junkie when he first discovered the thrills of fighting gravity by climbing mountains: later his addiction developed towards flowing with gravity to get his kicks from running rivers around the world. He lives in a village in Oxfordshire and supports his habit by work as a photographer, consultant and trainer.

Mike and Sarah Brewer are New Zealand kayakers who came on vacation to Nepal in 1990: Sarah describes it as 'the best trip we did'.

Anders Blomquist is two metres of river hippie that can't stay away from Nepal or his cameras. Anders has spent several seasons escaping Swedish winters in Nepal and Rum Doodle's Bar has almost become a second home.

Arlene Burns is a freelance adventurer who spends her life travelling the world. She first came to Nepal in the mid 1980's and fell in love with the country: we suspect that if we made her choose this would be her home. Arlene is a river and mountain guide, and a photo-journalist. She made the first descent of the upper Tsampo in Tibet and has spent several seasons river-running in Russia.

Mick Coyne is a freelance film producer who makes television documentaries to enable him to go on kayak trips . . . or is he a freelance paddler who goes on kayak trips to enable him to make T.V. documentaries? Anyway, whichever it is, he led the 'Kites and Kayaks' Dudh Kosi trip in 1986, the 'Taming of the Lion' Indus trip in 1990 and was Deputy leader of Paul Vander Molan's 'Iceland Breakthrough' expedition – all very memorable films. Mikes's previous experience included several years as a Royal Marine and a contract as safety adviser for one of the James Bond films.

Mieke de Moor is from Holland. She is a philosopher, mother of two marvellous daughters, and fell in love with Nepal during a kayaking trip in 1979. She teaches philosophy and organises kayaking courses on wild water. She feels at home in the French Alps where it seems possible to combine several worlds.

Whit Deshner is currently the beligerent dictator of the small principality of Freeloadia. An offbeat sense of humour can perhaps be blamed on working as a commercial fisherman in Alaska. In his spare time he travels around the world and causes havoc at airports with a plastic suitcase that looks suspiciously like a spud kayak. If you share his warped sense of humour then we recommend his book 'Does the wet suit you – the confessions of a kayak bum'.

Chris Dickinson looks forward most to two things in life – rainy days in Scotland, and sunny days in Nepal. He works as an outdoor activities instructor in the Highlands of Scotland and runs a small company 'Rapid River Runners' that offers guided kayak trips in Nepal – a good excuse to go to Nepal more often.

Alan Fox was founding Chairman of the D.K.C. (Deviants Kayak Club). A man of many talents, cartoonist, film maker, engineer, author, expedition organiser and lecturer. You'll meet him on a world river – or in some low bar. Alan has several books to his credit: his latest cartoon book is 'The Blind Probe'.

Wolfgang Haibach is one of the senior members of the A.K.C. (Alpina Kayak Club) from Germany and has led many overseas trips doing first descents of world rivers. He and the club have done much to encourage higher standards of river safety. He has been known to develop a morbid fear of dehydration on entering a bar – a fear that seems to have spread to other club members.

Mike Hewlett was the paddling star of the 'Kites and Kayaks' film, and was river leader of the 'Taming of the Lion' expedition. He is Managing Director of Porky Executive Services and his adonis-like body has featured on the cover of a certain exclusive catalogue. He keeps in shape with Karate and enjoys fixing cars.

Gudmund Host comes from Norway and likes Khukori XXX rum.

Mick Hopkinson lives in Christchurch, New Zealand, and is another veteran of the 1976 Dudh Kosi expedition. He partnered Mike Jones on their epic first descent of the upper Blue Nile in 1972. He has done many kayaking, caving and mountaineering trips since, including the Karnali in 1987. He was a leading paddler on the 'Taming of the Lion' expedition and recently did the first descent of 'Nevis Bluff' a major class 6 fall in New Zealand that international kayakers have been looking at and talking about for over a decade. Mick works as an outdoor activities consultant, advisor, and course organiser. He is also a star lecturer.

Roger Huyton was on the original Dudh Kosi expedition of 1976 and the follow up trip ten years later. He still paddles at a hard level and you'll probably bump into him on some class 5 river in Corsica or Idaho. He works as a film producer/director in London and lives in a quiet English village with a ruined castle as his next door neighbour. When he retires, a long way off, he talks of buying a caravan and going to rallies.

Nima Lama is one of the most experienced river guides in Nepal. Happily married with three children (probably more!) he runs the rafting company 'White Magic' and works in the off season in North America. He has led several exploratory rafting trips in Nepal and India and participated in the International Chuya Rally in Siberia in 1989.

Mike MacDonald works in Scotland as a teacher and yachtmaster instructor. A keen sailor he always says though 'that the smaller the boat, the more the fun!'. His extensive kayaking 'fun' includes nearly drowning in the Buri Gandaki in 1983, losing his boat and all gear at 4000 metres altitude in Ladakh, and coming last in the Arctic Canoe Race. Mike has a talented family who sensibly haven't taken up the 'fun' of kayaking.

Cam Macleay is a raft guide who has worked all over the world – from Russia to the Zambesi. He rowed the raft on the 'Taming of the Lion' Indus trip in 1990. He has an incredibly strong 'rafter's hand grip' developed from his early years wrestling sheep on a farm in New Zealand. Raft guides don't get paid that much and Cam likes variety and travelling, so spends about half the year working on temporary contract as a company accountant. His next trip could be New Guinea, Africa or Antarctica!

Bob McDougall comes from Seattle and is another famous name on the international kayaking circuit: a veteran of the Grand Canyon of the Stikine and co-founder of 'EPICS R

US' club – this concept was honed on the Na Ramro gorge on the upper Trisuli. Bob works as a consultant and designer for Patagonia. He was being interviewed after running a class 6 rapid and responded: 'If you can remember what happened you weren't there'!

Dave Manby started paddling at school: his parents sometimes wish he hadn't. Later he bumped into Mike Jones in a bar in Llangollen and ended up on the Dudh Kosi in 1976. Since then he has always found the second question on official forms difficult to answer but can usually be found in the summer on the Coruh river in Eastern Turkey running white water trips. Despite his gruff voice and shaggy exterior he really is a nice friendly chap and does like some post 1969 music.

Gabrielle Marges says 'I love to be in the mountains, walking, skiing, climbing and kayaking; but it seems ages ago that I felt the weight of my rucsack. Now that I have qualified as a physiotherapist I can start looking for my paradise!'

Louise Mathews is an Australian who has travelled and worked in Asia for the last ten years. She has come to love Nepal, its culture and landscape and is much in demand as a trekking leader. She has also kayaked and rafted many of its rivers and enjoys drawing along the way.

Frank Meyer lives in Seattle and was leader of the 1986 American Kayak Expedition to the Seti in Far West Nepal.

Barry Miller is based in Utah, and since 1981 has explored and run many of the rivers of the Far West of Nepal. Although helping with the river descriptions he has reservations about the negative effect of guide books like this one. He believes that: 'true adventure is being diluted by greater access to information – leading to increased exploitation and above all, change of experience for everyone involved'.

Gerry Moffat went out to Nepal as an 18 year old Scottish 'tear away' in 1983 and became the youngest ever rafter in Nepal. A friend reckoned that he's made more conquests in the Himalaya than Reinhold Messner. He went on to join the 'Taming of the Lion' Indus expedition and his experiences in Pakistan have tempted him and partners into setting up 'Kardkorum River Expeditions' to run trips in this dramatic area.

Jock Montgomery is from Maine. He started doing river trips when he was 11, developed webbed feet, and these force him to wear Tongs (flip flops, jangals,) – he's probably done more Himalayan treks wearing these than any other Westerner. Jock first came to Nepal in 1983 and has worked as a river guide and trekking leader. He is now a professional photographer (you'll find his pictures in other good guide books) and has taken up squirt boating for a sport.

Shyam Piya is one of the pioneers of white water rafting in Nepal. He has run exploratory rafting trips in Sikkim and Bhutan and particularly in the Far West of Nepal. His company 'Karnali River Tour and Expedition Pvt Ltd' was one of the first to run commercial trips on the Karnali. He is a founder Chairman of NARA.

Tim Raw had paddled in the Alps and New Zealand before Nepal. He owns up to spending many enthusiastic hours walking up valleys to look at potential rivers, only to realise that the rivers are all more improbable than he first thought – he enjoys laughing with good friends who have shared kayaking experiences all over the world.

Al Read used to be an American diplomat working in Asia. He is now a professional mountain climbing guide, Senior Vice President of InnerAsia Expeditions and a Director of

the American Alpine Club. He has been a member of several major mountaineering expeditions and was a leader of the 1979 Nepal-American Gaurishanker Expedition. He was one of the early explorers of Nepal's rivers and founded H.R.E. the first commercial rafting company in Nepal.

Guy Robbins started kayaking aged 14 at a drug and alcohol rehabilitation centre in Scotland. He then went boating in Southern Africa to dry out, moved on to the States but met the Moffat and was corrupted again and went to Asia. In Kathmandu he can be found hanging about in Rum Doudle's Bar drinking Khukuri XXX rum. Twice a year he heads to Pakistan to dry out and run trips with 'Karokorum River Expeditions'.

John Taylor is affectionately known as the Mr Fixit and Arthur Dailey of the kayaking world. He is often to be found in far flung corners of the world making top expedition films: by coincidence he always seems to be abroad when the tax inspector wants to talk to him. Friends say: 'he's always making pies so fast no-one else can get their finger in'!

Jim Traverso is a trekking leader, tour organiser, writer and part time kayaker with a deep knowledge and love of Nepal.

John Wasson started running rivers in Colorado in 1969 and has since run many rivers worldwide – he was on the first descent of Canada's Grand Canyon of the Stikine and was one of the first to kayak the Arun River and Modi Khola in Nepal. He lives in Idaho on the South Fork of the Payette River with his wife Jocelyn and a cat named Fenderskirts.

Jocelyn Wasson is a freelance illustrator (who also designs some wonderful T shirts). She has been keeping notes and drawings in her travel journals since she was a child and she has kindly let us use some of these drawings in our book. She enjoys kayaking, but occasionally at the top of a large rapid she wishes she was home with her cat Fenderskirts.

Andy Watt spent his formative years in Glasgow Canoe Club and occasionally at Glasgow Medical School: this explains his problems communicating – no one can understand his accent and few can read his hand writing. He has done a lot of kayaking all over the world and was featured as male 'pin-up' on the front cover of Canoeist Magazine. Andy is qualified in Internal Medicine, Tropical Medicine, and Immuniology and has a lot of Third World and expedition experience. He was last sighted in an Indian bazaar, carrying a battered dancer, and headed for a stint at the Mission Hospital in Manali.

Steve Webster first travelled out to the Himalaya in 1984 on what was meant to be a brief holiday but fell in love with Nepal – a beautiful girl called Neeru who was working for Royal Nepal Airlines. They married and Steve spent the next eight years in Nepal, much of that time working for Tiger Mountain in the Royal Bardia National Park. He has since returned to the U.K. and manages ExploreAsia's London office.

Don 'Kosi' Weeden is from a water lineage of ship captains, underwater demolition experts, and pool cleaners. He has been exploring Nepal's rivers since 1975, chiefly in pursuit of the ultimate 'rakshi', a potent local brew distilled on river banks. He is currently promoting river-based distribution of contraceptives in Northern India.

Ben Willems lives in Christchurch, New Zealand and works as an accountant. He has a sweet tooth and also likes the challenge of remote rivers: each year he flies in with a kit bag full of Mars Bars to run some more rivers in the Himalaya or Karakorams.

Nick Williams says he knows his mother and father and they were very disappointed that he took up kayaking. He started paddling when he was 16 and learnt to roll when he was 23: in the interim he swam most of the rivers in South Eastern U.S.A. He has swum on five continents but says his most enjoyable swim was on the Tamba Kosi in a relatively flat spot – he found he could swim to shore so did! Nick teaches kayaking at Nantahala Outdoor Centre and leads trips to Nepal most years.

Mike Wood first paddled in Nepal in 1980 and spent a lot of the next ten years working as a raft guide, trekking leader and rafting manager in Nepal. In his spare time he would be off exploring new rivers, like the Bhote Kosi and Tamba Kosi, and he became something of the resident kayaking expert in Kathnmandu – a walking guide book to be consulted in Rum Doodle's Bar. Mike now manages an outdoor store in Perth, Australia and is training for a 1993 Everest Expedition.

Mike Yager was the first professional rafting guide to work in Nepal and probably did more than anyone to develop rafting in the country. He was the first manager of H.R.E. and so trained many of the present senior river guides: they explored and developed rafting itineraries for many of the major rivers. After 20 years on rivers and mountains he is now on sabatical at the University of Utah: Once finished he plans to return to hard work, rivers and the four cardinal directions.

River running in other Himalayan Countries

Appendix F

In the Western Himalaya it can generally be said that most of the obvious sections of the main rivers have now been kayaked and many rafted, but many of the upper sections and the smaller tributaries remain to be explored. We have been river running in Pakistan and India, and travelled in Tibet; and in our experience, regardless of the country, most mountain people are invariably genuinely hospitable, friendly and honest. Nepal is still our first choice for river running, but if you ever get bored with this country then you won't be disappointed with the alternatives:

A useful map is published by Nelles maps and covers the whole of the Himalaya at a scale of 1:1,500,000.

India

Commercial rafting in India has taken off in the last few years. There are good safety standards controlled through the Indian rafting associations and you don't have the hassle of having to obtain permits. Main centre is Rishikesh on the holy Ganga (Ganges), conveniently situated some seven hours drive north of Delhi. Some kayaks are available for hire from rafting companies. Season here runs from October through to May and a one week raft or kayak trip down the holy Bhagirathi and Ganga can be particularly recommended. The Beas river near Manali is popular from April-June.

Ladakh (sometimes known as Little Tibet) is a fascinating region on the roof of the world that has Asia's equivalent of the Grand Canyon; the Zanskar Gorges. Here, there is some of the highest rafting in the world on the Zanskar and Indus rivers from July through September. Note that the road from Manali is no longer restricted and there is no need to go via strife torn Kashmir.

Sikkim has had some exploratory rafting and a New Zealand womens team kayaked there in 1991. The states to the east of Sikkim are restricted to foreigners and there has been little river running apart from a couple of rafting trips on the Brahmaputra.

Indian Rivers that have been run include: In Kashmir; the Sindh, Lidder, Warwan, and Chenab. In Ladakh; the Indus, Dras, Suru, Doda, Markha, Nubra, Shyok, Zanskar, Tsarap, and Lanakh (The Tsarap/Zanskar/Indus is a 'world classic' long kayak trip). In Himachal Pradesh; the Chenab, Chandra, Beas, Spiti, and Sutlej. In Uttar Pradesh; the Tons, Yamuna, Bhagirathi, Ganga, Alaknanda, Ramganga, and Kali (Sharda).

Although many rivers have been run, there is still probably more scope in India for 'first descents' and exploratory river running than in any other Himalayan country.

Bhutan

Rivers in this 'Shangri La' country are relatively short, steep, and powerful, and there appear to be only a few good multi-day raft trips. Short sections of the Mochu, Wangchu and Sang Kosh have been run. Note that Bhutan has a restrictive tourism policy designed to protect its unique culture: foreign tourists are only permitted in small organised groups and have to pay a substantial tourist tax.

Pakistan

Like India and Nepal, Pakistan welcomes foreign tourists and there are few restrictions. Permits are required if you want to raft the Indus, but a small group of kayakers is unlikely to encounter problems on other rivers.

Northern Pakistan has exciting white water in the heart of some of the world's most dramatic mountain scenery, the place to go if Nepal seems a bit tame! Commercial rafting has started up in the last two years based in Gilgit and running the Gilgit, Ishkoman, and Hunza rivers. Kayaks are available for hire to organised groups.

Best time of year is Sept-Oct or April-May in the windows between the cold of winter and summer spate. Note that all these rivers are snow melt, relatively high altitude (Gilgit is at 1500m) and the rivers are cold.

Jeep roads run up all the main valleys and most of the rivers have now been run: The Indus, Braldu, Astor, Laspur, Yarkhun, Mastuj, Chitral, Garam Chasma, Ludkho, Yasin, Hispar, Ghizar, Gilgit, Hunza, Shimshal, Ishkoman, Kandia, Kunhar, and Swat. The Kunhar, Ishkoman and Gilgit rivers can be particularly recommended.

Tibet

Tibet is a high arid plateau, with mountain ranges and rushing rivers that have a great deal of potential for rafting and kayaking. Sadly, this fascinating country, with its delightful people is now an occupied country under the harsh totalitarian regime of the Chinese Army. Latest reports suggest that many of the beautiful forested valleys of Eastern Tibet have been clear-felled by the Chinese and the rapids are blocked by huge log jams.

If you are prepared to ignore the human rights and environmental issues and can afford to pay several hundred thousand dollars to the Chinese for a permit then it is possible to organise an expedition; an Australian group rafted part of the Tsampo and there have been a few well-publicised rafting trips on the Yangtse and its tributaries.

The country is now only open to organised tour groups, but in 1987, when it was open to individual travellers, two American kayakers Arlene Burns and Dan Dixon smuggled their boats past the border and then hitch-hiked to near Mount Kailas. They then ran most of the upper reaches of the Tsampo down to near Lhasa – an epic adventure that cost them $40 each!

Glossary of river terms — Appendix G

Boulder garden – many rocks tastefully positioned in a rapid to give pleasure to boaters.

Boater/paddler – deviant form of human

Breakout – an 'eddy' that a boat can use to break out of the current and to then stop in.

Camera vulture – avaricious bird with a large black beak that hovers below rapids.

Canoe – an open or canadian style canoe. Note for American readers: Europeans often use 'canoe' as a generic name for all types of canoes and kayaks.

Chicken shoot – an easier way down a rapid that by-passes the main action.

Continuous – an over-used adjective in this book – denotes a sustained and unremitting stretch of river where the difficulty keeps at the same high level.

Eddy – an area of relatively slack water (or where the current re-circulates upstream) usually behind an obstruction in the river.

Eddy-line – the transition line between the main current and the slower calmer water of the eddy. Best crossed at speed!

Ender/endo/pop-out/loop – where kayakers use the force of a wave to drive their kayak vertically out of the water in a phallic-like display or kind of cart wheel.

Flip – a capsize of a raft: usually from hitting a hole or wave at the wrong angle/place: may be like an ender and quite spectacular.

Hole – normally formed on the downstream side of a rock or similar underwater obstruction. There is usually a 'stopper' / 'hydraulic jump' on the downstream side of the hole. Individual holes can be playful, tempting, humiliating, or downright dangerous.

High-siding – when a raft is caught broadside in a hole or against a rock the current presses down on the upstream side and tries to flip the raft – rafters need to quickly throw their weight onto the high side of the raft (the downstream side) to prevent this.

Kayak – small boat shaped like a banana, with a hole in the bottom from which the occupant hangs. Can be propelled the wrong way up by experts.

Kayaker – extreme form of deviant paddler (semi-human): uses a double ended paddle. Often called 'river maggots' by rafters because of their habit of infesting holes on a river. Canoeists and paddle rafters reckon that kayakers 'have twice the paddle but half the brains'.

Paddle – length of wood or plastic/metal: people hold one end and dip the other end in water to achieve a dramatic personality change.

Pin – where a boat is held by the current against a rock or other obstruction. May be vertical or horizontal, and underwater. Usually a serious incident and may be life-threatening. Low volume kayaks with sharp ends are particularly susceptible to vertical pins.

Playspot – section of water used by over-grown children for water play with rubber and plastic toys. Those playing should beware the enticements of 'camera vultures'.

Portage – favourite activity of canoeists: not so popular with rafters. Wise boaters portage when in doubt.

Pour-over – the current pours over the top of a rock and then drops vertically, usually into an evil hole. Hard to see from upstream until it's too late, so potentially dangerous.

Put-in – start of a river trip.

Raft – inflatable boat used for descending rivers: appeals to those with a rubber fetish. Referred to by kayakers as 'rubber bus', 'cattle wagon', 'pig boat', 'river barge', etc.

Roll – short for 'eskimo roll'.

Self-bailing raft – has an inflatable floor and holes to drain the water out. Recommended for more difficult rivers and high water conditions.

Scout – the act of inspecting a rapid or difficult stretch of river: 'When in doubt: get out and scout'.

Stopper (British) / Reversal (American) / Hydraulic jump (Engineering) – a breaking wave on the downstream side of a hole that re-circulates like a window blind rolling itself up: bad ones will do this to you!

Surf – kayaks, rafts, canoes, etc. can surf a river wave just like people ride ocean waves.

Take-out – finish point of a river trip.

The Hermitage on the Marsyandi

Useful names and addresses

Appendix H

Tourism Concern
Froebel College
Roehampton Lane
London SW15 5PU, U.K.

Gravity Sports
100 Broadway, Jersey City,
NJ 07306, U.S.A.
Ph: 800 346 4884 Fax: 201 860 9633

Nepalese Association of
Rafting Agents (NARA)
P.O. Box 3586
Kathmandu

Chrisfilm and Video Ltd
Glasshouses Mill
Pateley Bridge, Harrogate,
N. Yorks HG3 5QH, U.K.
Ph: 0423 711310 Fax: 0423 712493

Kites and Kayaks
521 Upper Brentwood Road
Gidea Park, Romford
Essex RM2 6LD
Fax: 07087 29173

Nepalese Embassies and Consulates

AUSTRALIA
377 Sussex St, Sydney 2000
Ph: 02 264 7197

CANADA
310 Dupont St, Toronto M5 RIV9
Ph: 416 968 7252

GERMANY
Im Hag 15, D-5300 Bonn 2
Ph: 0228 343097

U.K.
12a Kensington Palace Gardens
London W8 4QU
Ph: 071 229 1594

U.S.A.
2131 Leroy Pl, N.W. Washington,
DC 20008 Ph: 202 667 4550

473 Jackson St, San Fransisco,
CA 94111 Ph: 415 434 1111

Suite 110, 16250 Dallas Pkway,
Dallas, TX 75248 Ph:214 931 1212

212 15th St NE, Atlanta,
GA 30309 Ph: 404 892 8152

Subscribers

Appendix I

We would like to thank the following, who helped launch this book by subscribing prior to publication – and trusted us with their money!

Lloyd Allin
D.Alldritt
Nic Askew
Pete Atkinson
Marcus Bailie
Christine Baillie
Guy Baker
Marke Bankes
Bruce Barnes
Stephen Bates
Donald Bean
M.C. Beverly
Tim Biggs
Phil Blain
Tom Boise
Anne Butler
Pete Butler
Paul Buttin
Liz Campbell
Adam Campkin
Claire Carren
Kathy Carroll
Claire Cheong-Leen
Chris Clark
Robert Collins
Jel Coward
Fiona Cowie
Sally Cox
Peter Davies
Simon Drinkwater
Nigel Edwards
Alan Elsworth
Brenden Emery
Chuck Evans
Gill Farjounel
George Farquhar
Nico Fischbacher
Tony Ford
Chris Gash
Maggie Gosling
I. Greenhalgh
Terry Hailwood
Andy Halliday
Chris Hamblin
Chris Haresign
Robyn Harris
Rob Hastings
Mary Heffernan
Pete Higgins
Rob Hind
Larry Hopkins
John Hough
Horace
Dave Horrocks
T.J. Illston
Chris Ingram
John Jaques
Paul Jenkins
B.G. Jones
Mike Jones
Martin Keereweer
Peter Knight
Winni Kraus
Lionel Lafay
Robert Lewis
Roy Mackenzie
Ken McIlroy
Phil McClintock
Ian Marsh
Regina Maurer
Peter Midwood
Carol Midwood
Laura Millar
Donna Munro
Steve Neale
P.M.Neill
Chris Nichol
Mark Nichols
Chris Oliver
Brian Olyneck
Jim Orava
Jon Ord
Ren Owen
Tim Palmer
Nara Pandey
Paul Paree
Robin Parish
Chris Parker
Pete Patterson
T.F. Peacock
Mark Pedley
Adrian Pickup
Eric Plouviez
Christian Pohlschmidt
Sepp Puchinger
Radar
David Reed
Gianluca Ricci
Sue Richardson
Louis Rotter
Rupert Robin
Don Robinson
G. Roscoe
Dave Ross
Helen Rowlands
M.Rudd
Marcus Schmid
Ian Seed
Dave Simpson
John Sole
Paul Sujevich
Mike Sunderland
B.T. Smith
James Smith
Michael Smith
Howard Storey
Kevin Tandy
Chris Taylor
Norman Teasdale
Alan Tilling
Eric Totty
Sporting Travel
Jifi Vohradsky
Amalia Walther
Anthony Ward
Kirsty Wigglesworth
John Wilde
Clive Wilson
Mike Wood
Stuart Woodward

Index

...Innocently in search of pleasure, naively heading into total danger...
...and so I said 'its highly unlikely that you would get stuck in a canyon with an unrunnable rapid ahead and no possible portage'.... no sense of adventure, some people are just too cautious nowadays...
© foxy

Suppliers Directory

All of the following advertisers are well known to us. Usually they are products and services that we ourselves have chosen and used, and we can recommend them as reputable companies at the time of writing.

Himalayan River Exploration

Himalayan River Exploration are the pioneers of river rafting in Nepal, offering a wide choice of trips from a day excursion to ten days on the Sun Kosi shooting grade 4 to 5 rapids.

All rafts are of international quality, each outfitted to the highest safety standards. The guides are not only professional rafters, but also trained as Emergency Medical Technicians, not to mention their knowledge of local history, flora and fauna and Nepal's varied geology.

For more details contact:

ExplorAsia Ltd
13 Chapter Street
London SW1P 4NY
Tel: 071 630 7102
Fax: 071 630 0355

Himalayan River Exploration
P.O. Box 170
Kathmandu
Nepal
Tel: (977) 1 414073
Fax: (977) 1 414075

TREKKING & RAFTING (P) LTD.

N E P A L

JYATHA, THAMEL, KATHMANDU, P.O. BOX NO. 2118, TEL. : 226885

FAX : 977-1-226885 OR 977-1-227372 ATTN : WHITE MAGIC TREK

HIMALAYAN *encounters*

In Nepal you can't do better than contact HIMALAYAN ENCOUNTERS

Our experience of running the rivers of Nepal dates back to 1978. The organisation has a team of river-running specialists (both Nepali and non-Nepali) and inflatables and other equipment for long and short river journeys throughout the Nepal Himalaya.

Our association is largely with travellers unfamiliar with whitewater who are combining an encounter on one of the rivers of Nepal with some 'high adventure' trekking amongst the mountains. Many 'crews' are formed overseas where Himalayan Encounters is represented and other crews are formed as a result of people contacting us in Kathmandu.

Our experience on the Sun-Kosi river in particular is well-known, being the only organisation which runs this mighty river on a fairly regular basis - at least 8 or 9 times between October and April. This is a 10 day expedition setting out from Kathmandu. (After the final descent, many participants go on to trek with us due north to Everest Base Camp)

Clubs and other groups work with us; involving special itineraries, permits, service, equipment, etc. Also growing is cooperation with club and individual kayakers.

The specialness of Nepal and her peoples is not to be taken for granted nor taken advantage of selfishly. The sole purpose of Himalayan Encounters is to introduce people to the wonders of Nepal - always with conservation of the countryside and betterment of the people uppermost.

IN NEPAL:
HIMALAYAN ENCOUNTERS
Kathmandu Guest House
Thamel
Kathmandu, Nepal
Phone: (1) 432632 or 417426

IN UNITED KINGDOM:
ENCOUNTER OVERLAND
267 Old Brompton Road
London SW5 9JA
England
Phone: (071) 370 6845

IN AUSTRALIA:
SUNDOWNERS TRAVEL CENTRE
108 Albion Street
Surry Hills NSW 2010
Phone: (02) 281 4066

IN NEW ZEALAND:
SUNTRAVEL
P.O. Box 12 424
407 Great South Road
Penrose, Auckland
Phone: (09) 525 3074

IN USA:
ADVENTURE CENTER
1311 63rd Street
Suite 200
Emeryville CA 94608
Phone: (510) 654 1879

IN CANADA:
TREK HOLIDAYS
8412 - 109 Street
Edmonton Alberta
T6G 1E2
Phone: (403) 439 9118

NATIONAL WHITE WATER CENTRE

Britain's No 1 White Water Rafting , Canoeing & Kayaking Site - 2 Km of Grade III / IV White Water

Top Training Site for all International Expeditions

Frongoch , Bala
Gwynedd ,North Wales , LL23 7NU
0678 520826 (Water Information)
0678 521083 (Bookings)
0678 521158 (Fax.)

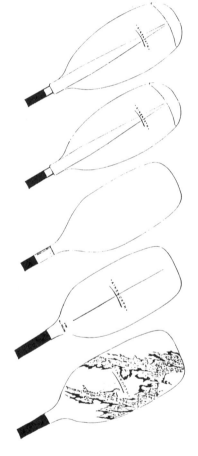

GREEN SLIME THROWBAGS

FAST, SIMPLE, WATER RESCUE

With over 10 years of expertise in design and manufacture our throwbags are justly world renowned and market leaders.

Chosen by numerous international expeditions canoeists, rafters and a wide range of other users.

Features include:

* Quality Rope
* Easy to throw
* High visibility
* Clear instructions

RESCUE RESCUE

For details and stockists contact:
SUZY, 2 Victoria Close,
Molesey, Surrey KT8 ISQ.
UK. Tel: 081 941 2714

RAPID TRANSIT EQUIPMENT FOR THE WORLD'S PROFESSIONAL RIVER RUNNERS

urocraft specialises in the manufacture of a wide variety of self-bailing and tandard White Water craft from their back-packable, 2 person, Rapid Explorer hrough a full range of expedition and commercial rafts to the mighty Grand Canyon -rigs made in England using quality Hypalon. Accessories are also available. urocraft White Water rafts are in daily service from the Alps to the Andes.

or further information please contact Chris Burrows:- Eurocraft (GB) Ltd, Unit , Dunkirk Hall Ind. Est, Dunkirk Lane, Leyland, Lancs, PR5 3SQ, U.K.
Tel (44) 772 622856 Fax (44) 772 622857

SEALLINE™ DRY BAGS

Oh for a dry sweater when you're wet and cold!.
No matter what your sport, Sealline dry bags are a must.
Sealline dry bags work! Now you can relax in the knowledge that even in heavy weather or white water, your clothing valuables and equipment stay dry.
From the makers of Therm-a-Rest, Cascade Designs Ltd., you can rely on Sealline dry bags to seal out water and keep your gear dry.

For Free Colour Brochure write to:

Cascade Designs Ltd.,
Dwyer Road, Midleton, Co. Cork, Ireland.

or phone

Mobile Adventure, Leicester, LE2 6GI
Tel. 0533 – 830659 Fax 0533 – 440454

Photo: Keith Gunnar

Specialist, High-Performance River Running and Playboating Equipment.

For full details please contact - Playboater Ltd, The Haymill Centre, Burnham Lane, Slough SL1 6LZ. Tel. (0628) 667507